DEFENDING THE REICH

5

120223

DEFENDING THE REICH

THE HISTORY OF JAGDGESCHWADER 1 "OESAU"

ERIC MOMBEEK

Translated from the French by John. J. Vasco

JAC PUBLICATIONS

CONTENTS

Published by JAC Publications
28 Bellomonte Crescent
Drayton
Norwich, Norfolk
England NR8 6EJ

Printed in England by
M. F. Barnwell
Aylsham
Norfolk NR11 6ET

ISBN 0 9515737 1 3

British Library cataloguing in Publication Data:
A catalogue record for this book is available from the British Library.

Cover portrait:
2nd May 1943. Leutnant Rudiger von Kirchmayr, Technical Officer of II. Gruppe, shoots down a Spitfire IX of 332 Squadron. The RAF pilot made a successful belly-landing.

Page 1:

Excellent in-flight view of Unteroffizier Alois Job in his Fw 190 A-4, "Black 6". In this machine Job scored his first victory on 12/1/43 over a Spitfire.

Page 2 top:

This Bf 109 E, "White 5", of 10th Staffel is possibly that of Oberfeldwebel Georg "Murr" Schott, an old Legion Condor pilot and one of the most experienced pilots of the Gruppe. Almost hidden by the ground mechanic leaning on the port wing is the Maltese Cross emblem beneath the cockpit. It would appear that IV. Gruppe adopted the III. Gruppe emblem at some time.

Page 2 bottom:

Ludwiglust, end of April 1945. He 162 A-2, "White 1", W.Nr. 120223 of 1st Staffel.

Page 3:

Posted to Rheine in mid-July 1943, II. Gruppe had to share their aircraft with II./JG 300, a "Wilde Sau" night fighting unit who did not possess their own aircraft until February 1944. This Fw 190 A-6 seen at Rheine in autumn 1943 belonged to II. Gruppe, Jagdgeschwader 1, but was also flown by Oberfeldwebel Richard Löfgen of II./JG 300.

FOREWORD
BY
EBERHARD BURATH
FORMER ADJUTANT OF JAGDGESCHWADER 1

As a former member of Jagdgeschwader 1, I am very pleased to see in print this work on JG 1, a Geschwader, which for a long time, has remained on the periphery of literature of the period. It had the thankless task for the whole of the war of defending the north-west flank of the Reich, which, until the entry of the Americans, earned little notice. The Geschwader came to the fore with the start of "Reichsverteidigung", which could be likened to a bloodletting.
What did that mean for the men, who with dogged bravery battle against superior forces ?
Heady recollections of combat surface from the heat of the battle. As the aircraft became a small part of one's self, so must the fighter, with its fixed armament, attack, and in its turn fly through the heavy return fire of the enemy. The attack was necessary against the bomber, in order to prevent it unloading its deadly cargo, or to prevent it making a further raid, if it was the return flight.
We sought only to serve our country, and thought little about the politics involved, the many threads of which this war drew together.
We listened, and flew. So Jagdgeschwader 1 fought, almost to the last man, until the end came. The He 162 came much too late. The die was cast.
Today, we flyers of all nations put our hands together in remembrance of our fallen comrades, in the hope that future generations will be spared such a war as we endured.

EBERHARD BURATH

INTRODUCTION

During the first campaigns of the Second World War, the Luftwaffe fighter force achieved overwhelming success. However at this time, the premier fighter unit, Jagdgeschwader 1, was only in the throes of formation. It only reached full complement when the allies began their raids on occupied Europe.

From 1942 to 1944 Jagdgeschwader 1 was based principally in Holland. Being the first line of defence of the Reich, it had the heavy responsibility of daylight interception of enemy formations generally superior in numbers, more appropriately equipped, and whose attack tactics were never thwarted. The pilots of Jagdgeschwader 1 returned surprising successes in spite of the imbalance of numbers, but nevertheless their losses were often heavy.

From June 1944, Jagdgeschwader 1 was engaged in the Normandy campaign in summer; defence of the Reich in Autumn, and the Ardennes offensive in Winter. When it was transferred to the east in January 1945 it was so weakened, like the Luftwaffe in general, that its influence on the front was minimal. It followed the general retreat until the war's end.

Aside from the historical and political interest which comes from studying a Luftwaffe fighter unit, the human interest is important. A unit theoretically comprised of between 50 and 100 pilots, but each faced danger alone, isolated in their aircraft. The reactions were very different: uncontrollable fear to unthinking heroism; attitudes which, in certain instances, left a bitter taste. Pilots of the Second World War knew one of the first forms of total war. One did not see the adversary whom one killed. The enemy was a terrifying machine with an invisible crew. Knowing that he would be saving his own people if he eliminated the bomber, the German fighter pilot attacked like an unforgiving jouster. On each mission, an internal conflict unfolded. Their personal conscience became tangled: fear of the enemy which often appeared technically superior; the role of defender of the population and its leader; the respect for orders .... A heavy burden for a young man of twenty to carry!

It is the history of these young men that this book deals with.

Certainly this work will contain gaps, which I hope the reader will understand.

ERIC MOMBEEK
IXELLES
AUGUST 1992

GLOSSARY

A/B Schule	Flying School
Deutsche Kreuz in Gold	German Cross in Gold
Eichenlaub	Knights Cross with Oakleaves
Einsatz	Combat
Eisernen Kreuz (I und II)	Iron Cross (1st and 2nd Class)
Ergänzungsgruppe	Replacement Wing
Fähnrich	Officer Cadet
Feldwebel	Warrant Officer
Flak	Anti-aircraft artillery
Führer	Leader
Gefreiter	Leading Aircraftsman
Geschwader	Roughly equivalent to 3 RAF wings
Gruppe	Roughly equivalent to a RAF wing
Gruppenkommandeur	Commander of a Wing
Hauptmann	Captain
Herausschuss	The act of forcing a bomber out of its formation
Jagdbomber	Fighter-bomber
Jagdgeschwader	Roughly equivalent to 3 RAF fighter wings
Jagdwaffe	Fighter Arm
Kampfgeschwader	Roughly equivalent to 3 RAF bomber wings
Kommodore	Commanding Officer of a Geschwader
Leutnant	Lieutenant
Luftwaffe	Airforce
Major	Major
Maschine Gewehr	Machine Gun
Nachtjäger	Night fighter
Oberfähnrich	Senior Cadet
Oberfeldwebel	Senior Warrant Officer
Obergefreiter	Corporal
Oberleutnant	First Lieutenant
Oberstleutnant	Lieutenant-Colonel
Reflex Viseur (Revi)	Gunsight
Ritterkreuz (träger)	Knights Cross (holder)
Schwarm	Section of four aircraft
Schwerten	Knights Cross with Oakleaves and Swords
Stab	Staff Flight
Staffel	Roughly equivalent to a RAF Squadron
Staffelkapitän	Commander of a Squadron
Sturmstaffel	Assault Squadron
Unteroffizier	Sergeant
Viermots	Four-engined bombers
Zerstörergeschwader	Bf 110 unit roughly equivalent to 3 RAF wings
Zweimots	Twin-engined bombers

A propaganda shot for the victory of 18th December 1939 with Oberstleutnant Schuhmacher in his Bf 109 E-3. Note the rear view mirror.

Kommodore Carl Schuhmacher in the cockpit of his Bf 109 E upon his return from a mission.

CHAPTER 1 - 1939

GENESIS

In 1939 the German Bight represented the Achilles heel of the Third Reich. It was through that area that the major part of commerce and essential materials passed, for a nation pursuing a course of power. From 1934, when the Luftwaffe hardly existed, Germany had sited their foremost fighter units in this area. The German Bight was protected by the greatest concentration of units in the whole of Germany.
In 1939 the Luftwaffe was far more powerful than the allies believed. On 3rd September 1939, two days after German forces entered Poland, France and Great Britain declared war on Germany. In the hours following, the RAF mounted a reconnaissance mission over the German Bight. Its purpose was to pinpoint the German fleet anchored off Wilhelmshaven. On the day after, the first bombing operation of the war in the west was launched. Carried out without fighter escort, this raid was a failure and the British bombers paid a high price. German fighters and anti-aircraft defences claimed two Wellingtons and five Blenheims.
On 12th September 1939, nine days after the fateful declaration of war, Oberstleutnant Carl Schumacher was handed the task of reorganising and unifying the defence of this strategically important area. Staffeln were placed under the control of the Stab, Jagdgeschwader Schumacher, also known as Stab, Jagdgeschwader Nord.
The Stab could muster few aircraft, but the following units were immediately placed under Schumacher's control:

II./JG 77 of Major Harry von Bülow-Bothkamp
II./Tr. Gr. 186 of Hauptmann Heinrich Seeliger;
I./ZG 76 of Major Reinecke; and
Gruppe 101 of Major Reichardt.

On 18th December 1939, the aerial conflict in the area erupted again, with Schumacher's units gaining the first major victory in air combat in the west. On that day, Major von Bülow-Bothkamp, Gruppenkommandeur of II./JG 77, was visiting his superior, Oberstleutnant Schumacher. Towards 13:00 hours word was received from Wangerooge that British aircraft were heading towards the Bight. Leutnant Steinhoff and his 10th Staffel, Jagdgeschwader 26, took off immediately. They made contact with the raiding force, and were soon joined by other units, including the Stab led by Schumacher personally.
"On 18th December 1939 when radar control called us up, no one could believe it. Many enemy aircraft were en route for our sector - it must have been some kind of interference. However a few minutes later, a naval "Freya" radar gave us identical information, which was confirmed by eye-witness sightings. This time, there was no doubt. The alarm was raised ...." On the different aerodromes, mechanics operated the inertia starters. The engines of the Bf 109s and 110s turned, then spat out short blue flames. Pilots slid into cockpits and quickly checked the instruments. A mechanic helped to tighten the harness. Then, facing the wind, aircraft took off in pairs. Course:Heligoland Bight. The pilots quickly saw the enemy bombers flying as though on parade. The Germans dived on the English formation. It was slaughter! Several German pilots soon had a Wellington framed in their gunsights. On the joy-sticks, fingers pressed the trigger. The bursts hit their target. The bombers which were hit staggered, and some set down on the icy waves. The Messerschmitts pulled away and searched for other targets.

Bf 109 E-3 of Oberstleutnant Carl Schuhmacher at Jever in December 1939. The eagle looks out onto the German Bight.

"It was madness!", recounted Oberstleutnant Schumacher. "The tommies were chased in all directions by our fighters. I also attacked an English bomber. He defended himself well and hit my machine on three occasions. One of the bullets, moreover, passed very close to my head. The bomber was finally in the centre of my sights. I fired at point-blank range, and continued to follow my victim. There were no more than several metres between the two of us - I had to pull away quickly. I was preparing for another attack after a wide turn when I saw the aircraft fall into the sea like a stone. My wingman immediately confirmed my victory.

"The combat had already taken us more than thirty kilometres to the west of Heligoland Island, and we were always on the tails of the English. We switched over during attacks, and chased them out as far as 150 kilometres before returning".

It is difficult to strike a balance in recounting this action, as the British information service played down the magnitude of the defeat. The RAF admitted the loss of twelve Wellingtons (out of 24 engaged), as well as claiming the same number of victories. In reality, the Germans lost two aircraft. In their turn, the Germans claimed 38 victories, of which 26 were officially acknowledged. What were the exact figures? More than 50 years after the event, historians continue to try to find the truth. The most recent studies show that at least 33 bombers were involved on 18th December 1939. The uncertainty concerning this initial point should at least ensure that care is taken against accepting too lightly the victory claims of the belligerent nations.

The heat of the "Great Battle of Heligoland Bight" had hardly died down when a further incursion by ten bombers occurred on 27th December. In spite of the season, the reception was as hot as that of 18th December. Kommodore Schumacher returned to base with a second victory.

This later combat seems to have dissuaded the British from undertaking further similar operations. The pilots passed a freezing winter in peace. Their unit would be renamed Stab, Jagdgeschwader 1 by the time spring 1940 brought further action.

September 1939, Allenstein. Bf 109 E-1s of I. Gruppe prepared for a mission against Poland. Extreme left is Hauptmann Wilhelm Balthasar, Staffelkapitän of 1st Staffel.

Paradoxically, while the Stab of Jagdgeschwader 1 was being formed, I. Gruppe of Jagdgeschwader 1 had existed from early 1939! It evolved from one of the oldest Gruppen of the fighter arm of the Luftwaffe: I. Gruppe, Jagdgeschwader 131 formed on 1st April 1937 at Jesau, near Königsberg, under Major Bernhard Woldenga. Renamed I. Gruppe, JG 130 seven months later, it was given the designation I. Gruppe, Jagdgeschwader 1 on 1st April 1939.

Under the dynamic direction of its leader, who was approaching 40 years of age, the Gruppe fared so well that it was split into two. I. Gruppe, Jagdgeschwader 21 was born out of Jagdgeschwader 1's I.Gruppe.

I. Gruppe of Jagdgeschwader 1 possessed a solid nucleus of pilots who had previously fought in the Spanish Civil War. Included in the ranks were such excellent pilots as Schlichting, Balthasar and Adolph. Towards the end of Summer 1939, rumours of war increased right up to the invasion of Poland. The 54 Bf 109 Es of I. Gruppe based at Seerappen alongside I. Gruppe, Jagdgeschwader 21 were given the rôle of protecting East Prussia. The Gruppe launched several missions over Polish territory, but their recall to Germany was rapid, and I. Gruppe took up residence at Gymnich, near Köln. Further training soon followed.

In the west, the war settled down to a long waiting game. Occasionally, enemy aircraft were reported, but because of the time required to gain height to intercept, the enemy had usually escaped. Nevertheless, on 28th September 1939, Feldwebel Klaus Faber opened the Gruppe's account by shooting down a reconnaissance Blenheim over Osnabrück. Oberleutnant Walter Adolph did likewise three days later. A similar victory recorded on 16th October south of Lingen by Leutnant Rosenbroom rounded off the claims for the year.

Leutnant Ludwig Franzisket salutes Hauptmann Bernhard Woldenga. In the guard of honour, from left to right: Feldwebel Junuschwski; Feldwebel Braxator; Feldwebel Faber; unknown, and Feldwebel Dobrick.

Gymnich, end of April 1940. Four officers of I. Gruppe beside Bf 109 E-3 "White 11" of 1st Staffel. From left to right: Leutnant Herbert Wasserzier; Leutnant Hans Lass; Leutnant Ludwig Franzisket and Oberleutnant Erwin Mann. Note the Gruppe emblem slightly ahead of the cockpit: a black cross on a white background, with three small gold coloured aircraft. During this period the aircraft of I. Gruppe carried their identification numbers on the engine cowlings, a practise which continued throughout the Battle of Britain and beyond when the Gruppe became III. Gruppe, Jagdgeschwader 27.

Erbo Graf von Kageneck of 2nd Staffel, seen here in his Bf 109 E-3, scored his first two victories, two Blenheims over Maastricht, on 12th May 1940. He was shot down and wounded while serving with Jagdgeschwader 27 in December 1941, and later died of his wounds in hospital.

CHAPTER 2 - 1940

LOOKING TOWARDS THE WEST

On 1st February 1940 an important change occurred at the head of the Gruppe. Major Woldenga handed over command to Hauptmann Joachim Schlichting, who was celebrating his 26th birthday on that date. His Staffelkapitäne were:

1st Staffel - Oberleutnant Wilhelm Balthasar;
2nd Staffel - Oberleutnant Walter Adolph; and
3rd Staffel - Oberleutnant Max Dobislav.

If the various units of the Luftwaffe proceeded with the training of its pilots, the high echelons of the army were not idle. After the conquest of Poland, The Wehrmacht moved its forces westwards. It was there that the next objective lay. As yet, there was no precise plan for conducting this campaign, only an idea based largely on the "Schlieffen Plan" of 1914, an ultra-classic attack which in no way would take the western forces by surprise. It consisted of a feint attack taking German troops to the northern French coast after crossing Belgium. This done, the forces would then strike to the west of Paris. At least two were not convinced of this tactic. Hitler himself, and a young general, Erich von Manstein, who profited from the delay to put forward a quite audacious and revolutionary idea. The main idea consisted of using large concentrations of armour as a spearhead. Tanks would open a corridor in the centre of the allied defences:the Ardennes region, an area considered almost impenetrable and therefore lightly defended. The breach accomplished, "Army Group A" would head towards Calais. The first pincer in the encircling movement would be in place. Simultaneously, "Army Group B" would roll across Holland and northern Belgium to join up with "Army Group A" and complete the pincer movement.

History shows the success of the plan. Faced by the French, Belgian and Dutch armies, and the British Expeditionary Force, the German army, although inferior in numbers, was better equipped, better led and more imaginative. The Luftwaffe was on this occasion

Feldwebel Klaus Faber opened the Gruppe's account when shooting down a Blenheim over Osnabrück on 28th September 1939. He is seen here in his Bf 109 E "Yellow 8" of 3rd Staffel.

able to lighten the burden of the ordinary soldier. This had already been shown during the Spanish Civil War and the attack on Poland.

From the first day of the campaign in the west, the Gruppe was in action with its old friends from the previous winter from Jagdgeschwader 27. I. Gruppe, as well as I. Gruppe Jagdgeschwader 21 and I. Gruppe Jagdgeschwader 52, was placed under the control of the Kommodore of Jagdgeschwader 27, Oberst Max Ibel, and were under the overall control of VIII. Fliegerkorps. The war in the west took off very quickly. In the early hours of 10th May 1940 German paratroopers overcame the Belgian fort of Eban-Emael and more importantly captured two of the three bridges over the Albert canal. These bridges were vital for the German advance. Jagdgeschwader 27 and its subordinate units were responsible for their defence.

I. Gruppe's first mission was in the early morning of 10th May. Nineteen Bf 109 Es escorted around forty Junkers 52/3 transport aircraft who dropped dummy parachutists between St. Trond and Tongres. An apparently strange operation but vital, because attention was diverted from the main target : the Albert canal. In the skies, combat had commenced. German fighters reported meeting five Gladiators. They were, in fact two patrols of Fiat CR 42s, of 3/II/2 of the Belgian Air Force. One of these aircraft was shot down. The pilot, Premier-Sergeant Roger Delannay was able to extricate himself from his stricken machine. He landed by parachute in a field of Terkelen Castle near St. Trond. Hit by a bullet in the spine, he was conscious, but completely paralysed. He died shortly after reaching hospital. His wingman, Lieutenant Charles Goffin, claimed a Bf 109 E. A pilot of II. Gruppe Jagdgeschwader 1 had to abandon his aircraft over Aachen. He bailed out safely.

The following day, 11th May, I. Gruppe were on "Freie Jagd" to cover the bridges. German interception services announced an imminent attack by Belgian aircraft. On this morning, a formation of nine Fairey Battles took off to attack the bridges with small sized 50 kilogram bombs. Escort was provided by six Gladiators. During the combat which followed, Leutnant Ludwig Franzisket recorded his first victory: "From 01:45 hours we were alerted at Gymnich that an aerial attack was being prepared in order to destroy the bridges over the Albert canal. The intercepted message stated that at 07:00 hours Belgian aircraft would attack the objective. At 06:09 hours, two Schwarme, each of four Messerschmitt 109 Es, took off with instructions to protect the area in front of Maastricht. The first Schwarm was led by Oberleutnant Balthasar. The second, which I led, was charged with the task of top cover. Arriving at our destination, we waited like guard dogs, in front of the bridges".

On the Belgian side, six Gloster Gladiators, in two sections, the first led by Sergeant Denys Rolin, the second by Capitaine Guisgand, approached the rendezvous point with the Battles charged with carrying out the attack. Rapidly, Rolin's gaze took in four, then eight black dots. As they became larger there was no longer any doubt: squared-off wingtips meant they were Bf 109s. Leutnant Franzisket had already spotted the enemy, who were approaching at the same altitude. Without waiting for assistance from the pilots of the other Schwarm, Franzisket and the pilots of his Schwarm turned to attack.

Rolin, in order to carry out his mission in protecting the bombers, tried to avoid combat. He climbed towards a layer of cloud at 1,200 metres, passed through it and then dived rapidly towards the enemy. He found himself practically on the tail of a Bf 109. He fired. The German did a barrel roll, condensation trails streaming from his wingtips. Missed! The Bf 109 E had escaped. Quickly, Rolin glanced behind him. In his gunsight, Franzisket lined up the Gladiator. A finger pressed the trigger on the joystick. The wing Kanone lit up. 20mm. rounds hit the Gladiator and exploded on the rear fuselage. The biplane, out of control, dived down in a tight spiral.

In the cockpit, Rolin realised that his aircraft no longer responded. The shells had cut through the control wires. Rolin undid his straps, opened the cockpit door and jumped. After counting to three, he pulled the ripcord and the parachute deployed. Under the force of it opening, one of his shoes came off, and it disappeared under the void. Rolin's misfortunes did not end there. After reaching the ground, he came face to face with a Belgian soldier. Suspicious, the soldier took him to his superiors, who panicked, taking him for a German agent. Although

tied up with electric wire, and with a pistol in his back, he did not remain long in this state. A soldier returned shouting in Flemish: "The Germans are coming". Everyone took refuge in a cave. German fire hit the ground around them. The Belgians surrendered. The Germans released Rolin, taking him for one of their own, but this mistake did not last long. Rolin eventually found himself in a prisoner-of-war camp.
Apart from Franzisket, four other pilots of I. Gruppe claimed victories: Hauptmann Balthasar two, and Leutnant Mann, Feldwebel Gillert and Unteroffizier Clade each claimed one. Contrary to German claims, four, not six, Gladiators were lost; the other two which escaped returned to their base badly damaged.
On the morning of the 11th, German pilots faced the Belgians. By the evening, they were facing the French. Thirteen Léo 451 bombers of bomber groups 1 and 2/12, escorted by Morane 406s, attacked bridges and vehicle columns. I. Gruppe were credited with three Léo 451s, one Blenheim(sic) and one Morane.
In spite of the many attacks, the bridges had still not been destroyed. Nothing could stop the passage of vehicles and soldiers, who were able to exploit the spearhead Panzer divisions. For I. Gruppe, the balance sheet looked excellent for this second day of the campaign: eleven victories and not a single loss.
On 12th May, Hauptmann Schlicting and his I. Gruppe were charged with protecting the bridges, with I. Gruppe, Jagdgeschwader 27 taking up the "Freie Jagd" rôle. During the early hours of the morning nine Blenheims of 139 Squadron launched an attack as desperate as those that had gone before. In five minutes, the Staffelkapitän of 2nd Staffel, Oberleutnant Walter Adolph, shot down three of the seven bombers lost during this raid. At 09:00 hours the Gruppe took off again to strafe the aerodrome of Diest, where sixteen aircraft out of twenty six were destroyed on the ground. Towards 11:00 hours I. Gruppe once again surprised aircraft of the RAF over Maastricht. Two squadrons of Blenheims were intercepted and only ten of the twenty four aircraft returned. Two bombers fell to the guns of young Leutnant Erbo Graf von Kageneck.
The days following were very quiet for the Gruppe, still based at Gymnich. The other units based closer to the front saw far more action, I. Gruppe, Jagdgeschwader 53 claimed 39 victories on 14th May. Finally, on 16th May, I. Gruppe moved into Belgium and operated from there for first time against France. They immediately recorded four victories in the area of Laon/Compiègne.
Mission followed mission: "Freie Jagd", escort, ground strafing. On 19th May, for example, the aerodrome of Soissons was strafed and four Potez were destroyed. On the same day, the Gruppe also recorded seven aerial victories. However, on 20th May, the day when German tanks reached the Channel coast, the Gruppe recorded its first loss - Leutnant Horst Braxator of 3rd Staffel, a promising pilot with two victories, fell in combat north of Amiens.
The battle moved quickly. On 23rd May, German aerial attacks reached the French channel ports. While escorting Bf 110s, two pilots of I. Gruppe were killed and two

Oberleutnant Wilhelm Balthasar of 1st Staffel in front of his "White 1" at Dummersee in late 1939. He had just received the Iron Cross, II. Class, which can be seen attached to his tunic button. The pennant on the radio mast denotes a Staffelkapitän, and the fuselage cross carries a thin white border common to German aircraft in the early months of the war.

others were wounded. The Gruppen under the control of Jagdgeschwader 27, on the other hand, claimed 27 victories. Oberleutnant Balthasar added three, and Leutnant Franzisket two, to their accounts. On 28th May Belgium sued for peace.
On 14th June the Gruppe celebrated the award of the Ritterkreuz to Oberleutnant Wilhelm Balthasar. He was only the second pilot of the Jagdwaffe, Werner Mölders being the first, to receive the Ritterkreuz. The award came following his success in scoring 23 aerial victories and destroying fourteen aircraft on the ground.
On 15th June, the Gruppe found itself at Romily-sur-Seine, but on the same day moved to Auxerre. On 16th June tragedy struck when the aircraft of Unteroffizier Stahn and Unteroffizier Brandt collided. Both pilots were killed.
On 22nd June the armistice between Germany and France was signed. The pilots of I. Gruppe, Jagdgeschwader 1 were on Nevers aerodrome when the victorious

end to the campaign was announced. Euphoria was widespread, and it was time to take stock of victories: Jagdgeschwader 27 claimed 235 victories, of which I. Gruppe, Jagdgeschwader 1 contributed 82. Hauptmann Balthasar was recognised as top scorer in the campaign, ahead of a certain Hauptmann Adolf Galland! Leutnant Franzisket and Oberleutnant Adolph recorded nine and six victories respectively.

However, just like Balthasar, the Gruppe had a career as brief as it was glorious. During the reorganisation of the fighter arm following the Battle of France, the large neighbouring unit absorbed it. On 5th July, I. Gruppe, Jagdgeschwader 1 became III. Gruppe, Jagdgeschwader 27. I. Gruppe, in its initial form, had disappeared. What was the connection between I. Gruppe and Stab of Jagdgeschwader 1? On the surface, none, save having the same name, and sharing recognition in the victory communications of the Luftwaffe. Throughout the Battle of Britain period, there was little activity in the old area occupied by the Stab of Jagdgeschwader 1. It was almost as though the war had passed it by.

However, it is with the coming of 1941 that the history of the unit as a complete Jagdgeschwader takes shape, with the official decision to form the unit.

Bf 109 E-4, "Black 14" of the unit carrying the unit emblem and a fuselage bomb rack.

Bf 109 E-4, "Black 13" again showing the unit emblem on the starboard side, and a 250 kilogram bomb on the ETC 500 bomb rack.

Pilots and pets lounge in the sunshine beside Unteroffizier Hans Schubert's "Yellow 4".

Summer 1941 at De Kooy. Unteroffizier Hans Schubert at cockpit readiness in his "Yellow 4". Note the unusual style of numeral.

Unteroffizier Heinrich Nöcker with two Bf 109 Es of 3rd Staffel at De Kooy, 1941. To the left is Oberleutnant Paul Stolte's "Yellow 1". Although taken in 1941, the Bf 109 E's carry a camouflage pattern which was largely superseded during the Battle of Britain in the summer of 1940.

CHAPTER 3 - 1941

JAGDGESCHWADER 1 REFORMED - 1941

Autonomous Jagdstaffeln formed the basis of the reconstituted I. Gruppe. Jagdstaffel Holland, formed from pilots of IV. Gruppe, Jagdgeschwader 2; Jagdstaffel Münster-Loddenheide and Jagdstaffel Wedding formed the new Gruppe. Young pilots fresh from training schools were also incorporated.

In 1941, activity was rare on this sector of the front. After the Battle of Britain, which Winter had consigned to the pages of history, the RAF and the Luftwaffe were left licking their wounds. Among the fourteen victories recorded by I. Gruppe in 1941, Feldwebel Mickel was the pilot who opened the Gruppe's account with the shooting down of a Blenheim on 13th January. Eight days later, his Rotte, comprising himself and Unteroffizier Krause, shot down two Blenheims. Another pilot of I. Gruppe came to the fore in spring 1941 : Oberfeldwebel Gerhard. After a victory over a Blenheim on 14th February, he followed up in April with another Blenheim victory on the 14th, and two Spitfireson the 28th. Unteroffizier Noecker also scored, with two claims against Blenheims on 4th June. In spite of that, the area remained relatively calm! Little by little, most German units departed from Western Europe. The next action would be in the east. Hardly had the clamour surrounding fresh victories in the Balkans subsided, than the news of the invasion of Russia dropped like a bombshell. The Reich was taking on the Soviet Union, with its immense territory. The attack opened on a 1,600 kilometre front. The news which came from that distant front was of the irresistible advance of German forces.

Oberleutnant Wolfgang Wedding recalled the formation of 2nd Staffel: "After having made my début as a fighter pilot with III. Gruppe, Jagdgeschwader 26, I accompanied my Gruppenkommandeur, Hauptmann Kienitz, to III. Gruppe, Jagdgeschwader 3 on 31st October 1939. We went there to form a Staffel which was destined for service aboard our unique aircraft carrier, the Graf Zeppelin, presently under construction. The campaign in the west changed that, and III./JG 3 was in combat over Belgium and France. They distinguished themselves

Unteroffizier Hans-Günther Wennekers poses on the cowling of his Bf 109 E-4 at Katwijk in August 1941. He joined 2nd Staffel on 17th June 1941. Comparison of the sun emblem on different aircraft shows different styles and faces, as well as the addition of girlfriends/wives names alongside. In this shot Wennekers partly covers the name.

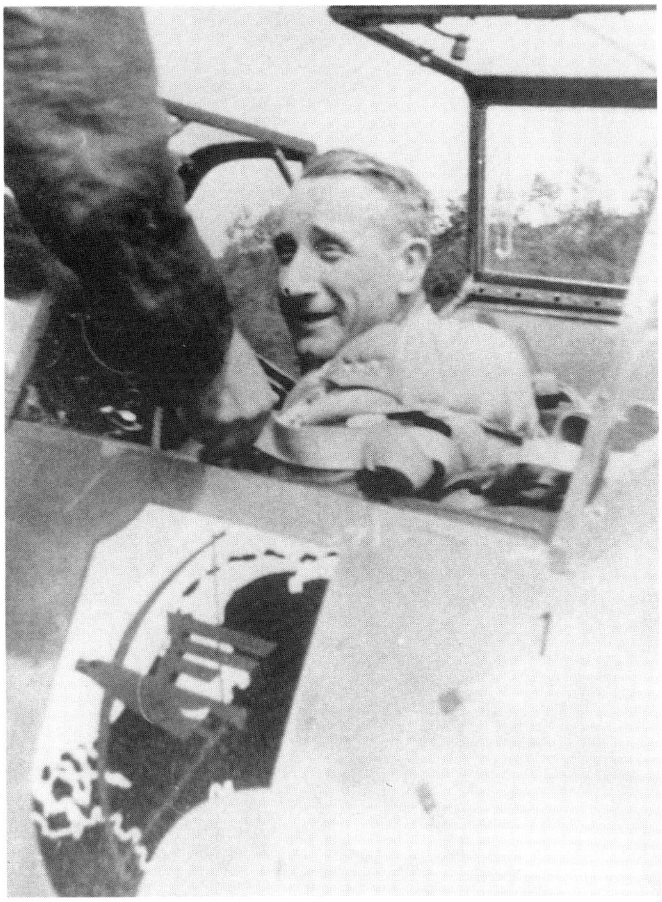

After holding the post of "Nachtjagdführer Holland" since November 1940, Major Dr. Erich Mix, seen here in his Bf 109 F at Bergen aan Zee, took charge of I. Gruppe on 7th July 1941 at Husum. During the transfer flight, he shot down his final victim, a Bristol Blenheim, 35 Kilometres from Den Haag. This victory was not, however, confirmed.

with many victories. At the beginning of summer 1940 I was withdrawn from the front and at Dortmund was given command of a dozen pilots, the majority having seen action in the west; the rest fresh from fighter training school. Our remit was to protect the Ruhr area, the nerve centre of Germany. In effect, while the Battle of Britain was raging, a system for defending the Reich was almost non-existent. In June 1941 the unit moved to Katwijk. Numerous problems then arose, above all the standard of the equipment: neighbouring units had priority and it became extremely difficult to obtain even the least material. It was the time of the formation of Jagdgeschwader 1, and I learned with great relief that our unit, "Jasta Wedding" would be incorporated into it. It could, at last, enjoy being part of an adequate infrastructure".
In July 1941 Oberstleutnant Schumacher received a new posting, being transferred to the General Staff. Major Erich von Selle, former Gruppenkommandeur of

Oberleutnant Paul Stolte, Staffelkapitän of 3rd Staffel, poses at De Kooy beside the rear of his Bf 109 E which carries two victory markings, the second being a Blenheim brought down on 22nd March 1941.

De Kooy, 4th June 1941. Unteroffizier Heinrich Nöcker stands proudly before the rudder of his Bf 109E sporting two victories. Nöcker was killed in action on 26th November 1942 in North Africa, shortly after arriving at that front.

The rudder of Oberleutnant Paul Stolte showing four victory bars with British cockades. The dates are: 22/3/41; 23/3/41; 25/5/41 and 28/5/41. Stolte was killed on the Russian front on 18/10/43 with II./JG 3, having at that time 43 victories.

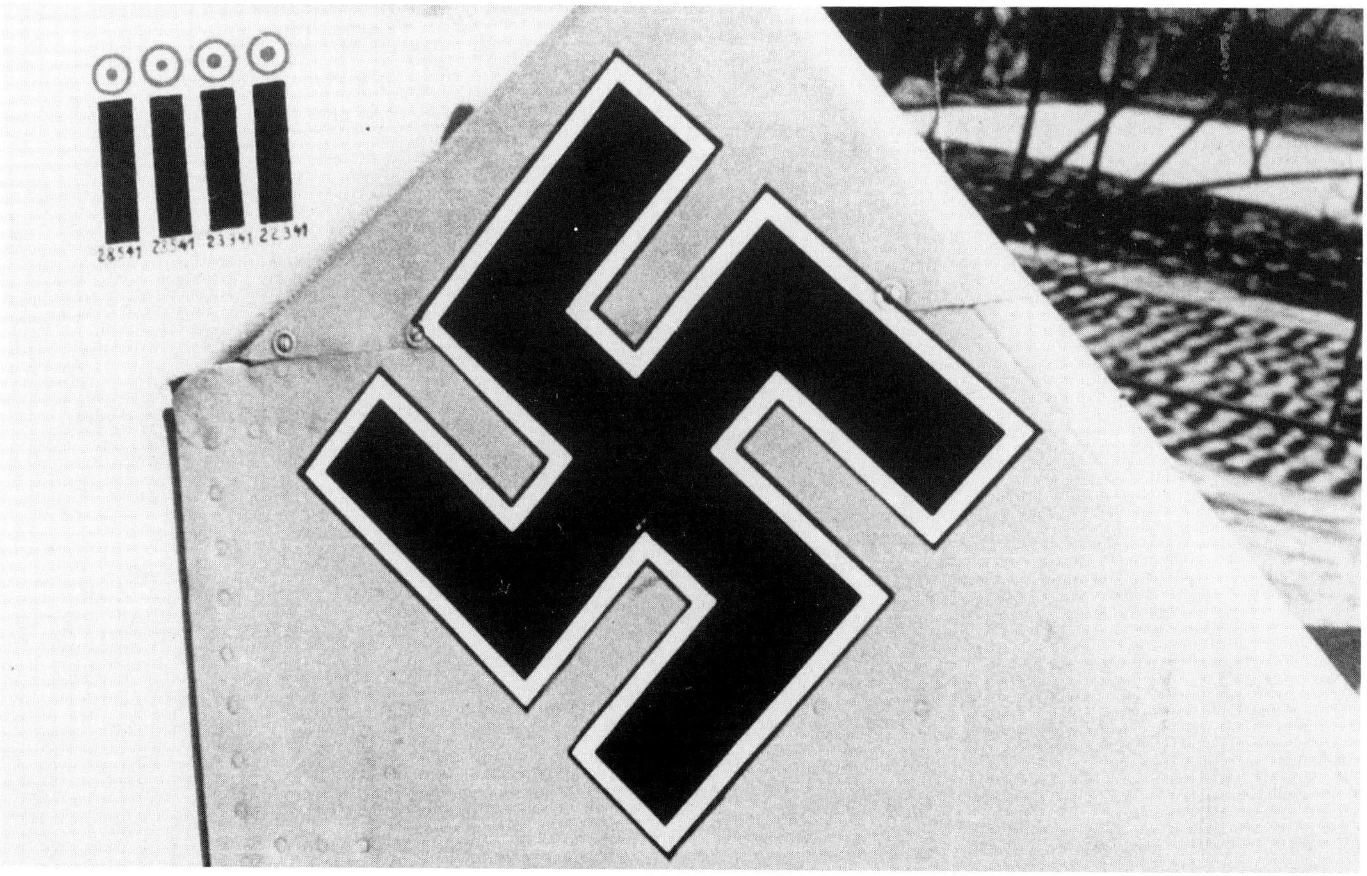

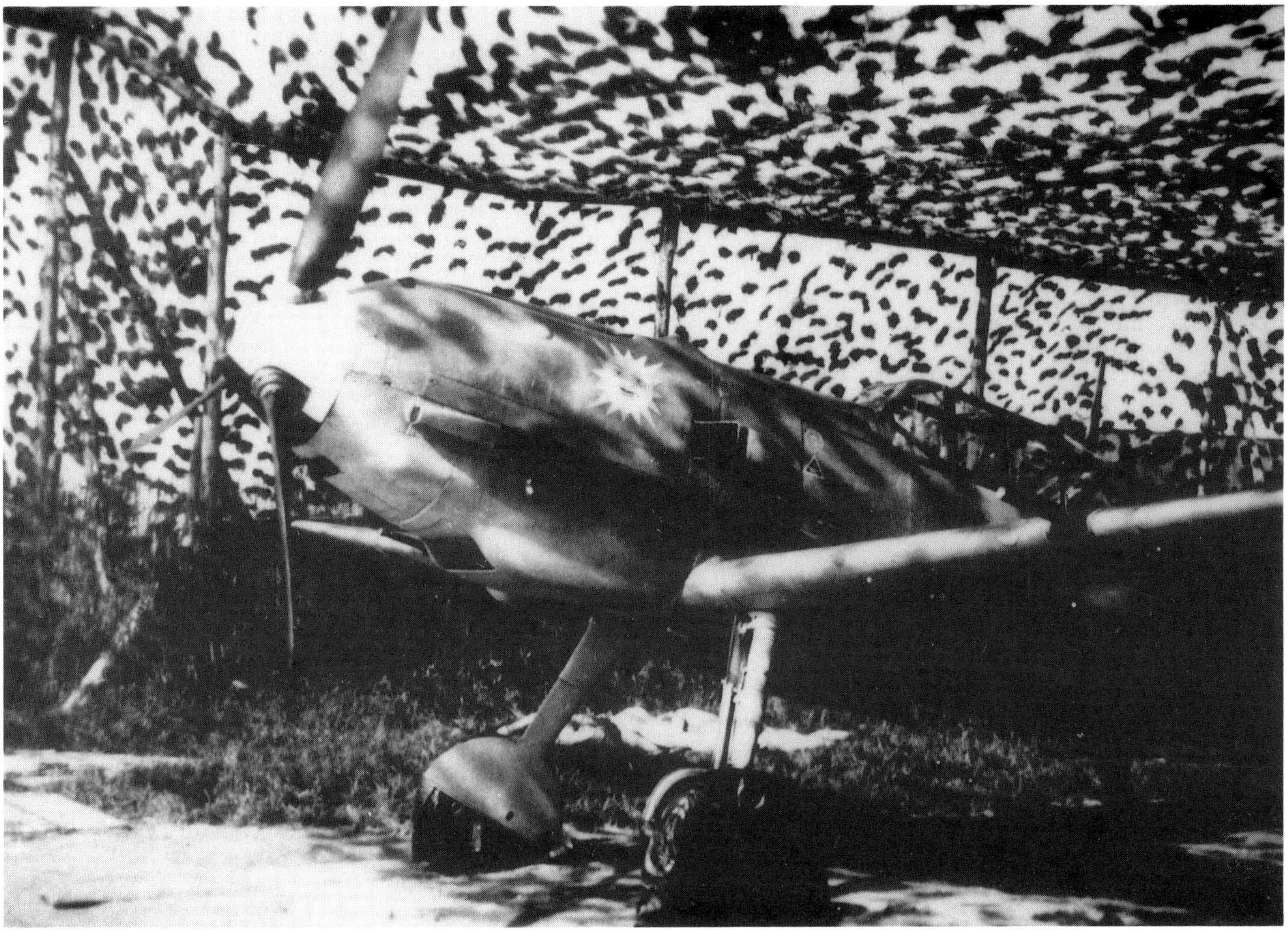

A Bf 109 E-4 of 2nd Staffel in its blast pen at Katwijk in the summer of 1941. The "sun" Staffel emblem can be clearly seen. This emblem was carried over by the Staffel from their days as "Tag Jagdstaffel Münster-Loddenheide".

II. Gruppe Jagdgeschwader 3, then I. Gruppe Jagdgeschwader 54, succeeded him at the head of the unit. He had nine victories to his credit.
On 26th September 1941 I. Gruppe found itself a Gruppenkommandeur in the shape of Major Dr. Erich Mix. Working at Fighter Headquarters in Holland, he had been connected with Jagdgeschwader 1 for several months. On 7th July 1941 he recorded his thirteenth and last victory over a Bristol Blenheim, shot down into the sea off Holland. He was a veteran of World War I, scoring three victories in that conflict. Mix was over forty years of age when he arrived at Jagdgeschwader 2 during the French campaign and the Battle of Britain.
His Staffelkapitäne were:

Oberleutnant Müller - 1st Staffel;
Oberleutnant Wolfgang Wedding - 2nd Staffel;and
Oberleutnant Paul Stolte - 3rd Staffel.

The Staffeln of I. Gruppe were dispersed on different aerodromes in northern Europe. They were thus found on the Frisian islands of Borkum and Wangerooge, and bases at Jever, Valkenburg, Bergen and De Kooy, the latter three being in the Netherlands. The Low Countries would be the home of Jagdgeschwader 1 for a long time, occupying as it did a vital strategic position, as events would prove.

In spite of his age - he was born in 1898 - Mix flew several combat missions with JG 1. His wingman, seen here with him, was Oberleutnant Hotari Schmude, who was killed on 18/3/43.

Düsseldorf, June 1941. View of a Bf 109 E of 2nd Staffel showing once again the sun emblem and the name Ingeborg on the cowling. Note the technical marking behind the supercharger air intake.

Ground personnel pose on a Bf 109 E of 2nd Staffel in the summer of 1941.

Major Erich Mix (holding the flowers) takes command of I. Gruppe at Bergen-aan-Zee in Summer 1941. In the background is one of the first Bf 109 Fs delivered to the unit.

Three pilots of 2nd Staffel pose in front of a Bf 109 E-5.

Oberleutnant Helmut Meckel scored steadily in the early part of the war. Fourteen victories in the east were added to eleven in the west before he returned to the western front. Meckel is on the extreme right.

Autumn 1941. When the weather was not too bad, the pilots took off on routine flights: escort; flying techniques; courier duties including occasionally the transportation of the sick and wounded. Contact with the enemy was, in general, rare. Nevertheless several victories were recorded. However everyone was aware that this period of relative calm would not last. The British had begun to come out of their defensive shell. Already to the south, over France, offensive incursions had become more frequent.

The area required to be covered by the Stab and I. Gruppe continued to grow, due, in no small part, to the fact that elements of Jagdgeschwader 53, based in Holland, were progressively moved to the eastern or mediterranean fronts. Jagdgeschwader 1 needed reinforcing.The eastern front would provide them with part of their requirements. After about three months of combat in Russia, I. Gruppe Jagdgeschwader 3 had recorded 293 victories. The highly-prized decoration, the Ritterkreuz, had been awarded to five of its pilots: Hauptmann Hans von Hahn (25 victories) and Oberleutnant Robert Olejnik (32 victories) in July; Oberleutnant Max Bucholz (27 victories) and Helmut Meckel (25 victories) in August, and Oberleutnant Detlev Rohwer (28 victories) in October. However, continuous combat,

Jever, summer 1941. On 2nd July 1941 Heinz Knoke joined 2nd Staffel. Knoke sits on the cockpit sill of this Bf 109 F while his Staffelkapitän, Oberleutnant Wolfgang Wedding, stares out from the cockpit. The aircraft carries the double chevron of Gruppenkommandeur, Major Erich Mix.

Leutnant Heinz Knoke's Bf 109 E "Black 3" displaying the sun emblem and his fiancée's name, Lilo, whom he later married.

rapid advancement, and the climate had resulted in the exhaustion of both men and machines. At the end of August the Gruppe had only two aircraft available for combat! On 14th September the order came for them to be rested. They were sent to the rear, at Madgeburg. From 10th October to 9th November the pilots were given leave. On 10th November the Gruppe received 40 Bf 109 F-4s. Ten days later they were put at the disposal of II. Fliegerkorps. Until 9th December 1941, there was uncertainty for the pilots: there was a rumour of posting to the south, in the Ruhr area, or to the Channel front. At 21:30 hours the news arrived: Stab, as well as 1st and 3rd Staffeln were to move to Katwijk; 2nd Staffel to Vlissingen. The defence of Holland was devolved to them. The following day, the advance guard led by Oberleutnant Borchers set off. On 13th December, 28 brand new Bf 109 Fs landed at Katwijk and twelve others at Vlissingen. They were then distributed to Leeuwarden and Woensdrecht. First of all it was necessary to become familiar with the area, then to start escort missions for small convoys. Winter was hard. Snow covered everything.

Among the young pilots with 2nd Staffel in 1941 was Unteroffizier Albin Wolf, seen here with his Bf 109 F-2 at Jever. This aircraft carries an unusually long aerial mast.

LOSS TABLES - 1941

Date	Name of Crew and Rank	Staffel	Fate	Aircraft, W.Nr & Code	Damage /Loss	Reason for Casualty	Place
04.01.41		1		Bf 109 E-1 (6018)	40%	Damaged taking off.	Bergen
14.02.41	Uffz. Wilhelm Schmidt	1	Killed	Bf 109 E-4 (6073)	100%	Collided in fog with wingman.	De Kooy
23.02.41	Fw. August Hofer	1	Killed	Bf 109 E-4 (5337)			De Kooy
26.02.41		1		Bf 109 E-4 (1780)	20%	Damaged taxiing. Pilot unhurt.	Schipol airfield
06.03.41		1		Bf 109 E-4 (5361)	10%	Damaged on landing. after combat mission.	Schipol airfield
13.03.41		Stab		Bf 109 E-1 (6056)	100%	Crash-landed on non-combat flight. Pilot unhurt.	Jever
31.03.41		I. Gruppe		Bf 109 E-7 (1272)	40%	Crash-landed on non-combat flight. Pilot unhurt.	Bergen
14.04.41		1		Bf 109 E-4 (1582)	35%	Damaged taking off. Pilot unhurt.	Katwijk
17.04.41	Ofhr. Friedheim Gottschalk	1	Killed	Bf 109 E-4 White 9 (1146)	100%	Crashed in the sea followed engine damage.	North Sea
05.06.41		I. Gruppe		Bf 109 E-4 (1524)	100%	Shot down into the sea. Pilot rescued unhurt.	North Sea
07.06.41		3		Bf 109 E-7 (1933)	70%	Returned damaged from combat mission. Pilot unhurt.	De Kooy airfield
08.06.41		I. Gruppe		Bf 109 E-1 (4069)	10%	Belly landing on non-combat flight. Pilot unhurt.	Near Breda
11.06.41		1		Bf 109 E-7 (3174)	35%	Damaged taking off. Pilot unhurt.	Katwijk airfield
17.06.41		1		Bf 109 F-4 (7057)	40%	Crash-landed after combat mission. Pilot unhurt.	De Kooy airfield

Bergen-aan-Zee, Summer 1941. Gruppenkommandeur Mix's Bf 109 F receiving attention from groundcrew. Note the victories marked on the rudder.

Date	*Name of Crew and Rank*	*Staffel*	*Fate*	*Aircraft, W.Nr & Code*	*Damage /Loss*	*Reason for Casualty*	*Place*
18.06.41	Fw. Friedrich Hermann	1		Bf 109 E-4 (1512)	40%	Belly-landed after combat mission. Engine damage.	Bergen airfield
22.06.41		1		Bf 109 F-4 (7052)	15%	Damaged due to technical problem.	Katwijk airfield
23.06.41		Stab		Bf 109 F (12765)	30%	Crashed taking off. Pilot unhurt.	Jever airfield
23.06.41		1		Bf 109 E-4 (936)	70%	Crash-landed after combat mission.	Bergen airfield
27.06.41		1		Bf 109 E-7 (5188)	40%	Crashed on landing on non-combat flight.	Katwijk airfield.
03.07.41		I. Gruppe		Bf 109 F-2 (2854)	15%	Damaged while taxiing.	Bergen airfield.
03.07.41	Major Erich Mix	I. Gruppe		Bf 109 F-4/B (7059)	30%	Crash-landing on non-combat flight.	Katwijk airfield
03.07.41		1		Bf 109 F-1 (5712)	45%	Damaged due to servicing fault.	Luck
15.08.41		I. Gruppe		Bf 109 E-7 (6179)	35%	Damaged due to servicing fault.	Husum
16.08.41	Lt. Heinz Knoke	1		Bf 109 F-2 (12866)	25%	Airframe damage.	Husum
29.08.41	Oblt. Joachim Klug	Stab	Wounded	Bf 109 E-7 (1360)	90%	Crash landed on non-combat flight due to engine damage.	Husum airfield
02.09.41		Stab		Bf 109 F-2 (12775)	100%	Crashed on non-combat flight.	Near Wittmund.
12.09.41	Lt. Siegfried Lüken	3	Killed	Bf 109 F-2 (12862)		Crashed on take-off.	West of Jever
17.09.41		I. Gruppe		Bf 109 E-7 (6110)		Emergency landing after combat mission.	Deventer

Pilots of 2nd Staffel with a Bf 109 F-2. On the aircraft, from left to right: Unteroffiziers Zick, Wennekers and Wolf. Standing, left to right: unknown; Oberfeldwebel Maul; Leutnant Steiger; Hauptmann Dolenga; Leutnant Knoke; Leutnant Gerhard and Feldwebel Dobrick.

Date	Name of Crew and Rank	Staffel	Fate	Aircraft, W.Nr & Code	Damage /Loss	Reason for Casualty	Place
24.09.41		I. Gruppe		Bf 109 F-2 (8967)	75%	Emergency landing after combat mission.	Wangerooge airfield
23.10.41		I. Gruppe		Bf 109 F-2 (6822)	100%	Emergency landing in the sea after combat mission.	North Sea
27.11.41	Gefr. Josef Schmitz	I. Gruppe	Killed	Bf 109	100%	Damage to propellor caused crash.	Venlo airfield
25.12.41		1		Bf 109 E-7 (7476)	60%	Damaged on non-combat flight.	Near Bergen

In mid-December 1941 the first Bf 109 F-2s arrived for I./JG 3, who in a matter of days would become II./ JG 1. The lack of a horizontal bar behind the fuselage cross of "Yellow 7" shows that it was first painted in its former unit's style. This aircraft would soon carry the bar.

Two views of Bf 109 Fs of I. Gruppe at Bergen-aan-Zee in summer 1941. The forward fuselage appears to be painted yellow.

SS-Major Reinhard Heydrich (centre) with members of JG 1 in front of the wing of a Bf 109 E.

Two views of a Bf 109 F-2 during the winter of 1941/42. Snow covering the airfield at Jever made take-offs and landings hazardous.

Unusual form of marking on this Bf 109 E of JG 1: a white chevron followed by an SS rune. The pilot of this aircraft was SS-Major Reinhard Heydrich. Seeking to gain combat experience, he was ultimately banned from flying by the Führer personally.

Two views of Unteroffizier Siegfried Zick and his Bf 109 E-4 carrying the sun emblem and the name "Inge" on the engine cowling.

On 3/7/41 Major Erich Mix belly-landed his Bf 109 F-4, W.Nr. 7059, at Katwijk.

One of the first Bf 109 F-2s to arrive at I. Gruppe was flown by Leutnant Heinz Knoke on 16th August 1941. W. Nr. 12866 was classified as 25% damaged as a result.

Jever, winter 1941/42. Oberfeldwebel Maul, Unteroffizier Zick and Unteroffizier Wolf in front of a Bf 109 F-2.

Groundcrew with a Bf 109 F in the winter of 1941/42.

Major Dr. Erich Mix heads towards his aircraft after leaving the operations room.

Wennekers with "White 2" of 2nd Staffel at Katwijk. The white numeral is unusual for a 2nd Staffel machine, perhaps a carry-over from the Staffel's previous status. This 109 has the early 'E-1/E-3' cockpit canopy, with an armoured windscreen. The supercharger air intake also looks the worse for wear.

Bf 109 F-2, "Yellow 6" sporting the yellow "Tatzelwurm" emblem and armoured windscreen.

Pilots of I. Gruppe JG 3, to be redesignated II. Gruppe, JG 1, arrived from the eastern front with an impressive array of victories. The rudder of Oberleutnant Robert Olejnik's Bf 109 F shows 37 victories, the majority recorded in the east.

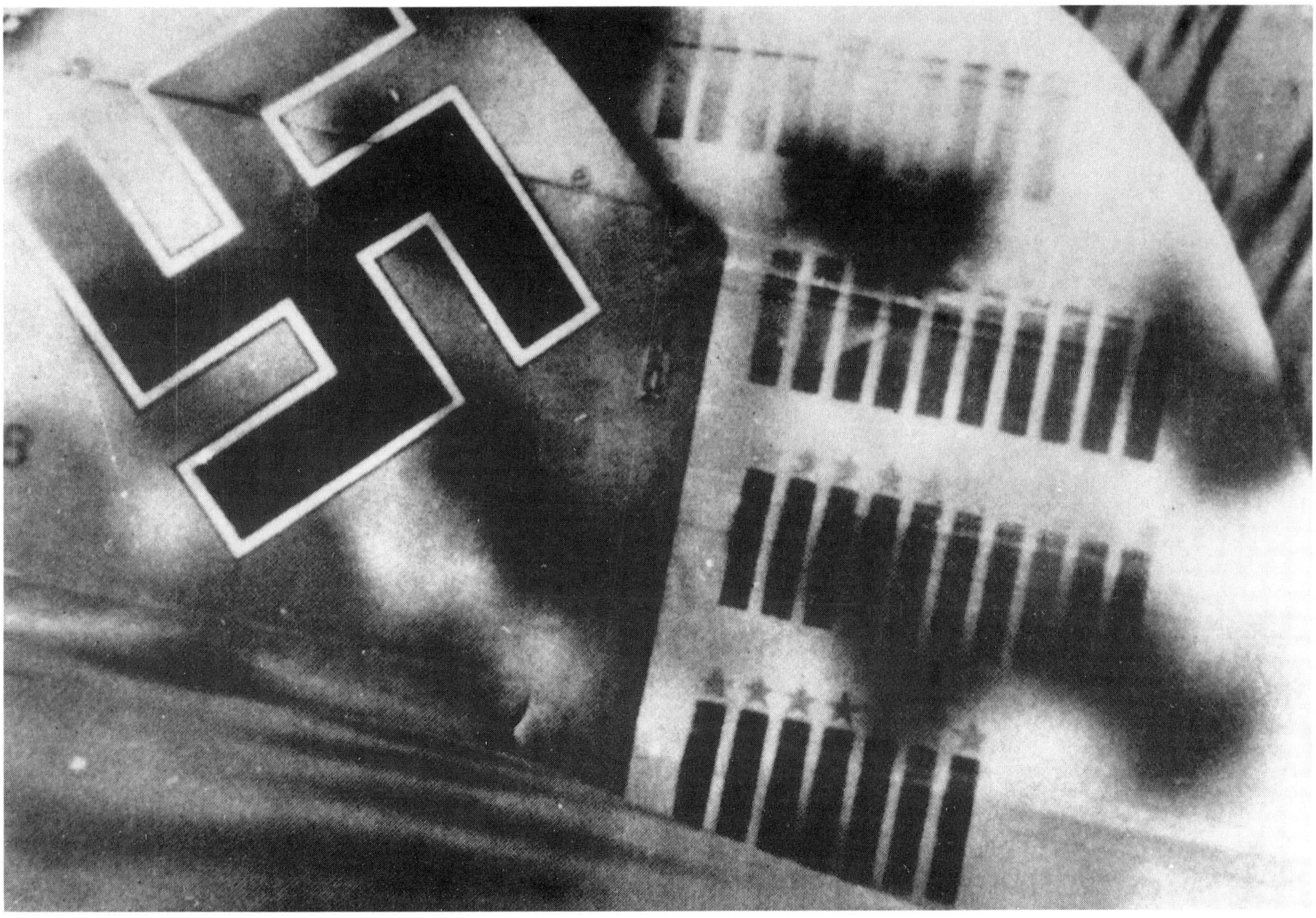

Aircraft of the unit seen at Bergen-aan-Zee in January 1942. This served as the base of 7th Staffel up to 8/2/42, when they moved to Husum.

Bf 109 E of 7th Staffel at Bergen-aan-Zee, January 1942. Note the armoured windscreen, capped spinner and protective cover over the engine cowling.

Aalborg, February 1942. Bf 109 Es of Kommando Losigkeit. Note the high numbers and radio codes on the fuselages, indicating they have been drawn from training units.

CHAPTER 4 - 1942

FORMATION OF II. GRUPPE - EARLY 1942

On 6th January 1942 the order was issued by the Reichsluftfahrt Ministerium, that from 15th January 1942 I. Gruppe, Jagdgeschwader 3 would officially become II. Gruppe, Jagdgeschwader 1. The commands remained unchanged:

Stab, II. Gruppe - Hauptmann Hans von Hahn;
4th Staffel - Oberleutnant Robert Olejnik;
5th Staffel - Oberleutnant Max Bucholz;
6th Staffel - Oberleutnant Eberhard Bock.

At the start of February the majority of pilots were sent to Hamstede. On 7th February, during a transfer flight, contact was made with the enemy for the first time. Oberfeldwebel Detlev Lüth was directed by night fighter operators onto the track of three Hampdens. He shot down all three of them. Laconically, the writer of the unit's war diary noted: "At last the first successes since Russia". Up to this date, the Gruppe had recorded 421 victories. On 8th February, the aircraft complement at Hamstede was as follows;

Stab - three Bf 109 F-4s;
4th Staffel - seven Bf 109 F-4s;
5th Staffel - six Bf 109 F-4s; and
6th Staffel - nine Bf 109 F-4s

On 6th January 1942 the Reichsluftfahrt Ministerium

Oberleutnant Robert Olejnik, the first Staffelkapitän of 4th Staffel.

Hauptmann Fritz Losigkeit was charged with the task of creating a "Kommando" to protect shipping passing the Norwegian coast. He wears the Iron Cross, First Class and Frontflugspange on the left side of his jacket, and the Spanish Cross (awarded to those participating in the Spanish Civil War) on his right.

Feldwebel Küpper of 5th Staffel was one of the victorious pilots during "Operation Donnerkeil". Unfortunately his claim for a Vickers Wellington was not confirmed.

also announced the creation of a III. Gruppe for the unit. It was formed from small units already in existence:

Stab, Erg. Gr. JG 52 became Stab, III./JG 1;
Erg. Gruppe 1 (Vannes) formed the basis of 7./JG 1;
Eins. St. Erg. Gr. JG 27 became 8./JG 1;
Eins. St. Erg. Gr. JG 52 became 9./JG 1.

Commanding officers were:
Stab - Hauptmann Herbert Kijewski;
7th Staffel - Oberleutnant Harry Koch;
8th Staffel - Hauptmann Julius Henschel; and
9th Staffel - Oberleutnant Werner Gutowski.

Hauptmann Herbert Kijewski already had a fine career as a fighter pilot behind him. Staffelkapitän of 5./JG 3, then Gruppenkommandeur of III. Gruppe of that unit, he left the eastern front at the end of 1941 to take up a new post in the west. He had 24 victories to his credit.

Unteroffizier Alois Job recalled the creation of 7th Staffel: "Being on the ground personnel of JG 26 at Werl in 1939, I volunteered to be a fighter pilot. I made my first flight on 26th April 1940 at Breslau. I then passed through Stephansdorf, Breslau, Vienna, and Düsseldorf. In mid-October 1941 I was assigned to the Ergänzungsgruppe at Vannes. There, my war missions would finally begin: submarine escort. Thankless and stressful tasks; overflying the sea is always a risky affair. Five weeks later, a dozen comrades and myself received the order to take our Bf 109 Es to Berlin/Döberitz: the unit was going to receive the new Bf 109 F. Arriving at Döberitz, our group was put under the control of Oberleutnant Koch and transferred to Bergen aan Zee via Hanover. Without realising it, from our arrival in Holland, on 25th December 1941, we formed the substance of 7th Staffel, Jagdgeschwader 1".

Regarding the 9th Staffel, Oberleutnant Werner Gutowski recalled: "After having taken part in the western campaign and the Battle of Britain with 5th Staffel, Jagdgeschwader 52, then the Geschwaderstab, I was given command of 3rd Staffel of EJG 52. With this Gruppe, whose task was to finish off the training of young pilots, we took up quarters at Elbing, in East Prussia, in June 1941. On 22nd June, the same day as the invasion of Russia, I learned that my Staffel had to return to the west, to Jever. I presented myself before Kommodore Schumacher, who informed me that henceforth my Staffel came under his jurisdiction. It was renamed 9./JG 1 shortly afterwards and moved to Husum. My unit was dispersed on different aerodromes.

Placed further north than other Gruppen of the unit, III. Gruppe took over the protection of southern Norway and Denmark, a very calm area which had been so for a long

Trondheim, February 1942. A Bf 109 of Kommando Losigkeit with damage to the undercarriage and propellor blades. The high numeral "Yellow 25" and radio code are evident.

Bleak weather conditions for groundcrew of Kommando Losigkeit working on this Bf 109 E.

On 6/3/42 the work of Kommando Losigkeit was complete at Trondheim. In front of their Bf 109 Es, pilots of JG 1 make preparations to return to their unit via Oslo-Fornebu.

On 6/3/42 at 16:10 hours, after two hours flying time, two 2nd Staffel pilots, realising they did not have sufficient fuel to reach Oslo, made a fortunate landing on a frozen lake near Wesbyen. As well as Hauptmann Dolenga, who is seen here sitting forlornly on the wing of his Bf 109 E, Unteroffizier Wennekers also crash-landed, several metres away. Leutnant Knoke managed to get further, but eventually suffered the same fate as his comrades. Dolenga's Bf 109 E carries the numeral "Black 1" denoting the Staffelkapitän of 2nd Staffel, and is fitted with an armoured windscreen. The engine cowling can be seen in the left foreground.

Same place, same circumstance - the Bf 109 E, "Black 16" of Unteroffizier Wennekers, whose three bent propellor blades show that the engine was turning as it landed. This aircraft also has an armoured windscreen, and carries two victory markings on the rudder.

Unteroffizier Alois Job of 7th Staffel in his Bf 109 E, which clearly shows the III. Gruppe emblem of a Maltese cross in a shield.

time. Vigilance flights and escort to shipping was the lot of the pilots. They had to wait until 17th August 1942 before Unteroffizier Heinz Born opened the Gruppe's account. The second victory did not arrive until 1943.
The same order of 6th January also announced the formation of IV. Gruppe. It was also created from training units:
Stab, Erg. Gr. JG 53 became Stab, IV./JG 1;
Eins. St. Erg. Gr. JG 77 became 10./JG 1;
Eins. St. Erg. Gr. JG 26 became 11./JG 1; and
Eins. St. Erg. Gr. JG 51 became 12./JG 1.
Commanding officers were:

Stab - Hauptmann Günther Scholz;
10th Staffel - Oberleutnant Diethelm von Eichel-Streiber;
11th Staffel - Oberleutnant Hermann Segatz; and
12th Staffel - Oberleutnant Herbert Huppertz.

This fourth Gruppe was formed at Brest, to be then transferred to Jever. Sent further north, to Norway, it would serve as the backbone of Jagdgeschwader 5 upon that unit's creation.
February 1942. Winter, with a savagery rarely reached, cut off the islands. Every day, in the early morn, the mist took over. No chance of taking off. If it was really necessary, visibility, which rarely exceeded 50 metres, transformed what would normally be a routine flight into

Feldwebel Hutter (left) and Ritterkreuzträger Oberleutnant Max Bucholz in the sunshine outside the operations room. On 12/2/42 Bucholz recorded his last victory, a Blenheim. Several weeks later he was posted to head of a flying school. He would then be in this line of duty until the end of the war.

March 1942. Unteroffizier Heinz Hanke sits proudly on Bf 109 F-2, "Black 7", of 8th Staffel.

Bergen-aan-Zee, early 1942. Hauptmann Harry Koch, Staffelkapitän of 7th Staffel poses with a Staffelhund beside the rudder of his Bf 109 F, W.Nr. 5477. There are 13 aerial victories shown, four fighter-bomber missions and a ship sunk.

Early 1942 at Aalborg. Hauptmann Harry Koch in discussion with pilots of the newly-formed 7th Staffel.

This emblem, a pink demon emerging from clouds against a blue background, was first seen on a Bf 109 in 1939. Hauptmann Wilhelm Moritz apparently re-introduced it in 1942 as the IV Gruppe emblem, and it could still be seen on aircraft of Jagdgeschwader 1 in 1945.

7th Staffel emblem which adorned the engine cowlings of their Bf 109 Es in 1942.

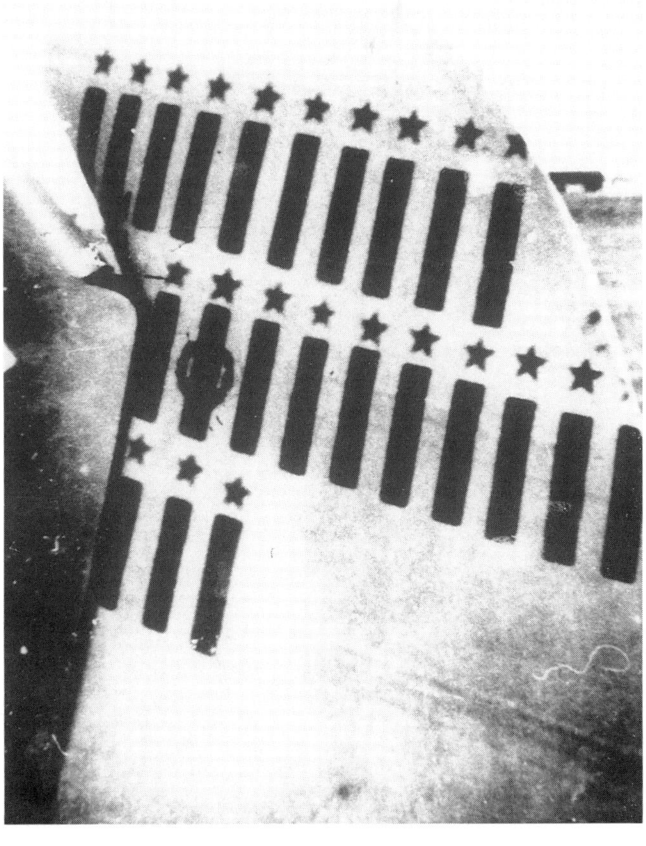

Haamstede, early 1942. 23 "kills" adorn the rudder of Oberleutnant Eberhard Bock's Bf 109. Withdrawn from frontline action following the death of his brother, he was killed bailing out when he collided with the rear of his aircraft.

The Fw 190 A-2, "White 7", W.Nr. 418, of Hauptmann Robert Olejnik, Staffelkapitän of 4th Staffel, with a Tatzelwurm in the Staffel colour of white.

a deadly exercise. One pilot noted in his diary: "Here, one could be on the steppes of Siberia. The storm, without respite, sweeps across the runways, hurls itself around buildings, hammers at doors and windows. The squalls reach speeds of up to 120 kilometres per hour".

The unit was stood down until the storms had subsided. However, on 11th February, they were placed on readiness. At 19:00 hours, the code word "Donnerkeil" reached the unit.

Bf 109 Es of 11th Staffel in the spring of 1942. With cockpits open, they are ready for take-off at a moment's notice.

OPERATION "DONNERKEIL" - FEBRUARY 1942

Since March and June 1941, the major units of the Kriegsmarine had been blocaded in the naval dockyards at Brest. Since that time they had met with over 300 aerial attacks, and it was time to find refuge elsewhere. The General Staff decided that they should be sheltered in the deep fjords of Norway. To do that, it required an audacious move: to clear the Pas-de-Calais under the nose and whiskers of the British. Fighters were tasked to provide aerial cover for the convoy. On board every large ship there was placed a fighter liaison officer. For example, on board the Scharnhost was Ritterkreuzträger, Oberst Max Ibel. Jagdgeschwader 2, 26, and 1, together with twelve aircraft from the Paris fighter school and 30 Bf 110 night fighters, would successively provide the aerial cover. The co-ordination of the Luftwaffe units was given to Adolf Galland, who had just succeeded Oberst Mölders as Generall der Jagdflieger.

On 11th February 1942, at 20:00 hours, the battle cruisers Scharnhost and Gneisenau, heavy cruiser Prinz Eugen, five destroyers and an escort flotilla appeared. However an aerial attack surprised them and they returned to their anchorage. At 22:00 hours, the order to depart was issued again, and shortly before 23:00 hours the convoy left Brest. At 09:00 hours the following day the convoy passed Cherbourg. During the first part of the journey, the British made no response. The bad weather undoubtedly helped the fugitives. At 11:00 hours the convoy was spotted by two British reconnaissance aircraft returning from a flight over northern France.

At 13:16 hours the convoy drew the fire of the British coastal batteries. Eighteen minutes later, the action began: six Swordfish torpedo aircraft and their escort of Spitfires approached. The Swordfish pilots showed great courage, but every single aircraft was shot down, either by naval defensive fire, or the aircraft of Jagdgeschwader 2. The Spitfires, held at bay by III. Gruppe, Jagdgeschwader 26, could not help. Presently the convoy approached the Scheldt estuary. Jagdgeschwader 1 would take over aerial escort duties.

At 15:30 hours an explosion shook the Scharnhorst: it had been damaged by a mine and remained immobilised off Holland for an hour. By chance, the mist became thick at that time.

Since 14:00 hours 27 Bf 109 Fs of II. Gruppe were ready to take up the escort rôle. However, the weather prevented any take off. It was only at 16:30 hours that the first aircraft could leave the ground. An hour later 4th and 6th Staffeln took off for action.

Identified by colour flares, II. Gruppe immediately entered combat, intercepting bombers. The courage of the British pilots was not sufficient, and their attacks became almost suicidal. When the Bf 109s of II. Gruppe landed towards 18:30 hours, they had returned seven victories and one probable. Among those victorious were Oberleutnant Bucholz (his 28th and last victory); Feldwebel Küpper (13th); Unteroffizier Kirchner (1st) and Oberleutnant Bock (22nd). The following is Oberleutnant Bock's account of the action: "On 12th February 1942 I took off at 17:20 hours from Haamstede aerodrome. The Schwarm's mission was to escort a large naval convoy up to Den Haag. The weather was so terrible that immediately after taking off I lost sight of the second Schwarm, which one of my pilots had erroneously chosen to follow. Due to the rain, visibility was about 2 kilometres.

I headed on the bearings indicated by the ships, but nevertheless had to head in the direction of the coast, as the weather rendered precise directing impossible. I wanted to pick up a course which was in a general easterly direction, at 50 metres altitude, when I saw an aircraft flying to the north of the coast 50 metres higher than myself. This difference of altitude allowed me to identify it as a Handley-Page Harford. After changing course, I was able to attack it from below. I fired while turning towards it, and kept on up to the last moment. I did a half turn in the clouds, and when I came out, I could see to my left the aircraft sinking in the waves, its right engine on fire. It was 17:37 hours and we were 7 kilometres to the west of Katwijk. My two wingmen were still far away from me when I saw 100 metres above me an Armstrong Whitley flying northwards. After changing direction I attacked it from below and behind. The enemy was so slow compared to me that I could only a fire a short burst before overtaking it. My victim then turned towards the Dutch coast, and I was able to attack again. During this attack, the enemy began to burn. It exploded and fell like a torch at an angle of 45 degrees. It crashed about 7 kilometres to the west of Katwijk. It was 17:39

Spring 1942, probably at Woensdrecht. Groundcrew pose in front of a Bf 109 F of 4th Staffel.

The emblem of IV. Gruppe, seen here on a Bf 109 E of 10th Staffel: a demon coming out of the clouds.

This pilot in Bf 109 E, "White 5", of 7th Staffel has just completed the 1,000th mission of the Staffel. There is evidence of a painted-out II. Gruppe bar aft of the fuselage cross.

hours. During these attacking manoeuvres I had lost my two wingmen. Shortly after my second victory I joined up with them in the area of the crashes. I then flew at 20 metres above the waves in order to find the ships to escort. The poor weather persisted: ceiling was about 50/100 metres. The rain and snow prevented forward vision in excess of one kilometre. The rain rendered the windscreen more and more opaque. However, I met up with the vessels at the head of the convoy. They greeted me with a very hot reception! I immediately drew away, and lost my wingmen once again. Alone, I remained ahead of the convoy for ten minutes to protect it. The weather got worse, so I set course for Haamstede where I landed at 18:15 hours".

On the following day, following the progress of the ships, II. Gruppe landed at the base at Uetersen, which was covered in snow. On 14th, the pilots were at Stade, from where they were dispersed to Lister and Aalborg. On 25th, they returned to Holland: Stab (3 aircraft) and 5th Staffel (8 aircraft) returning to Katwijk, the 12 aircraft of 4th Staffel to Leeuwarden and 10 Bf 109 Fs of 6th Staffel to Haamstede.

Although the Scharnhost was slightly damaged by a mine, the convoy passed almost unharmed. Eventually, the ships announced that they were in sight of Norway. They were safe. For the time being ...

Jagdgeschwader 1's involvement in Operation Donnerkeil did not finish there. At Jever, forces were rapidly assembled to protect those vessels which could not enter the deep waters of the fjords. The pilots were charged with aerial security until an effective and autonomous defence force could be put in place. I. Gruppe furnished the ground personnel, as well as several pilots of 2nd Staffel. The unit was given the name "Kommando Losigkeit", being named after its commanding officer. It was composed as follows:

1st Staffel - Oberleutnant Strössner;

2nd Staffel - Hauptmann Dolenga; and

3rd Staffel - Oberleutnant Eberle (who also was head of the Fighter Training Staffel Nr.1, which was also integrated in to the "Kommando").

From 15th to 20th February, the pilots were based in Denmark in Aalborg and Esjberg. They then moved to Gardermoen in Norway, and on 24th February, Trondheim. Evidently the British paid great attention to these battleships in the fjords. They continually launched photographic reconnaissance missions (under the code name "Chamberlain") over the Trondheim area. They sought to keep track of the slightest movement of the ships, and to evaluate their strength. These missions were not enjoyed by allied pilots: they were extremely long, on average 5¼ hours, there were frequent climatic changes, and often the target would be shrouded in mist. There was also the constant threat of murderous flak and enemy fighters. The allied fighters had, however, a trump card: they were flying a Spitfire which was so streamlined as to give them sufficient speed to evade enemy fighters.

Spring 1942. Bf 109 F, "Yellow 3", of 6th Staffel.

Unteroffizier Heinz Hanke of 7th Staffel in Bf 109 E, "White 6", early 1942.

Katwijk, April 1942. Pilots grouped around a Bf 109 F carrying a spiral spinner.

On the ground, when the weather was clear, the German pilots could see the condensation trails. They would jump into their machines, but by the time they had gained sufficient altitude to intercept, the Spifire would have disappeared. However, on 5th March 1942 Leutnants Knoke and Gerhard managed to catch one. The allied pilot bailed out and was captured.
On 6th March, Losigkeit's unit set off for home. However, a misfortune attended three of the pilots. An officer had misjudged the distance and the three aircraft had to put down as a matter of urgency on a frozen lake, near Wesbyen, out of fuel. Hauptmann Dolenga, Leutnant Knoke and Unteroffizier Wennekers were unhurt but their aircraft were submerged. The pilots rejoined the rest of the Kommando at Oslo. Aalborg and Jever were the final stop-over places. The men finally reached their respective units.
"During the operation to secure the safety of our ships in Norway, General Galland rejoined us at Esjberg where I led a training unit. I proposed to him that we convert our combat Staffeln into an effective fighter Gruppe. This proposition was studied and taken on board. The formation of the Gruppe took place at Döberitz a few weeks after this." - Hauptmann Wilhelm Moritz.
Hauptmann Losigkeit had proved his ability to lead a fighter Gruppe. On his return to Germany, he was entrusted with the creation of the new IV. Gruppe, Jagdgeschwader 1.

Oberleutnant Olejnik being congratulated by a member of the ground personnel upon return from combat.

THE REBIRTH OF IV. GRUPPE - APRIL/JULY 1942

On 4th April 1942 this Gruppe officially came into existence at Döberitz and Werneuchen, made up primarily of young pilots from training schools. Nevertheless the Gruppenkommandeur was surrounded by men who already possessed considerable experience:

10th Staffel - Oberleutnant Fritz Eberle;
11th Staffel - Hauptmann Wilhelm Moritz; and
12th Staffel - Oberleutnant Franz Eisenach.

These pilots carved out an excellent career in the Luftwaffe; the latter two would receive the Ritterkreuz.
Apart from taking part in Operation Donnerkeil, the early part of 1942 was very calm for II. Gruppe. There were certain noteworthy events: On 13th March, Feldwebel Winkler shot down a Spitfire, whose pilot was captured. However two days later a Rotte of 6th Staffel disappeared over the sea, victims, it would appear, of Spitfires. On 9th May two Spitfires fell to the guns of Oberfeldwebel Lüth and Feldwebel Hutter.
Changes also took place. From 12th May, their mounts were changed. The Bf 109 F-4s were exchanged for Focke Wulf 190 A-2s and A-3s which the neighbouring unit, Jagdgeschwader 26, had employed with success for nine months. This change also involved a change at the head of 6th Staffel: Oberleutnant Bock handed over command to Oberleutnant Detlev Rohwer who arrived from Rothenburg with the first Fw 190 A-2s and A-3s.

Excellent close-up view of the Tatzelwurm emblemof II. Gruppe.

Line-up of Bf 109 Es of 9th Staffel at Lister, 17/5/42.

Two views of a Bf 109 E of IV. Gruppe in its blast pen at Bergen-op-Zoom in Spring 1942.

Feldwebel Küpper poses on his Bf 109 F. Just visible is the left wing of a rather large bird emblem on the fuselage.

On 17th May Oberleutnants Olejnik and Rohwer carried out a comparison test of performances of the two fighter aircraft. The first-named flew a Bf 109 F, the second a Fw 190 A-3. It appeared that the Fw 190 had greater speed in the dive; could turn tighter, and was faster in level flight. On the other hand, at over 8,000 metres the greater weight of the Fw 190 became a handicap. The view was that the Fw 190 meant real progress.

There were also changes in personnel. Gruppenkommandeur Hans von Hahn received a new posting. After service in the east and west, he was to move north to take up a post in the Geschwaderstab of Jagdgeschwader 5. His place would be taken by Hauptmann Herbert Kijewski, who would move from III. Gruppe. Oberleutnants Olejnik and Rohwer, the most experienced Staffelkapitäne of II. Gruppe, took care of the day-to-day business in the interim period; Kijewski did not take up post until 15th October.

In his duties, the new Gruppenkommandeur would be assisted by an Oberleutnant, 27 years old, with a strong personality: Dietrich Wickop. He had fought with I. Gruppe, Jagdgeschwader 2 from December 1940. In July 1942 he was posted to the General Staff of Fighters - Holland, and then posted to Jagdgeschwader 1.

An unknown pilot of the unit smiles from the cockpit of his Bf 109 F.

Two views of a Bf 109 F of II. Gruppe at Katwijk, May 1942. Oberfeldwebel Georg Hutter perches on the cowling of his Bf 109 F peering at something of obvious interest through binoculars. Note the spiral spinner, and chevron indicating the Gruppenadjutant's machine of II. Gruppe. The Tatzelwurm emblem would be in green.

Katwijk, early summer 1942. Fw 190 A-2, "Black 8", of 5th Staffel shortly before take-off. Note the lower engine panel painted in the Staffel colour of red, and the Tatzelwurm in the same colour.

THE GROWTH OF II. GRUPPE - MAY/JUNE 1942

At the beginning of June the II. Gruppe commanders were as follows:
Stab - Oberleutnant Detlev Rohwer;
4th Staffel - Oberleutnat Robert Olejnik;
5th Staffel - Oberleutnant Max Bucholz; and
6th Staffel - Oberleutnant Detlev Rohwer.
Stab, 4th and 6th Staffeln were based at Woensdrecht; 5th Staffel at Katwijk.
Schwärme were regularly posted for several days to the aerodromes of Haamstede, Venlo, Schipol and Vlissingen. The detachments for the latter base became more and more rare, as the space was too small for a formation of Focke Wulf 190s.
Woensdrecht, the principal base of the Gruppe, was no more than a grass covered clearing surrounded by woods, with the village which gave its name to it to the south-west.
On 19th June the first major engagement for the Fw 190 A-2 took place. Seventeen aircraft (nine from 4th Staffel and eight from 6th Staffel) took off to patrol the Belgian coast. They were led by Oberleutnant Rohwer towards a British formation. The clash with the Spitfires of 152 Squadron took place at about 11:20 hours in the Zee-

Denmark, spring 1942. Unteroffiziere Reichenstein and "Napp" Rudschinat pose for the camera with Bf 109 E, "Black 10" as a backdrop.

The emblem of 9th Staffel was carried on the fuselage aft of the cross as well as on the engine cowling. The words translate as: "He who shoots first lives longest".

This Bf 109 E-7 is that of Staffelkapitän Oberleutnant Werner Gutowski of 9th Staffel, the 9th Staffel being formed from EJG 52. Of interest is the small fairing under the fuselage, which was the protective cover for a camera.

brugge area. The combat was violent, with aircraft going down in flames. The British lost five aircraft to the Germans two. Victories were claimed by Oberfeldwebel Ehlers (2 Spitfires); Leutnant Leonhardt; Unteroffizier Flecks and Unteroffizier Brakebush, killed shortly after. The four pilots, as well as the two losses, all came from 6th Staffel. II. Gruppe was launched on its combat road. From mid-June, IV. Gruppe began conversion to the Fw 190. Several pilots were sent to Rothenburg. Unteroffizier Fritz Haspel of 10th Staffel, for example, carrying out six take-offs before nightfall on 20th June, ferried his Fw 190 to Bergen.

Afterwards several pilots went to train their colleagues of 8th Staffel, at Leeuwarden. The compliment was repaid by some pilots of III. Gruppe who had earlier been trained at Rothenburg in May 1942 - they helped the conversion of another Staffel of IV. Gruppe.

A Bf 109 E of 9th Staffel carrying the emblem on the engine cowling.

Two views of a Fw 190 A-3 of 5th Staffel at Katwijk in summer 1942.

4th Staffel pilots at Woensdrecht in June 1942 relax in deckchairs alongside a Fw 190 A-3 of their Staffel.

Leutnant Rüdiger von Kirchmayr poses on his Fw 190 A-3 of 4th Staffel after being posted-in on 4/6/42. It would be the start of a brilliant career with the unit.

In summer 1942 4th and 6th Staffel were based at Woensdrecht, which explains the presence of 4th Staffel pilots Leutnant von Kirchmayr and Unteroffizier Niedereichholz in the shade near a 6th Staffel Fw 190 A-3.

Erich Friedrich, BMW mechanic attached to 5th Staffel, supervises the fitting of a Fw 190 A engine at Katwijk in summer 1942. The layout of the engine can be clearly seen. Note the twin-coloured spinner.

Four Fw 190 As of 4th Staffel at Woensdrecht in June 1942. The engines of the furthest three are running. In the distance, four pilots head towards the aircraft.

Fw 190 A's well hidden under cover of trees. The second aircraft carries a red Tatzelwurm, denoting 5th Staffel. Of interest are the different white markings on the spinners.

Unteroffizier Günter Kirchner, killed in the last weeks of the war, poses beside his Fw 190 A-3, W.Nr. 336 at Katwijk in June 1942.

Bf 109 E, "Yellow 7", of 12th Staffel in its blast pen in June 1942, probably at Mönchen-Gladbach.

Mönchen-Gladbach in the summer of 1942. A view of the operations room with blast pens alongside for aircraft of 11th Staffel.

Fw 190s of 11th Staffel in their blast pens at Mönchen-Gladbach, summer 1942.

The first Fw 190 A-3s to equip 11th Staffel. In the foreground, "Black 1", W.Nr.422, of the Staffelkapitän. The second aircraft in the line-up still carries radio codes.

JULY TO DECEMBER 1942

IV. Gruppe, and in particular 10th Staffel, encountered the enemy for the first time on 4th July. The airfields of Katwijk and Bergen aan Zee were attacked by Douglas DB 7s. Two pilots of IV. Gruppe took off as the bombs rained down. Unteroffizier Johannes Rathenow caught and shot down one of the bombers, registering the first success of the Gruppe. The first loss was suffered also. Unteroffizier Erwin Grütz was mortally hit by defensive fire and his Bf 109 F-4 crashed near his base. A technician on the ground was killed, and several were wounded.

The début of the Fw 190 was difficult. Unteroffizier Alois Job of 7th Staffel recalled that it was rare for a Focke Wulf engine to last more than ten flying hours! They caught fire regularly. However, by the end of summer, only I. Gruppe still flew the Bf 109.

27th August saw the first victory of III. Gruppe: Unteroffizier Heinz Born of 9th Staffel shot down a reconnaissance Spitfire piloted by the Belgian Pilot Officer Andrée Cantillion. On 27th August the Geschwaderkommodore, Major von Selle, handed over command of the unit to Major Dr. Erich Mix, formerly Gruppenkommandeur of I. Gruppe. Hauptmann Günther Beise, a 30 year-old pilot became Gruppenkommandeur of I. Gruppe. During summer '42, the various Staffeln of the unit continued to prepare for combat. Formation flying was perfected; training of the young pilots who continued to fill the ranks continued apace. Although the sector covered by Jagdgeschwader 1 was relatively quiet, events further south were hotting up, with allied troops landed at Dieppe on 19th August 1942. However during that month a greater menace appeared in the skies in the shape of Boeing B-17s, "Flying Fortresses" as they were known. Jagdgeschwader 1 had its first brush with a formation of B-17s who were out to attack Rotterdam. Nine Fw 190s led by Oberleutnant Olejnik attacked a formation of a dozen B-17s. Without loss, the Americans repulsed the attacks of the Germans. Oberfeldwebel Lüth, whose engine had been hit, had to make a belly landing.

On 7th September II. and IV. Gruppen were scrambled to intercept an enemy formation. 29 bombers were on the way to Rotterdam and Utrecht. The take off for the Germans went without problems, but not without fear. What had been heard about these four-engined aircraft (Viermots) had been unnerving. The strength of their defensive armament was incredible: each aircraft was equipped with ten heavy machine guns of 0.5 inch calibre. Also, they flew in compact groups (boxes), mutually covering each other, and were well escorted.

Two views of a damaged Bf 109 F in its blast pen.

Two views of a Bf 109 F of 12th Staffel with engine cowling removed receiving attention from groundcrew in the early summer of 1942 at Mönchen-Gladbach.

The result of this interception was poor: not only did the bombers pass without being troubled, but the escort of 20-30 Spitfires shot down and killed Leutnant Endrizzi of 4th Staffel, and another Fw 190 returned to base with damage.

Few events of note happened to disturb the second half of the year. I. Gruppe were re-equipped with the Bf 109 G-1, which superceded the Bf 109 F-4. Several disquieting accidents occurred, put down to teething problems with a new version. Engines caught fired without apparent reason which could lead to catastrophe. On 2nd October Unteroffozier Wennekers was fortunate. His engine caught fire suddenly whilst chasing a Mosquito. He managed to bail out unhurt. In spite of this fault, which was soon rectified when it was found the engine was overheating, the "Gustav" was well thought of. The increased performance allowed it to catch and shoot down the Mosquito, the fast, light British reconnaissance aircraft, which was considered almost impossible to catch. In 2nd Staffel, Oberleutnant Heinz Knoke showed his talents by recording his second and third victories: a Blenheim on 31st October and a Mosquito on 6th November.

In the matter of "chasing Mosquitos", II. Gruppe made its point on 11th October: Unteroffiziers Kolschek (4th Staffel) and Kirschner (5th Staffel) each claimed one shot down over the sea. In IV. Gruppe nine pilots received the Eisern Kreuz II. Klasse before the end of the year. Among them were Unteroffizier (later Feldwebel) Karl Bugaj, who had claimed a Mosquito on 28th July

Unteroffizier Alois Job of 7th Staffel with his Bf 109 E, "White 9" at Aalborg in July 1942. Note the III. Gruppe emblem beneath the cockpit and the pilot's head armour. One of the first Fw 190 As delivered to III. Gruppe can be seen in the background.

1942 and a Wellington on 31st October. There were also first victories with the unit for Feldwebel Rudolf Piffer of 11th Staffel - a Mosquito on 19th September, and Oberleutnant Hugo Frey of 10th Staffel - a Douglas on 4th September. Mosquitos were also claimed by three pilots of 12th Staffel: Feldwebel Roden on 6th September; Oberleutnant S'trohall on 8th September and Feldwebel Timm on 9th October.

IV. Gruppe continued its build-up. Leutnant Eberhard Burath, a young pilot fresh from training, described his arrival at IV. Gruppe: "I was completely dizzy, but proud. I had finally arrived! More than two years after the start of my training as a pilot, here I was at the front. I presented myself before Hauptmann Losigkeit in IV. Gruppe's command quarters at Mönchengladbach. He lobbed his favourite words at me to ensure I realised there were no easy times ahead: "Ich heisse Losigkeit, wie "Arbeitslosigkeit", aber ohne "Arbeit". He seemed to have a sense of humour. I was to find that out often. Meanwhile, I was posted to 11th Staffel. My room-mate was Leutnant Munz. I found him to be an excellent friend. A certain Toni Piffer, future recipient of the Ritterkreuz, also belonged to 11th Staffel, under the command of Oberleutnant Framm. As it happened, there was not a lot of contact with the enemy, at least not until the end of November '42".

Tatzelwurm on the starboard engine cowling, with access panels removed for maintenance/repair work.

Fw 190 A-2, W.Nr. 327, of 5th Staffel at Katwijk in summer 1942.

On 4/7/42 Unteroffizier Johannes Rathenow recorded the first victory of IV. Gruppe when Bostons were involved in a mission against Bergen-op Zoom airfield. His Fw 190 A-3, W.Nr.437, is met by his comrades on his return from action.

Rathenow leaps from the cockpit of his Fw 190A "White 12".

Rathenow poses proudly beside the fin of his Fw 190, which clearly shows the W.Nr.437.

Rathenow receives the congratulations of his colleagues from 10th Staffel. From left: Unteroffizier Haspel; Unteroffizier Bucek; unknown; Unteroffizier Rathenow; Feldwebel Snaidero; Feldwebel Laun and an unknown member of the ground personnel.

Two excellent views of Rathenow's Fw 190 A-3, "White 12", W.Nr.437.

Three pilots and a Staffelhund in front of the rudder of the victorious machine. From left: Unteroffizier Bucek; Unteroffizier Rathenow and Feldwebel Snaidero.

Excellent shot of Unteroffizier Snaidero sitting beside Fw 190 A, "White 12". Snaidero was badly wounded in the leg in combat on 15/5/43.

Shortly after IV. Gruppe's first victory, the victorious pilot received the Iron Cross,Second Class, from Gruppenkommandeur Major Losigkeit.

The first victory coincided with the first loss. Unteroffizier Erwin Grütz took off at the same time as Rathenow but his aircraft was hit. Mortally wounded, he crashed in his Bf 109 F-4, "White 6", W.Nr. 7423.

The end of July 1942 was a period of change for IV. Gruppe. Fw 190s progressively replaced their Bf 109 Es. A Bf 109 E is in the right foreground while pilots examine a brand new Fw 190 A.

Unteroffizier Erwin Grütz was buried with full military honours. Note the light colour on the underside of the wing of the Fw 190.

Fw 190 A-3, "White 1" of Hauptmann Friedrich Eberle being pushed into its blast pen by groundcrew.

Two views of a line-up of Fw 190 A-3s of 4th Staffel.

General Schwabedissen of 2nd Jagddivision visiting the Danish base of Esbjerg in summer 1942. He is met by some of the principal officers of III. Gruppe. From left to right: Schwabedissen; Hauptmann Gutowski (Staffelkapitän of 9th Staffel); Hauptmann Kijewski (Gruppenkommandeur) and Leutnant Deterra (Gruppenadjutant). Note the Bf 109 and the Fw 190 in the background; the visit coming at the time of changeover from one type to the other.

First victory for 11th Staffel (and second victory for IV. Gruppe) was recorded by Unteroffizier Karl Bugaj over Mönchen-Gladbach on 28/7/42. The victim was a Mosquito, which crashed near Tilburg. Bugaj is seen here upon his return to Mönchen-Gladbach being congratulated by other members of his Staffel.

On 7th November an accident at Stavanger resulted in Hauptmann Julius Henschel (Staffelkapitän of 8th Staffel) losing his life. He sought to be first to take off, without first checking on the position of his other pilots. Leutnant Richter crashed into his Fw 190, and the two A-3 versions burned immediately. Only Richter survived the inferno.

A move took place before the end of the year. Following the allied landings in North Africa on 8th November, a half dozen pilots from I. Gruppe, drawn mainly from 3rd Staffel, were sent to reinforce German fighters engaged on this front. They were led by Oberleutnant Werner Heidrich and left for Tunisia on 26th November. Heidrich, with five victories, had some experience, but the majority of his men had hardly any. Even less so on African soil! The Staffelkapitän fell in combat on 13th January 1943 after adding three more victories to his tally, when his unit, or what was left of it, was integrated into Jagdgeschwader 51.

There were some final important combats for II. Gruppe before the year's end. On 6th December 4th and 6th Staffeln based at Woensdrecht were called to combat far to the south. 85 B-17s and B-24s of the 1st and 2nd Bomb Wing were attacking Lille and Abbeville. Oberfeldwebel Ehlers and Unteroffizier Wloschinski, both of 6th Staffel, each recorded a victory. During their absence, at around 12:30 hours, two formations of Venturas, each flying at low altitude, overflew the base at Woensdrecht. One aircraft was shot down by the airfield defences and burned out near the runway. After combat in French skies, the first Kette of 6th Staffel returned to base quickly. They arrived just in time near Woensdrecht to shoot down one of the Venturas. It was also at that moment that 5th Staffel, called to the rescue from Schipol, arrived. Four victories in as many minutes were recorded, Oberfeldwebel Heeson and Unteroffizier Kirchner being among the victors.

Shortly afterwards, Hauptmann Moritz, Staffelkapitän of 11th Staffel, offered his congratulations to the successful pilot.

Two views of Feldwebel Franz Snaidero about to vacate the cockpit of his Fw 190.

Four ground personnel pose on the engine cowling of a Bf 109 F at Mönchen-Gladbach.

LOSS TABLES - 1942

Date	Name of Crew and Rank	Staffel	Fate	Aircraft, W.Nr & Code	Damage /Loss	Reason for Casualty	Place
10.01.42		I. Gruppe		Bf 109 E (7681)	80%	Crash landed due to engine problems.	Hannover-Fahrenwald
17.01.42		I. Gruppe		Junkers W-34 (1507)	65%	Crash landed due to engine problems.	Jever
21.01.42	Uffz. Bruno Wolny	2	Killed	Bf 109 E-4 Black 5. (4892)	95%	Crashed on take-off	Near Jever
23.01.42		IV. Gruppe		Bf 109 E-7 (7669)	30%	Crashed on landing.	Beaumont-le-Roger airfield.
24.01.42		9		Bf 109 E-4 (918)	80%	Crashed on landing.	Borkum airfield
28.01.42	Uffz. Robert Stellfield	5		Bf 109 F-4 (7427)	50%	Crashed on take-off.	Katwijk airfield.
29.01.42		8		Bf 109 E-7 (3520)	65%	Emergency landing due to fuel shortage.	Oldenswort
06.02.42	Oblt. Hermann Segatz	IV. Gruppe		Bf 109 E-7 (856)	75%	Emergency landing due to engine damage.	Near Brest-Süd
07.02.42	Paul Messner	IV. Gruppe	Wounded	Bf 109 E-7 (6518)	75%	Belly landing due due damage caused by ship's A-A fire.	Near Brest
12.02.42		I. Gruppe		Bf 109 F-4 (7053)	20%	Damaged on landing.	Raversijde
12.02.42	Fw. Beyer	IV. Gruppe		Bf 109 E-4 (777)	50%	Crash landed due to engine trouble.	Octeville airfield
14.02.42	Lt. Bergmann	II. Gruppe		Bf 109 (8600)	80%	Severely damaged on landing.	Stade
14.02.42		5		Bf 109 F-4 (6801)	20%	Take off aborted. Faulty servicing found to be the cause.	Stade

Obergefreiter Schmaul reads a paper on the wing of a Bf 109 F of 12th Staffel. Note the pilot's head armour, the IV. Gruppe emblem on the cowling and the Maltese Cross emblem beneath the cockpit.

Date	Name of Crew and Rank	Staffel	Fate	Aircraft, W.Nr & Code	Damage /Loss	Reason for Casualty	Place
21.02.42		2		Bf 109 F-2 (8097)	30%	Collided on landing with Bf 109 F-2, W.Nr. 8654.	Husum airfield
21.02.42		2		Bf 109 F-2 (5654)	60%	Collided on landing with Bf 109 F-2, W.Nr. 8097.	Husum airfield
21.02.42		II. Gruppe		Bf 109 F-1 (5629)	20%	Emergency landing due to fuel shortage.	Near 's-Hertogenbosch
21.02.42		8		Bf 109 E-7 (5796)	15%	Emergency landing due to fuel shortage.	Darmstadt
04.03.42		IV. Gruppe		Bf 109 F-1 (5682)	20%	Crash landed on non-combat flight.	Lade airfield
05.03.92		II. Gruppe		Bf 109 F-4 (8612)	45%	Crash landed on airfield.	Haamstede airfield
07.03.42		IV. Gruppe		Bf 109 F-1 (5616)	30%	Crashed into stationary aircraft on landing.	Lade airfield
07.03.42		IV. Gruppe		Bf 109 E-7 (1126)	20%	Crashed into stationary Bf 109 E-7 while landing.	Lade airfield
07.03.42		IV. Gruppe		Bf 109 E-7 (6473)	15%	Aircraft landing crashed into this aircraft.	Lade airfield
10.03.42		IV. Gruppe		Bf 109 F-2 (5488)	40%	Emergency landing due to getting lost.	Gjemnes
13.03.42		II. Gruppe		Bf 109 F-4 (8610)	15%	Crashed on take-off	Vlissingen airfield
15.03.42	Fw. Konrad Nelleskamp	6	Killed	Bf 109 F-4 Yellow 12 (7425)	100%	Shot down by Blenheim and Spitfires	North-west of Haarlem

Pilots of 10th Staffel at Schipol at the end of July 1942 grouped around a Fw 190. On the aircraft, from left to right : Unteroffizier Knespel; :Unteroffizier Rathenow and Unteroffizier Kirchoff. On the ground are, from left to right: Oberleutnant Fritz (not a pilot, but wearing a life jacket for the photo) ; Hauptmann Eberle ; Unteroffizier Haspel ; Unteroffizier Platzer ; Feldwebel Flemming ; Feldwebel Snaidero and Unteroffizier Bucek.

View of the rear of the Bf 109 E-7, "White 1", W.Nr. 6412, of the Staffelkapitän of 10th Staffel, Hauptmann Friedrich Eberle. 12 "kills", gained with JG 51, adorn the rudder, of which mechanic "Bubbele" Roth appears to take great pride. This aircraft carries the IV. Gruppe "circle" symbol aft of the fuselage cross, and the pilot's head armour can be seen bolted to the open centre canopy.

View of the same aircraft in its blast pen from the front port side.

Date	Name of Crew and Rank	Staffel	Fate	Aircraft, W.Nr & Code	Damage /Loss	Reason for Casualty	Place
15.03.42	Ofhr. Wolfgang Schmidt	6	Killed	Bf 109 F-4 Yellow 3 (7429)	100%	Shot down by Blenheim and Spitfires	North-west of Haarlem
20.03.42		II. Gruppe		Bf 109 F-4 (8592)	10%	Belly landing due to engine trouble.	Terschelling island
22.03.42		II. Gruppe		Bf 109 (8597)	45%	Damaged on landing.	Katwijk airfield
30.03.42	Oblt. Walter Diesselhorst	5	Killed	Bf 109 F-4/Z (8604)	100%	Crashed into the sea.	North-north-east of Nordwijk
30.03.42	Uffz. Otto Hochsteger	I. Gruppe		Bf 109 E-7 (3340)	60%	Crashed on landing.	Leeuwarden airfield
03.04.42		Geschwader Stab		Bf 109 F-2 (12829)	25%	Crashed on landing.	Leeuwarden airfield
25.04.42	Uffz. Rudolf Rauhaus	II. Gruppe		Bf 109 F-4 (8591)	50%	Airframe damage.	Katwijk airfield
29.04.42		3		Bf 109 F-2 (12854)	20%	Damaged on landing due to servicing.	Wangerooge airfield
29.04.42	Oblt. Werner Gutowski (Staffelkapitän)	9	Wounded	Bü 131			
09.05.42	Fw. Josef Hamann	5	Killed	Bf 109 F-4 (7433)	100%	Airsickness.	Nordwijkerhout
09.05.42	Uffz. Herbert Purz	6	Killed	Bf 109 F-4 Yellow 1 (8603)	100%		West of Walcheren
09.05.42		II. Gruppe		Bf 109 F-4 (7432)	45%	Crashed on take off.	Katwijk airfield
12.05.42	Uffz. Frischlasky	4		Bf 109 F ( )	80%	Damaged on landing.	Woensdrecht
16.05.42		II. Gruppe		Bf 109 F-4 (8589)	80%	Crashed on landing. Servicing fault.	Woensdrecht

A meal taken at "readiness" at Schipol. Unteroffizier Kirchner received the Iron Cross, Second Class shortly after his first victory, a Vickers Wellington, on 23/7/42. He is seen here wearing his decoration with Unteroffizier Schmid. Note the red Tatzelwurm on the BMW side-car.

Fw 190 A-3 of 5th Staffel under camouflage netting at Schipol in the summer of 1942.

Fw 190 A, "White 3" of 4th Staffel which was totally destroyed in summer 1942.

Date	Name of Crew and Rank	Staffel	Fate	Aircraft, W.Nr & Code	Damage /Loss	Reason for Casualty	Place
24.05.42	Uffz. Karl Heinz Johnen	II. Gruppe	Wounded	Bf 109 F-4 (7428)	50%	Emergency landing due to engine problem.	Jever
24.05.42		IV. Gruppe		Bf 109 E (6413)	30%	Emergency landing due to engine problem.	Near Wijk a. Zee.
28.05.42		II. Gruppe		Bf 109 F-4 (8622)	75%	Overturned on landing.	Katwijk airfield
31.05.42	Fw. Johannes Schiffer	4	Killed	Bf 109 F-4 (7414)	100%	Shot down in combat with Spitfires.	Over North Sea
31.05.42	Uffz. Max Seehagen	4	Killed	Bf 109 F-4 (7437)	100%	Shot down in combat with Spitfires.	Over North Sea
03.06.42	Lt. Eberhard Eichner	4	Killed	Fw 190 A-2 (409)	95%	Crashed on take-off on combat mission.	Near Ossendrecht
04.06.42		IV. Gruppe		Bf 109 (12646)	20%	Emergency landing due to fuel shortage.	Döberitz airfield
10.06.42	Lt. Heinz Tröger	II. Gruppe		Fw 190 A (339)	90%	Crash-landed due to servicing fault.	Woensdrecht
12.06.42		1		Bf 109 E-7 (3618)	30%	Damage to airframe following combat mission.	Borkum
16.06.42		IV. Gruppe		Bf 108 B-1 (1138)	20%	Emergency landing due to engine problems.	Wesel
19.06.42		I. Gruppe		Bf 109 E-4 (2750)	10%	Emergency landing due to fuel shortage.	De Kooy airfield
19.06.42	Uffz. Erich Scheu	4	Killed	Fw 190 A-2 White 3 (413)	100%	Shot down in combat with Spitfires.	Over North Sea
19.06.42	Uffz. Herbert Brakebusch	6	Killed	Fw 190 A-2 Yellow 9 (285)	100%	Shot down in combat with Spitfires.	15 km. north-east of Zeebrügge
21.06.42		2		Bf 109 G-1 (14052)	90%	Crash landed due to engine damage.	Near Cloppenburg
22.06.42		II. Gruppe		Fw 190 A-2 (429)	35%	Crash landed due to servicing fault	Katwijk airfield

Fw 190 A-2, W.Nr. 0485, carrying the single chevron of the Gruppenadjutant of III. Gruppe. This aircraft was flown several times during August 1942 from Husum to Esbjerg by Unteroffizier Heinz Hanke of 9th Staffel.

A discussion group in front of a Fw 190. Second from right is the future ace, Oberfeldwebel Rudolf Piffer.

Husum, 17/8/42. Unteroffizier Heinz Born of 9th Staffel climbs out of his Fw 190 A-3, "Yellow 11" after scoring the first victory of III. Gruppe. The victim, a reconnaissance Spitfire, crashed on the island of Sylt.

On the ground, Born, in the life jacket, is toasted by his colleagues. Ground crew are already in attendance on his "Yellow 11".

Shortly after this victorious return, Staffelkapitän Hauptmann Werner Gutowski presented Born with the Iron Cross, Second Class. From left to right: Hautpmann Gutowski; Unteroffiziere Schramm; Born; Stöwer; and Hoës.

Fw 190 A of 4th Staffel partly under cover showing a colour division on the spinner.

Date	*Name of Crew and Rank*	*Staffel*	*Fate*	*Aircraft, W.Nr & Code*	*Damage /Loss*	*Reason for Casualty*	*Place*
01.07.42	Uffz. Helmut Porowarski	I. Gruppe	Wounded	Bf 109 F-2 (9628)	50%	Emergency landing due to dead engine following combat.	Terschelling
03.07.42		I. Gruppe		Bf 109 F-2 (9616)	20%	Airframe damage following combat mission.	Jever
03.07.42	Uffz. Karl Dietmaier	9	Wounded	Bf 109 E-7 (4077)	90%	Emergency landing due to technical problems.	Katwijk airfield
04.07.42		II. Gruppe		Fw 190 A-2 (391)	30%	Damaged on landing.	Katwijk airfield
04.07.42		7		Fw 190 A-2 (321)	20%	Damaged airframe due to servicing fault.	Aalborg airfield
04.07.42	Uffz. Erwin Grütz	10	Killed	Bf 109 F-4 White 6 (7423)	100%	Crashed on take-off.	Bergen airfield
05.07.42		7		Fw 190 A-2 (423)	15%	Damaged on landing.	Aalborg airfield
06.07.42	Uffz. Alfred Auer	4	Killed	Fw 190 A-2 (336)	100%	Crashed due to engine damage.	Woensdrecht airfield
07.07.42	Ofw. Rudolf Mickel	3	Killed	Bf 109 F-2 (8329)	100%	Crashed into the sea on combat mission.	South of Baltrum Island.
11.07.42	Uffz. Otto Werner	7	Wounded	Fw 190 A-2 (5473)	100%	Pilot wounded on combat mission.	40 Km. north of Bulbjärg, Denmark
11.07.42		2		Bf 109 G-1 (14047)	40%	Damage due to belly landing.	Near Emden
13.07.42		II. Gruppe		Fw 190 A-2 (427)	25%	Crash landing.	Katwijk airfield
14.07.42		IV. Gruppe		Fw 190 A-2 (477)	10%	Belly landing.	Bergen airfield
15.07.42		II. Gruppe		Fw 190 A-2 (379)	15%	Emergency landing due to engine problems.	Near Egmond

Fw 190 A-4s of 6th Staffel lined up outside the Gefechtsstand at Woensdrecht in summer 1942.

Posing in front of a Bf 109 F with an unusually-painted spinner are Unteroffizier Niedereichholz and Unteroffizier Winkler, both of II. Gruppe.

Excellent view of "White 1" of 4th Staffel.

Brand new Fw 190 A-3, "Black 4" of 5th Staffel at Katwijk in the summer of 1942.

Date	Name of Crew and Rank	Staffel	Fate	Aircraft, W.Nr & Code	Damage /Loss	Reason for Casualty	Place
19.07.42		12		Fw 190 A-3 (5462)	30%	Technical problems.	Mönchen-Gladbach
21.07.42		12		Fw 190 A-2 (2192)	35%	Crash landed due to servicing fault.	Mönchen-Gladbach
25.07.42		II. Gruppe		Fw 190 A-2 (2205)	15%	Emergency landing due to engine trouble.	Dülken
26.07.42		12		Fw 190 A-2 (5474)	15%	Emergency landing due to engine trouble.	Winke, near Hardt
26.07.42	Uffz. Georg Güthenke	9		Fw 190 A-3 Yellow 7 (5445)	25%	Belly-landing due to servicing fault.	Husum airfield
28.07.42	Gefreiter Gren	4		Fw 190 A-2 (358)	80%	Crashed after taking off.	Woensdrecht airfield
28.07.42		12		Fw 190 A-2 (380)	35%	Emergency landing due to engine trouble.	Mönchen-Gladbach airfield
30.07.42		8		Fw 190 A (0542)	50%	Engine damage.	Kjevik airfield
31.07.42		2		Bf 109 G (14056)	30%	Take-off accident due to faulty servicing.	Jever
31.07.42		II. Gruppe		Fw 190 A-2 (2201)	15%	Airframe damage.	Venlo airfield
01.08.42		2		Bf 109 G-1 (14031)	100%	Destroyed due to engine problems.	Jever
01.08.42	Lt. Heinrich Rösch	6	Missing	Fw 190 A-3 Yellow 12 (7001)	100%	Shot down in combat with Spitfires.	Walcheren Island
01.08.42	Uffz. Horst Hamann	6	Wounded	Fw 190 A-3 (5466)	65%	Wounded in combat with Spitfires.	Crash-landed on Woensdrecht airfield
01.08.42	Uffz. Felix Emerich	12		Fw 190 A-2 (2207)	60%	Engine damage in combat.	Near Viersen

Pilots of 5th Staffel, with female friends, wait for the order to take off, which will come through the loudspeaker system which is visible. On the right is Feldwebel Georg Hutter, and in the middle, Oberfeldwebel Ernst Heesen.

Katwijk, 6/8/42. From left: Oberleutnant Bucholz; Leutnant Tschira; Oberfeldwebel Heesen; Feldwebel Hutter; Unteroffizier Kirchner and Leutnant Buchholz of 5th Staffel watch with trepidation the approach of a Fw 190 piloted by a "green" pilot, Unteroffizier Kehrle.

Unteroffizier Josef Kehrle sits on the port wing of his Fw 190 A-3, "Black 2", W.Nr. 4027, after a successful crash-landing. All three propellor blades are bent, showing that the engine was still turning as he touched down.

Date	Name of Crew and Rank	Staffel	Fate	Aircraft, W.Nr & Code	Damage /Loss	Reason for Casualty	Place
02.08.42	Gefr. Gren	4		Fw 190 A-3 (2134)	30%	Damaged on landing.	Woensdrecht airfield
06.08.42	Uffz. Walter Müller	11	Killed	Fw 190 A-3 Yellow 3 (30428)	100%	Crashed into barrage balloon.	Gelsenkirchen
06.08.42	Uffz. Josef Kehrle	5	Wounded	Fw 190 A-1 (4027)	100%	Emergency landing due to technical problems.	
06.08.42				Fw 190 A-3 (465)	60%	Collided with Fw 190 while taxiing (see next entry).	Deelen airfield
06.08.42				Fw 190 A-2 (283)	30%	Collided with Fw 190 while taxiing (see previous entry).	Deelen airfield
07.08.42	Fw. Karl Decker	6	Wounded	Fw 190 A-2 (118)	40%	Crash-landed due to engine damage.	Near Woensdrecht airfield
07.08.42		IV. Gruppe		Fw 190 A-3 (2213)	95%	Crashed on non-combat mission.	Winkel/Hart
10.08.42	Fw. Erich Kaiser	4	Wounded	Fw 190 A-2 White 6 (2123)	15%	Overturned on landing.	Venlo airfield
11.08.42	Uffz. Martin Wolf	II. Gruppe	Wounded	Fw 190 A-2 (308)	45%	Emergency landing with engine trouble.	Schipol airfield
11.08.42		II. Gruppe		Fw 190 A-2 (391)	30%	Problem due to faulty servicing.	Schipol airfield
14.08.42	Uffz. Helmut Priwowarsky	3	Wounded	Bf 109 G-1 (14149)	85%	Crashed due to engine problems.	Jever
16.08.42	Uffz. Kurt Tiesler	8	Killed	Fw 190 A-2 (456)	85%	Crashed on return from escort mission.	Near Oslo

On 21/8/42 Fw 190s of II. Gruppe encountered American B-17s for the first time. Several attacks were made on the bombers without success. Oberfeldwebel Detlev Lüth had to belly-land his Fw 190 A-2, W.Nr. 2116 alongside the airstrip at Katwijk after receiving hits in the oil sump from return defensive fire.

Date	Name of Crew and Rank	Staffel	Fate	Aircraft, W.Nr & Code	Damage /Loss	Reason for Casualty	Place
18.08.42		IV. Gruppe		Fw 190 A-3 (5447)	25%	Belly-landed due to servicing fault.	Schipol airfield
21.08.42		1		Bf 109 E-7 (4222)	20%	Crashed on landing.	Heligoland airfield
21.08.42	Ofw. Detlev Lüth	4		Fw 190 A-2 (2116)	25%	Damaged engine due to enemy action.	Katwijk airfield
21.08.42		II. Gruppe		Fw 190 A-2 (2130)	60%	Crashed on landing due to faulty servicing.	Venlo airfield
24.08.42		3		Bf 109 F-2 (12861)	15%	Emergency landing due to servicing fault.	Wangerooge airfield
25.08.42	Uffz. Martin Lachler	11		Fw 190 A-4 (606)	50%	Crashed on take-off.	Mönchen-Gladbach airfield
25.08.42	Fw. Hans Fändrich	12	Killed	Fw 190 A-4 TF+SZ (578)		Mid-air collision on ferry flight.	Venlo
26.08.42		II. Gruppe		Fw 190 A-4 (7022)	10%	Damaged on landing.	Venlo airfield
31.08.42		II. Gruppe		Fw 190 A-4 (626)	35%	Airframe damage on landing due to technical problems.	Venlo airfield
01.09.42	Ofw. Wilhelm Schippers	12	Killed	Fw 190 A-4 Yellow 6 (575)	100%	Crashed	St. Trond
04.09.42	Uffz. Karl Dietmayer	9	Killed	Fw 190 A-3 (5465)	100%	Crashed on non-combat flight.	Esbjerg
06.09.42	Uffz. Alfred Fischer	5	Killed	Fw 190 A-2 Black 9 (411)	100%	Crashed.	South of Leeuwarden
07.09.42	Lt. Karl Endrizzi	1	Killed	Fw 190 A-4 White 1 (5566)	100%	Shot down in combat with fighters and bombers.	North-west of Leiden
07.09.42	Uffz. Franz Contzen	8	Killed	Fw 190 A-2 (0286)	100%	Crashed on escort mission.	North-west of Lister

The version which quickly followed the "A-3" in 11th Staffel was the "A-4". These are Fw 190 A-4s of 11th Staffel seen in August 1942.

Bf 109 E, "Yellow 8" of 12th Staffel.

Bf 109 F, "White 8", of 10th Staffel. The shadows of the camouflage netting give this machine an unusual mottled look.

Date	Name of Crew and Rank	Staffel	Fate	Aircraft, W.Nr & Code	Damage /Loss	Reason for Casualty	Place
07.09.42	Uffz. Ludwig Platzer	10	Killed	Fw 190 A-3 White 8 (5436)	100%	Shot down in combat with RAF fighters	1 Km. south of Nieuwkoop
09.09.42		IV. Gruppe		Fw 190 A-4 (601)	10%	Crash-landed due to faulty servicing.	Schipol airfield
11.09.42	Oblt. Hans Mohr	II. Gruppe	Wounded	Fw 190 A-4 (609)	80%	Crashed into the Fw 190 of Ofw. Lüth on landing.	Venlo airfield
11.09.42	Ofw. Detlev Lüth	4	Wounded	Fw 190 A-4 White 9 (7030)		Crashed into the Fw 190 of Oblt. Mohr on landing.	Venlo airfield
12.09.42		11		Fw 190 A-4 (608)	20%	Emergency landing due to fuel shortage.	Zoute airfield
19.09.42	Lt. Gerhard Steiger	2	Killed	Bf 109 F-4 Black 16 (8418)	100%	Shot down in combat.	Pfahlhaus, near Oldenburg
19.09.42		II. Gruppe		Fw 190 A-4 (661)	45%	Engine damaged.	Near Ede
27.09.42		4	Bailed out unhurt	Fw 190 A-4 (5569)	100%	Crashed due to technical problems.	Near Woensdrecht airfield
02.10.42	Uffz. Hans Wennekers	2		Bf 109 G-1 Black 12 (14082)	95%	Crashed due to engine trouble.	Behlenberg
04.10.42	Oblt. Hans Mohr	II. Gruppe		Fw 190 A-4 (634)	25%	Crash-landed due to brake problems.	Woensdrecht airfield
05.10.42	Uffz. Horst Hamann	6	Killed	Fw 190 A-4 Yellow 9 (631)	100%	Crashed on test flight.	North-west of Turnhout
05.10.42	Fw. Erwin Roden	12	Wounded	Fw 190 A-4 Yellow 6 (584)		Emergency landing due to fuel shortage.	Zierickzee
07.10.42		II. Gruppe		Fw 190 A-4 (5568)	20%	Belly-landing due to technical problems.	Woensdrecht airfield
09.10.42	Uffz. Bernhard Deklerk	8	Killed	Fw 190 A-2 (466)		Overturned when taxiing.	Lister airfield

The Iron Cross, Second Class, has just been awarded to these three pilots of 6th Staffel. From left : Unteroffiziere Brakebusch ; Meissner and Flecks.

Two unidentified pilots of 12th Staffel pose with a Fw 190 with a dented spinner showing the devil emblem.

Same time, same place. This pilot is almost certainly Unteroffizier Rudolf "Pedro" Mayer, a South American, who returned to his native land to fly and fight for it.

29/7/42. Leutnant Tröger (left) and Unteroffizier Haninger of 4th Staffel each shot down a Spitfire in mid-afternoon.

Date	Name of Crew and Rank	Staffel	Fate	Aircraft, W.Nr & Code	Damage /Loss	Reason for Casualty	Place
19.10.42		8		Fw 190 A-3 (418)	40%	Crashed on landing.	Kjevik airfield
24.10.42		10		Fw 190 A-4 (590)	10%	Damaged while taxiing.	Deelen airfield
25.10.42	Uffz. Reinhard Lätsch	1	Killed	Bf 109 G-1 White 11 (14041)	100%	Crashed into the sea.	North of Heligoland.
27.10.42		II. Gruppe		Fw 190 A-4 (618)	100%	Emergency landing on the sea.	Near Texel Island.
28.10.42		8		Fw 190 A-3 (2202)	50%	Damaged on landing.	Kjevik airfield
29.10.42		II. Gruppe		Fw 190 A-4 (5549)	40%	Engine problem.	Zwanenburg
31.10.42	Oblt. Walter Leonhardt	6		Fw 190 A-4 Yellow 6 (5533)	10%	Belly-landing due to servicing fault.	Woensdrecht airfield
03.11.42		1		Bf 109 E-7 (6466)	60%	Emergency landing due to bad weather.	Heligoland
06.11.42	Lt. Georg Herrman	1	Killed	Bf 109 G-1 Yellow 8 (14054)		Crashed on take off.	Wangerooge airfield
07.11.42	Hptm. Julius Henschel	8	Killed	Fw 190 A-3 (2204)		Collided on take-off (see next entry).	Stavanger airfield
07.11.42	Lt. Erhard Richter	8	Wounded	Fw 190 A-3 (5462)		Collided on take-off (see previous entry).	Stavanger airfield
22.11.42		IV. Gruppe		Fw 190 A-4 (571)	15%	Belly landing due to technical problems.	Deelen airfield.
22.11.42		3		Bf 109 G-2 (10655)	100%	Crashed in bad weather.	Wüstensachsen
27.11.42	Uffz. Hans Altmeyer	8	Missing	Fw 190 A-4 Black 7 (7090)	100%	Crashed into the sea.	South of Arendal
27.11.42	Uffz. Allan Gödecke	9		Fw 190 A-4 (5586)	80%	Belly landed due to motor trouble.	Husum airfield
06.12.42	Ogfr. Karl Lülter	9	Wounded	Fw 190 A-3 (5440)	80%	Damage due to technical problems.	Löwenstedt

Deelen, Autumn 1942. This Schwarm from 10th Staffel is ready to scramble.

Tatzelwurm seen in an unusual position: on the bonnet of Oberleutnant Max Bucholz's car.

A 6th Staffel Fw 190 A which has been badly damaged. The Tatzelwurm is in yellow, and the lower engine cowling is red.

Late summer 1942 at Woensdrecht. 4th Staffel take off, to be followed by 6th Staffel.

Excellent in-flight view of Fw 190 A-3, "White 8" of 4th Staffel with Unteroffizier Haninger at the controls.

Oberleutnant Hugo Frey of 10th Staffel about to be strapped into his Fw 190 by his mechanic.

A member of the ground personnel appears to be directing this Fw 190 A of 4th Staffel. This emblem on the cowling, and the II. Gruppe horizontal bar aft of the fuselage cross can be seen.

Two views of Fw 190 A-4, "Yellow 4", W.Nr. 614 of 12th Staffel at Mönchen-Gladbach. In the background is an "A-2", "Yellow 3", of the same Staffel.

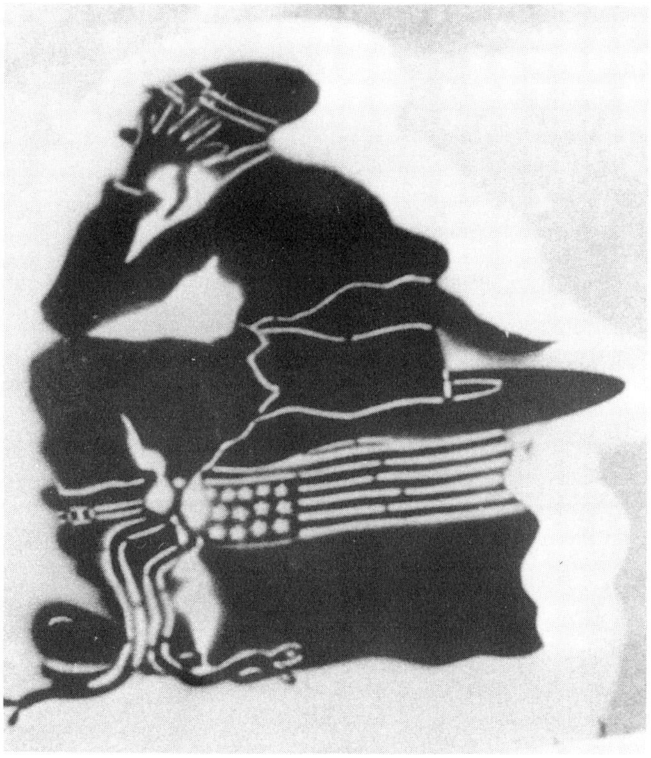

The insignia carried by the Fw 190s of 8th Staffel from summer 1942 requires no explanation.

Engine cowling of an 8th Staffel machine displaying the Staffel emblem with a member of the ground personnel in attendance.

Unteroffizier Franz Steiner of 8th Staffel in front of a Fw 190 of 8th Staffel carrying the emblem shown in the previous photograph.

Hauptmann Moritz, pictured shortly before leaving JG 1.

The successor of Hauptmann Moritz, who moved to JG 51, was Oberleutnant Rainer Framm, seen here with a Staffelhund. He took up post in early September 1942.

Feldwebel Fritz Timm with his Fw 190 A-5, "Yellow 7".

Fw 190 A-3 of 10th Staffel. The IV. Gruppe "circle" behind the fuselage cross can be seen.

Three views of Fw 190 A, "White 10" of 4th Staffel, with an unknown Obergefreiter in attendance.

Posing at the rear of his Fw 190 A-4, "Yellow 7", W.Nr. 585, is Feldwebel Fritz Timm, who is wearing the Iron Cross Second Class ribbon in his button-hole. This was awarded following his victory over a Mosquito on 9/10/42.

Two views of Fw 190 A-2, "Black 9" of 5th Staffel which has nosed-over - the likely cause of such accidents being too-heavy application of the brakes.

View of the revised emblem of the eagle overseeing the German Bight on a Bf 109 G-1 of the unit at Jever in the autumn of 1942. The eagle is now an arrow with the arc of a bow visible.

Bf 109 G-1 of Leutnant Knoke, showing his wife's name and two wedding rings intertwined. To the right, facing the camera, is Unteroffizier Wennekers.

Excellent view of the IV. Gruppe emblem on the engine cowling of a Fw 190 A.

Unusual head-on view of an unidentified pilot of 12th Staffel in his Fw 190. The bumps in the cowling just forward of the windscreen accommodated the breeches for the machine guns.

Unteroffizier Rudolf Rauhaus takes off in his Fw 190 A-2, "Yellow 4".

Fw 190 A-4, "White 7", W.Nr. 574, of 10th Staffel.

October 1942 at Mönchen-Gladbach. Three young pilots of 12th Staffel with their Adjutant. From left: Unteroffizier Anton Piffer; Oberfeldwebel Worth (Adjutant); Leutnant Eberhard Burath and Leutnant Hans Munz.

Feldwebel Fritz Timm of 12th Staffel receiving the Iron Class, Second Class from his Gruppenkommandeur, Hauptmann Losigkeit after shooting down a Mosquito on 9/10/42.

Unteroffizier Allan Gödecke of 9th Staffel belly-landed this Fw 190 A-4, "Yellow 2" on 27/11/42.

Two views of Unteroffizier Rudolf Rauhaus with his Fw 190 A, "Yellow 3", of 6th Staffel. On the port side is a personal emblem, on the starboard side, the coat of arms of his home city, Neuss.

Aalborg, late 1942. This Fw 190, "White 3" of 7th Staffel carries a slightly different style of Maltese Cross under the cockpit.

An excellent informal shot of 4th Staffel pilots Feldwebel Ernst Winkler (left) and Unteroffizier Heinz Fuchs. Around mid-day on 28/11/42 each shot down a Spitfire.

Two Fw 190 A-4s of 12th Staffel, late 1942.

A rather windswept pilot poses in the cockpit of his Fw 190 A.

Winter 1942/43. The pilot of Fw 190 A-4, "Yellow 6", of 12th Staffel is about to step off the wing onto firm ground again. Note the black triangular pattern on the forward fuselage which was used by several units to hide the heavy exhaust staining of the Fw 190.

Unteroffizier Niedereicholz in the cockpit of his Fw 190 A, "White 5" of 4th Staffel. Note that the numeral has not yet had its top part outlined in black, and the lower left side of the fuselage cross does not have the white outer marking.

Autumn 1942. Oberleutnant Witt, Gruppenadjutant of IV. Gruppe, leaves his Fw 190 A-4 in the hands of his mechanic. On 24/1/43 Leutnant Burath replaced Witt in the post of Gruppenadjutant.

Winter 1942/43. Pilots of 12th Staffel face the camera. From left to right: Leutnant Marxen (+30/7/43); Unteroffizier Meyer; Oberleutnant Becker (+30/7/43); Unteroffizier Emmerich (+10/10/43); Feldwebel Bach (+26/11/44) and Unteroffizier Küchler.

Pilots of 12th Staffel celebrate the new year (1943) with female friends at Mönchen-Gladbach.

CHAPTER 5 - 1943

THE PACE QUICKENS

Christmas 1942 passed in peace. On both sides, the 'truce' was honoured. In January 1943 there took place an important conference of allied leaders at Casablanca, where the future prosecution of the air war was determined. Matters were to develop to a point where aerial bombardment of the Reich would continue by day and by night, with the aim of destroying industrial production and communications. the German population would also become a target.

The first victory of the year went to III. Gruppe on 12th January, when Alois Job of 8th Staffel recorded the Gruppe's second victory overall. Contact with the enemy had been rare for III. Gruppe. "At 14:12 hours, my friend Reichstein and I scrambled from Kijevik. We were directed from Oslo, and it was not long before we sighted an aircraft coming straight towards us from the mist. We took it to be a Bf 109 first of all. However, as it tried to pass between us, we identified it: a Spitfire! We chased after it, and I managed to shoot it down without using my "Revi". Norwegian fishermen rescued the pilot" - Unteroffizier Alois Job. Job's victim was the Norwegian pilot, Pilot Officer Alex Andersens of No.1 PRU based at Benson.

It was with II. Gruppe that the first death in action for the year was recorded. This Gruppe endeavoured to maintain at least one Rotte in the air. It could then at least be prepared for a surprise attack. On 17th January, during one of the eight patrols of the day, two pilots of 6th Staffel were attacked by about twenty Spitfires. Feldwebel Flecks, an experienced pilot, managed to escape from the attack, but his partner, Unteroffizier Strunz, fell to the British guns.

II. Gruppe's first victories arrived on 20th January. Towards 15:00 hours, twelve Fw 190s of 5th and 6th Staffeln, accompanied by two pilots of 11th Staffel, attacked a formation composed of fifteen Lockheed Hudsons strongly escorted by Spitfires and Mustangs. Four Mustangs, two Spitfires and two Hudsons were shot down. Among the successful pilots were Oberleutnant Leonhardt (a Hudson and a Mustang, whose pilot was captured two days later), and Oberfeldwebel Heesen, and the two pilots of 11th Staffel, Feldwebel Bugaj and Unteroffizier Vorhauer, who flew regularly with II. Gruppe. Four days later, Bugaj and Vorhauer, always flying with II. Gruppe, were each accorded a victory over a Spitfire. However that was only the beginning.

On 27th January, the major turning point occurred. For

The end of an eventful combat for Feldwebel Kromer of 5th Staffel on 30/1/43. Following engine problems, he made a safe belly-landing near Woensdrecht in his Fw 190 A-4, "Black 10", W.Nr. 7032. The aircraft was assessed as 45% damaged. Note the red Tatzelwurm and the twin-coloured spinner.

Obergefreiter Pirkenseer (left) stands on the wing root of this Fw 190 with its pilot, Feldwebel Fritz Koch, who was killed in action on 27/1/43.

the first time, 91 bombers (84 B-17s of 1st and 2nd Bomb Wings and seven B-24s of 93rd Group) headed for Reich territory.

After attacks on France and Belgium on which techniques were perfected in formation flying and bombing, the time had arrived for strikes against Germany. The target was the port of Wilhelmshaven.

At Jagdgeschwader 1, the communications officer leapt to the tannoy: "Attention - large concentration of enemy in map-square 'Dora-Dora'. Immediate scramble. Hanni 8,000". The latter translates as: Hanni=Height; 8,000 = 8,000 metres (approximately 25,000 feet).

When the pilots reached their aircraft, the mechanics were already there, and helped them on with their parachutes. Then quickly into the cramped cockpit. Engines were started, aircraft moved off in a hellish din as canopies were closed. A green flare cleared them to take off. The thunderous noise accompanied the unit as aircraft took off one after the other.

The weather was beautiful, but cold. All of a sudden, a shout. A pilot had sighted the enemy. The B-17s and B-24s were flying as though on parade. The order to attack was given. The eagles pounced on their prey. However the assault was not strong enough and the allies repulsed it energetically. One Fw 190 was hit - it fell in flames. Formation leaders had trouble organising a further attack. These "boxes" had terrific defensive power! It was a veritable hail of fire which descended upon any aircraft which approached. However, it was certainly necessary to fly through it. A second aircraft

1st Staffel pilots following the award of the Iron Cross, Second Class to Unteroffizier Rudolf Hübl and Unteroffizier Bernhard Kunze. From left to right: Leutnant Berger (w. 29/11/43); Oberfeldwebel Kaiser (w. 4/10/43); Leutnant Lück (w. 9/4/44); Feldwebel Rathenow (+3/11/43); Unteroffizier Hübl (w. 8/10/43); Oberleutnant Schott (+27/9/43); Unteroffizier Kunze (+5/1/43); Oberleutnant Engleder (w. 16/12/43); Unteroffizier Rauhaus (+31/7/44) and Unteroffizier Knespel (+28/7/43).

A stern faced Leutnant Dieter Eberhard of 2nd Staffel prepares to take off.

was hit, then a third. It was necessary to organise properly if this was not to be a massacre. Pilots now regrouped to make a frontal pass. It was undoubtedly the only effective way. The front of the B-17 was its weak spot. The two neighbouring units, Jagdgeschwadern 2 and 26, more experienced, had tried this method of attack. It needed, however, a great deal of courage to see it through. Charge head-on, fire a burst, then pull away at the last second. The Focke Wulfs flew so close to the large propellors of the bombers that they were buffeted by the slipstream. Although two further fighters were shot down, the first successes were recorded. Four bombers went down to the guns of Oberleutnant Hugo Frey and Leutnant Dieter Gerhard of 2nd Staffel, and Unteroffiziers Haenel and Löhr, both of 12th Staffel. Haenel did not long survive this success. On 30th January, he shot down a Wellington, but was probably hit by the debris from his victim and he crashed into the North Sea.

Nevertheless, on return to base there was sadness. Five pilots of the unit did not return: two were killed, one missing and two wounded. A sad record. On the American side, three B-17s were missing, and 43 aircraft

The starboard undercarriage leg has collapsed on this 9th Staffel Fw 190 A-3, "Yellow 10", at Esbjerg on 27/1/43.

returned with damage.
The next combat occurred on 4th February. II. Gruppe was on a high. At 12:15 hours five Fw 190s of 5th Staffel led by Oberfeldwebel Lüth, took off from Schipol to intercept a formation of 65 B-17s en route for Emden. Twenty minutes later the battle began. Lüth and two other pilots each recorded a victory. A quarter of an hour after 5th Staffel, 6th Staffel also took off. Their seven Fw 190s made contact with the enemy forty minutes later. The enemy were no longer taken unawares and despite several attacks, only one Boeing was damaged. It continued to fly in spite of two engines having stopped! Another drama followed. Oberleutnant Walter Leonhardt, the successor of Rohwer at the head of 6th Staffel, separated from his pilots. Latching on to a "Viermot", he was not prepared, for all the world, to let this one return to England. The enemy aircraft fought back furiously. Leonhardt positioned himself for a second pass, the final thrust. Suddenly, his aircraft was transformed into a ball of flame. His Fw 190 A-4 disappeared forever with its pilot 100 kilometres north-west of Texel into the North Sea. On this day, IV. Gruppe also lost two pilots, including Unteroffizier Emmerich of 12th Staffel.
Matters were then calm for three weeks, and attention turned to reconnaissance missions in the area of the Thames estuary. Their purpose was to locate allied convoys: "Every day, our Gruppe sent at least two Rotten to the other side of the Channel. The first would take off in the morning, the other being sunset. The journey was undertaken at wave-top height in order to evade the British radar. The chalk cliffs would come into view, we would turn towards them, and switch on the camera. After seventeen minutes we would go up to the coast again. At this moment, we were more concerned about watching the skies rather than ensuring the quality of our reporting: the British were quick to work out our objective, and Spitfires patrolled in the area. We pilots took turns to fly these missions, which were not liked. One day, I left Woensdrecht with my wingman. We were surprised by enemy fighters. My wingman was immediately shot down and I was hit. I skimmed the waves but the Spitfire had spotted my move and followed. I sensed him on my back. The bursts of fire began. They passed quite close over the cockpit. To hit me the Spitfire would have to fly level with me, or even a little lower. Suddenly the bursts stopped. I glanced into the rear view mirror. The enemy had just hit the waves. It rebounded, turned over and disappeared into the waves. I took a deep breath. My aircraft controls still responded. Finally, I saw the coast of Holland and landed without difficulty" - Unteroffizier Hans Lehmann, 5th Staffel.
On 26th February there was glorious sunshine. Some pilots were stretched out on the airfield, others played cards. With such weather, it was certain that the heavy

Fw 190 A-4, "Yellow 4", with an unknown pilot in the cockpit and a mechanic on the wing root, in its blast pen at Mönchen-Gladbach in autumn 1942.

Fw 190 A-4, "Yellow 6" of 12th Staffel at Mönchen-Gladbach in autumn 1942.

Unteroffizier Heinz Hanke of 9th Staffel (extreme right) claimed his first victory on 26/2/43 over a Liberator in his Fw 190 A-4, W.Nr. 5701.

bombers would not be long in coming. At 10:00 hours IV. Gruppe were scrambled from Deelen and attacked a formation of four-engined bombers. Three victories were claimed by pilots of IV. Gruppe: Hauptmann Günther Specht of 10th Staffel and Oberfeldwebel Otto Bach of 12th Staffel.

Leutnant Burath, recently named Gruppenadjutant encountered Boeings for the first time: "In the search for, and the approach to, the enemy, I had become separated from the rest. I realised it too late, and tried to catch up. I eventually sighted them and headed for them at full gas. The silhouettes became larger and larger. They were enormous. Too big for fighters. How does one take them on, these Viermots? There must have been 60-70. Fear comes as a result of experience. I had neither. Without thinking I changed course to meet them head-on. All their arms opened up, and I felt I was flying through a cloud of bullets and tracer. I fired also, then suddenly, a burst came towards me. It came from the left, as red as a tomato. It was the colour which drew my attention, and I evaded it at the last moment. I recrossed the formation from one side to the other. Now it was time to meet it again. What did the "Amis" think of this great attack by a German fighter? At least they could say that they hit my Fw 190 with a good shot in the engine: I returned to base on 13 out of 14 cylinders".

At 10:50 hours, after waiting at cockpit readiness pilots of I. Gruppe also took off. This time, no question of failure. The lull had allowed time for full analysis of the correct method of attack. Everything seemed to be right. In effect, the combat against the 93 B-17s and B-24s sent to attack Wilhelmshaven went ideally for 2nd Staffel, who returned to base over an hour later with five victories against the bombers without loss to themselves. Leutnant Dieter Gerhard scored his seventh victory (of which two were four-engined bombers), Leutnant Hugo Frey his fifth and Heinz Knoke his fourth overall. Towards 14:15 hours Unteroffizier Meissner of 6th Staffel shot down a reconnaissance Spitfire flown by the Polish Flying Officer Xiezopolski of 542 Squadron.

Leutnant Dieter Eberhard of 2nd Staffel, with eight victories to his credit, was killed in action on 18/3/43.

9th Staffel carried its insignia from their Bf 109s to their Fw 190s. This Fw 190 A-3, "Yellow 7" shows the Staffel emblem aft of the fuselage cross. The chocks have been pulled away from the wheels with take off imminent.

FIGHTER-BOMBERS: MARCH 1943

On 9th March 1943 The unit's dispositions were as follows:
Stab at Schipol - 2 Fw 190 (1 serviceable);
II. Gruppe at Woensdrecht - 35 Fw 190 (29 serviceable);
4th Staffel at Schipol;
IV. Gruppe at Mönchengladbach - 30 Fw 190 (20 serviceable).
These units came under the control of General von Döring's 1st Fighter Division based at Deelen.
I. Gruppe at Jever/Wangerooge - 37 Bf 109 (28 serviceable);
III. Gruppe at Husum - 43 Fw 190 (31 serviceable)
These units came under the control of General Schwabedissen's 2nd Fighter Division at Stade.
The success of 26th February seemed to have inspired certain pilots of the unit. Certainly, they had scored a notable victory, but they needed not to be lulled into thinking it was always going to be easy. How would a dozen aircraft cope with the veritable torrent of aircraft which would soon be put over Germany at every opportunity when weather permitted? Another solution was required. Heinz Knoke and his friend Dieter Gerhard spent a night searching for the answer. "What if the bombers were to be bombed?". The calculations, ideas, problems, all were considered. Finally, as daft as it sounded, the idea could work. It only remained to convince the Gruppenkommandeur, then to obtain the bombs and await the other required material. It arrived on 8th March. Training began instantly. It took ten days before the bombs finally hit the target: large sandbags towed tirelessly by Junkers 88s.
On 18th March the order to scramble caught everyone by surprise. 103 American bombers were heading for Vegesack. At 14:14 hours - take off immediately. There was no time to fit the bombs to the aircraft of 2nd Staffel. The pilots took off for a conventional attack.
"Before Dieter closed his canopy he calls over to me that he wants to bag the enemy formation leader today. I ask him, laughing, if the Yanks have recently taken to painting the wings of their planes with rank badges.
"At an altitude of 25,000 feet we establish contact with the enemy in the Heligoland area. I lead the flight in close formation for a frontal attack.
"I opened fire on a Liberator from a little below. It immediately starts burning and sheers off to the right as it falls away from the formation. I come in again to attack

Unteroffizier Hermann Hoës of 9th Staffel stands to attention before his Staffelkapitän, Oberleutnant Werner Gutowski. Behind Gutowski is his Fw 190 A-3, "Yellow 1", showing the Staffel emblem was carried on the port side also.

Close-up of the 9th Staffel emblem carried on the engine cowling of a Fw 190. This emblem was carried over to 3rd Staffel, Jagdgeschwader 11, when 9th Staffel formed part of this new unit.

from above the tail, and then turn for another frontal attack, firing from ahead and below the steeply diving Liberator. My aim has never been better. Suddenly there is an explosion, and the blazing crate disintegrates into a shower of wreckage above my head. For a few minutes I am in danger of collision with falling engines or spinning flaming wings. That would mean certain disaster for me. Acting quickly, I slam the stick hard over into the left corner and go into a power dive. The falling fuselage of the Liberator misses me by inches as it hurtles into the depths. It falls into the sea some twelve miles south-east of Heligoland. That was my number five.

"I climb back to 25,000 feet for another attack at the massed enemy formation. Suddenly my heart almost stops beating. Dieter is in the middle of the Yank formation holding his aircraft steady following the same course. His first Liberator went down a few minutes ago. Now he wants to put the formation leader into the North Sea. The lad seems to have gone out of his mind. He keeps hard on the tail of a Fortress, blazing away at it. Tracers from every side converge upon its plane. He must have become completely insane.

"I dived down through the formation towards Dieter, firing indiscriminately at any of the Fortresses flying in the vicinity. Then Dieter suddenly breaks away in a steep dive. Three thousand feet below, his crate begins to emit a trail of smoke. He opens his canopy, then pushes himself up awkwardly in his seat, and the next moment is thrown clear. His parachute opens. I fly close to him. His face contorted with pain, he grips his body. Dieter is wounded.

"Fifteen minutes later he is down in the sea in map reference sector U-R-9. He succeeds in getting himself clear of the parachute, his rubber dinghy inflates, and he drags himself into it. I fly down low over his head and wave to him. He does not respond. He appears to be either unconscious or in utter pain. It looks as if he has been shot through the stomach.

"I immediately report by radio the position of our downed comrade and request help for him. Then I fly in and land. The mechanics look shaken at the news. I find no pleasure in my own success. If only Dieter is rescued alive ...

"Alone I fly out to sea again. The others have not yet returned. I can no longer find Dieter. One of the crash-boats patrolling the vicinity will have noticed his parachute descent and hurried to his assistance.

"Night falls. Still no news of Leutnant Gerhard.

"In his clothes locker I find a bottle of brandy. There is another such bottle in my own locker. We have once agreed that these bottles are to be drunk by the boys in memory of whichever one of us should first fail to return from a mission. What can have happened to Dieter?

"At midnight the telephone in my quarters rings.

Leutnant Heinz Knoke alongside the rear of Unteroffizier Wennekers Bf 109 which carried two victory markings: a Wellington on 23/8/42 and a Liberator on 26/2/43.

"Leutnant Dieter Gerhard was found by the crash-boat "Falke". He is dead.
"Slowly I replace the receiver. Dieter is dead. He was my closest friend.
"I remove the bottle from the locker and go across to Leutnant Frey. He is in his quarters with his wife and Lilo. They also have been waiting anxiously for news of Dieter. There is no need to say anything.
"I pass the bottle to Frey: "Come on: we may as well drink it up. We all feel the same - but that is the way we arranged it with Dieter, and that is the way it has to be."
The B-24 shot down by Knoke probably belonged to the 93rd Bomb Group. Although two B-17s were claimed by Oberleutnant Becker of 12th Staffel and Unteroffizier Hübl of 10th Staffel, of the eight German pilots who took off, only one B-17 was lost. However twenty three were seriously damaged.
II. Gruppe, which had taken off at the same time as IV. Gruppe, fell on a formation of about 40 Spitfires escorting 20 Ventura bombers. Three British fighters were shot down by Feldwebel Flecks, Unteroffizier Wlochinski and Oberleutnant Koch, whose aircraft was hit soon after. Koch bailed out over the sea and was recovered three hours later in his dinghy. He was taken to hospital in Amsterdam. For his first combat with Jagdgschwader 1, Feldwebel Leo Schuhmacher, who had been in action since Heligoland Bight in 1939, nearly suffered the same fate as Koch: his Fw 190 received 23 machine gun hits and one wing had a hole in it 30 centimetres in diameter. In spite of that, the pilot was able to make a belly-landing at Woensdrecht.
Dieter Gerhard was not to see the result of his efforts. On 22nd March there was a further alert. Once again there was insufficient time for the mechanics to fix bombs under the fuselage of the aircraft. Knoke passed control of 2nd Staffel to Feldwebel Wennekers and waited until a bomb was attached to his aircraft. Slowly he rolled along the strip. Suddenly the aircraft became unbalanced: a tyre had burst. Knoke fired a red flare and 20-30 mechanics came running. Under the direction of Knoke, they changed the tyre in record time. The Bf 109 finally took off. It took 25 minutes to reach 9,000 metres necessary for an attack. Finally he caught up with the enemy formation heading for England after having set fire to the docks at Wilhelmshaven. Knoke placed himself above the head of the formation. All around him bullets flew. His left wing was hit and slightly torn, but the aircraft still flew well. He was a thousand metres above the allied aircraft. Bomb away. It had fifteen seconds. Slowly it fell towards a group of three bombers. "... 10, 11, 12, 13, 14, 15". It exploded. The nearest bomber lost a wing and crashed into the sea. The other two turned in panic. On returning to base, everyone was excited. Göring himself called the pilot in the middle of the flight to congratulate him on his initiative. Finally, all talk was about this bomb.
On 3rd April, IV. Gruppe, including some Fw 190s "bombed-up" were scrambled from Deelen, but were unable to make contact with any enemy formation.
The next chance did not occur until elements of the unit had split away to form a new unit, among them, 2nd Staffel and their bomb-carrying Bf 109s.

On 25/3/43 the complete II. Gruppe was posted to Leeuwarden. These 6th Staffel Fw 190s are seen shortly after their arrival. The Bf 109s in the background belong to 2nd Staffel, Jagdgeschwader 27 who, for a short time, came under the control of the Gruppe.

In March 1943, Feldwebel Karl Bugaj received the Iron Cross, First Class. He stands before the rudder of his Fw 190 A-4, "Black 8", W.Nr. 663, in which he was killed on 12th April 1943.

Oberzahlmeister Selbach and Bugaj in front of the latter's Fw 190 A-4.

On 10/3/43 Unteroffizier Otto Schmid of 5th Staffel returned with damage to the windscreen of his Fw 190 A-4, "Black 8". He was lightly wounded as a result.

8th Staffel at Leeuwarden in March 1943 in front of Fw 190 A-4, "Black 8" which carries five kills on its rudder. Standing, left to right: Feldwebel Neuendorf; Unteroffizier Hentschel; Unteroffizier Job; Hauptmann Schnoor (Staffelkapitän); Unteroffizier Michalke; Leutnant Pancritius; Unteroffizier Steiner and Unteroffizier Rudschinat. Seated: Unteroffizier Doppler; Unteroffizier Reichenstein; unknown and Unteroffizier Spreckls.

Around March 1943 the Fw 190 A-4s of 10th Staffel had their engine cowlings and spinners painted white. Groundcrew pose with an aircraft of the Staffel.

Oberfeldwebel Leo Schuhmacher in front of a Fw 190 A of the unit.

Two views of the Fw 190 A-4, W.Nr. 555, of IV. Gruppe Gruppenadjutant, Leutnant Eberhard Burath on 11/3/43 after it had crashed on take off at Deelen. Burath escaped unhurt.

The idea of dropping a 250 kilogram bomb on American bombers was tried out in April 1943 by I. Gruppe. This Fw 190 A-4 was so equipped.

Fw 190 A-5 of 10th Staffel. The "A-5" reached IV. Gruppe in March 1943. Note the FuG 16 Z aerial beneath the fuselage. The lower engine cowling panel is a different colour to the rest of the undersides.

CHANGE IN STRUCTURE AND MANPOWER (APRIL/MAY 1943)

By April 1943 all Gruppen of the unit were ready for combat. Orders then arrived which all had long awaited: prepare for action - strengthening of the defence was imperative. On 1st April JG 1 was split in order to form a similar unit which was given the designation Jagdgeschwader 11.

I./JG 1 became II./JG 11;
III./JG 1 became I./JG 11;
II./JG 1 remained unchanged; and
IV./JG 1 became I./JG 1.
A new III./JG 1 was created.

At the head of the unit there was also a major change. On 1st April the veteran Commanding Officer, Dr. Erich Mix, handed over command to a pilot without equal, Major Hans Philipp. On 17th March 1943 he had become the second German ace to reach the incredible score of 200 victories. He came from the northern sector of the Russian front, where he was almost venerated by his men. Hans Philipp was just 26 years old.

In I. Gruppe there was also a change of leadership. Major Fritz Losigkeit was appointed Gruppenkommandeur of I./JG 26 and took up his new post on 1st June. His place as Gruppenkommandeur of I./JG 1 was taken by Hauptmann Emil-Rudolf Schnoor, from III./JG 1.

In II. Gruppe, Hauptmann Dietrich Wickop confirmed his ability as a fighter pilot. On 4th April he shot down a Spitfire; the following day he claimed a probable against a Boeing, and the day after two Spitfires fell victims to his guns. On this day, 6th April, when 4th and 5th Staffeln intercepted approximately 30 Spitfires (almost certainly those of 331 and 332 Squadrons, RAF) near Flessingue, radio contact was suddenly lost with the two aircraft of the Gruppenstab. Major Kijewski and Oberleutnant Mohr (Technical Officer) had taken off a little later than the other pilots - they were never to join up with them. They were almost certainly bounced by Spitfires. After a long search, the only thing found was some debris identified as being that of a Focke-Wulf 190. They were both listed as missing. Hauptmann Wickop thus took over leading the Gruppe, Oberleutnant von Kirchmayr became Technical Officer, and Leutnant Tschira took command of the 5th Staffel.

Once again the eastern front provided the pilot to take up a post of Gruppenkommandeur in the unit. Major Karl-

Heinz Leesmann was one of those experienced pilots who had learned their trade with JG 52, the unit which would ultimately claim the greatest number of Luftwaffe victories. When it appeared he had been heading for major honours, Leesmann had been struck down by serious injuries received in combat on 6th November 1941 near Klim leading I./JG 52. After returning to non-flying duties with I./JG 52, he returned to operational flying with his posting to III./JG 1 on 27th March 1943. He would prove his fitness for combat by notching up several victories in a short time.
With the new III. Gruppe formed at Leeuwarden Major Leesman was aided by three dependable Staffelkapitäne:
7th Staffel - Oberleutnant Heinrich Klöpper
8th Staffel - Oberleutnant Herwig Zuzic; and
9th Staffel - Oberleutnant Eugen Wintergerst.
Oberleutnant Klöpper was a Ritterkreuzträger from JG 51, arriving from the eastern front with over 80 victories. The destinies of Oberleutnants Zuzic and Wintergerst appeared to be firmly linked together. They both flew with 4./JG 77 on the eastern front, and collided on 24th September 1941 over enemy territory, both bailing out. Captured unhurt by the Russians, they submitted to five weeks of indoctrination, in order to be parachuted into Rumania as spies. Having done so, they immediately surrendered to the authorities, and recounted their tale.

Oberleutnant Harry Koch, Staffelkapitän of 6th Staffel at cockpit readiness. Note the unusual headgear worn by Koch.

Barred from further action on the eastern front for security reasons, they were therefore posted to IV. Gruppe on 6th January 1943, later moving to III. Gruppe, who required experienced personnel.
III. Gruppe were now up to strength, with Staffelkapitäne in post. They were strengthened by several 'old hands' from I. and II. Gruppe, who were distributed among the three Staffeln. Several pilots had also been posted to III. Gruppe following disagreements with their superiors.
Many new pilots fresh from training schools also arrived at Leeuwarden. The final stage of their apprenticeship had arrived: meeting their officers and colleagues, taking possession of their equipment, flights over the airfield, familiarisation of the surrounding areas, formation flying, and other tasks which would unite them into a fighting unit.
III. Gruppe was equipped with the Bf 109 G-6, whose performance at altitude was superior to the Fw 190. As it happened, each fighter unit operating on Reich defense duties had such a Gruppe. Their task was to provide top cover while the other units attacked in strength. However III. Gruppe did not take part in any major interceptions during the first two months of their existence.
The situation was different for the other two Gruppen. Periods of respite became rare. Every day, the enemy would come. On 2nd May I. Gruppe claimed three victories, by Major Losigkeit, Oberleutnant Framm and Felwebel Lacher. Geschwaderkommodore Phillip also logged his first 'kill' with JG 1 on this day. Hauptmann Wickop, Gruppenkommandeur of III. Gruppe, continued to dice with death, and on 2nd May he recorded another victory. The II. Gruppe report ran as follows: "On 2nd May 1943 Jafü Holland/Rhein ordered II. Gruppe to scramble, led by Hauptmann Wickop. Made up of the Staff Flight and the three Staffeln (24 Fw 190s), the

Oberleutnant Hans Mohr, Technical Officer of II. Gruppe seen here in the side-car, was posted missing in action together with his Gruppenkommandeur on 16/4/43.

This Fw 190 A-4 carries the markings of the Technical Officer of II. Gruppe as well as a personal emblem and Tatzelwurm. This is not, however, the aircraft in which Oberleutnant Hans Mohr was flying when he was lost. On that occasion he was flying a Fw 190 A-4, "Yellow 2".

complete formation had taken off by 19:13 hours. The Gruppe was directed from the ground by the 'Y-system' of ground control. At 19:30 hours at 6,500 metres the enemy formation was sighted. The formation consisted of about 40 Spitfires divided into several small units. They were flying at 7,000 metres in the opposite direction. The Staff Flight turned into the Spitfires as they changed course towards our formation. The first shots were fired almost simultaneously by the English leader and Hauptmann Wickop. The two pilots were between 100 to 150 metres apart. The Gruppe leader was hit in the left wing, undercarriage and in the cockpit. The Spitfire passed above the Fw 190 and dived on fire, in a short spin, to crash 1-2 kilometres north of North Beveland Island, near Wisserkerke. The pilot, Flight Lieutenant Marius Eriksen, leading a Norwegian flight, was able to bail out in time and was captured. The aircraft of Hauptmann Wickop, hit in the oil sump, was too badly damaged to continue combat. He was forced to make a belly-landing near Vlissingen at 19:45 hours. Hit by splinters from his canopy, Wickop was lightly wounded in the left arm. Eriksen had ten victories going into that combat; Wickop became his eleventh.

"After the head-on conflict of the leaders, further engagements took place. Unteroffizier Meissner (Rottenführer in 6th Staffel) attacked a lone Spitfire from behind firing at 5,000 metres. Immediately thick smoke was observed. For his second attack Unteroffizier Meissner attacked from the flank at a distance of 150 metres, the Spitfire, smoking heavily, dived at a steep angle and crashed into the sea at 19:36 hours, two kilometres north of Domburg, 70 metres from the shore. The pilot, saved

Large tents served as Operations Posts at Deelen in 1943. Here Kommodore Philipp stands at the entrance to a tent speaking to Leutnant Eugen Wintergerst.

Deelen, April 1943. 10th Staffel was re-numbered 1st Staffel. The IV Gruppe circle aft of the fuselage cross has been painted out. Note also the white painted engine cowlings.

Deelen, early 1943. These pilots of 12th Staffel pose near a Fw 190 A-4 for a group photograph. From left to right: Unteroffizier Emmerich; Feldwebel Timm; Unteroffizier Löhr; Feldwebel Nette; Oberleutnant Becker with "Moritz", the Staffelhund; Unteroffizier Lück and Unteroffizier Küchler.

Deelen, April 1943. Leutnant Ullmann in telephone conversation from a deckchair with his Gruppenkommandeur's Citroën a few yards away. In the background is a Fw 190 carrying Gruppenadjutant markings.

Hans Philipp (centre) with Hauptmann Herbert Kijewski of II. Gruppe.

by his parachute, was rescued by an air/sea rescue craft of the Rhine flotilla.

"After Hauptmann Wickop's victory, a section of Spitfires turned towards the Staff Flight, of which Leutnant von Kirchmayr led a Rotte. They (the Staff Flight) dived to avoid the attack. A circling combat then ensued. At 3,000 metres von Kirchmayr succeeded in getting behind an English aircraft, and fired two bursts which hit the right radiator. The Spitfire tipped on its right wing and dived, Kirchmayr followed until he saw its belly land on the coast east of North-Beveland Island. The pilot was captured after trying to flee.

"During the turning combat, Feldwebel Lacha, Rottenführer in the first Schwarm of 4th Staffel, managed to fire a burst from a distance of 100 metres into the left side of a Spitfire. A long plume of white smoke ensued. The aircraft dived, but righted itself 200 metres lower, carrying out a right turn. Lacha made a second attack from the right, hitting the wings and engine. Large flames spurted from it, and the Spitfire crashed into the waves. It was 19:40 hours. The pilot was unable to save himself. At the same time, Leutnant Wiegmann, Rottenführer of the Rotte from 4th Staffel providing high altitude cover attacked from behind the rear aircraft of a group of three Spitfires. Strikes were registered on the radiator. The allied fighter tried to evade a new attack by diving, but in the ensuing combat Wiegmann hit his target five more times. After the last attack at a height of 800 metres, the Spitfire did a half roll and crashed between the Islands of Walcheren and Schouwen. The pilot was almost certainly killed.

"Immediately following combat being joined, Leutnant Tröger, Staffelführer of 4th Staffel, saw a Fw 190 above him being attacked by three Spitfires. Tröger attacked them and separated them from the Fw 190. However, in his turn, he needed to be helped. Other Spitfires had singled him out as their target. Shortly afterwards, he spotted an isolated adversary heading westwards in a dive. This Spitfire was being attacked by a small boat of the Kriegsmarine, without any noticeable results. Leutnant Tröger pursued his quarry at wavetop height and launched into combat almost in the froth of the waves. He managed to hit the enemy aircraft in four attacks. At 19:34 hours the Spitfire lost its last ten metres of height and crashed 20 kilometres west of West-Kapelle.

"At 20:24 hours the last aircraft of II. Gruppe landed. Six pilots each lodged a claim for a single victory. Three Fw 190s were more or less severely damaged by enemy fire. Among them, one Fw, hit in the undercarriage and oil sump, made a belly landing."

WICKOP, Hauptmann and Gruppenführer.

In his report, Wickop did not mention the loss of one of his pilots killed during the combat: Oberfeldwebel P. Eberhardt, a Legion Condor veteran who later served as a flying instructor. 331 and 332 Squadrons RAF admitted the loss of four of their Spitfires.

On the 3rd, despite his injuries of the day before, Wickop shot down a Ventura, which was his 11th victory, the 99th of the Staff Flight and the 525th of the II. Gruppe. His wingman, Unteroffizier Rauhaus, did likewise and recorded his third victory. These aircraft were part of a dozen bombers heading for the region of La Haye. That allied unit was decimated: five other Venturas were credited to the Gruppe, Unteroffizier Meissner once again being victorious. The escort, made up of 40 Spitfires, was kept at bay by several pilots of all three Staffeln, during which engagement Oberfeldwebel Ehlers shot down two Spitfires. However on the German side two pilots were lost in this combat: Feldwebel Pfeiffer of 4th Staffel, and Oberfeldwebel Heesen of 5th Staffel, who had 28 victories to his credit.

On 4th May Wickop and Ehlers led off the 17 serviceable Fw 190s of II. Gruppe against a raiding force of some 80 Boeings escorted by an equivalent number of Spitfires, heading for Antwerp. Wickop and Ehlers each claimed an allied fighter. This success was, however, to come to a sudden end. On 16th May, towards the end of the day, 28 pilots of the unit took off, among them the majority of officers including Philipp, Schnoor and Wickop. At around 10,000 metres they saw approximately 50 Thunderbolts, these being part of a total force of 117 from the 4th, 56th and 78th Fighter Groups of the USAAF operating over northern Belgium. The latter Group, profiting from superior altitude, fell on the Germans. In the Vlissingen area, the crew of a ship suddenly saw a Fw 190 dive towards the sea, and finally crash with its pilot. It was the aircraft of Hauptmann Wickop. High above, the furious combat continued. Major Philipp shot down a P-47, Oberleutnant Harry Koch claimed likewise and Felwebel Lacha a probable. The Americans admitted one loss from the 78th Fighter Group and claimed three victories. Hauptmann Wickop claimed his last victory over a Spitfire shortly before being shot down himself. In a little more than three months he had registered 13 victories, three of which had been Flying Fortresses.

When all hope had faded for Hauptmann Wickop, the Geschwaderkommodore, Hans Philipp appointed Hauptmann Olejnik to temporary command of II. Gruppe. On 3rd June Hauptmann Walter Hoeckner was posted

This Fw 190 A-4 carries the chevron and bar of the Geschwaderadjutant. This aircraft was the mount of Hauptmann Hans Ehlers, who occupied this post from 1/4/43.

Oberstleutnant Günther Lützow, Commander of 1st Jagddivision talks with Leutnant von Kirchmayr (centre) and Hauptmann Wickop (right) during a visit to Woensdrecht on 4/4/43.

During a visit to the unit Oberstleutnant Lützow sits at the controls of Bf 109 G, "Yellow 4".

Deelen, April 1943. IV. Gruppe was re-named I. Gruppe. At this time the Gruppenstab adopted black and white stripes on their engine cowlings. Oberleutnant S'trohall (of Rumanian origin) is seen here with his Fw 190 A-5 which carries the stripes and the chevron and circle in front of the fuselage cross, denoting his rôle as Technical Officer of the Gruppe.

Second from left is Feldwebel Otto Bach, who would have a distinguished career with JG 1. Next to him, also facing the camera, is Hauptmann Günther Specht, who shot down his first "Viermot" with JG 1 on 26/2/43. Specht wears a patch over his left eye, having been blinded in combat during one of the many combats over the German Bight area.

Deelen, early 1943. Sitting on this ambulance wagon, which carries emblems on both mud guards are two of the well-established pilots of 12th Staffel, Oberleutnant Karl Becker and Oberfeldwebel Otto Bach.

Hauptmann Günther Specht (right) in discussion with Oberleutnant Herwig Zuzic at Schipol on 15th April 1943.

to JG 1. Hoeckner had been flying since 1940 and had 50 victories, the majority of which were scored in the east. He had previously been with JG 52, then JG 77, and had been Staffelkapitän of 1st Staffel, Jagdgeschwader 26 from early 1943. After a settling-in period, he took over command of II. Gruppe from Olejnik on 28th June.

On 17th May, a mission involving 26 Fw190s of II. Gruppe resulted in the interception of two Martin B-26s, and they were quickly despatched by Feldwebel Niedereichholz of the Staff Flight and Oberfeldwebel Winkler of 4th Staffel. However like all units, I. Gruppe were to know disappointment. On 21st May the 1st and 4th Bomb Wings divided two objectives between them: the submarine pens at Wilhelmshafen and Emden. Nearly 150 B-17s took part. Leutnant Eberhard Burath recalled this combat vividly:

"The 21st May 1943 was for me a major, but sad day. At 10:30 hours we were sent off to intercept a formation of "Viermots". As were unable to find them, we returned to Schipol at 11:13 hours. One hour eight minutes later, we took off once again to intercept the "boxes" on their return journey. This time we were well directed. 100 kilometres from Ameland Island we met up with them. We changed direction in order to attack from ahead. From an impossible angle I managed to shoot down a B-17. Upon landing I made an excited report to my Gruppenkommandeur, who congratulated me on my first victory. However, at this moment, another thought crossed my mind. Just before breaking off combat, I

General Galland visited 8th Staffel at Leeuwarden in early 1943. Extreme left is Hauptmann Schnoor; Galland is second from the right. In the background is "Black 5" of 8th Staffel.

Galland's personal aircraft, a Siebel 104, with his own Mickey Mouse emblem on the port engine, and on the fuselage, the winged "U" of JG 3 and the wolf's head of the Ergänzungs-zerstörergruppe.

Around May 1943 Oberfeldwebel Otto Bach left I. Gruppe to move to 5th Staffel. He is seen here with his Fw 190 of 5th Staffel which carries an unusual 'star' decoration on the nose of its spinner.

Cockpit readiness Leeuwarden in summer 1943. Kehrle's wingman, Unteroffizier Rudolf Einberger had a portly hunter as his Rotte emblem. Einberger was shot down and killed on 8/10/43.

saw a Fw 190 sink in the sea. A parachute was seen to come away from it. I immediately started the chronometer to determine the distance from the coast the unfortunate pilot found himself, and to help the rescue services. Back at base, Oberleutnant Munz, my old room mate was missing. I wanted to set off to look for him, and no sooner was my machine ready than I set off alone. I first of all headed for that part of the coast which I had crossed, and then started the 'chrono' and set off in the correct direction. When some time had elapsed, I began looking around to try to spot something. Finally I spotted a yellow spot tossing about in the waves. An inflatable dinghy! I drew nearer and what I had expected

Pilots released by I. and II. Gruppe formed the nucleus of III. Gruppe. They were given responsibility for a Schwarm (four aircraft), or a Rotte (two aircraft). Feldwebel Josef Kehrle of 5th Staffel was posted to 8th Staffel. The two Bf 109 G-6s of his Rotte carried a similar emblem: a hunter in a shield. Kehrle is seen in his aircraft with the emblem beneath the cockpit.

Full view of Kehrle's Bf 109 G-6, "Black 7", with the emblem visible, and an umbrella providing shade for the cockpit.

was confirmed - no-one on board. I flew in larger circles at wave-top height. Nothing - not the slightest sign. "Hans, my old friend, where are you?" The red light indicated it was time to return. 68 minutes already. An air/sea rescue aircraft had been called up in the meantime. I took off once again and joined up with it. Together we searched up for a long time. All the time, nothing. 73 minutes, time to return again. My companion also had to abandon the search as darkness began to spread over the sea. The sadness of it all literally shattered me. What if he had seen us during our searches? Six weeks later, his body was washed ashore on the beach at Sylt. There were none better than he."

Leutnant Georg Schott replaced Munz at the head of 1st Staffel. Schott, nicknamed 'Murr', was a veteran of the Spanish Civil War. He had been with IV./JG 1 since its formation at Döberitz. During this combat on 21st May, as well as Burath, Leutnant Krebs and Unteroffizier Rathenow each claimed a B-17. Five B-17s did not return to England.

Another view of Einberger's Bf 109 G-6, "Black 8". This is the aircraft in which he was shot down in on 8/10/43.

Leutnant Ernst Heesen of 5th Staffel, seen here at readiness. He was posted missing in action on 3/5/43 when his score stood at 28 victories.

Another great loss in May 1943 occurred on the 16th when II. Gruppe Kommandeur, Hauptmann Dietrich Wickop was lost in action following combat with P-47s.

For a month, until he was killed in action on 16/5/43, Hauptmann Dietrich Wickop led II. Gruppe. His aircraft carried the numeral "Black 1" and a large bird with wings spread under the cockpit. In the background is the Fw 190 A-5 of Leutnant von Kirchmayr.

Two views of the Fw 190 A-5 of Leutnant von Kirchmayr carrying the markings of Technical Officer of II. Gruppe. Kirchmayr succeeded Oberleutnant Mohr when the latter was lost in action. This aircraft was also used by II./JG 300 on Wilde Sau night sorties, as evidenced by the flame dampers fitted to the exhaust opening.

On 2nd May 1943 a violent combat took place over Holland. This Spitfire of 332 Squadron was the victim of Leutnant von Kirchmayr.

Tense faces at Woensdrecht following major combat on 2/5/43. In flying gear, Leutnant Tschira and Oberfeldwebel Hutter, both of 5th Staffel, show concern over the fate of the missing Oberfeldwebel Eberhard, who crashed into the sea.

One of the Fw 190s of Hauptmann Losigkeit. Under the cockpit are the flags of the nations he had fought against.

This Fw 190 carrying the double chevron of a Gruppenkommandeur was the aircraft of Hauptmann Fritz Losigkeit, Gruppenkommandeur of I. Gruppe. At the end of May 1943, he handed over command to Hauptmann Schnoor.

Leeuwarden, 23/5/43. The inaugural ceremony of III. Gruppe. Major Leesmann with Bf 109 G-6s, among which are the 'R-6' version equipped with MG 151 20mm. cannon in gondolas under the wings. They were very effective against bombers, but reduced the Messerschmitt's manoeuvrability.

Another view of the inaugural ceremony of III. Gruppe on 23/5/43.

Commanding officers of III. Gruppe in front of two Bf 109 Gs, one of which is a G-6/R6. From left to right: Leutnant Wintergerst (Staffelkapitän, 9th Staffel); Oberleutnant Klöpper (Staffelkapitän, 7th Staffel); Major Leesmann (Gruppenkommandeur); unknown; Oberleutnant Zuzic (Staffelkapitän, 8th Staffel) and Oberleutnant Hardt (Gruppenadjutant).

Two Bf 109 G-6s of 8th Staffel. "Black 5" is the aircraft of Feldwebel Alfred Miksch, who arrived from III./JG 3 with 48 victories. Note the white kill markings on the rudder.

High spirits at Woensdrecht in June 1943, with Staffelkapitän Leutnant Wilhelm Tschira pursuing Otto Bach with a hosepipe.

ZWEIMOTS - JUNE 1943

On 1st June, I. Gruppe moved to Schipol, in Holland. Their proximity to the coast allowed the Gruppe to undertake daily reconnaissance missions over the Channel. During this period also, the Gruppe tested the 21cm. rocket system. The 21 cm. 'Nebelgranaten', known as 'stovepipes' because of the shape of the tube from which they were fired, were secured under the wings of Fw 190 A-4s and A-5s. The projectile had a delayed fuse which detonated at a distance of about 800 metres after firing. Initial results were encouraging and the use of this weapon became general throughout the I. Gruppe.

The fighters of the unit did not only attack the American bomber streams in this year of 1943. They had also to reckon with raids by British light and medium bombers, under heavy escort, who made shorter distance attacks on the coast. A raid of 10th June was a typical example. For 98 Squadron based in Norfolk, the day's target was the electricity plant to the north of Ghent in Belgium. Six Mitchell IIs took part in the operation. For close escort, they had the Spitfires of 167 and 485 Squadrons. Four other squadrons covered the sector. The aircraft took off at 17:55 hours. Almost immediately one of the bombers separated from the formation and returned to base with mechanical trouble. The others reached the 'enemy' coast and drew the fire of the light flak batteries. The first hurdle had been overcome without any problems. However, on the horizon, there appeared a second, menacing sight. 28 Fw 190s of II. Gruppe were approaching. Combat was joined in the region of Eeklo-Zelzate, between Bruges and Ghent. The combat report of Feldwebel Kurt Niedereicholz illustrated perfectly the engagement: "I took off at 18:30 hours following the call to scramble, and was No.4 in the Staff Flight led by Hauptmann Olejnik. Over the radio, we were directed on a course of 240/280 degrees whilst climbing to 5,000 metres. A quarter of an hour later, we engaged a mixed formation of enemy, between 20-30 aircraft. I identified five aircraft as being Mitchell B-25 Cs. As they were flying in a south-easterly direction, Hptm. Olejnik turned us on the left flank of the enemy and gave the order to attack. I turned towards them out of the sun and attacked the B-25 at the right rear of the formation. I then observed hits on both engines, as well as a trail of white smoke. At this moment, I was brutally surprised by two Spitfires diving on me from above. In order to get rid of them I dived and returned to base at low level. I could not therefore observe the fate of the Mitchell. I landed at 19:34 hours without any hits, and Oberfeldwebel Ehlers was able to confirm my account".

Although the war diary of 98 Squadron attributed the loss

Another view of Miksch's "Black 5".

Two unknown pilots pose in the cockpit of Feldwebel Josef Kehrle's Bf 109 G-6.

The rudder of Feldwebel Miksch's Bf 109 F having the latest victories recorded.

Feldwebel Alfred Miksch poses by the rudder of his Bf 109 F, "Black 20", which carries 37 victories on it.

Leutnant Kurt Ibing poses in front of his Fw 190 A-4 of 5th Staffel, which carries a red Tatzelwurm. Note the single-coloured spinner, and what appears to be a white outline swastika on the fin.

Unteroffizier Hans Lehmann of 5th Staffel in front of his Fw 190 A-5, which carries a red Tatzelwurm.

of a Mitchell to flak, that of 167 Squadron acknowledged that the bomber had certainly been a victim of a Fw 190. The Mitchell crashed a short distance from Maldegem airfield, the four crew members being killed.

During the combat which followed, three other British aircraft were claimed shot down, by Leutnant Tröger (4th Staffel), Feldwebel Haninger (4th Staffel) and Oberfeldwebel Ehlers (6th Staffel); 167 admitted the loss of two aircraft. On the German side, three aircraft were lost. Unteroffizier Schnarski was killed; Unteroffizier Rost bailed out with slight burns, while Oberleutnant Koch's aircraft was 70% damaged when he made a crash-landing. He was safe and sound. Returning to England, one Mitchell, badly damaged by flak, just managed to reach Manston airfield.

The allies paid a heavy price this day. Apart from aircraft losses, the mission was not completed and the formation was split up once enemy fighters appeared. The only consolation was that three Fw 190s were written off.

A week later, the price paid by II. Gruppe was far greater. Twenty aircraft took off at around 09:30 hours. Landing again at 10:26, only fifteen returned. Two experienced pilots, Leutnant Heinz Tröger and Oberfeldwebel Ernst Winkler, had been killed, and three other wounded, in combat with Spitfires. On the German side, not a single victory had been claimed. The following is an extract from a letter written on 28th June by Hauptmann Olejnik to the father of Ernst Winkler:

"Dear Herr Winkler,

I have the sad task of advising you that your son, Ernst, did not return from a mission against the enemy on 17th

Arriving with II. Gruppe, Otto Bach progressively led a Rotte, a Schwarm, and eventually 5th Staffel. His first wingman was Leutnant Fritz Wegner. Although Wegner was superior in grade, the most experienced flyer always led the formation, a practise dating back to the Battle of Britain in 1940, at least. Wegner is seen here on the port wing helping Otto Bach out of his aircraft.

In early June 1943 the Fw 190 A-5s and A-6s (as seen here) of I. Gruppe were fitted with 21 cm. rockets under the wings in order to break up the American bomber formations. The results were encouraging, but less than two months later American escort fighters appeared over Europe in strength. Weighed down by these protuberances, the Fw 190 became easy prey for allied fighters.

June 1943. Ernst had been in my unit for a long time, and had gained the respect of his superiors. Everyone appreciated him, and looked on him as an excellent friend. The sad day of 17th June unfolded as follows:
The Gruppe took off to intercept an enemy incursion. Ernst was a Schwarmführer in 4th Staffel. Not long after taking off, we sighted enemy fighters. During combat, your son's aircraft was attacked and hit. Ernst was able to bail out, but he had been badly wounded, and had probably died while in his parachute. Falling into the sea, he sank immediately. A vessel was on the spot within a minute, but he could not be found. Up to date, the sea has not given up his body.

OLEJNIK
HAUPTMANN"

Hauptmann Olejnik rests between two officers of his Staff: Oberzahlmeister Hans Selbach on the left and Leutnant Halbey on the right.

Two views of another Fw 190 A-3 of 9th Staffel which has come to grief. This time it is "Yellow 5". Note the bent propellor blades.

Fw 190 A-5 of the Gruppenadjutant of II. Gruppe. The Tatzelwurm would be in green . Hauptmann Stärk, the one-time Adjutant, was not a pilot, so this aircraft would have been flown by others.

THE LOSSES MOUNT - MID 1943

On 10th June 1943 the Bf 109 G-6s of III. Gruppe were scrambled from Leeuwarden for the first time, but no contact was made with the enemy. However, on the following day, while I. Gruppe made no interception, III. Gruppe took part in their first engagement with a bomber force at around 18:00 hours. Gruppenkommandeur Major Leesmann and one of his Staffelkapitäne, Leutnant Wintergerst, set an example by each shooting down a B-17.

On 22nd June nearly 200 B-17s were sent to bomb the railway industries at Hüls in the Ruhr region. For the first time, Jagdgeschwader 1 operated as a complete unit. I. Gruppe recorded its best ever figures since its formation by shooting down ten B-17s. Feldwebel Piffer, Oberfeldwebel Laun, Leutnant Schott, Unteroffizier Kunze and Unteroffizier Rathenow were among the victors. They also recorded eleven Herausschüsse, Leutnant Engleder and Leutnant Schott being among the claimants. Five Fw 190s were damaged but without injury to their pilots. II. Gruppe established contact with the bomber stream shortly after 10:00 hours, but the Spitfire and P-47 fighter escort managed to keep them away from the bombers. Only Oberleutnant Harry Koch managed to pierce the cover, and he shot down a B-17. Oberleutnant Kotiza and Leutnant von Kirchmayr each claimed a Spitfire. III. Gruppe suffered their first losses: one wounded, but about ten Bf 109s damaged as a result of having to make emergency landings due to fuel shortage. However, Major Leesmann brought down another B-17. The next combat, on 25th June was even more painful. Although Major Leesmann, Feldwebel Lindenschmidt and Unteroffizier Hans Fordemann among others each shot down a B-17, the Gruppenadjutant, Oberleutnant Hardt, was killed after bringing down a B-17 at 08:50 hours, three of his colleagues were wounded and another posted missing.

Unteroffizier Hans Lehmann of 7th Staffel, who had six confirmed victories, recalled the action many years later: "On 25th June 1943, in the early morning, two Rotten of my 7th Staffel took off. The first was led by our Staffelkapitän, Oberleutnant Klöpper, I led the second. My Messerschmitt was hit and I had to make a forced landing. On my return to base I found out that Klöpper was wounded and he was in hospital. When I arrived in his room, he was only able to speak with difficulty - splinters of plexiglass had cut his face, "No question of

Two Ritterkreuzträger of III. Gruppe at Leeuwarden on 11/6/43 following combat against an allied raid against Wilhelshaven. Major Leesmann (left) and Oberleutnant Klöpper, Staffelkapitän of 7th Staffel.

Gruppenkommandeur and his Adjutant: Major Leesmann (left) and Oberleutnant Friedrich Hardt showing what a typical Luftwaffe fighter pilot wore for combat in the mid-war years.

Major Karl-Heinz Leesmann (second from left), discusses tactics with pilots after combat on 11/6/43 at Leeuwarden. Third from the right, wearing sunglasses, is Leutnant Wintergerst, and to his right, Feldwebel Meissner.

Waiting for III. Gruppe's first action, from left to right: Oberleutnant Hardt; Oberleutnant Zuzic and Hauptmann Luckenbach.

Major Karl-Heinz Leesmann (left) and two members of his Stabsschwarm: Adjutant, Hauptmann Hardt and Hauptmann Luckenbach (back to camera).

11th June 1943. Oberleutnant Wintergerst is carried in triumph after landing. He had just shot down one of the first two victims credited to III. Gruppe. Major Leesmann had brought down the other.

25/6/43. Leeuwarden. III. Gruppe losses were heavy. Gruppenadjutant Oberleutnant Hardt was killed and Unteroffizier Lehmann was badly wounded. Here, Oberleutnant Wintergerst pauses for a few seconds before climbing out of his Bf 109 G-6 on his return.

On 25th June 1943 Oberleutnant Klöpper was lightly wounded in action. His rudder is decorated with the Ritterkreuz, the number '50' beneath it, and further victory markings which include four 'Viermots' shown as claim numbers 82, 87, 88 and 89.

After the loss of Hauptmann Wickop, Hauptman Robert Olejnik took command of II. Gruppe, and passed control of 4th Staffel to Leutnant Heinz Tröger (seen here on the left in conversation with Leutnant von Kirchmayr). Tröger was found dead on 17/6/43 after bailing out of his Fw 190 A-5, "White 12" following combat with Spitfires. In this photograph, note the flying equipment of the two pilots, and the flares strapped around the waist and ankles.

Leeuwarden, shortly after the formation of III. Gruppe. Major Leesmann reports to a General of the Luftwaffe.

staying here, as soon as the opportunity arises, I'm away!"

"I got back to the airfield, and several hours later, I saw my Staffelkapitän's car. He had rejoined us in the operations room - he had indeed escaped. Our conversation was abruptly interrupted by a new order to scramble, as bombers were approaching. There was the usual intense activity before take off. As I no longer had an aircraft, I asked Klöpper to let me use his. "Of course, take it, but don't get shot down; the Ritterkreuz has just been painted on the rudder". I took off. His aircraft never did return. Half an hour later I was hanging on my parachute, badly wounded in the leg. The war was over for me - hospital martyrdom commenced. A year of intensive treatment. Over the years, I have only been able to walk with crutches".

"There were often moments of understanding, even assistance, between our enemies and ourselves. The British, particularly, were in general very correct. My God, we belonged to the same world, slightly different for those who were pilots. I recall times when life became normal. For example on 1st July 1943, between 10:00 and 11:00 hours, we engaged about 20 Spitfires about 10 kilometres to the west of the mouth of the Scheldt. A pilot of 3rd Staffel had been shot down. We took it in turns to fly over the spot in the hope of finding him. We flew at wave-top height, then up to 300 metres. Above us, a further 100 or 200 metres , the English were circling as well. No attacks, no animosity, they were also looking for one of their own. At about 20:00 hours, during my last sortie, I suddenly saw a coloured patch floating on the sea. I approached. An inflatable dinghy! The red vessel was being tossed around in the waves; the person on board was waving. We thought we had found our own companion, without realising he could be English. And that was indeed the case! One of our resue launches was able to rescue the pilot in distress, who turned out to be an English officer. All this took place within an sight of our opponents, who were no doubt as excited as ourselves."

Thus recalled Oberleutnant Rudolf Engleder of 1st Staffel. On 13th July, II. Gruppe were withdrawn to Rheine. Their place in Holland was taken by I./JG 26. During this time II. Gruppe began working with II./JG 300. This unit

Kommodore Philipp and several officers of III. Gruppe. From left to right: Hauptmann Luckenbach; Major Leesmann; Oberfeldwebel Husser; Major Philipp; Leutnant Halbey and Oberleutnant Reisinger.

employed the aircraft of II. Gruppe at night; their pilots had been trained from the beginning to fly single-seater fighters at night. This arrangement lasted until the beginning of 1944, bringing disagreements in its wake: losses due to night action reduced the fighting strength of II. Gruppe.
To cover losses, fresh pilots were continually being

Post-combat animated discussion. Centre is Unteroffizier Meissner talking to Oberleutnant Wintergerst (extreme right).

posted to operational units. Fritz Wegner recalled the attitude of experienced pilots to new recruits: "On 15th July 1943 after a long training period which I was impatient to finish, I was posted to 5./JG 1. 'Green' pilots were generally accepted very well by the old hands. Obviously it was all a question of personalities. Most of the 'old-timers' took the new boys under their wings to protect them. By contrast, others, on rare occasions, thought: "These young boys, how long will they survive? It's better not to get too attached to them. "Occasionally, they were rather unfriendly. Nevertheless, the great majority adhered to the family spirit of fighter pilots. It was a great strength. I remember for example the sensitivity of Oberfeldwebel Detlev Lüth. He was like a mother to us. His move to another Staffel was terrible for us, but when we found out he had been killed in combat we felt like orphans. Swoboda, Flecks, Ertmann, Hutter, Kirschner, all were fine men. I was nominated as wing man to Oberfeldwebel Otto Bach. He came straight to the point: being a 'green' pilot, I had only one thing to do - remain glued to him. "You get on my wing and stay there". It wasn't always very easy, but both our lives certainly depended on it. So we would go through the masses of 'Viermots'. I, thinking we would fall to the bursts of steel, he showing me not only the way to attack, but also the way to survive. It was like a big 'show', a very exciting experience which was also frightening". This

Bf 109 G of the unit with an unknown pilot in the cockpit.

Bf 109 G-6, "Black 1", of Oberleutnant Herwig Zuzic, Staffelkapitän of 8th Staffel. Note his personal emblem beneath the cockpit, and the Staffel emblem further forward on the fuselage.

Bf 109 G-6/R6 of 8th Staffel.

was how Fritz Wegner remembered his baptism of fire. He did not know then that he was at the start of a long career in military aviation which would take him as far as the rank of Lieutenant-General in the 1970s.

The air war took on monstrous proportions. The night of 24/25th July 1943 saw the beginning of "Operation Gomorrah". The city of Hamburg endured ten days and nights of almost constant attack from the RAF and the USAAF. Incendiary and explosive bombs caused the deaths of 42,000 civilians, the destruction of 250,000 homes and made one million people homeless. Jagdgeschwader 1 were regularly in action during this time.

On 25th July, during the raids on Hamburg and Kiel, Oberleutnant Koch and Oberfeldwebel Hutter (both of II. Gruppe) each shot down a B-17; a Herauschuss was also claimed by another pilot of the Gruppe. III. Gruppe also established contact with the enemy at about 17:30 hours, and Unteroffizier Fritz Haspel recorded a fresh victory over a B-17, which set down on the sea. III. Gruppe suffered a heavy loss: Gruppenkommandeur, Major Leesmann, crashed into the sea after an attack on Flying Fortresses. His wingman, Leutnant Ullman, also hit, could only report on the last sighting of his Commanding Officer: "The aircraft trailed a large banner of smoke, and he called to me over the radio that he had been hit. The aircraft turned east, then dived in a westerly direction and disappeared in the waves". A vessel was despatched immediately from Heligoland and quickly reached the crash area, but there was no sign of Leesmann. His body was washed ashore on 16th August. Hauptmann Olejnik took command of III. Gruppe. On 26th July, towards 11:50 hours, there were fresh victories over bombers attacking Hamburg and Hannover. Oberleutnant Koch and Oberfeldwebel Bach each claimed a B-17, and II. Gruppe also laid claim to two Herausschüsse. For their part, III. Gruppe established contact with a formation of about 100 B-17s around midday, with one pilot claiming a Herausschuss.

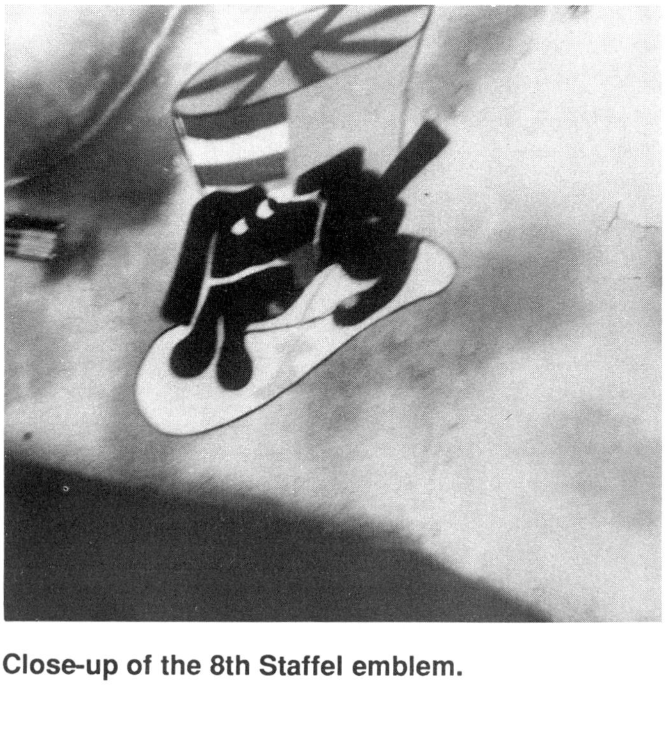

Close-up of the 8th Staffel emblem.

Hübl points out his third victory. The victim was a P-51 on 7/7/43, whose pilot was captured.

The personal insignia of Hübl: Grog, after the famous German comedian of the 1930's.

In July 1943 at Deelen two pilots of 1st Staffel, Leutnant Rudolf Engleder and Unteroffizier Rudolf Schnappauf received the Iron Cross, Second Class, from their Gruppenkommandeur, Hauptmann Schnoor. Engleder was ultimately proposed for the Ritterkreuz, and Schnappauf regularly flew as wingman to the last two Geschwaderkommodoren.

On 28th July the 8th USAAF attacked the Fieseler works at Kassel, and the aircraft works at Oschersleben. For the first time, P-47 Thunderbolt fighters carried auxiliary fuel tanks which extended their range. The pilots of Jagdgeschwader 1 were not seen by the escort fighters and at 10:13 hours II. Gruppe attacked a box of 60 B-17s head on. Three were shot down, Oberleutnant Koch claiming two of them.

Hauptmann Schnoor, Gruppenkommandeur of I. Gruppe, tried to explain how to attack these famous boxes. He confided to his assistant, Leutnant Burath the way to attack.

Burath recalled the action on 28th July 1943 as follows: "On this day, at about 10:00 hours, we overflew northern Holland to intercept Flying Fortresses. On sighting them, in the region of Leeuwarden, Hauptmann Schnoor detached himself from the unit and gained height to have a better view of the situation. "Right, on to them!". I took the lead and dropped the right wing to indicate to the others the direction of my flight to bring us head-on to the Americans. After a turn of 180 degrees I was in front of them. Everything went well, the position was perfect. A small glance to the side. Immediately the aircraft was hit by a burst of fire. I protected myself and attacked alone as the others had fallen back during the manoeuvre. I felt the tension in the pit of my stomach. The Americans, themselves, did not seem to have this problem; they fired continually. The fire, which usually went everywhere, was directed solely at me. I was the only target. All around me were streams of light and colour. I made myself small behind the double protection of the two

Formal photograph following the awards in front of Fw 190 A, "White 9". From left to right: unknown; Lück; Koeditz; Schnappauf; Schott; Engleder; Hübl; Rathenow and Kaiser.

Then followed the informal congratulations.

This Fw 190 A of 5th Staffel carries the red Tatzelwurm emblem and two-coloured spinner.

rows of cylinders (the 18 cylinders of the Fw 190 were arranged in two rows). I held a B-17 in my sights and with difficulty managed to give it several bursts. It defended itself with all its might. A real shooting gallery! My aircraft was hit all over, I needed to land.

"By chance, my mount behaved relatively well, and, above all, did not catch fire. The ground approached rapidly. I was pleased the Dutch had maintained such good fields. I selected a suitable one and headed for it. Now the aircraft became a little bit more unpleasant: it no longer wished to land. The whole field had nearly passed beneath me before I succeeded in getting down. The matter, however, was far from over. The belly-landing was violent and unending. The end of the field was approaching. My God, a canal! Damn the Dutch and their canals! The obstacle was approaching. The nose of the aircraft scraped along the soil. The tail appeared to be lifting - it looked catastrophic. Suddenly the left wing touched the soil and provoked a sudden change of direction. The nose of the aircraft dug deeper into the soil. On both sides of the cockpit , potatoes flew everywhere, as though imitating me. The crazy landing had finally ceased. The calm after the storm. I breathed a sigh of relief. Once again my guardian angel had rescued me from a perilous situation. I got out of the machine and found I was in a potato field near Buitenpost. With hands on hips, I looked over my aircraft. It seemed to be in a relatively good state. However it had lost 20cm. in length ...".

After having observed the attack, Hauptmann Schnoor joined in the attack on the Fortresses. He was credited with his third victory. Leutnant Schott, Staffelkapitän of 1st Staffel, and Oberfeldwebel Laun of 3rd Staffel also claimed a Fortress each. Two Herausschüsse were also

On 30/7/43 American P-47 escort fighters encountered I. Gruppe over Holland for the first time. Several experienced pilots, like Leutnant Peter Marxen, Staffelkapitän of 2nd Staffel, shown here, were lost.

Burial ceremony at Arnhem. Kommodore Hans Philipp lays a wreath at the graveside of his fallen comrades.

Bf 109 G-6 undergoing maintenance, with a mascot perched on the engine cowling.

recorded, one by Oberleutnant Becker, Staffelkapitän of 3rd Staffel. Along with them, II. Gruppe returned two victories, thanks to Oberleutnant Koch, Staffelkapitän of 6th Staffel, and Unteroffizier Wolschinski of the same Staffel.

On 30th July, the surprise was even worse for the unit. This time the escorting fighters, 107 P-47s, were totally effective during a raid on the Fieseler works at Kassel. At about 10:30 hours, the pilots of I. Gruppe with six of II. Gruppe alongside, were assailed over Holland by a horde of Thunderbolts. They put up an almost impentrable shield in front of the bombers. The hunters, the German fighters, became the hunted. The Staffelkapitän of 2nd Staffel, Leutnant Peter Marxen, had to bail out. In so doing, he hit the tail of the aircraft and was found dead on the ground. Oberleutnant Karl Becker, Staffelkapitän of 3rd Staffel, was killed shortly after announcing a victory. Oberfeldwebel Hans Laun of 3rd Staffel, one of the longest serving members of I. Gruppe was killed, as was Unteroffizier Karl Weninger of the same Staffel. Two other pilots were wounded. Four victories, one of which was by Fw. Rudolf Piffer, and four Herausschüsse, three of which were claimed by Leutnant Lück (2nd Staffel), Hans Feustel (2nd Staffel) and Rudolf Engleder (1st Staffel) were lodged by I. Gruppe. II.

Deelen, near Arnhem, July 1943. This Fw 190 A, "Yellow 8" of 3rd Staffel clearly shows the "stove-pipe" for the 21 cm. rockets.

A bomb is loaded onto a Bf 109 G-6 at Leeuwarden in July 1943.

On 28/7/43 after combat with B-17s, Unteroffizier Bernhard Kunze set his Fw 190 A-4, "White 12", W.Nr. 530135, down on the roof of Drachten swimming baths.

At the beginning of August 1943 the first Fw 190 A-6s arrived for II. Gruppe. The aircraft arriving at front line units still carried radio codes. Here, the latter part of the code: +HO can be seen on Leutnant Fritz Wegner's machine, W.Nr. 550740.

Deelen, summer 1943. Attempts continued to find effective firepower against American bombers. This Fw 190 A-6/R-1 of 1st Staffel certainly merits the name "Kanonenvogel", with two MG 17s over the engine, two 20 mm. MG 151s in the wings and four MG 151s in gondolas under the wings.

Rheine, summer 1943. The engine turns on Oberleutnant Rüdiger von Kirchmayr's Fw 190 A-5. Of interest is the lower engine cowling painted yellow, and the front of the engine cowling and Tatzelwurm in red.

Groundcrew of III. Gruppe working on the propellor of a Bf 109 G-6/R6 and (below and opposite page, top) posing with the aircraft on completion of their task.

Gruppe had one pilot killed; Oberleutnant Koch of 6th Staffel managed to reach the B-17s and shoot one down. III. Gruppe, who had joined battle with escort fighters composed of Spitfires and Thunderbolts towards 10:30 hours, did not suffer any losses. Leutnant Wintergerst brought down a P-47, Feldwebel Kehrle a Spitfire, and Feldwebel Miksch of 8th Staffel claimed a Herausschüss on a B-17.

On the American side, of the 134 bombers committed, 12 were lost. The fighters gained the honours on this day: Major Roberts of the 78th Fighter Group was credited with the first 'triplet' (three victories on one mission) of the 8th Air Force, while his colleague, Captain C. London, became the first American 'ace' of the 8th Air Force following his 4th and 5th victories (a Fw 190 and a Bf 109). American fighters claimed 24 victories for the loss of 7 of their own aircraft.

Following this deadly combat with the Thunderbolts, the Fw 190s were given better manoeuvrability: the rocket tubes of I. Gruppe were removed. The pilots of the unit would try to avoid the escort fighters before taking on the bombers later. The radius of action of the P-47 did not yet allow it to reach Reich airspace.

The next engagement took place on 12th August when the three Gruppen established contact with a formation of around 300 B-17s over the Ruhr area. Over Solingen the allies ran into an intense flak barrage, which disrupted the formation. It was at this moment that the pilots of II. Gruppe launched their attacks. The result was seven B-17s claimed as shot down or Herausschüsse, with Hauptmann Walter Hoeckner, Oberleutnant Harry Koch, Oberfeldwebel Detlef Lüth and Oberfeldwebel Otto Bach among the claimants. One pilot of II. Gruppe was killed, and 12 aircraft were damaged by return defensive fire. I. Gruppe lodged three victories (Hauptmann Schnoor, Oberfeldwebel Kaiser and Unteroffizier Swoboda) and two Herausschüsse (Oberleutnant S'trohall and Leutnant Eh). Unteroffizier Fritz Haspel, of 8th Staffel, whose III. Gruppe took on the escort fighters, was injured during a forced landing on Walcheren island.

Pilots of 8th Staffel at readiness. Feldwebel Miksch has his arm raised.

Three views of Unteroffizier Fritz Husser of 10th Staffel with Fw 190 A-4, "White 10", W.Nr. 583. On 28/7/43 this aircraft crashed, killing the pilot, Unteroffizier Karl Knesper.

Oberfeldwebel Georg Fröhlich of 8th Staffel on his Bf 109 G-6, "Black 6" in summer 1943.

Oberleutnant Zuzic in the cockpit of his Bf 109 G shortly before take-off.

Feldwebel Fritz Haspel (3rd from right in flying gear) reports to his Staffelkapitän, Oberleutnant Zuzic (centre, in flying gear). Extreme left is Feldwebel Kehrle.

Bf 109 G-6 at Leeuwarden.

THE DAY OF THE FIGHTERS - 17/8/43

On 17th August 1943 Jagdgeschwader 1 were led and equipped as follows:
Geschwaderstab and I. Gruppe based at Deelen;
equipped with Fw 190 A-4 and A-5s;
Geschwaderkommodore - Major Hans Philipp
Gruppenkommandeur - Hauptmann Emil-Rudolf Schnoor;
1st Staffel - Leutnant Georg Schott;
2nd Staffel - Leutnant Hans Feustel;
3rd Staffel - Oberleutnant S'trohall

II. Gruppe based at Woensdrecht;
equipped with Fw 190 A-4 and A-6s;
Gruppenkommandeur - Hauptmann Walter Hoeckner;
4th Staffel - Oberleutnant Eugen Kotiza;
5th Staffel - Leutnant Rüdiger von Kirchmayr
6th Staffel - Oberleutnant Harry Koch

III. Gruppe based at Leeuwarden;
equipped with Bf 109 G-6s;
Gruppenkommandeur - Hauptmann Robert Olejnik;
7th Staffel - Oberleutnant Heinrich Klöpper;
8th Staffel - Oberleutnant Herbert Zuzic;
9th Staffel - Oberleutnant Eugen Wintergerst

At 04:00 hours on the 17th August the pilots of I. Gruppe stirred: daybreak. As soon as their aircraft were ready, four pilots took off towards the sea for the first reconnaissance of the morning. During this time, the others had breakfast without suspecting that this would be their day. At Leeuwarden, the pilot's day began at 03:15 hours, a half hour before sunrise. They busied themselves checking their equipment and their aircraft. At 07:00 hours breakfast was taken at the dispersals of the various Staffeln. Shortly after 08:00 hours the pilots were dressed ready to take off instantly, on the first scramble.
At this moment, the German listening services were already on the alert. Towards 07:30 hours many important signals were heard: a large formation of enemy aircraft were forming to the west of Gt. Yarmouth. The information was immediately sent to the Luftwaffe authorities. In turn their orders were sent to the necessary locations.
In effect, at 06:45 hours, the first B-17s took off from England for a mission which, in terms of size, surpassed anything that had gone before. The attack of 17th August 1943 was carried out by two large formations. The first, comprising 146 B-17s of the 4th Bomb Wing would attack the Messerschmitt works at Regensburg-Prüfening and continue across southern Europe to land at bases in North Africa. The second formation, consisting of 230 aircraft of the 1st Bomb Wing had as its objective the ball-

17th August 1943 became known as the "Day of the Fighters". Many pilots were able to increase their scores, such as Unteroffizier Bernhard Kunze of 1st Staffel, shown on the right here beside his Fw 190 A-5, W.Nr. 410055. The five victories included B-17s, the last two recorded for 17/8/43.

bearing works at Schweinfurt.

However the unsettled weather over the south-east of England hampered take off. When it was thought that the missions would have to be aborted, the order to proceed was given. Precious time had been lost, and the raids had lost their synchronisation. It took more than an hour for the 146 first wave bombers to join up and get in combat formation. The fighter escort joined them over the North Sea, at cruising speed to maximise fuel economy. Shortly after 09:30 hours the formation crossed the Dutch coast south of the Scheldt estuary.

At the same time, the order for take off reached III. Gruppe. The 32 serviceable Bf 109 G-6s left Leeuwarden led by Hauptmann Olejnik and headed for Deelen airfield, there to await further orders.

The neighbouring unit, Jagdgeschwader 26, established contact with the allied armada over Anvers. From this moment on, German fighters followed the bombers along their complete route over Europe. III. Gruppe of Jagdgeschwader 1 took off again and intercepted as the escorting fighters turned back at the limit of their range, the Belgian-German border.

Hauptmann Olejnik recalled the interception thus: "Shortly after 11:00 hours the course taken by the enemy formation led us to believe with certainty that this attack would be against southern Germany. At that point, "cockpit readiness" was ordered. Shortly after mid-day, 31 Bf 109s took off. I was not among them, as I had radio problems during the earlier move. My oldest Staffelführer

Unteroffizier Schoenrock of 4th Staffel, seen here in May 1943 at Woensdrecht with his Fw 190 A-4, claimed two B-17s on 17/8/43, of which only one was officially acknowledged.

The very experienced Oberfeldwebel Hutter (left) explains a combat to a newcomer, Leutnant Schwarz. The latter recorded his first "Herausschuss" on 17/8/43.

During a patrol over the Channel in August 1943, Feldwebel Hempel and Oberfähnrich Herbert Eh of 3rd Staffel came across a large ship on the English coast. Hempel was able to identify it as the 'Exeter' thanks to the identification chart which pilots on reconnaissance missions carried. Herbert Eh approached it and was hit by the defensive fire. He managed to belly-land his aircraft in a Dutch meadow.

On 16th August 1943 the body of Leesmann was washed ashore on a beach. He was buried at Recklinghausen. The funeral cortege was led by Leutnant Düsterbeck, who carried his decorations on a cushion.

The checkerboard first appeared on the cowlings of Fw 190s of I. Gruppe in summer 1943. It helped identification in the air. It would appear that the squares adopted the same colours as the numerals on the sides of the aircraft: black/white for 1st Staffel; black/red for 2nd Staffel and black/yellow for 3rd Staffel.

took over leading the formation. Twelve minutes later, the fault was fixed and I took off with a pilot of I. Gruppe as my wingman. We reached 1,220 metres altitude and followed the course of my Gruppe over the radio. In spite of our efforts, we were unable to catch our comrades up. Suddenly, at a height of 7,500 metres, about 50-60 kilometres away, I sighted three formations of bombers. I changed course towards them. At this time we were over the Aachen region. The enemy were flying a south-easterly course. After a chase of 35 minutes, I made contact over Saarbrücken. By this time my Gruppe had already been in violent combat for a quarter of an hour, which had reverberated in my earphones.

"I gained height to weigh up the position. They were "Fortresses", with their very impressive defensive armament. These aircraft were better left alone! I attacked a bomber to the left of the formation from behind and slightly below. After my third attack, black smoke escaped from its right engine. Little by little the enemy aircraft became detached from its group, but managed to correct itself 100 metres behind, losing 80 metres of height in the process. A very uncomfortable position for it: it could no longer count on the protection of its colleagues. It released its bombs, which was the prudent thing to do.

"During my fourth attack, the aircraft went out of control. Engulfed in flames, it made three large turns to the left. Seven crewmen bailed out. At 4,000 metres, the turns became tighter. The right wing broke off, followed by the left wing. The fuselage continued to dive and hit the

Three views of a Fw 190, "White 4", of 1st Staffel after a taxing accident at Schipol in summer 1943.

ground in a wood near Darmstadt. Three men were probably still in the aircraft.
"It was high time for me to land. Towards 13:45 hours I landed at Mannheim-Sandhofen, where the aircraft could be re-fuelled and re-armed. I found several of my pilots there, who had also chosen this base as a landing place. We were soon ready for further combat. In spite of that, we were ordered to take off late, and we could not attack the "Amis" on their return flight. We therefore set off for Leeuwarden. At 20:00 hours, 22 pilots of the Gruppe had returned to base. Three others arrived the following day. We had four wounded, but claimed 12 victories, which led to interminable discussions".
After several passes, the pilots of the unit broke off combat. Apart from a B-17 credited to Olejnik, two others were claimed by Feldwebel Meissner and Feldwebel Fröhlich. Other units took up the pursuit, and Luftwaffe attacks were incessant as far as Regensburg. Nevertheless 126 bombers were able to unload their deadly cargo and damaged the factories. Their ordeal was not over: heading for Africa, they had to get through German units based in southern Europe. Exhausted, after a flight of 11 hours, the surviving crews finally touched down at Bone, Telerma and Berteaux. They had left 24 of their crews in Europe.
At 11:20 hours the 230 four-engined bombers of the second wave took off. They were to face German units which were once again ready for action. At 11:57 hours Major Hoeckner's II. Gruppe were brought to a state of readiness at Woensdrecht. Nineteen Fw 190s took off at about 14:30 hours and attacked a formation of about 100 B-17s. Shortly before 15:30 hours II. Gruppe reported seven Herausschüsse, of which 5 were officially credited. The successful pilots were Oberleutnant Koch; Oberfeldwebel Bach; Unteroffizier Schönrock (two, of which one was not granted); Leutnant Schwarz and Unteroffizier Scharler.
If the damage inflicted on the ball-bearing works was considerable, the losses for the bombers were heavy. Jagdgeschwader 1 alone claimed 21 B-17s, 12 by I. Gruppe. Among the victorious pilots were Oberleutnant Engleder, who claimed two B-17s, his 6th and 7th victories; Hauptmann Schnoor, his fourth official victory; Oberfeldwebel Piffer, his fourth; Unteroffizier Kunze, and a certain Oberfeldwebel Emil Demuth, of whom more will be heard of later. His first victory over a B-17 marked the beginning of an excellent career with Jagdgeschwader 1 starting on 27th July 1943 with 2nd Staffel. Feldwebel Hans Meissner also scored a victory over a B-17.
On the debit side, I. Gruppe mourned the loss of Leutnant Hans Feustel, Staffelkapitän of 2nd Staffel, who managed to bail out despite being badly wounded. Taken to hospital, he died four days later. Leutnant Hans Ehlers who had recently moved to I. Gruppe, took over 2nd Staffel.

Deelen, summer 1943. Fw 190 A-4, "Yellow 2" of 3rd Staffel being refuelled.

Jagdgeschwader 1 were not the only successful unit. In total, 60 B-17s were shot down and 168 damaged. Allied fighters lost three P-47s, three Spitfires and one Typhoon. In comparison, the losses of the German fighters were relatively light: six killed and twelve wounded. P-47 pilots claimed 20 victories. In the days which followed, III. Gruppe were hard hit. The sea finally gave up the body of Major Leesman. On 19th August Oberleutnant Herwig Zuzic, Staffelkapitän of 8th Staffel, was killed in combat over Knoke. Three pilots of 9th Staffel also did not return to base.

"In the afternoon of the 19th, I. Gruppe took off from Leeuwarden and headed for the centre of the Low Countries: an attack was brewing. Aircraft were prepared and we waited near our machines. Take off was at 19:30, hours. For technical reasons, Wintergerst did not take part, and I led 9th Staffel. Contact with the enemy was made in the area of Ostend. The Gruppe split into two: Zuzic's Staffel and mine attacked from the right; the rest, led by Olejnik from the left. Combat with Spitfires began and I quickly lost Zuzic from sight. It seems he had probably collided while turning before the attack . Spitfires came towards me. We were face to face and opened fire simultaneously. I was hit in the foot. My 109 was riddled but remained controllable, and I escaped from the English. My aircraft would not make it back to Woensdrecht, so I found a field and made a belly-landing. The aircraft bounced hard, the impact was very

Gedenket im Gebete und beim heiligen Opfer
meines lieben Gatten und Vaters, unseres guten
Sohnes und Bruders

Leutnant Eugen Wintergerst

Staffelführer in einem Jagdgeschwader
Inhaber des Ehrenpokals des Reichsmarschalls,
des E. K. 1. und 2. Kl., der goldenen Frontflug-
spange und des Verwundetenabzeichens
Teilnehmer an den Kämpfen in Frankreich,
im Osten und gegen England

geboren am 13. Juni 1915 in Lauben
gefallen am 4. September 1943 bei einem Feind-
flug gegen England

Wir wollten beide glücklich sein,
doch grausam griff das Schicksal ein,
nahm mir mein Liebstes auf der Erde,
wie kann es denn nur möglich sein?
Nun liegst du still in Feindesland begraben,
kein Fleh'n und Weinen gibt dich mir zurück!
Verloren ist mein Höchstes, was ich hatte,
vorbei ist Liebe - Hoffnung - Glück.
Mit Gott will ich in diesem Schmerz feststeh'n,
Bis wir bei Gott uns wiederseh'n. N/1162

Obituary card for Oberleutnant Eugen Wintergerst, Staffelkapitän of 9th Staffel, shot down and killed over Bergues, France, on 4th September 1943.

A pilot of 1st Staffel returns victorious to Deelen in summer 1943. The checkerboard marking is clearly visible as well as the pilot's personal emblem beneath the cockpit.

Oberleutnant Georg Schott, Staffelkapitän of 1st Staffel and victor in 19 combats (four of which were with JG 1) was killed in action on 27/9/43. His successor was Oberleutnant Robert Engleder. Schott (left) and Engleder are seen here in April 1943 in front of a Fw 190 A-4 with a white engine cowling. Both pilots wear life jackets due to combat often taking place over the North Sea.

The Belgian Feldwebel Guido Rombaut of 6th Staffel. He was with JG 1 for only a short time before he was killed in action in combat with Thunderbolts in Fw 190 A-6, "Yellow 12" on 27/9/43.

violent. Badly wounded, I was transported to the hospital at Anvers" -Feldwebel Hans Meissner of 9th Staffel recalling the loss of Zuzic, and his own harrowing combat experience. In fact Zuzic had collided with one of his comrades, who escaped the collision unhurt. The reaction of Eugen Wintergerst, Herwig Zuzic's friend, was prophetic: "Ever since we were at the front, we have always been together. Herwig is dead, I know I will not be long joining him". On 4th September 1943 Oberleutnant Wintergerst, Staffelkapitän of 9th Staffel was shot down by Spitfires over Bergues/Dunkirk. He bailed out too low. One of his pilots was killed and another wounded also. These major combats led to an important reinforcement of German fighters engaged on defence of the Reich duties. At the end of August, Jagdgeschwader 3 returned from southern Russia to bases on the Rhine, Jagdgeschwader 26 was based in Holland, and three Gruppen from the northern part of the Russian front were alloted new bases in Wiesbaden, Munich and Oldenburg. More than a month passed without an attack on Germany. The USAAF licked their wounds and concentrated its forces against objectives in France and Belgium. However, reconnaissance missions continued, and on 24th September Unteroffizier Rauhaus successfully shot down a Mosquito near Zwolle, in Holland. The victorious machine was one of four Bf 109 Gs delivered to II. Gruppe two weeks earlier. These Messerschmitts, passed on to 11th Staffel, were equipped with GM 1 engine-powerboost system, which gave the engine increased performance with the injection of Nitrous Oxide to the fuel. The Bf 109 G increased its top speed by nearly 30 kilometres per hour, and could attain this increased performance in around 5 minutes. These

Fw 190 A, "Black 3" of Leutnant Fritz Wegner.

Oberleutnant Georg Schott, Staffelkapitän of 1st Staffel, killed in action 27/9/43.

aircraft were allocated to high altitude duties, and represented a major threat to allied reconnaissance aircraft. It would be the 27th September before B-17s appeared over the Reich skies again. 308 bombers escorted by 262 P-47s headed for the industrial area of Emden. I. Gruppe took off from Deelen at 10:30 hours; II. Gruppe half an hour later. I. Gruppe were first to engage the "Viermots", but the latter defended themselves vigorously. The Fw 190, "White 11", of Oberleutnant Schott, Staffelkapitän of 1st Staffel was hit during this attack. He was found dead in his dinghy three weeks later. When II. Gruppe arrived in a position to attack, they were surprised by a formation of 30-40 P-47s coming out of the sun, and a dogfight ensued. Hauptmann Hoeckner and Leutnant von Kirchmayr each claimed an American fighter. Only Oberleutnant Kotiza and his Schwarm managed to reach the B-17s, claiming one. Four Fw 190s of II. Gruppe had to make belly-landings. One was missing: Unteroffizier Guido Rombaut of 6th Staffel. He represented a unique case in the annals of the Luftwaffe. A volunteer Belgian in the Flemish SS, through persistence he obtained a transfer to the Luftwaffe and was posted to Jagdgeschwader 1 only several days before his disappearance.

Groundcrew fill the supplementary fuel tank of "Black 3" under the watchful eye of Leutnant Fritz Wegner.

Excellent view of Fw 190 A-6, "Black 5", W.Nr. 550473, of 5th Staffel.

THE DEATH OF THE KOMMODORE

On 4th October 155 B-17s escorted by 223 P-47s had as their targets the industrial regions of Frankfurt and Wiesbaden, as well as the city of Frankfurt itself. Towards 11:00 hours II. Gruppe met and attacked a group of about 100 Boeings at an altitude of 8,000 metres over the Eifel/Weisbaden area. A pilot of II. Gruppe was killed by the return defensive fire, another of I. Gruppe was wounded. However two victories (one each to Hauptmann Hoeckner and Unteroffizier Fuchs) and one Herauschuss (Oberleutnant Kotiza) were claimed by II. Gruppe. Of the pilots of I. Gruppe, Oberleutnant Engleder, Oberfeldwebel Piffer and Unteroffizier Kunze each claimed a B-17 shot down; Leutnant Ehlers a Herausschuss.

"On 4/10/43 the USAAF launched a further large-scale attack directed this time against the region of Frankfurt-Hanau. A tough combat unfolded at an altitude of 9,000-10,000 metres. Once again, the imposing American fighter escort engaged us in a cloudless sky.

"The bombardment no doubt hit the Hanau industries hard, because those responsible for its defence and the district head of Frankfurt visited Göring and protested strongly asbout his fighters: "How is it possible that American bombers can fly over the city in almost parade-ground fashion? And further, German fighters were seen at altitude, not attacking!" Göring went into one of his mad rages in which he knew the answer, and he had despatched to all the fighter units responsible the following orders:

1. There are no meteorological conditions which could prevent fighters from taking off and engaging in combat.
2. Every fighter pilot taking off in a machine not showing any sign of combat, or without having recorded a victory will be prosecuted by a court-martial.
3. In the case of where a pilot uses up his ammunition, or if his weapons are unusable, he should ram the enemy bomber."

"On 8th October 1943 at about 10:00 hours, the Kommodore, Oberstleutnant Philipp, called together the post-holding officers of I. Gruppe. Present were Hauptmann Schulz, Geschwaderadjutant and Schnoor, Gruppenkommandeur of I. Gruppe, as well as Oberleutnants Engleder, S'trohall and Leutnant Ehlers. The Kommodore acquainted them with the head of the Luftwaffe's circular. He concluded with this remark: "As far as I'm concerned, I categorically refuse to allow myself to be held to such advice; I know what I have to do!" " Thus Oberleutnant Engleder recalled the early days of October 1943.

Towards mid-day the approach of a formation of bombers was reported. Cockpit readiness was ordered. The order for take off was issued to I. Gruppe at 12:45 hours.

Leeuwaden, autumn 1943. Bf 109 G-6/R-6 of 9th Staffel.

Just over an hour later, at about 14:00 hours, more than 300 B-17s were engaged over Münster. Geschwaderkommodore Philipp ordered 1st Staffel to attack with the command: "System 1, angreifen".
Feldwebel Reinhardt of the Geschwader Staff Flight recalled: "During this first wave attack, we were attacked by Thunderbolts. In spite of this, I clearly heard the Kommodore announce a further victory over the radio, his 206th. Also the orders which he gave me. A last phrase: "Reinhardt, attack!". Feldwebel Reinhardt, wingman of Philipp, saw his leader's aircraft dive towards a cloud and disappear into it. Shortly after, wounded from colliding with an enemy aircraft, he had to make a forced landing. After the combat, the aircraft set down at Deelen, and at around 15:30 hours the news came through: Kommodore Philipp had been shot down in the region of Nordhorn.
A pilot of I. Gruppe was killed and three others were wounded. Among the wounded were Leutnant Hans Ehlers, who had shot down a bomber and rammed another over Kalle, as well as Unteroffizier Rudolf Hübl, who was hit after having claimed his seventh victory, a B-17. Oberleutnant Engleder of 1st Staffel added two more B-17s to his account. Leutnant Lück, Oberfeldwebel Piffer and Feldwebel Rathenow among others each claimed a B-17 among the seven victories and five Herausschüsse claimed by I. Gruppe.
On Sunday 10th October, I. and II. Gruppen were joined at their bases at Deelen and Rheine by I. and II. Gruppen of Jagdgeschwader 26 respectively. Around 14:30 hours these Gruppen were scrambled. II. Gruppe of Jagdgeschwader 1 (comprising 30 Fw 190s and four Bf 109 Gs equipped with the 'Y'-system) and II. Gruppe, Jadgeschwader 26 were ordered to assemble over Münster. In this region there were also ten other Gruppen of fighters or 'Zerstörer'. Münster was the precise target for some 236 bombers. Well positioned, the defending German forces inflicted heavy losses: 30 four-engined bombers were shot down.
II. Gruppe of the unit launched its first head-on attack at 15:00 hours. After this first pass, the pilots regrouped. Under the leadership of Hauptmann Koch, they then attacked the right flank of the American formation. Hauptmann Höckner shot down a B-17, but his Fw 190 A-6, "Red 1", was hit in the engine. Oil obscured his windscreen and he had to bail out. Three other victories were claimed by II. Gruppe, including one by Leutnant Wegner, as well as five Herausschüsse (two for Hauptmann Koch and one each for Feldwebel Fuchs and Feldwebel Niedereicholz). In I. Gruppe, Oberfeldwebel Demuth, Oberfeldwebel Piffer and Feldwebel Rathenow each claimed a victory, and two Herausschüsse were also recorded.
III. Gruppe lost Unteroffizier Einberger over Bremen, a victim, it appeared, of his own flak. On the credit side, Hauptmann Olejnik shot down a B-17, his last victory with Jagdgeschwader 1, and Hauptmann Eberle, who had returned to the unit after 6 months with Jagdgruppe West, claiming a P-47.

Leeuwarden, autumn 1943. Three Bf 109 G-6s of 9th Staffel receiving attention from groundcrew. Note the "Erla Haube" canopies on two of the aircraft.

SCHWEINFURT - SECOND TIME

14th October, noon. The German listening services reported almost at the same instant an identical message: "Numerous echoes. Important formation of bombers. Direction Brussels".

At about 13:30 hours, II. Gruppe were the first Gruppe to engage the enemy. Two "boxes", each containing about 150 aircraft under strong escort were flying over the Eindhoven region. At an altitude of 8,000 metres, with auxiliary fuel tanks released, the Fw 190s turned into the attack. At this moment the escorting P-47s fell on the German pilots. The confusion was indescribable. Oberfeldwebel Detlef Lüth in his Fw 190 "White 9", escaped the Thunderbolts and found himself on the track of a B-17: "On 14/10/43, at 12:14 hours, I took off as No.3 in 4th Staffel, JG 1, following orders from Jafü 3. At about 13:32 hours we saw between 250-300 Boeings, split into two large formations. As I had not released my auxiliary fuel tank, I lost contact with the rest of the Gruppe. I approached three aircraft flying about 1,500 metres from the right of the formation. When I was sufficiently close to the three aircraft, I identified them as Thunderbolts. I got into position directly behind them, but at the same moment I was attacked by a fourth fighter, which pursued me down to 5,000 metres. Following that, still with plenty of fuel, I looked to make contact with my colleagues. After three or four minutes I realised that would not be possible. I had to attack alone. I placed myself above a group of 15-20 Boeings and dived on them from the right. In a wide curve, I passed under them to put myself in a position to fire on the last Boeing on the left side. I approached, firing all the time from 150 metres to 50. A part of its fuselage came away, the rudder tore off, as well as part of the wings. I followed the Boeing for a moment. Its guns continued to fire up to the point when it left the formation, making a turn to the left. Two men bailed out, and I noticed that during this turn, a Bf 109 made a fresh attack on the aircraft. I made a second pass, this time on the flank. Two further crew members took to their parachutes. The aircraft itself then began to fall. It lost its fin, appeared to steady itself for a second, before crashing from 3,000 metres. I would place the impact with the ground at about 10 kilometres south-east of Düren. I was then chased by two escort fighters. I no longer had sufficient ammunition to fight them. It was 13:40 hours. Thirty five minutes later, I landed at Köln-Ostheim airfield".

It is interesting to note that Lüth's aircraft, a Fw 190 A-6 fitted with two MG 151/20 Kanone and two MG 17 machine guns fired 280 rounds with the former weapon, and 550 with the latter.

Oberfeldwebel Leo Schuhmacher and Oberleutnant Eugen Kotiza each claimed a Herausschüss. The American force reached the Rhine, at which point their fighter escort had to turn back, having reached the maximum radius of action. II. Gruppe also had to turn back.

With I. Gruppe, Oberleutnant Engleder distinguished

On 23rd October 1943 there occurred a major meeting at Deelen. Hauptmann Schnoor (facing camera) presents his pilots to Göring on the occasion of the presentation of awards: the German Cross in Gold for Leutnant Ehlers; Iron Cross, First Class for Unteroffizier Kunze (shaking Göring's hand); Feldwebel Rathenow (to the left of Kunze); Oberleutnants Engleder and S'trohal. The Iron Cross, Second Class for Leutnants Dedow and Steffen, Oberfeldwebel Demuth (to the right of Kunze) and Unteroffiziers Lacher and Hempler.

himself once again by shooting down two B-17s. In fifteen days, he had destroyed ten Flying Fortresses - a record. Hauptmann Schnoor claimed one, his third victory. Oberfeldwebels Piffer and Demuth, Feldwebel Rathenow and Unteroffizier Kunze each claimed a Boeing. 7th Staffel were less fortunate: three of their pilots were killed, but Oberfeldwebel Fröhlich of 8th Staffel shot down a B-17.

Other fighter units appeared on the horizon. Bad news for the Americans! The second Schweinfurt raid was reaching a climax. Like a cursed city, it seemed to have cast a spell on the crews from the New World. On the airfield in England, everyone scanned the skies nervously. How many Fortresses would return? And in what state? How many wounded, or killed, on board? Like that of 17th August, the results of the raid were catastrophic. Sixty B-17s crashed on enemy territory, five others in England. Twelve others got down almost miraculously, but were written off. 121 other Boeings regained their bases with serious damage. Six hundred men were missing. Five dead and forty wounded were taken from returned aircraft.

From now on the bombers could not venture so deep into the skies of the Reich without fighter escort covering the whole route. The experts set about trying to increase the range of the American fighters. In the meantime, the USAAF contented itself with targets closer to home.

The German air defence celebrated. On 23rd October Reichmarshall Göring and senior offices visited Deelen to encourage the men and discuss new tactics. It was also the time to hand out decorations. Hauptmann Harry Koch and Leutnant Hans Ehlers received the Deutsche Kreuz in Gold, and several other pilots of the unit received the Iron Cross 1st or 2nd class.

Changes occurred in Jagdgeschwader 1. The new Kommodore was one of the greatest aces in the history of fighter aviation. Oberstleutnant Walter Oesau was famous since the Spanish Civil War, when he shot down ten aircraft. He was the third pilot to achieve the magical figure of 100 victories, and his success brought him the highest decorations: the Knights Cross, then Oakleaves, then Swords. Forbidden to fly combat missions, Oesau had been named Jagdfliegerführer 4 Brittany. He took over control of Jagdgeschwader 1 after the death of Philipp.

New Staffelkapitäne were appointed in I. Gruppe, all expert fighter pilots. On 6th November 1943 Hauptmann Alfred Grislawski took charge of 1st Staffel. This ace, from JG 52, had more than 100 victories. Aged 24, he had received the Knights Cross in July 1942. Four days

Photographs of checkerboard Fw 190's are rare. This is the final one. This destroyed Fw 190 could be the A-6, "White 10", W.Nr. 550795 of Feldwebel Wilhelm Hoge of 1st Staffel, which crashed due to mechanical failure at Deelen at 16:30 hours on 20/10/43. The pilot died shortly after the crash.

Oberleutnant Engleder of 1st Staffel took part in all of the major air battles, such as 17/8/43 and 14/10/43. In November he moved to 2nd Staffel, which explains the black number on the fuselage of this aircraft. Clearly visible is the flare chute below and forward of the cockpit canopy.

later, Oberleutnant Rudolf Engleder was named Staffelkapitän of 2nd Staffel. The following day, Leutnant Hans Ehlers took charge of 3rd Staffel.

On 3rd November 1943, the Americans took up once again the attack on the Reich. This time, it was the port of Wilhelmshaven which received a visit from the allied bombers. They were covered by P-38s of the 55th Fighter Group. Bf 109 G-6s of III. Gruppe took off from Leeuwarden at 12:43 hours. Visibility was poor, and the rain which soaked the airfields made take-off hazardous. When cloud base had been traversed, the drops of rain appeared like shot and shell: the escort fighters pounced on the Germans. It was a massacre! The Staffelkapitäne were the first victims: Oberleutnant Rainer Framm of 9th Staffel crashed in his Bf 109 G-6, "Yellow 1" near Bad Zwischenahn. Not long after, Hauptmann Alfred Faber of 8th Staffel and his Bf 109 G-6 "Black 1" disappeared into the North Sea near Ameland. Feldwebel Josef Kehrle of 8th Staffel was wounded. He returned to his Staffel after convalescence, and was finally rendered 'hors-de-combat' after being wounded in April 1944. At this time, Kehrle had forteen victories, of which twelve were four-engined bombers. In contrast 7th Staffel managed to evade the American defensive screen, and two pilots, one being Oberleutnant Klöpper, each claimed a B-17.

I. Gruppe took off at 12:26 hours and returned with two victories, but on the debit side they lost Feldwebel Johannes Rathenow, the pilot who had scored the first victory of the Gruppe. His Fw 190 A-6 "White 7" was a hit and exploded. Twenty two Fw 190s of II. Gruppe took off a t 12:55 hours. The Gruppe had one pilot killed and six aircraft were damaged or lost, like that of Oberfeldwebel Lüth who had to bail out after shooting down a B-17. Feldwebel Sauer also had to bail out on this mission. A P-38 Lightning was shot down by Oberfeldwebel Haninger. The Americans admitted the loss of seven bombers and two fighters. On this day, the unit counted at least 22 aircraft as written off or damaged.

Leutnant Hans Berger recalled his early days with the unit: "When I arrived at I./JG 1, on 12th June 1943, I was a very fearless pilot, and ten days later I shot down my first B-17. I saw several crew members bail out, and I followed the aircraft down until it crashed. I could therefore pinpoint its location precisely. The remains were where I had exactly indicated. However, without a witness, this victory was not credited. Being a young, inexperienced officer, I had little chance of having it confirmed. My first "kill" allowed an experienced pilot to move a little nearer to receiving the "Ritterkreuz". My first disappointment. The second was even worse. I had a very good friend, my Schwarmführer, Johannes Rathenow. He taught me a lot, and I appreciated his kindness. On 3rd November 1943, while manoeuvring into position to attack a box of Viermots, his aircraft received a direct hit and exploded before my eyes. I was only a few metres to his left.

These two events, and the realisation of the situation in which we fought, completely changed my view of the

On 11th November 1943 Feldwebel Max Sauer (seen here) was the only pilot of II. Gruppe to shoot down a B-17. Shortly after he would become the wingman of Kommodore Oesau.

war. Those who chased the honours list, would very quickly find their name on a loss list. My comrades laughed at me when they saw me underlining the different aerodromes on a map. I systematically remembered all the small landing grounds where I might eventually gain refuge, after pursuing a stream of bombers. We were often short of fuel and had to get down quickly. Frequently all these places were under surveillance from enemy fighters, who pounced on us as soon as our undercarriage came down. I, myself, contrived to remain alone and avoid these "hot" areas. Landing on a small base offered the following advantages:
- fighter pilots were always particularly well received there, and well fed;
- one did not have to take off immediately with unknown pilots who disappeared, leaving you alone to face the enemy;
- These small aerodromes often did not possess the special "C" fuel required by fighter aircraft. I could therefore expect a respite of two or three days.
It was perhaps because of this that I survived".
III. Gruppe were hard hit in November 1943. On the 29th,

On 11th November 1943 Oberfeldwebels Flecks and Schuhmacher each shot down a P-47 flying escort to 60 B-17s heading for Münster. Shortly after his victory, Oberfeldwebel Schuhmacher visited the crash site of his victim.

towards 14:00 hours, III. Gruppe were engaged by 20 Lightnings. At least seven were claimed, by among others Oberleutnants Klöpper, Bucholz and Feldwebel Miksch. A P-47 also fell to the guns of Oberleutnant Overhagen. When combat was broken off, Oberleutnant Heinrich Klöpper and his section of two dived at great speed through the clouds. They did not realise that cloud base was very low, and breaking through the clouds, they did not have time to pull out and all three crashed in the Westrand Zuiderzee. At that time Klöpper had 94 victories, gained mainly on the eastern front. This month of November had, however, resulted in additions to his score: a B-17 on the 3rd; another two days later; a B-24 on the 26th, and the P-38 to close the account.

THE YEAR'S END - 1943

On 1st December the 1st and 2nd Bomb Division headed for the industrial region of Solingen. Nearly 300 bombers took part, escorted by 374 P-47s and 42 P-38s. I.Gruppe were involved in the interception. Oberleutnant Rudolf Engleder added two more B-17s to his score, bringing it up to 25. Hauptmann Alfred Grislawski also claimed two Boeings and Unteroffizier Kunze, a Thunderbolt. II. Gruppe shot down three B-17s, two of them by Hauptmann Harry Koch. In III. Gruppe, one of their best pilots was lost: the Austrian Feldwebel Alfred Miksch of 8th Staffel, whose victory tally stood at 48, mostly gained on the eastern front.

On 11th December at about 11:00 hours, III. Gruppe were once again in action against the fighter escort of Thunderbolts on a raid against Emden. An hour later II. Gruppe reached the bombers and Hauptmann Koch, Oberfeldwebel Bach and Feldwebel Fuchs each claimed a B-17.

The hordes of bombers increased continually. On 16th December, nearly 550 B-17s and B-24s escorted by 200 fighters headed for the port of Bremen. "This day was rotten. The mist could be cut with a knife. Cloud base was at 150 metres. It was necessary to reach 2,800 metres to get through the clouds. The order for take off reached us at 13:00 hours. Course 300 degrees. At 7,000 metres over Den Helder (north of Amsterdam) we encountered the enemy. I led my seven men of 2nd Staffel. Straight on for two head-on attacks. After the first, I had obtained a victory; after the next pass, a second. The enemy flight had almost passed when my aircraft was hit in turn. Splinters of glass, like small pieces of ice, hit my right eye, and I was wounded on the left side of the head. I was

On 1st December 1943 Feldwebel Alfred Miksch of 8th Staffel was killed in action. With 48 victories gained mostly in the east, he was one of the most experienced pilots of III. Gruppe.

The end of 1943 saw changes of Staffelkapitän in I. Gruppe. Hauptmann Alfred Grislawski (left) took charge of 1st Staffel, and Leutnant Hans Ehlers, 3rd Staffel.

On 16/12/43 Oberfeldwebel Rudolf Piffer recorded his 7th and 8th victories over B-17s. He is seen here shortly after landing at Dortmund. He was awarded the German Cross in Gold on 29/3/44 and was promoted to Leutnant on 1/5/44. He was a brave and fearless pilot, but did not survive the Normandy campaign of summer 1944.

On 22nd December 1943 the unit suffered its last loss of the year. During combat with B-17s in the region of Badbergen, Hauptmann Harry Koch, Staffelkapitän of 6th Staffel with 28 victories collided with his wingman, Unteroffizier Mietho. Mietho bailed out to safety; Koch crashed to his death.

blind, alone, flying an aircraft in open sky. I informed my pilots of the situation and Oberfeldwebel Piffer, one of my Schwarmführers, took up station at my side. Over the radio, he guided me south, over the Zuiderzee. I thus reached the base at Twente. And it was only thanks to the radio that I could be assisted in accomplishing a blind landing". A very eventful combat and landing for Oberleutnant Rudolf Engleder, Staffelkapitän of 2nd Staffel. Toni Piffer thus extricated his Staffelkapitän from a perilous situation after registering his 7th and 8th victories. A total of nine victories were returned by I. Gruppe, Hauptmann Alfred Grislawski and Leutnant Hans Ehlers were among the victors.

On 20th December at 11:00 hours II. Gruppe, comprising 12 Fw 190s and two Bf 109 Gs of 11th Staffel, received the order to take off. The two Messerschmitts detached themselves from the rest and climbed to 11,000 metres. At 12:10 hours the pilots of this high-flying formation sighted the bombers flying a north-westerly course. One of the two pilots was unable to attack: ice formed on his windscreen had rendered it opaque. Unteroffizier Swoboda therefore attacked alone. He rapidly lost 5,000 metres in height, and came on to the formation from the rear. After several bursts, the 109 was hit by return defensive fire. His guns jammed, and four P-47s arrived on the scene. The German pilot realised he could not put up much resistance against his adversaries, and he decided to ram the B-17 he had attacked. He approached it at speed from the right and struck the rudder. The fin was also damaged, and instantly the Boeing dived out of control. It crashed on Norderney island, taking four crew members to their deaths. Swoboda managed to bail out and reached the ground unscathed. In the combat which followed, Hauptmann Koch and Oberfeldwebel Lüth each claimed a B-17.

On the 22nd December 1943 II. and III. Gruppen were scrambled at around 13:10 hours; the cities of Münster and Osnabrück were the targets. II. Gruppe suffered a very great loss: while his wife had arrived to pay him a visit, Hauptmann Harry Koch, Staffelkapitän of 6th Staffel and one of the most experienced pilots of the unit, was killed following an aerial collision with his wingman, Unteroffizier Mietho, during combat. In the previous eight months, he had scored nearly 20 victories, including thirteen B-17s. Unteroffizier Mietho, more fortunate, was able to bail out. While waiting for someone to succeed Koch, the two most experienced Schwarmführern, Oberfeldwebel Leo Schuhmacher and Oberfeldwebel Reinhard Flecks, led the Staffel in combat. On the ground, it was the Gruppenadjutant, Oberleutnant Stärk, who ran things in the interim. III. Gruppe were embroiled in combat with the escort. Two P-38s were shot down, including one by Gruppenkommandeur Hauptmann Eberle.

LOSS TABLES - 1943

Date	*Name of Crew and Rank*	*Staffel*	*Fate*	*Aircraft, W.Nr & Code*	*Damage /Loss*	*Reason for Casualty*	*Place*
03.01.43		II. Gruppe		Fw 190 A-4 (587)	10%	Emergency landing due to fuel shortage.	Near Gosselies
08.01.43		12		Fw 190 A-4 (5564)	25%	Airframe damage.	Deelen
11.01.43	Uffz. Heinz Born	9	Wounded	Fw 190 A-4 (5548)	20%	Damaged on escort mission.	Aalborg East
11.01.43		III. Gruppe		Fw 190 A-4 (7080)	80%	Belly landing.	Fredrikshaven
13.01.43	Uffz. Josef Kehrle	6		Fw 190 A-4 (5547)	10%	Damage on landing.	Woensdrecht airfield
15.01.43	Uffz. Robert Stellfield	5		Fw 190 A-4 (7032)	25%	Belly landing after combat.	Woensdrecht airfield
17.01.43	Uffz. Georg Strunz	6	Killed	Fw 190 A-4 Yellow 8 (628)	100%	Shot down in combat with Spitfires.	Wissekerke
21.01.43		II. Gruppe		Fw 190 A-4 (5573)	15%	Belly landing due to engine damage on combat mission.	North-east of Woensdrecht airfield
21.01.43		12		Fw 190 A-4 (563)	20%	Belly landing.	Deelen airfield
24.01.43	Uffz. Günther Kirchner	5	Wounded	Fw 190 A-4 Black 3 (5556)	100%	Crashed due to engine damage.	Near Anapolder
24.01.43	Uffz. Rudolf Rauhaus	6		Fw 190 A-4 (595)	70%	Emergency landing due to engine damage.	Haamstede airfield
27.01.43		Stab, I. Gruppe		Bf 109 G-1 (14078)	100%	Crashed due to engine damage.	North of Oldenburg
27.01.43	Uffz. Rolf Bölter	1	Killed	Bf 109 G-1 White 1 (14146)	100%	Crashed following combat.	North Sea
27.01.43	Ofw. Gerhard Witt	1	Missing	Bf 109 G-1 White 4 (14112)	100%	Crashed following combat.	North Sea
27.01.43		2		Bf 109 G-1 (14074)	100%	Crashed following combat.	Egglingen
27.01.43	Fw. Helmut Speckhardt	3	Killed	Bf 109 G-1 Yellow 8 (14085)	100%	Crashed following combat.	North Sea
27.01.43	Uffz. Gerhard Bruhnke	4	Wounded	Fw 190 A-4 White 10 (629)	100%	Crashed following combat with USAAF B-24.	South-west of Sneek
27.01.43	Fw. Fritz Koch	12	Killed	Fw 190 A-4 Yellow 3 (5604)	100%	Crashed on combat mission.	Terschilling
27.01.43		12		Fw 190 A-4 (614)	20%	Belly landed due to fuel shortage.	Oldebroek
30.01.43	Gefr. Anton Worm	3	Killed	Bf 109 G-1 Yellow 10 (14092)	100%	Shot down in combat with RAF Wellington.	North Sea
30.01.43	Fw. Kromer	5		Fw 190 A-4 (7032)	45%	Belly landed due to servicing fault.	Woensdrecht airfield
30.01.43	Uffz. Herbert Hänel	12	Killed	Fw 190 A-4 Yellow 6 (574)	100%	Shot down in combat with RAF Wellington.	North Sea
03.02.43		I. Gruppe		Fw 190 A-4 (607)	30%	Emergency landing due to engine damage.	North of Lemec
04.02.43		I. Gruppe		Bf 109 G-1 (14081)	40%	Emergency landing due to fuel shortage.	Near Quakenbrück
04.02.43		I. Gruppe		Bf 109 G-1 (14117)	50%	Emergency landing due to engine damage.	Osterlog
04.02.43		I. Gruppe		Bf 109 G-1 (14108)	90%	Damaged on combat mission.	Maroardsmon
04.02.43	Oblt. Walter Leonhardt	6	Killed	Fw 190 A-4 Yellow 6 (5533)	100%	Shot down in combat with USAAF B-17.	North Sea
04.02.43		II. Gruppe		Fw 190 A-4 (579)	20%	Emergency landing due to engine damage.	Geesteren

Date	Name of Crew and Rank	Staffel	Fate	Aircraft, W.Nr & Code	Damage /Loss	Reason for Casualty	Place
04.02.43		II. Gruppe		Fw 190 A-4 (561)	10%	Emergency landing due to fuel shortage.	Near Medemblik
04.02.43		II. Gruppe		Fw 190 A-4 (603)	10%	Belly landing due to fuel shortage.	Near Hogmade
04.02.43	Uffz. Werner Hitzke	10	Killed	Fw 190 A-4 White 4 (567)	100%	Crashed on combat mission.	Achmer
04.02.43	Uffz. Rudolf Mayer	12	Killed	Fw 190 A-4 Yellow 7 (585)	100%	Shot down on combat mission.	East of Leen
11.02.43		I. Gruppe		Bf 109 G-1 (14128)	85%	Crashed due to servicing fault.	Borkum
12.02.43		I. Gruppe		Bf 109 E-7 (5196)	30%	Emergency landing due to fuel shortage.	Auschwitz
12.02.43	Lt. Heinrich Overhagen	II. Gruppe		Fw 190 A-4 (623)	10%	Belly landing due to servicing fault.	Wateringen
12.02.43	Fw. Heinz Küpper	12	Wounded	Fw 190 A-4 Yellow 5 (588)	100%	Pilot bailed out due to engine fire.	Near Leeuwarden
14.02.43	Uffz. Franz Scharler	5	Wounded	Fw 190 A-4 Black 12 (5533)	80%	Emergency landing on non-combat mission.	Woensdrecht
20.02.43		1		Bü 131 (4035)		Emergency landing due to engine problems.	Wangerooge
26.02.43		II. Gruppe		Fw 190 A-4 (5574)	25%	Crashed on take off due to technical airfield problems.	Woensdrecht
26.02.43	Uffz. Hans-Georg Lehmann	5		Fw 190 A-3 (5456)	10%	Emergency landing due to engine problems.	Near Osterholt
26.02.43	Oblt.Herwig Zuzic	IV. Gruppe	Wounded	Fw 190 A-4 (586)	80%	Emergency landing due to engine problems.	Near Grootebroek
03.03.43		9		Fw 190 A-4 (5570)	15%	Overturned on landing.	Husum airfield
04.03.43		3		Bf 109 G-1 (14086)	30%	Emergency landing following combat.	Near Herbern
04.03.43	Uffz. Max Kolschek	4		Fw 190 A-4 (562)	80%	Belly landing due to engine damage.	Leeuwarden
07.03.43		11		Fw 190 A-4 (565)	10%	Belly landing.	Mönchen-Gladbach airfield
08.03.43		2		Bf 109 G-1 (14134)	25%	Crashed on take-off.	Jever airfield
08.03.43	Uffz. Friedrich Knorr	9	Killed	Fw 190 A-4 (5548)	100%	Crashed on non-combat flight.	North of Aalborg
08.03.43		IV. Gruppe		Fw 190 A-4 (587)	20%	Technical problems to aircraft on airfield.	Deelen airfield
10.03.43		I. Gruppe		Bf 109 G-1 (14051)	100%	Crashed.	Near Jever
11.03.43	Uffz. Max Kolschek	4	Killed	Fw 190 A-4 White 1 (7026)	100%	Shot down in combat with Spitfires.	North Sea
11.03.43		III. Gruppe		Fw 190 A-4 (587)	15%	Technical problem on take off.	Deelen airfield
11.03.43		10		Fw 190 A-4 (5587)	25%	Belly landing.	Deelen
11.03.43	Lt. Eberhard Burath	IV. Gruppe		Fw 190 A-4 Chevron (5555)	70%	Crashed on take-off.	Deelen
14.03.43		12		Fw 190 A-3 (5486)	25%	Belly landing.	Deelen airfield
16.03.43		IV. Gruppe		Fw 190 A-4 (562)	20%	Belly landing due to engine damage.	Deelen airfield
18.03.43	Oblt. Hotari Schmude	1	Wounded	Bf 109 G-1 (14145)	100%	Shot down in combat with USAAF B-17s.	North Sea
18.03.43	Lt. Dieter Gerhard	2	Killed	Bf 109 G-1 Blue 6 (14150)	100%	Shot down in combat with USAAF B-17s.	North Sea
18.03.43		2		Bf 109 G-1 (14057)	20%	Damaged on landing following combat.	Jever airfield
18.03.43	Oblt. Harry Koch	6		Fw 190 A-4 (5592)	100%	Shot down in combat with Spitfire.	North Sea

Date	Name of Crew and Rank	Staffel	Fate	Aircraft, W.Nr & Code	Damage /Loss	Reason for Casualty	Place
18.03.43	Lt. Ludwig Gottschling	10	Missing	Fw 190 A-4 White 9 (590)	100%	Shot down in combat with USAAF B-17s.	North Sea
18.03.43		IV. Gruppe		Fw 190 A-5 (7253)	80%	Emergency landing following combat mission.	Near Groningen
21.03.43		IV. Gruppe		Fw 190 A-4 (6034)	100%	Airborne collision. See next entry.	Eindhoven
21.03.43		IV. Gruppe		Fw 190 A-4 (61210)	100%	Airborne collision. See previous entry.	Eindhoven
21.03.43		IV. Gruppe		Fw 190 A-4 (612)	100%	Airborne collision other aircraft less than 10% damaged.	Near Eindhoven
22.03.43		IV. Gruppe		Fw 190 A-4 (568)	15%	Airframe damaged on landing due to technical problem.	Deelen airfield
24.03.43	Lt. Paul Dietrigkeit	III. Gruppe		Fw 190 A-5 (52638)	80%	Damaged on landing.	Stade airfield
28.03.43		II. Gruppe		Fw 190 A-4 (5601)	60%	Damaged while taxiing.	Leeuwarden airfield
01.04.43		3		Fw 190 A-5 (2603)	50%	Airframe damage.	Deelen airfield
03.04.43		IV. Gruppe		Fw 190 A-4 (593)	10%	Belly landing due to technical problems.	Deelen airfield
05.04.43	Hptm. Dietrich Wickop	II. Gruppe		Fw 190 A-4 (5552)	20%	Airframe damage.	Woensdrecht airfield
05.04.43		II. Gruppe		Fw 190 A-4 (568)	80%	Emergency landing due to engine damage.	Near Middelburg
06.04.43		3		Fw 190 A-4 (589)	20%	Damaged while taxiing.	Deelen airfield
06.04.43		6		Bf 109 G-1 (14079)	50%	Engine damage.	Jade Bay
06.04.43	Lt. Schwarz	5		Fw 190 A-4 (5558)	80%	Belly landing due to servicing fault.	Woensdrecht airfield
06.04.43		II. Gruppe		Fw 190 A-4 (20240)	50%	Emergency landing due to engine	Near Haamstede airfield
06.04.43		II. Gruppe		Bf 109 G-4 (19391)	100%	Crashed after getting lost.	Near Eindhoven
09.04.43	Uffz. Robert Stellfeld	5	Wounded	Fw 190 A-4 Black 9 (662)	90%	Emergency landing due to engine trouble.	Near Waarde
10.04.43	Oblt. Buchholz	5		Fw 190 ( )	35%	Overturned on landing.	Woensdrecht
12.04.43	Lt. Karl Bugaj	2	Killed	Fw 190 A-4 Black 8 (663)	100%	Crashed on non-combat flight.	Achmer
13.04.43		Stab, II. Gruppe		Bf 109 G-6 (16470)	30%	Crash landing on non-combat flight.	Near Gladbach
15.04.43	Fw. Georg Hutter	5		Fw 190 A-4 (5557)	10%	Airframe damage.	Woensdrecht airfield
16.04.43	Major Herbert Kijewski	Stab, II. Gruppe	Killed	Fw 190 A-5 Double Chevron (7203)	100%	Shot down on combat mission	North Sea
16.04.43	Oblt. Hans Mohr	Stab, II. Gruppe	Killed	Fw 190 A-4 Yellow 2 (610)	100%	Shot down on combat mission.	North Sea
17.04.43	Uffz. Hans Pelzer	3	Killed	Fw 190 A-4 Yellow 12 (566)	100%	Shot down on combat mission.	Bahlum
17.04.43		3		Fw 190 A-4 (2640)	40%	Emergency landing following combat.	Near Wittmundshafen
19.04.43	Gefr. Gerhard Hopf Fw. Hermann Brackhagen	4	Wounded Wounded	Bf 108 B-1 RJ+AZ (1138)	50%	Emergency landing due to fuel shortage.	Near Rechlin
25.04.43		II. Gruppe		Fw 190 A-5 (7202)	45%	Damage due to servicing fault.	Woensdrecht
27.04.43	Lt. Eberhard Burath	I. Gruppe		Fw 190 A-4 Chevron (7202)	45%	Belly landing on Deelen non-combat flight.	
29.04.43	Lt. Leopold Zaus	2	Killed	Fw 190 A-5 Black 9 (2615)	100%	Pilot lost consciousness and aircraft crashed.	Vaassen

Date	Name of Crew and Rank	Staffel	Fate	Aircraft, W.Nr & Code	Damage /Loss	Reason for Casualty	Place
29.04.43	Uffz. Wloschinski	6		Fw 190 A-4 Yellow 1 (605)	30%	Belly landing due to servicing fault.	Woensdrecht airfield
02.05.43	Uffz. Andreas Banz	2	Killed	Fw 190 A-5 Black 10 (1302)	100%	Shot down by Spitfires.	Near Schipol
02.05.43	Uffz. Erhard Bruhnke	4		Fw 190 A-3 (5438)	30%	Problem on take-off. Turned back and crashed on landing.	Woensdrecht airfield
02.05.43	Lt. Heinrich Völler	5	Killed	Fw 190 A-4 Black 11 (5605)	100%	Crashed following take off.	1 kilometre south of Woensdrecht
02.05.43	Ofw. Peter Eberhardt	5	Killed	Fw 190 A-5 Black 2 (7224)	100%	Shot down by Spitfires.	North Sea
03.05.43	Lt. Wolfgang Steffen	1	Wounded	Fw 190 A-4 White 6 (602)	90%	Emergency landing due to engine damage.	Thiel
03.05.43	Lt. Hermann Dumm	2	Wounded	Bf 109 G-3 SP+EM (16292)	60%	Overturned on landing.	Rechlin
03.05.43	Fw. Willi Pfeiffer	4	Killed	Fw 190 A-4 White 8 (5567)	100%	Shot down by Spitfires.	North Sea
03.05.43	Lt. Ernst Heesen	5	Killed	Fw 190 A-5 Black 7 (1191)	100%	Shot down in combat.	North Sea
03.05.43	Ofw. Georg Hutter	5	Wounded	Fw 190 A-5 (2652)	100%	Shot down in combat.	Haarlem-Zandvoort.
13.05.43		I. Gruppe		Fw 190 A-5 (152630)	15%	Engine damage.	Near Wageningen
13.05.43	Uffz. Häusler	6		Fw 190 A-4 (7021)	25%	Damaged on landing.	Woensdrecht airfield
14.05.43	Uffz. Willi Lück	3	Killed	Fw 190 A-4 Yellow 13 (563)	100%	Shot down in combat with fighters.	East of Gent.
14.05.43		I. Gruppe		Fw 190 A-4 (140592)	35%	Belly landing following fighter action.	Deelen
14.05.43	Lt. Wolfgang Grimm	4	Wounded	Fw 190 A-4 (42230)	80%	Emergency landing following combat with P-47.	Woensdrecht airfield
14.05.43	Lt. Schermann	II. Gruppe		Fw 190 A-4 (1349)	25%	Emergency landing following strafing attack on boat.	Woensdrecht airfield
15.05.43	Fw. Franz Snaidero	1	Wounded	Fw 190 A-4 White 3 (2342)	60%	Damaged on combat mission.	North-west of Borkum
15.05.43	Uffz. Willi Herzog	2	Wounded	Fw 190 A-4 (40617)	30%	Emergency landing due to fuel shortage.	Nordeney airfield
16.05.43	Hptm. Dietrich Wickop	Stab, II. Gruppe	Killed	Fw 190 A-5 Black 1 (7328)	100%	Shot down on combat mission.	North Sea
17.05.43		II. Gruppe		Fw 190 A-5 (1188)	40%	Damage due to servicing fault.	Woensdrecht airfield
21.05.43	Oblt. Hans Munz	1	Killed	Fw 190 A-4 White 2 (5589)	100%	Shot down on combat mission.	North-west of Groningen
21.05.43	Flgr. Richard Ankersen	1		Fw 190 A-5 White 1 (2631)	45%	Damage due to servicing fault.	Leeuwarden airfield
22.05.43	Uffz. Günther Rost	4		Fw 190 ( )	20%	Damaged on landing on non-combat flight.	Münster
22.05.43	Fw. Rudolf Haninger	II. Gruppe		Fw 190 A-4 (632)	40%	Damage due to servicing fault.	Woensdrecht airfield
27.05.43	Lt. Friedrich Wiegmann	4	Killed	Fw 190 A-5 White 1 (7208)	100%	Shot down in combat with Spitfires and Thunderbolts.	North-east of Ecloo
27.5.43	Lt. Egon Besgen	5	Killed	Fw 190 A-4 Black 10 (2291)	100%	Shot down in combat with Spitfires.	South-south-east of Ecloo

Date	Name of Crew and Rank	Staffel	Fate	Aircraft, W.Nr & Code	Damage /Loss	Reason for Casualty	Place
28.05.43		III. Gruppe		Bf 109 G-6 (1558)	10%	Damage due to servicing fault.	Leeuwarden airfield
31.05.43		2		Fw 190 A-4 (140593)	30%	Damage due to servicing fault.	Bergen airfield
01.06.43	Uffz. Karl Wenzlik	III. Gruppe	Wounded	Bf 109 G-4 (19383)	75%	Belly landing on non-combat flight.	Woensdrecht airfield
02.06.43	Albert Lindenschmidt	III. Gruppe	Wounded	Bf 109 G-6 (19361) (19361)	80%	Emergency landing due to engine problems.	Near Stens, Leeuwarden
03.06.43		I. Gruppe		Fw 190 A-5 (410950)	65%	Struck obstruction on landing.	Katwijk airfield
03.06.43		I. Gruppe		Fw 190 A-5 (410050)	60%	Damage due to servicing fault.	Katwijk airfield
04.06.43		I. Gruppe		Fw 190 A-5 (7333)	40%	Damage due to servicing fault.	Schipol airfield
05.06.43		I. Gruppe		Bf 109 G (14104)	10%	Belly landing due to servicing fault.	Schipol airfield
06.06.43	Stabsing. Gustav Schwarz	III. Gruppe	Wounded	Bf 109 G-6 (15458)	30%	Engine problems.	Mooleneind
10.06.43		I. Gruppe		Bf 109 G-6 (15364)	20%	Damage to tyre on landing.	Leeuwarden airfield
10.06.43	Uffz. Günter Rost	4	Wounded	Fw 190 A-4 White 9 (7029)	100%	Shot down in combat with Spitfires.	Stuijenkenskerke
10.06.43	Uffz. Georg Pissarski	5	Killed	Fw 190 A-4 Black 9 (6571)	100%	Shot down in combat with Spitfires.	North of Gent
10.06.43	Oblt. Harry Koch	II. Gruppe		Fw 190 A-5 (7345)	70%	Emergency landing following combat.	Hülst
11.06.43	Lt. Kurt Ibing	4		Fw 190 A-3 (5439)	30%	Belly landing due to servicing fault.	Woensdrecht airfield
12.06.43		I. Gruppe		Fw 190 A-4 (145574)	20%	Overturned on landing in bad weather.	Köln-Butzweilerhof
12.06.43	Lt. Günther Buchholz	6		Fw 190 A-4 Yellow 11 (7024)	10%	Damaged on landing.	Woensdrecht airfield
13.06.43	Lt. Walter Herrmann	5	Killed	Fw 190 A-4 Black 15 (7032)	100%	Shot down in combat with Spitfires.	Ooltgenplaat
13.06.43		III. Gruppe		Bf 109 G-6 (15396)	50%	Belly landing due to engine fire.	Quakenbrück
16.06.43	Uffz. Alfred Behr	2	Wounded	Fw 190 A-4 Black 4 (7033)	70%	Emergency landing due to engine damage.	Katwijk airfield
17.06.43	Ofw. Ernst Winkler	4	Killed	Fw 190 A-4 White 5 (622)	100%	Shot down in combat with Spitfires.	South of Vlissingen
17.06.43	Lt. Heinz Tröger	4	Killed	Fw 190 A-5 White 12 (410044)	100%	Shot down in combat with Spitfires.	Ijzendijke
17.06.43	Lt. Günther Buchholz	6	Wounded	Fw 190 A-4 Yellow 11 (7024)	100%	Shot down in combat with Spitfires.	Ritem
17.06.43	Fw. Rudolf Haninger	4		Fw 190 A-4 (7022)	100%	Emergency landing following combat.	Gröde
18.06.43		II. Gruppe		Fw 190 A-4 (5701)	20%	Emergency landing following combat.	Woensdrecht airfield
21.06.43	Lt. Wilhelm Tschira	5	Killed	Fw 190 A-5 Black 7 (7340)	100%	Crashed on landing.	Woensdrecht
22.06.43		2		Fw 190 A-4 (140625)	90%	Emergency landing due to fuel shortage.	Boukamp
22.06.43		2		Fw 190 A-4 (142337)	30%	Damage following combat.	Near Münster
22.06.43		3		Fw 190 A-5 (2630)	50%	Engine damage.	Schipol airfield
22.06.43		3		Fw 190 A-5 (410194)	20%	Damaged in combat.	Near Kleve
22.06.43		I. Gruppe		Fw 190 A-5 (3630)	50%	Belly landing due engine damage.	Schipol

Date	Name of Crew and Rank	Staffel	Fate	Aircraft, W.Nr & Code	Damage /Loss	Reason for Casualty	Place
22.06.43		I. Gruppe		Fw 190 A-4 (625)	90%	Emergency landing due to fuel shortage on combat mission.	Near Arnhem
22.06.43		II. Gruppe		Bf 109 G-6 (1593)	30%	Belly landing due to combat damage.	Vierlingbeek
22.06.43		III. Gruppe		Bf 109 G-4 (19361)	10%	Emergency landing due to fuel shortage.	Near Ede
22.06.43		III. Gruppe		Bf 109 G-4 (15373)	25%	Damage to tyre on landing.	Twente airfield
22.06.43		III. Gruppe		Bf 109 G-4 (15445)	20%	Damaged in combat.	Deelen airfield
22.06.43		III. Gruppe		Bf 109 G-6 (19867)	20%	Damaged in combat.	Deelen
22.06.43	Fw. Georg Fröhlich	III. Gruppe		Bf 109 G-6 (19854)	80%	Overturned on landing due to fuel shortage.	Maasdijk
22.06.43		III. Gruppe		Bf 109 G-6 (15390)	30%	Belly landing due to fuel shortage.	Nimmwegen
22.06.43		III. Gruppe		Bf 109 G-6 (15395)	40%	Emergency landing due to fuel shortage.	Genemuiden-Zwolle
22.06.43		III. Gruppe		Bf 109 G-6 (19611)	70%	Belly landing due to fuel shortage.	Bodegraven-Gouda
22.06.43		III. Gruppe		Bf 109 G-6 (15412)	80%	Belly landing due to fuel shortage on combat mission.	Leiden-Alfen
24.06.43	Lt. Richard Haug	6	Killed	Fw 190 A-5 White 1 (7202)	100%	Crashed on non-combat flight.	South of Woensdrecht
25.06.43		1		Fw 190 A-4 (140601)	15%	Damaged while taxiing.	Schipol airfield
25.06.43	Uffz. Kurt Lessnitz	I. Gruppe	Wounded	Fw 190 A-5 (840191)	10%	Belly landing due to servicing fault.	Schipol airfield
25.06.43	Oblt. Friedrich Hardt	III. Gruppe	Killed	Bf 109 G-6 Chevron 1 (15394)	100%	Shot down on combat mission.	North-west of Cloppenburg
25.06.43	Uffz. Hans Lehmann	7	Wounded	Bf 109 G-6 White 4 (15397)		Pilot wounded in combat.	Oldenburg
25.06.43	Uffz. Albert Oexle	8	Missing	Bf 109 G-6 Black 10 (20103)	100%	Pilot missing in combat.	Leer
25.06.43	Ofw. Fritz Timm	9	Wounded	Bf 109 G-4 Yellow 28 (19432)		Pilot wounded in combat.	Wilhelmshaven airfield
25.06.43	Lt. Helmut Müller	9	Wounded	Bf 109 G-6 Yellow 29 (19613)	85%	Pilot wounded in combat.	Aschendorf airfield
25.06.43		III. Gruppe		Bf 109 G-2 (20032)	100%	Crashed following combat.	Terborg
25.06.43	Oblt. Klöpper	III. Gruppe		Bf 109 G-6 (15442)	15%	Belly landing following combat.	Oltmansfehn
25.06.43		III. Gruppe		Bf 109 G-6 (15481)	10%	Damaged following combat.	Leeuwarden
27.06.43		1		Fw 190 A-4 (140630)	20%	Damaged following combat.	Schipol
27.06.43		2		Fw 190 A-4 (140570)	20%	Damage following combat.	Schipol
27.06.43		I. Gruppe		Fw 190 A-5 (150217)	20%	Airframe damage.	Schipol airfield
29.06.43	Lt. Hermann Dumm	9	Killed	Bf 109 G-6 Yellow 10 (15454)		Crashed on non-combat flight	Leeuwarden
01.07.43	Uffz. Karl Walz	2	Killed	Fw 190 A-5 Black 5 (410198)	100%	Shot down in combat with USAAF fighters.	North Sea
01.07.43		I. Gruppe		Fw 190 A-4 (140614)	35%	Belly landing following combat.	Schipol airfield
01.07.43		3		Fw 190 A-4 (0614)	40%	Emergency landing following combat.	Schipol
10.07.43	Lt. Horst Ertmann	II. Gruppe	Wounded	Fw 190 A-5 (55573)	60%	Crashed due to engine problem.	North of Woensdrecht

Date	Name of Crew and Rank	Staffel	Fate	Aircraft, W.Nr & Code	Damage /Loss	Reason for Casualty	Place
16.07.43	Uffz. Georg Wilhelm	9	Killed	Bf 109 G-6 Yellow 3 (15481)	100%	Crashed on bombing practise.	
16.07.43		III. Gruppe		Bf 109 G-4 (19361)		Belly landing due to servicing fault.	
17.07.43	Uffz. Helmut Tumann	II. Gruppe	Wounded	Fw 190 A-4 (1188)	15%	Belly landing following combat.	Schipol
17.07.43	Lt. Hans Thorwarth	7	Killed	Bf 109 G-6 White 11 (15440)	100%	Shot down on combat mission.	North Sea
17.07.43	Ofw. Kurt Gewiss	8	Killed	Bf 109 G-6 Black 2 (15611)	100%	Shot down in combat with four-engined bombers.	North Sea
18.07.43	Fw. Erwin Roden	7	Killed	Bf 109 G-6 White 8 (19853)	100%	Shot down in combat with four-engined bombers.	North Sea
18.07.43	Uffz. Günther Hasenfuss	7	Killed	Bf 109 G-6 White 2 (20085)	100%	Shot down in combat with four-engined bombers.	North Sea
18.07.43		III. Gruppe		Bf 109 G-6 (15441)	15%	Damage due to combat.	De Kooy
20.07.43	Gefr. Hubert Obiltschnig	2	Killed	Fw 190 A-5 Black 5 (530128)	100%	Shot down in combat.	East of Amselveen
25.07.43	Maj. Karl-Heinz Leesmann	Stab, II. Gruppe	Killed	Bf 109 G-6 (20073)	100%	Shot down in combat with four-engined bombers.	North Sea
25.07.43	Uffz. Hans Fordemann	7	Wounded	Bf 109 G-6 White 3 (15368)		Crash-landed after combat with four-engined bombers.	Heligoland
26.07.43	Uffz. Willy Kühn	2	Killed	Fw 190 A-5 Black 13 (410196)	100%	Shot down in combat with four-engined bombers.	Hattendorf
26.07.43	Uffz. Werner Wiegand	2	Wounded	Fw 190 A-5 Black 4 (410244)		Belly-landed after combat.	Detmold
26.07.43	Fw. Hans Hattendorf	2	Killed	Fw 190 A-4 (45574)	100%	Crashed due to fuel shortage.	
26.07.43	Uffz. Wolfgang Knobloch	II. Gruppe	Wounded	Fw 190 A-5 (710013)		Crashed due to fuel shortage.	Altenrhein
26.07.43	Uffz. Heinrich Oberjürgen	7	Killed	Bf 109 G-6 White 3 (20114)	100%	Shot down in combat with four-engined bombers.	Nessmersiel
27.07.43		3		Fw 190 A-4 (140664)	15%	Airframe damage.	Deelen airfield
28.07.43	Uffz. Karl Knespel	1	Killed	Fw 190 A-4 White 10 (583)	100%	Shot down in combat with four-engined bombers.	Groningen
28.07.43		I. Gruppe		Fw 190 A-4 (5570)	60%	Damaged in combat.	Leeuwarden
28.07.43	Fw. Franz-Wilhelm Heck	9	Wounded	Bf 109 G-6 Yellow 7 (15694)	100%	Pilot wounded in combat - bailed out.	
28.07.43	Uffz. Norbert Preussler	9	Wounded	Bf 109 G-6 (15442)	100%	Pilot wounded in combat - bailed out.	
28.07.43	Uffz. Alfred Thieme	9	Killed	Bf 109 G-6 Yellow 4 (15438)	100%	Shot down in combat.	
28.07.43		III. Gruppe		Fw 190 A-4 (640)	35%	Damaged on landing.	
30.07.43	Ofw. Hans Laun	1	Killed	Fw 190 A-5 Yellow 5 (1751)	100%	Shot down in combat with USAAF P-47s and bombers.	Arnhem
30.07.43	Lt. Peter Marxen	2	Killed	Fw 190 A-5 Black 3 (410193)	100%	Shot down in combat with USAAF fighters and bombers.	Deelen
30.07.43	Lt. Hans Windbichler	2	Wounded	Fw 190 A-5 Blue 4 (410231)		Shot down in combat with Spitfires.	Deelen
30.07.43	Oblt. Karl Becker	3	Killed	Fw 190 A-5 Yellow 14 (410005)	100%	Shot down in combat with USAAF P-47s and bombers.	Holland

Date	Name of Crew and Rank	Staffel	Fate	Aircraft, W.Nr & Code	Damage /Loss	Reason for Casualty	Place
30.07.43	Uffz. Karl Weninger	3	Killed	Fw 190 A-5 Yellow 12 (840133)	100%	Shot down in combat with USAAF P-47s and bombers.	Hengelo
30.07.43	Uffz. Rudolf Lacher	3	Wounded	Fw 190 A-4 Yellow 10 (658)		Emergency landing due to fuel shortage.	Groningen
30.07.43	Lt. Josef Wieser	5	Killed	Fw 190 A-4 Black 9 (623)	100%	Shot down in combat with USAAF P-47s and bombers.	Lith
30.07.43		III. Gruppe		Bf 109 G-6 (15365)	80%	Damaged in combat.	Near Soesterberg
09.08.43	Uffz. Erich Landgrebe	6	Wounded	Fw 190 A-6 PT+XY (550454)		Crashed on non-combat mission.	Rheine
11.08.43		III. Gruppe		Bf 109 G-6 (15472)	20%		South of Texel
12.08.43	Uffz. Kurt Brumund	6	Killed	Fw 190 A-4 Yellow 12 (7021)	100%	Shot down in combat with USAAF four-engined bombers.	Düren
12.08.43	Uffz. Fritz Haspel	8	Wounded	Bf 109 G-6 Black 2 (15645)		Belly landing following combat.	Vlissingen
12.08.43		III. Gruppe		Bf 109 G-6 (15445)	15%	Belly landing due to fuel shortage.	Woensdrecht airfield
17.08.43	Lt. Hans Berger	1		Fw 190 A White 10 ( )		Overturned due to running short of fuel.	Odheim
17.08.43	Lt. Hans Feustel	2	Killed	Fw 190 A-6 Black 8 (550467)	100%	Shot down in combat with USAAF bombers.	Löwen
17.08.43	Fw. Bodo Nette	3	Wounded	Fw 190 A-5 Yellow 14 (840131)	100%	Shot down in combat with USAAF bombers.	St. Trond
17.08.43	Ofw. Bernard Liper	4	Wounded	Fw 190 A-4 White 4 (5565)		Emergency landing following combat.	Maastricht
17.08.43	Ogefr. Hermann Gottwald	6	Wounded	Fw 190 A-6 Yellow 6 (550152)		Emergency landing on non-combat flight.	Dortmund
17.08.43		II. Gruppe		Fw 190 A-6 (550443)	50%	Crashed into another aircraft while taxiing.	Deelen airfield
19.08.43	Oblt. Herwig Zuzic	8	Killed	Bf 109 G-6 Black 1 (15367)	100%	Shot down in combat.	Knoke
19.08.43	Lt. Horst Bork	9	Killed	Bf 109 G-6 Yellow 3 (20498)	100%	Shot down in combat.	Neussen
19.08.43	Lt. Han-Joachim Niemeyer	9	Killed	Bf 109 G-6 Yellow 11 (20092)	100%	Shot down in combat.	Vlissingen
19.08.43	Fw. Hans Meissner	9	Wounded	Bf 109 G-6 Yellow 12 (19992)		Emergency landing following combat.	Vlissingen
20.08.43	Ufz. Ewald Thiele	8	Killed	Bf 109 G-6 (19848)	100%	Crashed through engine damage.	Zuiderzee
31.08.43	Fw. Erhard Bruhnke	4	Killed	Fw 190 A-5 Black 2 (7212)	100%	Shot down in combat.	Koblenz
-4.09.43	Lt. Eugen Wintergerst	9	Killed	Bf 109 G-6 Yellow 1 (15609)	100%	Shot down in combat with Spitfires.	Bergues
04.09.43	Uffz. Horst Seemann	9	Killed	Bf 109 G-6 Yellow 2 (220021)	100%	Shot down in combat with Spitfires.	Channel
04.09.43	Uffz. Heinz Biesenbach	9	Killed	Bf 109 G-6 Yellow 10 (20520)	100%	Shot down in combat.	St. Omer
04.09.43	Ofw. Fritz Timm	9	Wounded	Bf 109 G-6 Yellow 11 (15911)	100%	Shot down in combat with Spitfires.	St. Omer

Date	*Name of Crew and Rank*	*Staffel*	*Fate*	*Aircraft, W.Nr & Code*	*Damage /Loss*	*Reason for Casualty*	*Place*
05.09.43	Uffz. Erwin Mietho	6	Wounded	Fw 190 A-4 Yellow 7 (7031)		Overturned on landing.	Rheine
05.09.43	Uffz. Siegfried Weberitsch	9	Killed	Bf 109 G-6 Yellow 4 (20506)	60%	Crashed on take-off.	Woensdrecht airfield
07.09.43	Fw. Herbert Herglotz	7	Missing	Bf 109 G-6 White 13 (20585)	100%	Shot down in combat with Spitfires.	North Sea
10.09.43	Fw. Gustav Schulze	III. Gruppe	Wounded	Bf 109 G-6 (15365)	100%	Hit obstruction on take-off.	Eelde
22.09.43	Uffz. Gustav Frey	9	Wounded	Bf 109 G-6 Yellow 9 (20531)	100%	Received direct hit from own flak.	Near Enkhuizen
23.09.43	Lt. Ernst Eser	6	Killed	Fw 190 A-6 Yellow 8 (550519)		Crashed on non-combat flight.	Rheine
27.09.43	Oblt. Georg Schott	1	Killed	Fw 190 A-6 White 11 (550476)	100%	Shot down in combat with USAAF bombers.	German Bight
27.09.43	Uffz. Rudolf Schnappauf	1	Wounded	Fw 190 A-4 White 6 (630)		Emergency landing following combat.	Wittmundhaven
27.09.43	Ofw. Willy Ulrich	5	Wounded	Fw 190 A-4 Black 8 (2572)		Crashed on landing following combat with B-17s.	Hage
27.09.43	Fw. Hans Becker	6	Wounded	Fw 190 A-5 Yellow 7 (7232)		Crash landing due to fuel shortage.	Diepholz
27.09.43	Fw. Guido Rombaut	6	Killed	Fw 190 A-6 Yellow 12 (550523)	100%	Shot down in combat with P-47s.	West of Norden
04.10.43	Ofw. Erich Kaiser	1	Wounded	Fw 190 A-5 White 8 (410192)		Emergency landing following combat.	Eschborn
04.10.43	Fw. Wloschinski	6	Killed	Fw 190 A ( )	100%	Shot down in combat.	
04.10.43		II. Gruppe		Fw 190A ( )		Emergency landing. following combat.	
04.10.43		II. Gruppe		Fw 190 A ( )		Emergency landing following combat.	
05.10.43	Uffz. Herbert Reichel	3	Killed	Fw 190 A-5 Yellow 8 (410191)	100%	Crashed on non-combat flight.	Ailertchen
08.10.43	Obstlt. Hans Philipp	Gesch. Stab	Killed	Fw 190 A-6 Red 3 (530407)	100%	Shot down on combat mission.	Nordhorn
08.10.43	Fw. Hans-Günther Reinhardt	Gesch. Stab	Wounded	Fw 190 A-6 (550733)		Emergency landing following combat and ramming.	Dielingen
08.10.43	Uffz. Rudolf Hübl	1	Wounded	Fw 190 A-6 White 5 (550490)		Emergency landing	Nienburg
08.10.43	Uffz. Johannes Kreimeyer	1	Killed	Fw 190 A-6 White 6 (550729)	100%	Shot down in combat.	Vroomschoop
08.10.43	Lt. Hans Ehlers	2	Wounded	Fw 190 A-6 Black 5 (530175)	100%	Pilot bailed out after ramming USAAF bomber.	Kalle
08.10.43	Uffz. Alfred Hoyer	3	Wounded	Fw 190 A-4 Yellow 15 (591)		Emergency landing following combat.	Vesepe
08.10.43	Oblt. Eugen Kotiza	4		Fw 190 A ( )		Belly landing following combat.	
08.10.43	Uffz. Franz Scharler	5	Killed	Fw 190 A-6 Black 1 (550513)	100%	Shot down in combat with B-17.	Löningen
08.10.43	Lt. Bernhard von Kortzfleisch	6	Wounded	Fw 190 A ( )		Shot down in combat	
08.10.43	Uffz. Rudolf Einberger	8	Killed	Bf 109 G-6 Black 8 (26052)	100%	Shot down, probably by own Flak.	Bremen

Date	Name of Crew and Rank	Staffel	Fate	Aircraft, W.Nr & Code	Damage /Loss	Reason for Casualty	Place
09.10.43		I. Gruppe		Fw 190 A-6 (530379)	60%	Damage due to engine problem.	Deelen airfield
10.10.43	Uffz. Hans Vorhauer	2	Killed	Fw 190 A-6 Black 2 (530112)	100%	Shot down in combat with USAAF fighters.	Emeloe
10.10.43	Uffz. Paul Habranke	2	Killed	Fw 190 A-5 Black 4 (2632)	100%	Shot down in combat with USAAF bombers.	Greven
10.10.43	Fw. Felix Emerich	3	Killed	Fw 190 A-5 Yellow 4 (937)	100%	Shot down in combat with USAAF bombers.	Haaksbergen
10.10.43	Uffz. Swoboda	I. Gruppe	Killed	Fw 190 A ( )		Shot down in combat	
10.10.43		II. Gruppe		Fw 190 A ( )	80%	Belly landing following combat.	
10.10.43		II. Gruppe		Fw 190 A ( )	90%	Overturned on landing following combat.	
10.10.43		II. Gruppe		Fw 190 A ( )	90%	Shot down in combat.	
10.10.43	Lt. Wilhelm Hermannes	7	Killed	Bf 109 G-6 White 6 (20495)	100%	Shot down in combat.	Esmdetten
14.10.43	Fw. Kurt Niedereicholz	5	Wounded	Fw 190 A-6 Black 5 (550740)		Belly landing following combat with USAAF bombers.	Niedermendig
14.10.43	Fw. Wolfgang Brunner	6	Wounded	Fw 190 A-6 Yellow 1 (550757)		Overturned on landing following combat with USAAF bombers.	Mainz-Finthen
14.10.43	Uffz. Hubert Swoboda	II. Gruppe		Bf 109 G ( )	40%	Belly landing following combat.	
14.10.43	Ofw. Otto Langenbach	7	Killed	Bf 109 G-6 White 5 (20464)		Shot down in combat with USAAF bombers.	North-east of Hasselt
14.10.43	Fw. Helmut Brinkmann	7	Killed	Bf 109 G-6 White 12 (15389)		Shot down in combat with USAAF bombers.	North-east of Hasselt
14.10.43	Uffz. Friedrich Gaber	7	Killed	Bf 109 G-6 White 13 (160342)		Shot down in combat with USAAF P-47s.	North of Hasselt
14.10.43	Fw. Albert Lindenschmidt	9		Bf 109 G-6 ( )	100%	Shot down in combat.	
18.10.43	Ofw. Rudolf Piffer	2	Wounded	Fw 190 A-6 Black 3 (530720)		Emergency landing due to engine damage.	Terwolde
18.10.43		I. Gruppe		Fw 190 A-5 (410037)	100%	Shot down in combat.	Brunswick
19.10.43	Ofw. Fritz Bahl	I. Gruppe	Wounded	Fw 190 A-5 (410055)	65%	Overturned on landing due to servicing fault.	
20.10.43	Fw. Wilhelm Hoge	1	Killed	Fw 190 A-6 White 10 (550795)	100%	Crashed due to engine problems.	Deelen
20.10.43	Hptm. Harry Koch	6		Fw 190 A ( )		Belly landing following combat.	Woensdrecht
20.10.43	Uffz. Zinkl	II. Gruppe		Fw 190 A ( )	100%	Shot down in combat with USAAF B-17.	
22.10.43		III. Gruppe		Bf 109 G-6 (19643)	50%	Damaged due to hitting obstruction on airfield.	Deelen
23.10.43		III. Gruppe		Bf 109 G-4 (19611)	40%	Damage due to technical problems.	Eelde
31.10.43		1		Fw 190 A-6 (550783)	25%	Damaged due to engine problems.	Deelen airfield
03.11.43	Fw. Johannes Rathenow	1	Killed	Fw 190 A-6 White 7 (550785)	100%	Shot down in combat with USAAF bombers and P-38s.	Bad Zwischenahn
03.11.43		I. Gruppe		Fw 190 A-6 (550784)	15%	Belly landing due to fuel shortage.	Near Leeuwarden
03.11.43		I. Gruppe		Fw 190 A-4 (571)	15%	Belly landing due to fuel shortage.	Near Meppen
03.11.43	Ofw. Detlev Lüth	4		Fw 190 A-6 (550741)	100%	Shot down in combat.	Wesermünde

Date	Name of Crew and Rank	Staffel	Fate	Aircraft, W.Nr & Code	Damage /Loss	Reason for Casualty	Place
03.11.43	Uffz. Günther Schieweck	5	Killed	Fw 190 A-4 White 11 (621)	100%	Shot down in combat with USAAF bombers and P-38s.	Paddingbütte
03.11.43		II. Gruppe		Fw 190 A (550465)	10%	Belly landing following combat.	Near Emden
03.11.43		II. Gruppe		Fw 190 A (550154)	100%	Shot down in combat with USAAF bombers and P-38s.	Westerlok
03.11.43		II. Gruppe		Fw 190 A (550741)		Damaged in combat with USAAF bombers and P-38s.	Schiffdorf
03.11.43	Lt. Kurt Ibing	II. Gruppe		Bf 109 G-5 (15718)		Damaged in combat.	Near Oldenburg
03.11.43		II. Gruppe		Fw 190 A (2333)	100%	Shot down in combat.	Near Brake/ Oldenburg
03.11.43	Lt. Freimut Ullman	Stab, III. Gruppe	Killed	Bf 109 G-6 Chevron 2 (20527)	100%	Shot down in combat with USAAF bombers and P-38s.	Holland
03.11.43	Fw. Wilhelm Schneider	7	Killed	Bf 109 G-6 White 8 (20535)	100%	Shot down in combat with USAAF bombers and P-38s.	Holland
03.11.43	Hptm. Alfred Faber	8	Killed	Bf 109 G-6 Black 1 (15935)	100%	Shot down in combat with USAAF bombers and P-38s.	Holland
03.11.43	Uffz. Georg Riehs	8	Killed	Bf 109 G-6 Black 3 (160349)	100%	Shot down in combat with USAAF bombers and P-38s.	Holland
03.11.43	Fw. Josef Kehrle	8	Wounded	Bf 109 G-6 Black 10 (27023)	10%	Emergency landing following combat with USAAF bombers and P-38s.	Nieuw-Beerta
03.11.43		8		Bf 109 G-6 (19867)	100%	Shot down in combat.	Near Westerstede
03.11.43	Oblt. Rainer Framm	9	Killed	Bf 109 G-6 Yellow 1 (140018)	100%	Shot down in combat with USAAF bombers and P-38s.	Holland
03.11.43	Gefr. Günther Ewald	9	Killed	Bf 109 G-6 Yellow 10 (27133)	100%	Shot down in combat with USAAF bombers and P-38s.	Holland
03.11.43	Uffz. Gustav Frey	9	Killed	Bf 109 G-6 Yellow 12 (410212)	100%	Shot down in combat with USAAF bombers and P-38s.	Holland
03.11.43	Fw. Erich Matern	III. Gruppe		Bf 109 G-6 (15429)	100%	Shot down in combat with USAAF bombers and P-38s.	Marx
03.11.43		III. Gruppe		Bf 109 G-6 (15439)	10%	Emergency landing due to fuel shortage following combat.	Vosha
03.11.43		III. Gruppe		Bf 109 G-6 (410200)	60%	Belly landing following combat.	Oldenburg
03.11.43		III. Gruppe		Bf 109 G-6 (27134)	100%	Shot down in combat with USAAF bombers and P-38s.	Zwischenahn
05.11.43		1		Fw 190 A-6 (550799)	100%	Crashed due to engine problems.	South of Zwolle
05.11.43	Uffz. Gerd Ungering	3	Killed	Fw 190 A-4 Yellow 5 (670)	100%	Shot down in combat with USAAF bombers and P-38s.	Düsseldorf
05.11.43	Uffz. Rudolf Lacher	3	Killed	Fw 190 A-5 Yellow 6 (919)	100%	Shot down in combat with USAAF bombers and P-38s.	Düsseldorf
05.11.43	Ofw. Fritz Timm	9	Wounded	Bf 109 G-6 Yellow 2 (140013)	100%	Shot down in combat with USAAF bombers and P-38s.	Greffrath
11.11.43	Fw. Wilhelm Knöller	1	Wounded	Fw 190 A-4 White 5 (2359)	100%	Shot down in combat with USAAF bombers	Lüdinghausen
11.11.43	Gefr. Helmut Kock	1	Killed	Fw 190 A-6 White 8 (530362)	100%	Shot down in combat with USAAF bombers.	Senden

Date	*Name of Crew and Rank*	*Staffel*	*Fate*	*Aircraft, W.Nr & Code*	*Damage /Loss*	*Reason for Casualty*	*Place*
11.11.43	Ofw. Rudolf Piffer	2	Wounded	Fw 190 A-6 Black 12 (550512)		Pilot wounded in combat with USAAF bombers and fighters.	Deelen
11.11.43	Lt. Friedrich Heinrich	3	Killed	Fw 190 A Yellow 9 (150933)	100%	Shot down in combat with USAAF bombers.	Ascheburg
11.11.43	Uffz. Erwin Wessely	5	Killed	Fw 190 A-6 Black 4 (550883)	100%	Shot down in combat with P-47s.	Limbergen
11.11.43		II. Gruppe		Fw 190 A-6 (550878)	65%	Belly landing following damage in combat.	Glize-Rijen
11.11.43	Uffz. Knut Busch	9	Killed	Bf 109 G-6 Yellow 7 (15441)	100%	Shot down in combat with USAAF bombers.	North-west of Arnhem
13.11.43		I. Gruppe		Fw 190 A-4 (601)	45%	Belly landing following combat.	Near Bielefeld
13.11.43	Uffz. Günther Weber	7	Wounded	Bf 109 G-6 White 2 (20502)	100%	Shot down in combat with USAAF B-17s and fighters.	Near Rheine
13.11.43		III. Gruppe		Bf 109 G-6 (20272)	15%	Emergency landing due to fuel shortage.	Kamper-Nieustadt
13.11.43		III. Gruppe		Bf 109 G-6 (27136)	15%	Emergency landing due to fuel shortage.	Fechtern
13.11.43		III. Gruppe		Bf 109 G-6 (20472)	80%	Emergency landing due to engine problem.	De Punt
15.11.43	Fw. Bruno Nette	3	Wounded	Fw 190 A-6 (550781)	100%	Emergency landing on non-combat flight.	Zwolle
16.11.43	Fw. Paul Pfing	III. Gruppe		Bf 109 G-6 (410248)	75%	Belly landing on non-combat flight.	Schipol airfield
16.11.43		III. Gruppe		Bf 109 G-6 (15389)	60%	Overturned on landing.	Volkel airfield
17.11.43	Fw. Walter Hermann	II. Gruppe	Killed	Fw 190 A-6 (550460)	90%	Crashed due to engine problem.	Rheine
18.11.43	Lt. Werner Deppe	II. Gruppe		Fw 190 A-5 (7220)	45%	Emergency landing due to bad weather.	Goslar
24.11.43		I. Gruppe		Bf 109 G-6 (15392)		Emergency landing due to engine problem.	Eelde airfield
25.11.43	Lt. Claus Jürgen Dedow	2	Killed	Fw 190 A-6 Black 10 (550554)	100%	Crashed on non-combat flight.	Hoendelo
26.11.43	Uffz. Walter Ruttau	4	Killed	Fw 190 A-5 White 21 (410251)	100%	Shot down on combat mission.	Near Cloppenburg
26.11.43		II. Gruppe		Fw 190 A-6 (550888)	70%	Damaged on combat mission.	Oldenburg
26.11.43		II. Gruppe		Fw 190 A-5 (410000)	25%	Damaged due to engine problem.	Harpstedt-Bassung
26.11.43		II. Gruppe		Fw 190 A-5 (410009)	55%	Emergency landing due to engine problem.	Near Bussum
29.11.43	Oblt. Wilhelm Krebs	I. Gruppe	Wounded	Fw 190 A-6 Chevron 0 (530378)	100%	Shot down on combat mission.	Holthausen
29.11.43	Lt. Hans Berger	1	Wounded	Fw 190 A-6 White 1 (530374)	100%	Shot down in combat with USAAF bombers.	Delmenhorst
29.11.43	Fw. Ferdinand Gauster	2	Killed	Fw 190 A-6 Black 9 (550797)	100%	Shot down on combat mission.	Cloppenburg
29.11.43	Uffz. Heinz Lieschke	3	Killed	Fw 190 A-6 Yellow 1 (1188)	100%	Shot down on combat mission.	South-west of Bremen
29.11.43	Oblt. Hans-Joachim Harder	6	Killed	Fw 190 A-6 Yellow 5 (550510)	100%	Shot down in combat with P-47s.	Harpstedt
29.11.43	Uffz. Reinhard Ehelich	6	Killed	Fw 190 A-4 Yellow 3 (7027)	100%	Shot down on combat mission.	Near Attendorn
29.11.43		II. Gruppe		Bf 109 G-5 (15342)	30%	Belly landing due to engine problem following combat.	Westerode

Date	Name of Crew and Rank	Staffel	Fate	Aircraft, W.Nr & Code	Damage /Loss	Reason for Casualty	Place
29.11.43		II. Gruppe		Fw 190 A-4 (2553)	20%	Belly landing due to engine problem following combat.	Vörden airfield
29.11.43	Oblt. Heinz Klöpper	7	Killed	Bf 109 G-6 White 1 (410106)	100%	Misjudged height and crashed.	West of Zuider Zee
29.11.43	Ofhr. Manfred Spörk	7	Killed	Bf 109 G-6 White 3 (510930)	100%	Misjudged height and crashed.	Zuider Zee
29.11.43	Ofw. Hermann Brackhagen	7	Killed	Bf 109 G-6 White 5 (510285)	100%	Misjudged height and crashed.	Zuider Zee
29.11.43	Lt. Franz Koplik	III. Gruppe		Bf 109 G-6 (19913)	60%	Emergency landing due to fuel shortage following combat.	Bergen
29.11.43		III. Gruppe		Bf 109 G-6 (410281)	15%	Emergency landing to fuel shortage following combat.	Heereveen
30.11.43	Fw. Helmut Lotterer	2	Killed	Fw 190 A-4 Black 4 (589)	100%	Shot down in combat with USAAF fighters.	Deelen
30.11.43	Fw. Florian Ernst	2	Killed	Fw 190 A-6 Black 12 (550512)	100%	Shot down in combat with USAAF fighters.	Deelen
30.11.43	Uffz. Rudolf Schnappauf	1	Wounded	Fw 190 A-6 (550793)	100%	Shot down in combat.	East of Deelen
30.11.43		III. Gruppe		Bf 109 G-6 (27029)	25%	Airframe damage following non-combat flight.	Leeuwarden
01.12.43	Uffz. Rudolf Kirchmayer	3	Wounded	Fw 190 A-5 Yellow 5 (7333)	100%	Shot down on combat mission.	Aachen
01.12.43	Lt. Friedrich Scheemann	4	Killed	Fw 190 A-5 White 5 (7228)	100%	Shot down in combat with USAAF bombers.	Near Köln
01.12.43	Lt. Horst Ertmann	II. Gruppe	Wounded	Fw 190 A-6 Red 11 (550794)	60%	Belly landing following combat.	Menden/Bonn
01.12.43	Ofw. Benno Liper	4		Fw 190 A-5 (410007)	100%	Shot down on combat mission.	Near Arnberg
01.12.43	Fw. Alfred Miksch	8	Killed	Bf 109 G-6 Black 13 (140007)	100%	Shot down on combat mission.	South Holland
01.12.43	Uffz. Helmut Johanning	8	Wounded	Bf 109 G-6 Black 7 (410098)	75%	Emergency landing following combat.	Near Mol
10.12.43	Uffz. Richard Farnick	7	Killed	Bf 109 G-6 White 10 (15439)	100%	Crashed on non-combat flight.	Nistelrode
11.12.43		3		Fw 190 A-6 (551104)	70%	Belly landing on non-combat flight.	Near Oldenburg
11.12.43	Ogefr. Rottorosky Ogefr. Kneller	I. Gruppe "	Wounded Wounded	Go 242 (952)	100%	Crashed due to servicing fault.	Dortmund airfield
11.12.43		III. Gruppe		Bf 109 G-6 (20218)	80%	Crashed following combat	Vlieland island
11.12.43		III. Gruppe		Bf 109 G-6 (20087)	100%	Shot down on combat mission.	Harlingen
13.12.43		II. Gruppe		Bf 109 G-5 (15716)	20%	Crashed on take off.	Rheine airfield
13.12.43		III. Gruppe		Bf 109 G-6 (410138)	25%	Damaged while taxiing.	Volkel airfield
16.12.43	Lt. Martin Lacha	1	Wounded	Fw 190 A-7 White 1 (430162)	100%	Shot down in combat with USAAF bombers.	Menaldum
16.12.43	Oblt. Rudolf Engleder	2	Wounded	Fw 190 A-6 Black 7 (430177)		Wounded in combat with USAAF bombers.	Twente
16.12.43		3		Fw 190 A-5 (2639)	30%	Damaged on combat mission.	Near Twente
16.12.43	Fw. Klaus Holz	III. Gruppe	Wounded	Bf 109 G-6 (20528)	55%	Collision on take-off.	Volkel airfield

Date	Name of Crew and Rank	Staffel	Fate	Aircraft, W.Nr & Code	Damage /Loss	Reason for Casualty	Place
16.12.43	Uffz. Heinz Hartung	III. Gruppe	Wounded	Bf 109 G-6 (110003)	80%	Emergency landing due to fuel shortage following combat.	Deventer
20.12.43	Uffz. Erwin Franz	2	Killed	Fw 190 A-6 Black 10 (531089)	100%	Shot down in combat with USAAF bombers.	Delmenhorst
20.12.43	Fw. Gerhard Giese	3	Wounded	Fw 190 A-6 Yellow 6 (31086)	100%	Shot down in combat with USAAF bombers.	Mulberg
20.12.43		3		Fw 190 A-6 (551117)	100%	Crashed following combat.	South-west of Bremen
20.12.43	Uffz. Hubert Swoboda	11	Wounded	Bf 109 G-5 White 4 (15339)	100%	Rammed B-17 during combat.	Nordeney Island
21.12.43	Lt. Wolfgang Steffen	2	Killed	Fw 190 A-6 Black 5 (550792)	100%	Crashed on non-combat flight.	Dortmund
22.12.43	Fw. Rudolf Lehmann	4	Wounded	Fw 190 A-6 (550465)	90%	Belly landing following combat.	Near Werlte
22.12.43	Hptm. Harry Koch	6	Killed	Fw 190 A-6 Yellow 11 (550751)	100%	Collided with aircraft of Uffz. Mietho during combat.	Badbergen
22.12.43	Uffz. Erwin Mietho	6		Fw 190 A-5 (7215)	100%	Collided with aircraft of Hptm. Koch during combat.	Near Hesepe
22.12.43		III. Gruppe		Bf 109 G-6 (19094)	100%	Shot down on combat mission.	North of Nordhorn
22.12.43		III. Gruppe		Bf 109 G-6 (19993)	100%	Shot down on combat mission.	Nordhorn
22.12.43		III. Gruppe		Bf 109 G-5 (27120)	15%	Belly landing following combat.	West of Lingen
30.12.43		1		Fw 190 A-6 (550721)	20%	Damaged following combat.	Near Aachen

"Black 3" of 2nd Staffel takes off across a snow-covered runway.

Dortmund, early 1944. Fw 190 A-6s of I. Gruppe take off wingtip-to-wingtip.

At the end of 1943, Oberstleutnant Walter Oesau introduced a new emblem for JG 1: a red, winged "1" in a white diamond, which was enclosed in a red circle. This was to be applied to both sides of the engine cowling. This Bf 109 G-6 of 7th Staffel carries the red JG 1 "defence of the Reich" band on the rear fuselage. Note also the small aerial mast, DF loop, and the Erla Haube cockpit canopy.

On 11/1/44 II. Gruppe had their first major action in three weeks. Eleven B-17s were claimed by ten of the fifteen pilots led by Oberleutnant von Kirchmayr. All the pilots seen were victorious; from left to right: Leutnant Wegner; Oberfeldwebel Schuhmacher; Oberleutnant von Kirchmayr; Oberfeldwebel Haninger; Oberleutnant Burath; Feldwebel Sauer; Stabsfeldwebel Martens and Feldwebel Schoenrock.

CHAPTER 6 - 1944

YEAR OF DECISION

On the threshold of the new year, the hour had come. 1943 had been a decisive turning point for Jagdgeschwader 1, for German fighter aviation, and for the Reich itself.

On the ground, the Wehrmacht was retreating on all fronts. Russia, assisted by the industrial might of the United States, had succeeded in building up a formidable army equipped with the latest materials. German forces could only attempt to hold up Soviet efforts at reconquering their territory, presently concentrated in the Kiev region. On the Mediterranean front, the Germans held, at great cost, the centre of the southern Italian front to prevent allied forces streaming north. In the west, they were making preparations to repel an invasion, which would, almost certainly, determine the outcome of the war.

On the aerial front, German fighters continued to record important victories. In the east, the figures spoke for themselves: on 14th October 1943 Walter Nowotny became the first pilot to reach 250 victories. Less than two months later, Jagdgeschwader 52 celebrated its 8,000 success. Nevertheless, German losses rose, and the Luftwaffe no longer had mastery of the skies. In the west, the fighter arm was seriously ill-used. However, 1943 had not finished too badly for them. The progressive reinforcement of 'defence of the Reich' units allowed them to still score well during large raids.

If about 1650 German fighter aircraft were assembled in the west, the times did not bode well for them. On the allied side, attempts were made to extend the radius of action of the escort fighters. On 13th December 1943 they were able to reach Kiel. In March 1944 they could accompany the bombers as far as Berlin. This formidable and effective allied escort altered the balance between the opposing forces. The beginning of 1944 was the turning point. If Jagdgeschwader 2 "Richthofen" (based in the Brittany-Normandy region) and Jagdgeschwader 26 (in northern France and Belgium) celebrated their 2,000th victories on 15th January and 24th February 1944 respectively, they would soon be disappointed: all realistic hope of resisting the allied armada would progressively disappear.

Oberleutnant Eberhard Burath recalled those days: "From the beginning of 1944, the war became extremely hard for us. The time had long since gone when we entered combat "fresh and happy". It wasn't exactly a feeling of fear, but rather a state of excitement, of extreme tension. Calmness and joking had totally disappeared. In spite of that, there remained a firm resolution to overcome fear and to do our duty, even unto death. In flying, when the enemy were found, and combat could no longer be delayed, all sentiment disappeared. One became a war machine. We became all-powerful. Shortly after landing, we were worn out by the change. One tried to overcome things in drink. We sometimes did not know how we could carry on ...

"We did not sleep a lot: we would drink and talk for a great part of the night. On early morning scrambles, I often took off with my flying gear rapidly slung over my pyjamas. A good whiff of oxygen quickly woke me up. Our way of life was very special, and that is why we stayed, in the main, on our airfield. Even during times of respite, there was a certain tension: an alert could surprise us at any moment. In this case, the contrast was enormous: we would leave our chairs to enter into murderous combat several minutes later; less than two hours later, we would once again be stretched out in the sun. It was even harder to take when a friend's chair remained empty".

After the new year revels (I. Gruppe had been provided with 5,000 litres of beer!), it was difficult to get back to the serious business of fighting a war. At the start of the year III. Gruppe, and, above all, I. Gruppe suffered under the weight of combat. Two black days, 4th and 5th January, cost I. Gruppe five pilots, including the very experienced Feldwebel Bernhard Kunze of 2nd Staffel.

On 11th January, II. Gruppe re-entered the fray. At around 10:30 hours, all three Gruppen of the unit took off. Fifteen pilots of II. Gruppe met up with sixty B-17s over Paderborn (1st, 2nd and 3rd Bomb Divisions sent nearly 600 bombers over the aircraft industries of Oschersleben and Halberstadt, as well as different cities in the centre of Germany). Three successive head-on attacks of II. Gruppe led by Oberleutnant von Kirchmayr resulted in the impressive statistic of nine B-17s claimed as shot down, although only one was officially credited. Among the claimants were Oberleutnant Burath; Oberleutnant von Kirchmayr (two); Leutnant Wegner and Oberfeldwebel Schuhmacher. There were two losses for the Gruppe, one killed and one wounded. III. Gruppe also recorded successes over a P-47 and a B-17 (claimed by Oberleutnant Overhagen). One pilot of the Gruppe was killed. Towards 13:30 hours, during their second action of the day, five pilots of I. Gruppe (including Hauptmann Grislawski and Leutnant Berger) recorded three victories and two Herausschüsse over Zwolle in central Holland. Twenty American bombers did not return on this day.

On 21st January 1944 a strong personality arrived at the unit from the fighter training school at Orange in France. Known for his straight-talking throughout the Luftwaffe, Major Heinz Bär was well received by II. Gruppe. Göring had not showered many honours on him, in spite of his being credited with nearly 200 victories on all fronts, in spite of being Staffelkapitän and Gruppenkommandeur in several units. Here he was a simple pilot in 6th Staffel, the result of several pronouncements well spoken, but badly received by the head of the Luftwaffe, who did not wish to face up to reality. Many pilots of great renown gravitated to this Staffel. After the accidental death of Oberleutnant Harry Koch, Oberleutnant Lutz-Wilhelm Burckhard, a Ritterkreuzträger with over 50 victories in the east, was destined to take over the Staffel. However, having always flown the Bf 109, he moved to III. Gruppe on 9th February 1944 to become Staffelkapitän of 7th Staffel, depleted in recent actions: in two and a half

Stabsfeldwebel Martens leaves his Fw 190 A-6, "Black 9", W.Nr. 550755 at Dortmund after combat on 11/1/44. Thirteen days later he was shot down and killed by P-47s near Tournai in this machine.

Oberleutnant Alfred Grislawski explains his latest combat in front of "White 9". On 24/1/44 he was wounded in action and had to bail out of his Fw 190 A-7.

Supplementary fuel tanks were fitted under the belly before take off against the American "box" formations. Unteroffizier K. Ell, mechanic, is seen working on the engine of this Fw 190 A-6 of 1st Staffel.

months three Staffelkapitäne had been lost. Oberleutnant Georg "Schorch" Eder took over 6th Staffel. He left hospital after being wounded with Jagdgeschwader 2, whose 5th Staffel he led. He had more than 30 victories when continuing his career with Jagdgeschwader 1.

In spite of their ability, these pilots acknowledged the prowess of Bär. It was he who led II. Gruppe from the time he joined it. Moreover the Gruppenkommandeur, Hauptmann Walter Höckner, was in the throes of being transferred to Jagdgeschwader 4, and his successor, Hauptmann Hermann Segatz, from Jagdgeschwader 5, was a man of good sense. The pilots were unanimous: Bär was the natural choice to lead the Gruppe in combat. On 24th January, heavy combat took place in the Belgian skies. 563 bombers escorted by 678 fighters were sent to the Frankfurt area, but the bad weather disorganised the armada. The bombers were recalled and returned to England - nevertheless one group of 60 bombers drop their bombs on an electricity complex near Eschweiler. Twenty one pilots of II. Gruppe met up with around fifty bombers over Belgium. Three P-51s and one P-47 were claimed for the loss of three pilots killed and two wounded on the German side. Among those killed was a Schwarmführer of 5th Staffel, Stabsfeldwebel Rudolf Martens and his wingman, shot down by P-47s in the Tournai area. I. Gruppe, led by the Staffelkapitän of 1st Staffel, Hauptmann Alfred Grislawski, were also in action, with Grislawski being shot down and bailing out

Apart from the new emblem and Reich defence band, I. Gruppe also re-introduced black and white bands around the engine cowlings. Note, however, that the undersurface access panel for the engine did not carry the bands.

wounded after claiming a fresh victory. The Gruppe also claimed three Herausschüsse, Leutnant Hans Berger laying claim to one.

On 30th January, the three Gruppen were once again in action. This time they were up aginst 777 bombers and 635 fighters whose objectives were Brunswick and Hannover. Several pilots increased their victory tally: Leutnant Hans Ehlers recorded his 34th and 35th; Oberfeldwebel Toni Piffer his 12th and 13th; Feldwebel Rudolf Hübl his 10th and Hauptmann Emil Schnoor his 6th. On 30th January four pilots of II. Gruppe, Feldwebel Sauer, Unteroffizier Rauhaus, Unteroffizier Swoboda and Unteroffizier Negressus, each claimed a B-17. II. Gruppe thereby celebrated its 600th victory. In contrast, III. Gruppe, sorely tested, suffered the loss of six pilots killed, among them the Staffelkapitän of 7th Staffel, Hauptmann Albert Kind. There were also three wounded, including Gruppenkommandeur Hauptmann Friedrich Eberle. His place was taken by Major Hartmann Grasser, an Eichenlaubträger with close on a hundred victories gained in both the east and west theatres. He had been in action from the start of the war.

On 8th February the three Gruppen were in action

I. and II. Gruppe machines also carried the red winged "1". This Fw 190 A of II. Gruppe has the emblem partly completed.

Major Emil Schnoor, Gruppenkommandeur of I. Staffel takes an interest in the preparations of his machine at Dortmund in early 1944.

A mechanic checks the engine cowling of this Fw 190 A-6 of I. Gruppe.

towards mid-day. Leutnant Hans Berger of I. Gruppe claimed a B-17, and a II. Gruppe pilot claimed a P-47. One could not talk of normal things, in the face of death and the losses of friends and enemy. The list grew longer and longer, names and figures without end.

"Even the most experienced of us lost our calm. Before take off, one risked getting lost in the cigarette smoke. The majority of pilots were withdrawn, unapproachable. There was only Major Bär who did not change.

"At every stage of "alert", we were waiting to get off quickly. At 30 minutes readiness we could still circulate on the airfield. At 15 minutes, we remained near dispersal and checked our equipment. At 3 minutes, we put on our flying suits and leather boots, life jacket, flask of colourant, pistol and flares if we were near the coast; around the waist went the compass; the map, paper with the codes as well as the chocolate and pervitine in the knee pouch. Orders were passed by loudspeaker or by telephone.

"In the case of a scramble not involving cockpit readiness, we would run to our machines. Between two and four mechanics would help us. One would be on the left wing to help us to get into the aircraft and attach our parachute which was already in place on the seat. The rest of the equipment had been prepared in advance: dinghy, earphones, sunglasses ... we tested the radio and checked the oxygen. During this time two other mechanics helped to start the engine. We then taxied to the take-off point, and then took off. If the Gruppe took off in formation, different coloured flares indicated in which order the different Staffeln took off.

"On 10th February, it happened once again. It was a memorable day. I flew as wingman to an experienced Oberfeldwebel. We met up with a formation of "Viermots" over Brunswick. My comrade attacked alone and immediately shot down a B-17. "Now, you can also do it, go on, after them!" I approached very close to my victim and fired a long burst at him. His right wing was badly hit, and flames spewed forth. Nevertheless the Americans did not give up and continued to fire at me. Better and better! My aircraft was hit all over. Like lightning flashes, the bullets ripped into the fuselage. Soon, there was no response from the joy-stick, or from the other controls. I did not know what to do to get out! I had already jettisoned the canopy but, like a stamp on an envelope, I remained stuck to the armour plate in the cockpit. My right arm was finally out, but, forced by the wind, it was pushed backwards. I forced my head out and to the side. I felt that my nostrils resembled those of a charging stallion. My left hand caught hold of the front of the canopy and I pulled. In this situation, the force was enough, and I was carried clear by an air current. My

Fw 190 A-6 of I. Gruppe near one of the hangars at Dortmund, early 1944.

Rheine, early 1944. II. Gruppe had shared its Fw 190s with II. Gruppe, JG 300 since summer 1943. This Fw 190 A-6, which carries the winged "1", is about to take-off on a "Wilde Sau" mission.

Volkel, 19/2/44. Leutnant Hans Halbey, Technical Officer of III. Gruppe, proudly hands over the 500th aircraft sent to the Gruppe to Gruppenkommandeur, Hauptmann Friedrich Eberle.

An in-flight view of a Schwarm from 3rd Staffel, early 1944.

breathing was blocked, and the wind played with my jacket and tore it. One of my boots was forced off, and I was thrown about like a vulgar table-tennis ball.
"Don't pull, don't pull! Pulling the ripcord just after bailing out would be foolish. I was falling very fast, I was too high, and furthermore the sky was full of enemy aircraft. I had already personally seen how they machine-gunned defenceless pilots hanging on their parachutes. Faster, faster, lose altitude!
Things calmed down a bit. The speed decreased and I pulled myself together. i had time to observe that I was falling head first. My legs were tossing about above me. Above all, remain calm. The top of the clouds spread out for about 2,000 metres. At this height I could open the parachute. A 4,000 metre parachute descent is not too bad! I approached the clouds. No fighters in sight, so I pulled the ripcord and the canopy deployed. I felt the shock which happened as a parachute opened! Everything went fine. I was suspended for several moments when my attention was drawn to a sound. A small black spot fell in front of me. I wanted to put out my hand and catch my boot. In the clouds, my anxiety returned. I could see nothing. How do I get out of this? Shortly afterwards, a dull colour came towards me: the earth was in view.
"My adventure was reaching the end, even if there still was a little more to come. Where should I land? On the ground, there were woods everywhere, and I had no desire to pin my backside to one. Up to present, every-

Oberleutnant Helmut Biederbick, an experienced pilot with JG 54 on the eastern front, replaced his friend, Hauptmann Harald Römer, who was killed in action on 20/2/44, as Staffelkapitän of 2nd Staffel. Biederbick is seen here in his Fw 190 A-7, "Black 7".

Aircraft of I. Gruppe, as seen here, occupied the airfield of Hopsten (Rheine) from 12th to 24th February 1944.

Several aircraft are in flames after P-47s machine-gunned the airfield of Hopsten.

thing had gone well, but this was rather bad ... I then felt a small fresh breeze which, without effort, pushed me further on. Roofs, a church, a complete village. This did not look too good. I saw people in the street and I cried. Some looked up with fear on their faces. The village disappeared beneath me and a freshly ploughed field came into view. A few seconds later I reached earth. There at last! I was sprawled on my stomach, full length. There was no way of releasing the parachute, the mud had blocked up the buckle. I was there, on all fours in a field, the silk wrapped all around me. I looked like a pig trying to find a truffle. The ground was covered in snow ..." Eberhard Burath's rather amusing account of an attack on a bomber formation, and the events following his bailing out.

Higher up, combat continued. Major Heinz Bär, who was leading II. Gruppe, shot down a B-17 as well as a Thunderbolt. The final reckoning was seven victories against two German pilots of the unit killed. Feldwebel Fritz Haspel of III. Gruppe claimed his second confirmed victory - a Thunderbolt.

On 19th February 1944 the allies launched their gigantic week-long aerial offensive, code named "Big Week", designed to paralyse the German war industries. During "Big Week" nearly 20,000 tons of bombs were dropped on the aircraft industries of the Reich.

On 20th February, after ten days pause in combat, the three Gruppen were in action against an armada of1003 bombers escorted by seventeen squadrons of American fighters and sixteen British. Twenty Fw 190 A-6s and A-7s made three passes against the bombers. The third, at about 13:00 hours in the region of Muhlouse, was the most effective: three B-17s and two P-38s were claimed (Oberfeldwebel Reinhold Flecks claiming a B-17 and a P-38). I. Gruppe were also engaged, Oberfeldwebel Rudolf Hübl claiming a B-17, but 2nd Staffel lost their Staffelkapitän, Hauptmann Harald Römer, killed. His place was taken by a veteran of Jagdgeschwader 54, Oberleutnant Helmut Biederbick, who recalled: "I was on the eastern front with JG 54 when victories were still relatively easy ... Less problem for others, because I myself was not an aggressive pilot at heart; I was too concerned about watching my rear, and did not concentrate enough on my prey.

"I was posted to Schleissheim as an instructor, and from there to Manching, where I met Harald Römer. Römer left us to return to the front - he was posted to JG 1. He could not have served long in his rôle as Staffelkapitän because soon, to avoid a court-martial following several pranks, I in my turn had to return to action and learned unfortunately that the Staffel I had been given was that of my friend Harald, who had fallen shortly beforehand. "Reichsverteidigung" was a terrible period. The eastern front, which I had known, was far less dangerous. In the case of an alert (in the west), we usually had five minutes to prepare ourselves, put on the obligatory life jacket, and go to the toilet as nerves took a hold.

"Loudspeakers blared out military marches. We would

Volkel, February 1944. Six officers of III. Gruppe: Hauptmann Marschall; Hauptmann Eberle; Oberleutnant Buchholz; Oberleutnant Overhagen; Lt. Göhre and Leutnant Reimann.

gather near our aircraft, accompanied by the music which was sometimes interrupted by news concerning the advance of the "Dicke Autos" or "Indianer". We followed their progress on a map. Each Squadron Leader had a telephone on the wing of his aircraft and linked to the Stab section. The music was interrupted: "Sitztbereitsschaft" - cockpit readiness. At any moment we could be taking off. A green flare over the airfield was the signal; engines would be started and we would take off.

"When the enemy were sighted, we flew for several seconds parallel to the formation in order to evaluate its strength and direction. We were aware of the escort fighters, but often they did not attack at this moment. We picked up speed, swept wide of our target, and carried out a 180 degrees turn. We were then head-on, and opened fire while traversing through the bomber stream. During this move, our formation lost cohesion, and that was what the enemy fighters were waiting for. They then picked us off at the rear of the "Viermots".

On 21st February the cities of Brunswick and Hannover, as well as about fifteen aviation plants in central Germany, were the focus of attention for 861 bombers. Sixteen of them were shot down, of which five were claimed by II. Gruppe. Major Heinz Bär claimed three, taking his tally to 185; Oberleutnant von Kirchmayr and the official leader of II. Gruppe, Hauptmann Segatz, each claimed a single victory. On the debit side, the Gruppe lost five pilots killed and four wounded, Feldwebel Otto Schmid, with seven victories, of which five were Viermots, being among the wounded. He managed to get his Fw 190 A-7 down at Rheine in spite of a bad wound to his leg. Having received the distress message from the pilot, the airfield commander fired a red flare to prevent other aircraft from landing. Medical services were with him immediately he landed, but in spite of all assistance, Schmid's leg was amputated in June.

The pilots of III. Gruppe, who had taken off shortly after 15:00 hours, were taken by surprise by P-47s coming out of the sun. Two pilots were killed. The Bf 109 G-6 of Feldwebel Fritz Haspel of 8th Staffel, who had not managed to release his supplementary fuel tank before attacking, lost contact with his comrades. Suddenly his aircraft received a burst of fire in the engine. Haspel immediately began the procedure for a crash-landing. A second burst hit his machine. There was no question of a crash-landing now - he had to bail out quickly. Haspel bailed out after jettisoning the canopy. The latter hit the propellor of the Thunderbolt, and it in turn went down out of control. The American pilot managed to bail out, but,

Pilots of 1st Staffel pose around a pennant which carries their Staffel emblem at the end of February 1944 at Hopsten. From left to right: Unteroffizier Kubon (+29/3/44); Unteroffizier Altenhain; Unteroffizier Manikowski (+11/4/44); Unteroffizier Kenzler; Unteroffizier Martin (+29/3/44); Unteroffizier Schulze; Leutnant Lück (w. 9/4/44); Unteroffizier Talbat; Fahnenjunker Junge (w. 14/8/44) and Feldwebel Kaiser.

deploying his parachute too quickly, the silk tore, and he broke both legs due to a rapid descent. Haspel was credited with the victory, but he suffered second degree burns to his face which required four weeks of treatment.
On the following day, it was the turn of the aero industries in the centre of Germany and the industrial region of Schweinfurt to suffer attack. The three Gruppen of the unit were in action. Among the victorious pilots were the usual two "Aces" of II. Gruppe, Major Heinz Bär, and Hauptmann Hermann Segatz, who claimed two B-17s. Oberfeldwebel Rudolf Hübl of I. Gruppe also claimed his thirteenth victory, a B-17.
On 24th February, after a rest day, I. Gruppe encountered 809 bombers over Holland en route for Rostock, Schweinfurt, Gotha and Eisenach. Several victories were claimed: two B-24s by Hübl, one by Oberfähnrich Toni Piffer of 2nd Staffel, and a B-17 by the Gruppenkommandeur Emil Schnoor. However, on the debit side, I. Gruppe lost three pilots killed and one wounded. In spite of the intervention of the fighter escort, II. Gruppe launched an attack on the bombers, and succeeded in shooting down two B-24s (Oberleutnant von Kirchmayr claiming one of them), as well as two P-47s. Three pilots were killed, however, among them the experienced Feldwebel Heinz Fuchs of 4th Staffel. III. Gruppe were in action towards 15:00 hours. No pilot was lost, and the Technical Officer of the Gruppe, Leutnant Hans Halbey, scored his first victory, a P-47.
On 25th February the unit once more engaged the enemy. 754 bombers escorted by 899 fighters. Heinz Bär recorded three victories over four-engined bombers and one probable; von Kirchmayr - one B-17; Segatz - one B-17, and Oesau - one B-17 and a B-24. On this occasion there were no losses to the unit.
"Big Week" had cost the allies dear: 160 four-engined bombers shot down by German fighters, which in turn lost 165 pilots, 99 of them killed.
On 1st March Oberleutnant Burath took charge of 4th Staffel. However, in spite of the impressive number of victories registered by the Staffel, he noted with sadness that in three months of action, 36 pilots had passed through the Staffel - three times normal strength!

March 1944, Rheine. After the death of Hauptmann Hermann Segatz on 8/3/44, Major Bär officially took over II. Gruppe. He is seen here giving instructions to his pilots. From left to right: Oberleutnant von Kirchmayr; Oberleutnant Burath; unknown; Leutnant Schwarz; Leutnant Wegner; Leutnant Deppe; Leutnant Terborg; Oberfeldwebel Bach; Oberfeldwebel Flecks; Oberfeldwebel Niedereicholz; Feldwebel Sauer and Unteroffizier Zunkl.

BERLIN PREMIERE - 6th MARCH 1944

The "Big City", as the Americans called it, had not, as yet, been seriously troubled by bombs during the day, and no one could say who (the allies or the Germans) was the more surprised. The thousand miles which separated the capital of the Reich from the mainland of Great Britain was no longer an obstacle to the realisation of the prophesy of Churchill: "For every bomb dropped on England, we will repay with a thousand". In the line of Maxims, Göring, for his part, had said that if Berlin suffered bombardment, he could be called "Meier". The Reichmarschall would need re-naming!

Jagdgeschwader 1 were part of 3rd Fighter Division, led by General Major Walter Grabmann, whose quarters were at Deelen. On 6th March 1944 Jagdgeschwader 1 lined up as follows:

Stab: Oberst Walter Oesau - 3 Bf 109 G-6s based at Rheine;

I. Gruppe: Major Emil Schnoor - 19 Fw 190 A-7s based at Twente;

II. Gruppe: Hauptmann Hermann Segatz - 21 Fw 190 A-5 and A-7s based at Rheine; and

III. Gruppe: Hauptmann Hartmann Grasser - 13 Bf 109 G-5 and G-6s based at Mönchen-Gladbach.

On the other side of the Channel, since dawn, there was frenzied action around the bombers which, in several hours time, would take the war in the air a stage further. 730 bombers escorted by 801 fighters would take part. At 08:50 hours the first aircraft took off. From that moment the German listening services were continually tuned into the 250th bombing mission. More than an hour before the first American aircraft crossed the Channel, orders had been issued to the German fighter units. For this attack, the units would work closely together: 2nd and 3rd Fighter Divisions would fight together, led by the Gruppenkommandeur of I. Gruppe, Jagdgeschwader 11, Hauptmann Rolf Hermichen. This move had been used several days earlier over Steinhuder Lake and allowed a concentration of a sizeable force which caused disquiet among the allied armada.

The first Boeings reached the coast of Holland at 10:52 hours. With engines at cruising speed to conserve fuel, the escort fighters slowly made up the distance between

Major Bär (centre) discussing tactics with his pilots in front of a model of a Spitfire. To his left is Oberleutnant von Kirchmayr; facing him is Oberfeldwebel Leo Schuhmacher and, second from right, Oberfeldwebel Bach.

themselves and the bombers.

The interminable "Sitztbereitsschaft" finally ended on the majority of bases on the west European continent. At Twente, Major Schnoor's I. Gruppe took off at 10:55 hours, setting course for Steinhuder Lake. I. Gruppe was joined over Rheine by the 21 Fw 190s of II. Gruppe, led by Bär. The two Gruppen were the last to arrive over the Lake, meeting with 50 Bf 109s and Fw 190s of Jagdgeschwader 11 and twenty Bf 109s of III. Gruppe, Jagdgeschwader 54. Jagdgeschwader 1's addition meant that a concentration of more than 100 fighters would go into action. A force which far exceeded usual fighting strength. A feeling of invulnerability was held by many of the young German pilots. However, their numbers could not compare with those put into the fray by the Americans.

At 11:40 hours the German formation set course westwards. The search began. The advantage was with those who saw the enemy first. A shout: silhouettes appeared in the distance. There they are! Part of the

On 6th March 1944 Leutnant Hans Berger of 1st Staffel took off from Twente at 12:10 hours to intercept the first large-scale American raid on Berlin. He shot down a B-17, but his Fw 190 A-7, W.Nr. 340016 was hit. Nevertheless he was able to return to Twente at 13:33 hours. His mechanic "Kari" Ell is with him near the damaged rudder of his aircraft. The red fuselage band can be clearly seen.

Dortmund, early 1944. Five renowned pilots of I. Gruppe are seen discussing tactics. From left to right: Oberfeldwebel Piffer; Leutnant Eh; Leutnant Berger; Hauptmann Schnoor and Leutnant Ehlers.

force, at least, as an instrument problem had resulted in half of the bombers deviating to the south. Noticing their error, the American navigators changed course northwards. Without a doubt they sought to evade contact with enemy fighters. The second formation of bombers had less chance. It found itself among the German fighters, who tried to deceive the side gunners of the bombers. The time for manoeuvring was past - targets were chosen. The German fighters pounced. At this moment the bombers could only rely on the quality of their defensive armament, and to luck. They had to withstand the force of this first frontal attack, the escort would not intervene until after it had happened: the frontal pass would break up the German formation and they would be far less dangerous. Muscles tense - perspiration on every brow. Hauptmann Rolf Hermichen gave the order to attack. Choose a target quickly, don't let it go, and go in right to the last moment.
The first blazing victims fell away from the bomber stream. The debris of around ten fortresses fell in the Quackenbrück area. However, it was then the turn of the German fighters to be boxed in, as the escort reacted. One of the first victims was the Fw 190 A-7 of Oberleutnant Wolfgang Kretschmer (recently arrived from Jagdgeschwader 54) who lost contact with the rest of II. Gruppe after probably shooting down a "Viermot" during the frontal attack. Alone, he was preparing for a second attack from the rear. At full throttle, Colonel "Hub" Zemke, commander of 56th Fighter Group, led his P-47s towards Kretschmer. The latter realised the gravity of the situation too late, and his despairing manoeuvres could not get him out of the line of fire when the American leader opened up. The fuselage was hit; the aircraft began to break up and burn. Kretschmer had to get out quickly before the fuel tank exploded. Blinded by the flames, deafened by the noise around him, Kretschmer managed to extricate himself with difficulty from the inferno. Finally clear, the shock of the parachute opening brought home to him that he was still alive. On the ground, he was found in a terrible state: face, hands, garments, all were ravaged by fire. An ambulance took him away for treatment, and ten weeks convalescence in Quackenbrück.
High above, the action continued. Fahnenjunkeroberfeldwebel Emil Demuth suffered a similar fate to Kretschmer. After having shot down a B-17 on his first pass, Demuth and his wingman lined up a second B-17. It would have been a possible victory had it not been for the intervention of 56th Fighter Group. Demuth's Fw 190 A-7 caught fire. He managed to jettison the canopy.

5th April 1944. I. Gruppe evacuate their base at Twente. Ground personnel render the airstrip unusable.

On 9th April 1944 following violent combat with four-engined bombers in deplorable weather two Fw 190 A-8s of I. Gruppe, "White 3" and "White 8", belly landed on the small island of Erö at around 12:30 hours. Note the shields over the machine gun ports.

Hauptmann Lutz-Wilhelm Burckhardt (right) converses with his Gruppenkommandeur, Hauptmann Friedrich Eberle in front of a Bf 109 G. Note the "Erla Haube" canopy on this machine.

Instantly, the rush of air fanned flames around his face. He vacated the cockpit and jumped. The parachute opened, but the flames continued to devour his clothing. Struggling like a demon, he managed to extinguish the flames before reaching the ground in the Minden area.
The bomber stream approached Berlin. The German fighters were now running short of ammunition and fuel. It became necessary to get down quickly. Of the twenty-one Fw 190s of II. Gruppe which took off, only two managed to regain home base. Seventeen others landed at various aerodromes in north-west Germany. Apart from the loss of Oberleutnant Kretschmer, II. Gruppe also lost the experienced Oberfeldwebel Detlev Lüth, still trapped in his aircraft when it crashed at Eydelstadt. During this action I. Gruppe also had two pilots killed.
Other units took up the attack, and more bombers were sent crashing down. Berlin's air raid warning sirens sounded at 12:47 hours. Thirteen minutes later, the surviving bombers appeared, dropping 1,200 tonnes of bombs on the capital. 345 civilians were killed.
It was then time for the return flight to England, and for several pilots of Jagdgeschwader 1, a second chance to attack the bombers. At 14:20 hours at Rheine, Major Heinz Bär led off three Fw 190s. Shortly before 15:00 hours, he re-established contact with the enemy in the Lingen area. In the same way, a similar number of pilots of I. Gruppe found themselves once again locked in combat. Jagdgeschwader 1 returned a good score. Inevitably Bär and Segatz each shot down two B-17s. Kommodore Oesau claimed a B-17 and a P-47; Oberleutnant von Kirchmayr a B-17 and a P-51. Other pilots were also victorious: Oberfeldwebel Otto Bach-one B-17; Unteroffizier Helmut Stiegler two B-17s; Unteroffizier Hubert Swoboda one B-17; Oberfeldwebel Leo Schuhmacher (Bär's wingman) one B-17; Leutnant Hans Berger one B-17 and Oberfeldwebel Rudolf Hübl one B-17.
In England, there was the habitual waiting and worrying on the airfields. The survivors eventually, appeared, and a count was made of missing aircraft. 80 did not return: 69 bombers and eleven fighters.
The run of victories eventually came to an end for one of the "aces" of II. Gruppe. Having recovered from the action of two days previous, twenty-one pilots of II. Gruppe took off on 8th March at mid-day. The Focke-Wulfs met up with the enemy three-quarters of an hour later. Ten minutes of weighing-up the situation, and manoeuvring into position, then the attack. Five pilots returned victories: Oberleutnant von Kirchmayr and Hauptmann Segatz each a B-24 and Unteroffizier Stiegler a P-47. Nevertheless this latest victim to his account marked the end of the road for Hauptmann

Fw 190 A-7, "Black 3", W.Nr. 430352, of 2nd Staffel. This aircraft carries the black and white bands on the cowling with the unit emblem, and defence of the Reich band on the rear fuselage.

Segatz. The Gruppenkommandeur of II. Gruppe was shot down and killed in his Fw 190 A-7, "white 23" over Luckau by an American fighter. Segatz had at least 34 victories to his credit. I. Gruppe was also successful, Oberfeldwebel Hübl claiming a B-17.
"Shortly after taking over the Gruppe, Major Bär wanted us to change our ideas. We were totally exhausted with combat. On the occasion of a transfer of base, he took us to dine in the best restaurant in Wiesbaden. We were fairly embarrassed following him into the main room. What would people think? Our leaders had said we were slovenly, incapable. Also, a few days before, the city had suffered a heavy raid which we were unable to prevent. Would we also be insulted here? A great surprise awaited us. First of all there was silence, then applause! A feeling of pride came over us. There were still people who recognised our sacrifices. The service was exemplary, and we ate with the civilians. The last glass was emptied late into the night". - Oberleutnant Eberhard Burath, Staffelkapitän, 4th Staffel.
The rest of March was fairly calm. Victories and losses became a confused jumble. Bär, Eder and von Kirchmayr consulted frequently, and their victory tally increased regularly. Oberleutnant Eder, Staffelkapitän of 6th Staffel, recorded nine victories in April: four B-17s; two B-24s and three P-47s. Oberleutnant Rüdiger von Kirchmayr had recorded eleven victories from the start of the year to the end of April, nine of them being four-engined bombers. Young pilots also knew good periods. During the month of April, for example, while Bär claimed five victories and von Kirchmayr four, Unteroffizier Helmut Stiegler was credited with the destruction of four enemy aircraft and a "Herausschüss". All things considered, a creditable performance. Nevertheless, Stiegler was still inexperienced, and did not have the chance to be lucky, like the major aces. He was killed in action on 12th May 1944, having recorded seven victories while serving with Jagdgeschwader 1.
However there was another side to the coin. Oberleutnant Hans Ehlers and Hauptmann Emil Schnoor, officers of I. Gruppe, were both wounded within three days of each other. On 13th April after a major conflict aimed at protecting central Germany from a force of some 626 bombers escorted by 566 fighters, the unit

The two major personalities side-by-side. Kommodore Walter Oesau (left) and Gruppenkommandeur, II. Gruppe, Heinz Bär. The Fiesler Storch in the background was frequently used by them to visit the crash sites of their victims.

registered heavy losses. Four killed and two wounded, including Oberleutnant Ehlers, who had to make a forced landing after having shot down a P-51 and a B-17. The injury was superficial. During this combat, Hauptmann Schnoor claimed his sixteenth and last victory. The injuries to Schnoor were far more serious. On 16th April, engine failure on a local flight marked the end of his career with Jagdgeschwader 1. The supply officer of I. Gruppe, Hauptmann Ludwig Siegfried, recalled: "On Sunday 16th April 1944 Hauptmann Schnoor came to see me to ask if, as usual, lunch would be served at 13:00 hours. I said it would. It was mid-day. There was an hour for him to do some local flying. No one knew exactly what had happened. Schnoor tried a forced landing in a field. The undercarriage could not take the force of the landing and snapped. He was badly wounded in the head. Taken to hospital at Detmold, he remained there for six weeks. His marriage had been arranged for this time, and he almost literally went from his hospital bed to the ceremony".

On 22nd April 803 bombers once again overflew the Reich, the majority in the region of Hamm. All units of Jagdgeschwader 1 took off shortly before 18:00 hours. III. Gruppe came off worst in the ensuing combat: the fighter cover provided by 242 P-51s was formidable. Seven pilots of III. Gruppe were killed and two wounded. Among the victorious pilots of II. Gruppe were Oberleutnant Georg Eder, one P-47, Oberfeldwebel Otto Bach (one P-47) and Reinhard Flecks (two P-47s), and Flieger Blech, two B-17s. The latter, after having shot down the first B-17 from behind, collided with the rudder of a second in breaking off combat with the first. Both aircraft fell. Blech, as well as seven Americans of the second aircraft, managed to bail out.

Armourers working on a Fw 190 A-6 of I. Gruppe.

"Yellow 6" of 3rd Staffel sporting black and white bands and the "Reichsverteidigung" marking, but without the Geschwader emblem on the engine cowling.

On 16th April 1944 Hauptmann Schnoor, Gruppenkommandeur of I. Gruppe, took off on a routine flight. Shortly afterwards, his Fw 190 A-7, "White 20", W. Nr. 340035 crashed near Detmold. Schnoor was badly wounded, his place at the head of the Gruppe being taken by Leutnant Ehlers.

In I. Gruppe Oberleutnant Biederbick claimed a B-17, and on this day Major Heinz Bär recorded his 200th victory shortly before 20:00 hours. He took off quickly from Störmede after seeing a B-24 heading due west. He moved in behind the "Liberator" and one attack from his Fw 190 A-7, "Red 23" was sufficient to bring it down. Four bailed out.

The young Oberfähnrich Herbert Neuner remembered his early combat experience: "Born in 1924, I was eighteen when I volunteered for service. My aim: to become a pilot. After doing four months of drill, I was posted to the Luftkreigschule 4, then to pilots school where I received accelerated training. In August 1943 I was at fighter training unit, Jagdgeschwader 104 at Herzogenaurach. In March 1944 I arrived at Orange where Jagdgruppe Sud was situated, from where the fighter units in the west drew fresh pilots from the pool of reserves. At this point, every young pilot hoped for the order to arrive for their posting to the front. Mine arrived quickly: I had to join JG 1, via Paris. My dream was realised, with at first a stop-over in Paris. After a train journey in the company of Fähnrich Gustav Knoll, I arrived at Rheine on 5th April 1944. Hauptmann Schnoor received us, and then separated us: I was posted to 2nd Staffel, Knoll to 3rd Staffel. We had to learn to fly the Fw 190; neither of us had had it in our hands before. Oberfeldwebel Demuth was my tutor, even after my first take-off when I nearly killed myself. Three take-offs in a day and it was felt I was ready. The following day, I was presented to the Kommodore, the famous Walter Oesau who received us warmly and left a lasting impression. Shortly after, the Gruppe left for Rheine for the combat area of Bad Lippspringe. It was a large field with an imposing building, a boarding house where we pilots were billeted. In the morning a wagon or coach came to collect us and take us to the airfield. Waiting for the "Alert", we passed the day playing cards, some fished, others listened to records. The most popular type was "swing"; the discs had been "liberated" from France and they were listened to with great pleasure, ignoring the ban on this kind of music. My first combat mission petered out: I. Gruppe were badly directed, and we returned disappointed. The second was certainly more eventful. On 22nd April the Gruppe was scrambled. The Stab took off first, then each Staffel in turn, Schwarm by Schwarm. Like a long ribbon, our formation climbed for sufficient altitude. I was far from being afraid. It was a new, exciting experience. We attacked the Viermots head-on. After this pass our formation was split up, but I managed to join a comrade who appeared to have been hit. After that, I can't remember anything. My aircraft was hit, almost certainly by our own Flak. In spite of the danger of explosion, and the orders of his superiors, a Feldwebel from a nearby battery succeeded in getting me out of my burning Fw 190. I was hospitalised until 5th July".

On 24th April the unit sufferred no losses in combat and recorded claims over B-17s by, among others, Oberleutnant Georg Eder, Leutnant Hans Berger and Oberfeldwebel Georg Hutter. There was also a probable claimed over a Thunderbolt by Unteroffizier Fritz Haspel of 8th Staffel.

Five days later, the complete Geschwader, including 27 Fw 190s of II. Gruppe, took off shortly before 10:00

This Fw 190 A shows clearly the lack of continuation of the black and white bands onto the lower engine panels.

22nd April 1944 was a notable day for II. Gruppe. Shortly after landing after combat, Major Bär took off once again. He returned 27 minutes later with his 200th victory. These views show his victorious return.

The normal mount of Oberfeldwebel Leo Schuhmacher, "Red 23". Major Heinz Bär recorded his 200th victory in this machine.

Rheine, spring 1944. Major Bär (centre, with back to camera) converses with pilots of 6th Staffel. To his right is Oberleutnant Eder. On the left of the group are Oberfeldwebels Bach and Schuhmacher.

Fw 190 A of I. Gruppe in early 1944.

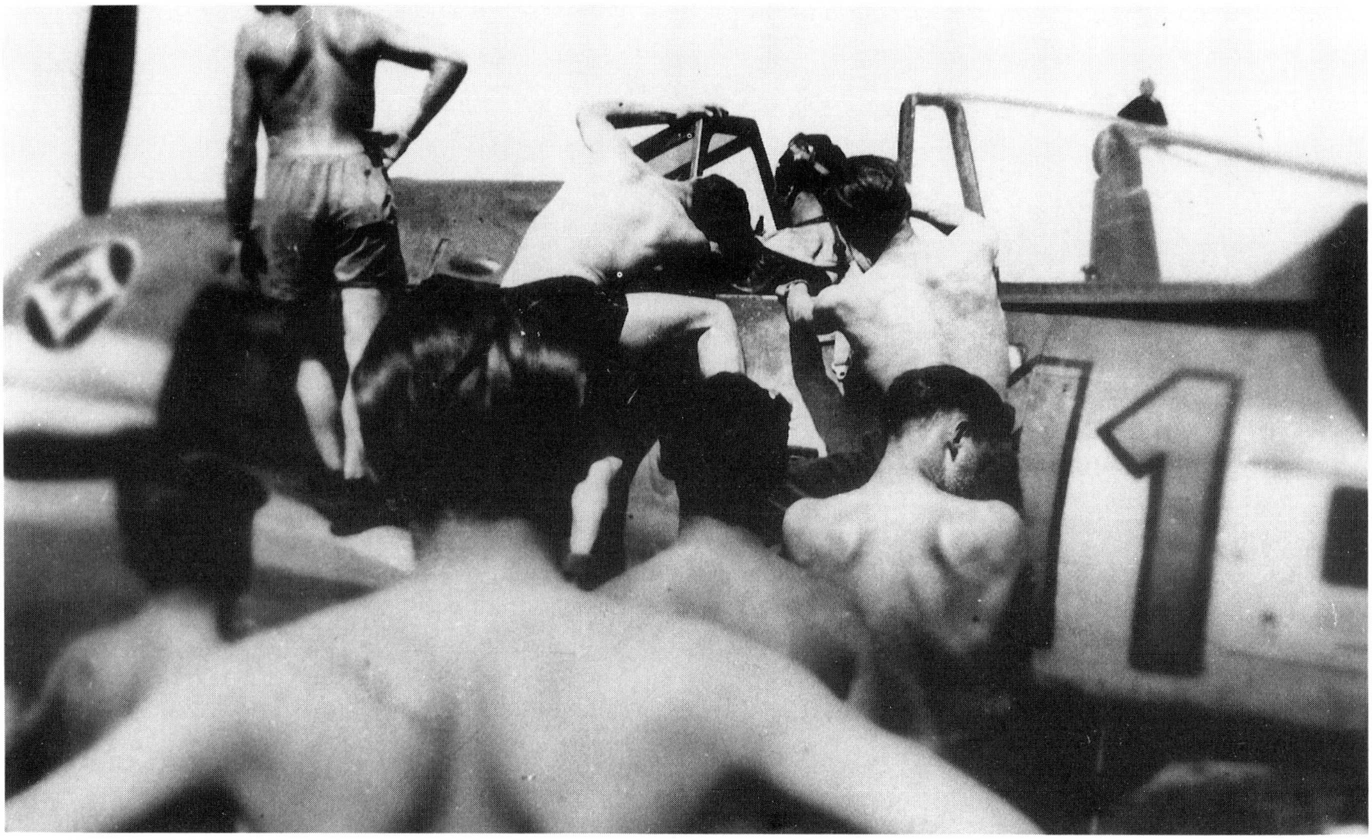

A pilot of 6th Staffel upon return from combat in "Yellow 11" in the spring of 1944. This is possibly Oberfeldwebel Flecks, who brought down two P-47s on 22/4/44.

hours. Although 6th Staffel lost two pilots, there were fresh victories for Bär (a P-47 and a B-24), Eder (a P-47 and a B-17) and von Kirchmayr in two actions (a P-47, a B-17 and a B-24). The latter two were recorded at 13:15 hours. Von Kirchmayr took off from Salzwedel at the head of a Schwarm to catch the bombers on the return flight. He recorded the 700th victory of II. Gruppe, and the 195th of 5th Staffel. Oberfeldwebel Hübl also claimed a B-17 at 11:01 hours.
Heinz Bär reported: "On 29/4/44 I was at cockpit readiness in my "Red 13". I took off with the Gruppe at 09:40 hours. In concert with I. and III. Gruppe, we headed in the direction of Kassel, via Paderborn, and reached 7,000 metres. On a course of 130 degrees in the Hannover region we saw the enemy formation made up of Boeings and Liberators with a strong fighter escort. They were heading due east. We gained height and opened our attack near Brunswick. After I had shot down a Liberator, our formation, assailed by the fighter escort, entered into a merciless combat. I tried to regain height in a sharp climb. At this moment, above me, I spotted a Fw 190 with its right undercarriage leg hanging down. It was being chased by a Thunderbolt. I got directly behind the latter and opened fire at a distance of 150 metres. The P-47 exploded. Its debris was scattered to the south of Brunswick. It was 10:56 hours. Height 7500m. Witness: Ofw. Schuhmacher".
For the moment, the main aim of the allied airforces was the preparation for landings, a decisive stage in the liberation of Europe. The communications network of the occupiers had to be destroyed, or at least seriously disrupted. The superiority of the allies was overwhelming, but on the German side, the units on "Defence of the Reich" duties and the Western front were being reinforced.
Profiting from a relative calm in the East, the Luftwaffe was able to amass some 1,675 aircraft in Germany and the western countries. All the units based in the west were however quite worn out in dealing with a fighter escort. The first half of 1944 was a murderous time for the day fighters: from January to May nearly 1850 fighter pilots had been killed. Each unit was regularly weakened by the loss of experienced officers. For example, Jagdgeschwader 2 lost two Kommodore (Oberstleutnant Mayer and Major Ubben) in just less than two months. These type of experienced flyers would be sorely missed when the allied invasion began on the Normandy coast. An order was issued to German pilots to evade combat with the escort fighters. The bombers remained the primary objective. From then on, the allied fighters, whose range allowed them to reach every corner of the Reich, could fly almost with impunity. Their numbers and their quality contributed to their forming a screen for the bombers which became harder and harder to penetrate.
On 8th May Berlin and Brunswick were the targets for 807 bombers escorted by 729 fighters. Towards 08:40 hours, the three Gruppen took off and assembled over Paderborn. Four B-24s and one B-17 were claimed by the pilots of II. Gruppe, the familiar names of Eder, von Kirchmayr and Schuhmacher among the claimants.
I. Gruppe were involved mainly with B-24s. Unteroffizier Geberth of 1st Staffel shot down one and recorded a Herauschuss over another. Feldwebel Just also shot down a B-24 while other pilots of his Staffel were credited jointly with bringing down another. Oberfeldwebel Piffer was victorious over a P-51 and Oberfeldwebel Hübl, a B-17.
At 11:42 hours von Kirchmayr took off once again with his wingman and shot down a further B-17. His companion, Flieger Blech, shot down a P-51 over Cloppenburg. On the debit side, seven pilots were killed and five others wounded, Oberfeldwebel Rudolf Hübl being among the wounded after adding a further B-17 to his tally.

Each victory claimed by a Luftwaffe pilot had to be confirmed and accepted by the Oberkommando der Luftwaffe. This often took several months and on many occasions the pilot had been lost in the meantime. This is an example of the confirmation form received, in this instance, by Oberleutnant Helmut Biederbick of 2nd Staffel.

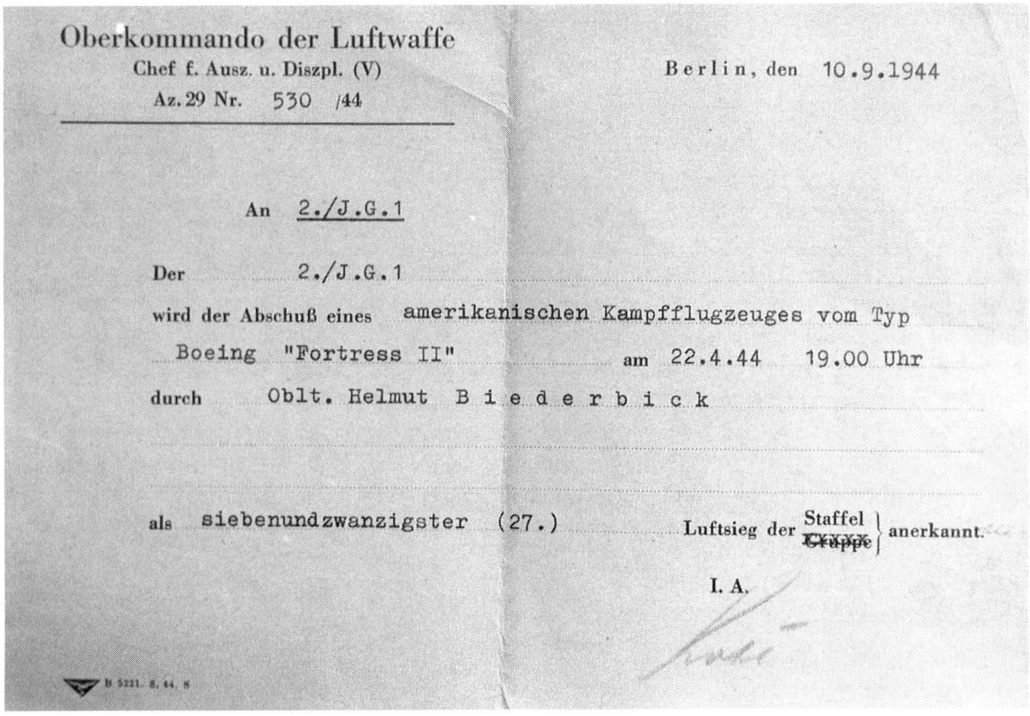

Oberkommando der Luftwaffe
Chef f. Ausz. u. Diszpl. (V)
Az. 29 Nr. 530 /44

Berlin, den 10.9.1944

An 2./J.G.1

Der 2./J.G.1
wird der Abschuß eines amerikanischen Kampfflugzeuges vom Typ
Boeing "Fortress II" am 22.4.44 19.00 Uhr
durch Oblt. Helmut Biederbick

als siebenundzwanzigster (27.) Luftsieg der Staffel ~~Gruppe~~ anerkannt.

I. A.

May 1944, Störmede. Fw 190 A-8s of 6th Staffel carrying the Geschwader emblem and defence of the Reich band. Note the light fuselage camouflage on "Yellow 5", which is somewhat unusual.

JG 1 "OESAU"

11th May 1944 was a black day for Jagdgeschwader 1. The 8th USAAF carried out their 350th Bombing mission (since their first raid in mid-August 1942), with an attack in the area of north-eastern Belgium and Luxemburg. Nearly 900 bombers took part, and the fighter escort flew over 1,000 sorties. At Paderborn, the Bf 109 Gs of Stab and III. Gruppe took off, Kommodore Walter Oesau leading off three aircraft of the Stabsschwarm. Oesau, with 125 victories to his credit, was taking off on what was to prove his final action: "The four machines of the Stabsschwarm were diving towards the bombers when they were pounced on by a horde of American fighters, the majority being P-38s. Oesau was forced into a circling combat, alone against five aircraft. His wingmen, themselves fully occupied in action, could do nothing to help him. Trying to escape his opponents, and defend himself, Oesau progressively lost height". Oberfeldwebel Leo Schuhmacher recalled: "Several times I had said to Oesau that the Fw 190 was better than the Bf 109, but being an old pilot of the 109, he preferred it. On 11th May Bär remained on the ground because of technical problems and Oesau led the formation totalling thirty aircraft. At high altitude we spotted the enemy fighters and Oesau ordered me over the radio to take II. Gruppe with me. As I was later told by his wingman, a young Oberfeldwebel, Oesau was attacked by P-51s who forced him into a turning dogfight. Each turn became tighter, and the Bf 109 slowed down, more so than his adversaries. Oesau was probably shot down near the ground. I saw Oesau's body: the whole left side appeared to have been hit by a burst. Thus wounded he no doubt tried to carry out a makeshift landing".

The remains of his Bf 109 G-6 AS, "Green 13" were found several kilometres from St. Vith. Not far away, his body was found - it had been flung clear on impact. Major Bär had the sad task of identifying it. Several years after the war, Major Hartmann Grasser also commented on the loss of Oesau: "At that time, Oesau was physically and mentally exhausted. The German fighter pilots, like their officers, had to fight right through the war, without respite. I consider it a grave error on the part of our High Command. I personally took part in the combat when Oesau was lost. Alone, chased by Lightnings and Mustangs, he had no chance of escaping. Neither did we. It was in this way that we lost the majority of the best among us."

Much research has been carried out to establish Oesau's victor. Nothing certain has been resolved. One theory is that the canopy was hit during the attack on the bombers by a shell fired by the American, Colonel James

One of the last photographs of Oberst Walter Oesau. He is seen with Oberleutnant Hans Ehlers during a visit to I. Gruppe.

Kommodore Oesau chats with members of the Gruppenstab of II. Gruppe. From left to right: Hauptmann Stärk; Feldwebel Sauer; Oesau and unknown.

L. "Pappy" Doyle. Oesau tried to break off combat, and was followed by five P-38s, holding his own against them for ten minutes, before trying to land as a matter of urgency, and being shot down as a result. By a sad twist of fate, several hours after the disappearance of Oesau, a letter signed by Adolf Galland, the General of Fighters, arrived at the Stab of the unit. It was an order posting Oesau to the headquarters Staff of Galland. Too late! All that could be done was to honour the fallen hero. From henceforth the premier fighter unit would be called "Jagdgeschwader 1 Oesau".
Major Heinz Bär, the most experienced pilot, instantly became Kommodore. In effect he became Kommodore of Jagdgeschwader 3, as he remained with Jagdgeschwader 1 for another ten days only before moving to his new unit. Oberleutnant Georg Eder became Gruppenkommandeur of II. Gruppe in the interim. He had a heavy responsibility, as the day following the loss of Oesau, the 8th Air Force launched a major raid into eastern Germany.
12th May cost the unit seven pilots killed (including the promising Unteroffizier Stiegler) and two wounded. However the balance was somewhat redressed by a victory for Eder (a B-24) and five other pilots of II. Gruppe, who laid claim to a B-24, three Herauschüsse and a P-47.
A week later, on 19th May towards mid-day, the unit gathered over Paderborn to face a further raid on Berlin. The escort managed to prevent the first head-on attack. The Germans turned east before launching a second frontal attack. Oberleutnant "Schorch" Eder continued his success, adding a B-24 and two P-47s to his score. Four other P-47s were claimed by pilots of II. Gruppe, including Oberfähnrich Swoboda and Oberfeldwebel Schuhmacher.
Walter Oesau's successor was another top quality fighter pilot. Like those who had preceeded him (Philipp, Oesau and Bär), he had received the highest awards of the German forces: the Ritterkreuz with Oakleaves and Swords. Officially named Kommodore of Jagdgeschwader 1 on 20th May 1944, Oberstleutlant Herbert Ihlefield had great experience of command. Jagdgeschwader 1 was the fifth unit of which he had taken command. Over 1,000 combat missions since the Spanish Civil War; nearly 130 victories, including 15 Viermots.
Another notable change occurred within the unit: in III. Gruppe the Gruppenkommandeur, Major Hartmann

Major Bär's Fw 190 A-8, "Red 13", with its rudder decoration showing 200 victories.

Two views of a Fw 190 A-6, "Yellow 13" of Oberleutnant von Kirchmayr. Note the Defence of the Reich band and the II. Gruppe bar on it.

Oberst Walter Grabmann, Commander of 3rd Jagddivision under whose control JG 1 came, frequently visited the unit. Here he is seen (centre) with Bär (left) and Oesau in front of his personal Fw 190, "White X".

Excellent view of Unteroffizier Erwin Steeb in his Fw 190 A in the spring of 1944.

This view shows two of the most successful pilots of II. Gruppe; Oberfeldwebel Leo Schuhmacher is on the extreme left, and Oberleutnant von Kirchmayr on the extreme right. Both would receive the Ritterkreuz in the last weeks of the war. Between them are Unteroffizier Hauptmann (second from left) and Oberfeldwebel Dietrich (third from left).

Grasser passed command over to another veteran of the "Legion Condor" - 32 year-old Hauptmann Erich Woitke, formerly of Jagdgeschwader 3 and 52. Hauptmann Woitke was a veritable phenomenon: an athlete, 1.85 metres tall, he had taken part in the 1936 Olympics in the decathlon. In action from the start of the war, he had been demoted several times due to his straight-talking nature. On the last occasion, after having received the "German Cross in Gold" from Göring personally, he threw it to the ground while making disparaging remarks. On each occasion, his courage and experience in combat resulted in his eventual advancement once again.
On 24th May Jagdgeschwader 1's strength was as follows:

Stab	Bad Lippspringe	no aircraft on strength;
I. Gruppe	Bad Lippspringe	28 aircraft (11 available)
II. Gruppe	Störmede	27 aircraft (16 available)
III. Gruppe	Paderborn	48 aircraft (21 available)

10 Fw 190s of II. Gruppe took off from Salzwedel and formed up with Jagdgeschwader 3. Because of intense flak, an assault Gruppe was not able to be formed. Attacks were therefore made in pairs or Schwarm formation. A B-17 each was claimed by Leutnant Bach and Oberleutnant von Kirchmayr; the latter's claim, however was not confirmed. III. Gruppe was also in action, with Leutnant Koplik, who had moved to 9th Staffel, claiming a B-17 and one of his comrades a P-38.
On 25th May I. and III. Gruppen were in action, Leutnant Koplik recording his 3rd victory in 12 days: a P-51.
On 28th May, the three Gruppen of the unit took off at 13:05 hours and assembled over Paderborn led by Oberleutnant von Kirchmayr. II. Gruppe returned an impressive score, claiming eight B-17s. In Stab, III. Gruppe, Leutnant Halbey recorded his second victory, a P-51. However losses were high: three wounded and three killed, including the experienced Oberfeldwebel Fritz Timm in Bf 109 G-6, "Yellow 3", who had moved from I. Gruppe to III. Gruppe when the latter Gruppe was formed.
On 29th May from 08:15 hours, the German listening monitored bombers forming up over Ipswich. At 11:01 hours after waiting for a quarter of an hour in their aircraft, 20 pilots of II. Gruppe took off towards Paderborn. They formed up there with the other two Gruppen of the unit. At mid-day the unit located the enemy. After flying parallel to the force for several minutes, speed was increased, the bombers were overtaken and the Ger-

Oberfeldwebel Ottto Bach of 5th Staffel climbs out of his Fw 190 A-7 at Rheine in early 1944. Note the flame dampers over the machine guns on top of the engine cowling.

man formation turned in for a frontal attack. Oberleutnant Eder, Leutnant Bach and Leutnant Swoboda, as well as two of their comrades of II. Gruppe shot down five B-17s. II. Gruppe also claimed four Herauschüsse. Short of fuel, three Fw 190 landed at Cottbus. A pilot was killed on landing, while Eder and Bach were wounded.
At the end of spring 1944, the German Air Ministry decided to reinforce all the units based in the west. I. Gruppe were supplemented by 9th Staffel, Jagdgeschwader 77 of Oberleutnant Wolfgang Ernst, a veteran of that unit since 1941. Recently wounded in combat over Rumania, he left convalescence to take up his new posting at an airfield near Uelzen where his pilots were to be trained on the Fw 190 A-8. Jagdgeschwader 77 had only flown the Bf 109. The conversion was completed in three days.
7th Staffel, Jagdgeschwader 51 were allocated to II. Gruppe. The order to transfer reached them at Terestopol near Brest-Litwosk where the front was fairly calm. The Staffelkapitän was Ritterkreuzträger Hauptmann Karl-Heinz Weber. With 136 victories in the east, he would soon succeed Major Bär as Gruppenkommandeur of II. Gruppe. Pilots started arriving at the II. Gruppe airfield of Störmede on 29th May. Here also, the pilots had to adjust from flying the Bf 109 to the Fw 190. This transition passed without any major problems as the Staffel had previously flown the Fw 190.
III. Gruppe were provided with bomber pilots who had converted to fighters, a transfer which became more prevalent as losses mounted in the Jagdwaffe. These bomber pilots often did not have the experience or qualities required of fighter pilots. Therefore these excellent bomber pilots were converted to a rôle which was unfamiliar to them. 1st Staffel, Kampfgeschwader 2 released 62 Unteroffiziere and ground personnel to III. Gruppe. They became effective from mid-October.
These three reinforcement Staffeln were re-named 4th, 8th and 12th Staffel from 15th July. These changes did not take effect until September. The men had other matters to occupy them.

A Fw 190 A of the Gruppenstab of II. Gruppe in the spring of 1944, probably at Rheine.

Fw 190 A-7, "Yellow 7", of Unteroffizier Walter Köhne of 3rd Staffel in the spring of 1944. Note the name beneath the cockpit.

Fw 190 A,"White 7" of 1st Staffel with a name under the cockpit in similar written form to that shown on the previous photograph.

Fw 190 A-7 of 6th Staffel receiving maintenance inthe spring of 1944.

Fw 190 A of 3rd Staffel having a propellor put in place.

INVASION FRONT - JUNE 1944

On 6th June 1944 the allied landings took place in Normandy. Certainly, everybody waited for such an attack, but the date and place was not known. Once it had started, orders were sent out immediately, but with little effectiveness. Hundreds of possibilities were studied: for every case there was an opposite argument. Previously planned troop movements were put into effect.
With regard to the German fighter force, the General Staff had counted on calling upon 1,000 aircraft to combat the allied airforces. At 05:00 hours on the morning of 6th June, Stab, I. Gruppe received the following coded message: "Einsatz West - Einsatzort Le Mans" : "Combat West - Operations Base Le Mans". Half an hour later, Gruppenkommandeur Hauptmann Ehlers assembled his officers and gave the order to prepare to leave the airfield of Bad Lippspringe. Several hours later, 31 Focke-Wulf 190 A-8s took off for Montdidier, a stopping-off place on the journey. Early the following day they reached Le Mans. Hauptmann Ludwig Siegfried, supply officer of the Gruppe, took command of fifteen wagons from the supply depot. He did not reach Le Mans until the evening of 9th June. A further two days were required for the majority of the equipment.
In the late afternoon of 6th June, several Ju 52s taking technicians and important equipment took off from Bad Lippspringe. Arriving in the Coulommiers area (40 kilometres to the east of Paris), the formation was intercepted by British night-fighters. A Ju 52, with sixteen members of ground personnel on board (including Leutnant Sommer, the Intelligence Officer of I. Gruppe) was shot down. The other aircraft set down quickly as a matter of urgency.
On 6th June, II. Gruppe left Störmede for Normandy. "Major Bär, recently transferred to Jagdgeschwader 3, alerted us by telephone that the invasion had begun. He advised us to prepare to move to the front. Our 32 Focke-Wulfs took off from Störmede at 16:25 hours. We had a re-fuelling stop-over at Mondidier. This airfield did not have sufficient re-fuelling vehicles, so we had to stay overnight. On the following day, shortly after take-off, we were advised by radio that Flers, the airfield we were heading for, had been bombed. We therefore had to set course for Le Mans. When we arrived, there was indescribable chaos: the ground was completely covered by the sudden influx of masses of aircraft." - Leutnant Fritz Wegner, 5th Staffel.
The Normandy campaign for II. Gruppe began at 18:00 hours on 6th June. Seventeen Bf 109 G-6s carried out a transfer flight of 55 minutes from Paderborn to Beauvais. Before the invasion, a high-altitude unit had been created. It comprised of four Gruppen, whose rôle it was to

Oberleutnant Alfred Grislawski, Staffelkapitän of 1st Staffel, watches a mechanic work on his Fw 190 A-7. Note the flame dampers on this machine as well as the armoured windscreen. This aircraft also carries the red "defence of the Reich" band on the rear fuselage, and the lower engine cowling panels in red. The spinner appears to be in the Staffel colour of white.

On 9th June 1944 Oberleutnant Hans Ehlers of I. Gruppe received the Ritterkreuz. He celebrates the event here with ground personnel and female companion.

take on the bomber escort. III./JG 1; I./JG 5 and II./JG 11 were the units involved. Placed under the control of Oberst Herbert Ihlefeld, they often occupied the same airfield. Nevertheless, III. Gruppe often operated independently.
The day of 7th June began tragically at Le Mans: groundcrew of I. Gruppe arrived totally exhausted during the night, and slept in the aircraft. In the early morn, American fighter-bombers attacked the base and machine-gunned several Ju 52s. Ten bodies were recovered from the fuselages.
Simultaneously, 7th Staffel, Jagdgeschwader 51, destined to join II. Gruppe, left their base to the north of Paris. At a height of about 600 metres, the last Schwarm was attacked by Mustangs. Hit, Leutnant Johann Brünnler had to leave the formation. Six P-51s pursued him. His colleagues, hampered by additional equipment in their cockpits, formed a defensive circle. They were too occupied in defending themselves, and could do nothing for Brünnler. His body, and the wreckage of his Fw 190 A-8, were found near Chateaudun. After extricating themselves from the assault of the Mustangs, the pilots set down on a part of the famous automobile circuit of Le Mans. They made their quarters there.
On 7th June, on the ground as well as in the air, the centre of gravity of the battle was centred on Caen. I. and II. Gruppen twice flew escort to fighter-bombers. III. Gruppe carried out a mission in the same region and clashed with P-47s in the Rouen area, resulting in one pilot being wounded and Hauptmann Weber killed. Two pilots of 9th Staffel shot down a P-51 and a P-47.
During the whole campaign take-offs and landings were critical times for the German pilots: their bases were under continual surveillance. This was well illustrated on 7th June. P-47s shot down the Bf 109 G-6 of Gefreiter Penke as it was taking off from Beauvais. Penke was the pilot who had earlier the same day shot down the P-51.
On 8th June an astonishing order arrived at I. and II. Gruppe. It came as a result of a surprise discovery: an important bomb dump was at Le Mans with 250 kilogram bombs. As it was felt that these should be used, the two Gruppen were to take up the rôle of fighter-bombers. This at a time when some pilots even lacked the rudiments of formation flying!
"Astonishing and even depressing, we were to become fighter-bombers. None of us had received such training. From then, we were sent "Jabo" types, and someone from a Jabo unit arrived and read a text to us, which was supposed to teach us how to use aircraft with bombs.. They were suspended under the fuselage, attached to the connecting point for the supplementary fuel tank. Under these conditions, reaching Normandy from Le Mans was no easy matter. It was necessary to economise on fuel, and above all avoid being intercepted. To

On 11th June III. Gruppe lost many aircraft following a raid on their base at Beauvais. The pilots returned to Wunsdorf to re-equip. It was there that General Galland visited them.

surprise the enemy, we flew due north over the coast. We hoped to come at them from behind. The coast could be clearly seen ahead. Trouville and Deauville. Obviously we had an embarassment of choice of targets, but the anti-aircraft fire from the ships was intense. The sky was saturated with the black puffs of Flak. I attacked a ship, but what could a measly 250 kilogram bomb do against such a giant. After the attack, we headed due south at low level to pick up course for Le Mans. Judging by the shouts over the radio, the red lamps on the fuel gauges were lighting up soon afterwards. We finally reached Le Mans. I seem to recall that two of our pilots did not return from this attack." - Leutnant Fritz Wegner.
The results of this attack were insignificant. Two other missions of this type, without incident, were carried out on 9th June by first twelve, then ten, Fw 190s of II. Gruppe. I. Gruppe was only able to carry out a single mission carrying bombs.
On 8th June III. Gruppe lost its Gruppenkommandeur when his Bf 109 G-6 was shot down near Pont Laverne. Hauptmann Woitke bailed out but he dislocated both shoulders and was "hors de combat" for three months.

"In the evening of 9th June we joined our pilots based at Le Mans. I immediately camouflaged the vehicles in a wood. That proved to be sensible, as shortly afterwards at around 01:00 hours the airfield was the subject of a serious attack. On the airfield and its surroundings, about 50% of the Focke-Wulfs were either destroyed or badly damaged. Those which had escaped were grounded. There was no chance of taking off from the badly cratered field. All through the night we were active, seeking out the unexploded bombs, or watching for another raid. We spent the following hours with shovels and pickaxes to make the airfield serviceable (more than 300 craters were counted). After becoming serviceable again, I. Gruppe was finally able to take off for the airfield at Cuissai, several kilometres to the north-west of Alençon. Of the airfield, it was that in name only. It consisted of two large fields joined one to the other by a small road. On 12th June after a lot of work, this "base" was operational. These were our famous preparations for combating the invasion" - Hauptmann Ludwig Siegfried, Oberzahlmeister, I. Gruppe.
In fact, on 10th June at 01:00 hours, RAF bombers, Pathfinder Mosquitos and 109 Lancasters and Halifaxes successfully bombed Le Mans aerodrome.
"The situation of our II. Gruppe during combat on the invasion front was certainly desperate. I know it was the same for the neighbouring units. When we landed, after the senseless "Jabo" attacks, there were nearly always enemy aircraft circling over the aerodrome. That was when we had to run like rabbits. For several days, we only ate tinned meat, like tinned beef. Morning, mid-day and evening. Occasionally, our cook would be able to bring us eggs. He would place them carefully in what served as a kitchen. During the night, as though helping us to make omelettes, the Americans would come to bomb us. After they left, the airfield was no more than a cratered field with unexploded bombs strewn around it. They could do it with impunity. The following day, we discovered that one of them had singled out the kitchen! We could see, just to one side, a plate of intact eggs. There followed a serious discussion: we were hungry. Suddenly Swoboda and I sprinted to take possession of the plate. We returned to the cheers of our comrades" - Leutnant Fritz Wegner, 5th Staffel.
The Fw 190s of II. Gruppe dispersed 500 metres east of the aerodrome were spared. Nevertheless the pilots were unable to take off due to the state of the airfield. On 12th June, after being repaired, twelve Fw 190 A-8s of I. Gruppe took off and took up residence in a field at Cuissai/Lonrai, near to Alençon. They were progressively brought up to strength, reaching 32 Fw 190s twelve days later. In the afternoon of 12th June I. Gruppe flew two patrols.
Shortly after, II. Gruppe took possession of a small improvised airstrip on the edge of the village of Essay, situated ten kilometres from Cuissai.
On 9th and 10th June, III. Gruppe launched several missions from Beauvais. On 11th June, 2nd Bomb Division of the 8th USAAF sent 584 B-24s to several French aerodromes. The base of Beauvais-Tille was

attacked by twelve B-24s, who dropped thirty tons of bombs. The headquarters of the unit was destroyed, as well as numerous aircraft of III. Gruppe, who then progressively returned its pilots to Wunstorf in order to re-equip. In ten days they had lost a half-dozen men, including the experienced Oberfeldwebel Gustav Dilling. The revitalised Gruppe did not reappear until July. By contrast, the Geschwaderstab remained in France, albeit without aircraft. On 15th June it was to be found at Clastres, near St. Quentin.
Large formations of German fighters were inevitably spotted by the allies. For that reason, the German pilots usually operated in small numbers on "free chase" missions. On 13th June, at 19:00 hours, eight Fw 190s of I. Gruppe were in action in the St. Lô/Ste. Mère Eglise region. Leutnant Siegfried Stoffel and Unteroffizier Walter Dobrath, both of 1st Staffel, recorded I. Gruppe's first victories of the campaign: two Thunderbolts. The two sorties of the 14th were uneventful, but those of the following day in the region of Ste. Mère Eglise and Carenten brought four victories to four of the most effective pilots of June: an Auster for Leutnant Anton-Rudolf Piffer and three Thunderbolts for Leutnant Siegfried Stoffel, Unteroffizier Fritz Rathofer and Unteroffizier Walter Dobrath. However two pilots of I. Gruppe were killed.
On 16th June six Spitfires were credited to I. Gruppe following combat over a German column in the Valognes sector. Leutnant Piffer shot two down, with Stoffel, Rathofer and Dobrath victorious again. During the combat Unteroffizier Fritz Hofmann of 3rd Staffel shot down a Spitfire, but had to bail out at a height of 150 metres. Wounded and taken to hospital, he was posted missing by the unit owing to the poor state of communications at the time. He did not return to the unit until October. The letter sent to his parents by Staffelkapitän Horst Maier describes the action: "In the region of Caen-Tilly, known for its violent combats, my unit was attacked at about 300 metres by six Spitfires with superior height. All the enemy aircraft were shot down, but they managed to shoot down two of ours. The pilots saw one bail out. The parachute opened, and we overflew where he landed. We hope that he survived.
"In spite of intensive checks, we still do not have news of Fritz, which has obliged me to report him as missing. The possibility remains that having been saved by his parachute, he is presently in hospital, and communication difficulties prevent us from knowing more...".
On the following day Fritz Rathofer claimed a "probable" Mustang, but the road came to an end for the young Austrian, Anton-Rudolf Piffer. Thunderbolts caught him unaware in his Fw 190 A-8 "White 3" near Argentan. He was posthumously awarded the Ritterkreuz on 20th October 1944 for his 26 victories in the west. Among the victories were 20 four-engined bombers as well as three aircraft in the Normandy campaign.
"The Gruppenkommandeur of our Gruppe, Hauptmann Hans Ehlers, was really exceptional. Always leading his men, he cared for them individually, in the sky as well as on the ground. One day our secretary told me that he had seen bizarre signals from a neighbouring hill through his binoculars. On the following day our Gruppenkommandeur assembled about 20 volunteers and set to see what it was about. They found no-one, only branches set out in such a way as to be able to guide aircraft, and evidence of several impacts on the ground. Obviously materials had been dropped for partisans, and this only a short distance from our base. The fact was quickly confirmed, for two or three days later we were fired upon by machine guns from an apparently harmless car. The bullets spread everywhere, but no-one was wounded. Likewise our precious radio-wagons parked nearby also escaped damage. Ehlers immediately set up a heavy machine gun battery to protect the site.
"It was also around this time, on the morning of 17th June, that he found me and said: "Siegfried, a bottle of Champers, I have just been awarded the "Dödel", (the slang term applied to the "Ritterkreuz"). At the time he had 52 victories, including 20 Viermots. Several days later, two Mosquitos flew over the airfield. Flying at a height of 50 metres, they dropped six bombs. Ehlers told us not to disturb the craters: the Staffeln, passing to the left and right of them, could still take-off and land. A sensible direction because Mosquitos frequently passed over our camouflaged installations without realising our activities continued" - Hauptmann Ludwig Siegfried, Oberzahlmeister, I. Gruppe.
On 17th June, the 8th USAAF launched a fresh series of attacks on the airfields used by German aircraft. Lonrai and Essay were among the targets. The latter was badly damaged, and II. Gruppe had to move to Semallé several kilometres distant.
"We put in a lot of effort to get our airfield into shape. Everything had not been finished when, on 17th June, a

View of Fw 190s of II. Gruppe destroyed on the ground at Semallé on 25th June 1944 by allied fighter-bombers. The German pilots had to return to Germany to re-equip.

new attack caught us by surprise. The Viermots were flying due south. We thought they were heading for Paris. Suddenly someone shouted: "Listen, the noise is increasing!" We then saw the enemy aircraft execute a turn and fly right over the airfield from the south. At this moment, sitting on a case of bombs, I was discussing our next mission. I shouted: "Everyone head south off the airfield!" The men jumped into a wagon, which took off like a whirlwind! I was unable to catch it up. I was trapped, and was soon joined by an old soldier. We had only a few seconds to get as far away as possible from our own bombs. We were going to receive enough of them! Hardly had we flattened ourselves on the ground than the heavens opened on us. An eternity later, we were still alive, but in a different world. Everything was in chaos. Our case of bombs had certainly vanished. An hour passed before the men returned. They did not think they would find us alive" - Leutnant Fritz Wegner, 5th Staffel.

On the same day, 7th Staffel, Jagdgeschwader 51 lost three pilots during a combat with about twenty Mustangs near Alençon. The fact that a mechanic was found in one of the Fw 190s led one to believe that a small group were moving to a new base. Activities re-commenced on 20th June.

"After changing base, our formation was dispersed in the Alençon region. My Schwarm settled in the large grounds of a château. There were four pilots and we lodged in tents near the aircraft, which were hidden in a wood. On the other side of the airfield another Schwarm led the same lifestyle: three or four times a day the telephone would ring with orders for a mission. The experience gained on the eastern front was beneficial: there we had always fought in small formations against the elite pilots of the "Red Guard". We quickly learned the rules for survival in Normandy. Mustangs and Thunderbolts continually circled and dived as soon as they saw their prey. The only possibility of escaping them was to bank and engage them in a turning dogfight. Nerves of steel were required. Pilots who tried to flee had no chance; the Americans would catch them in seconds. Typhoons, Tempests and Spitfires were the aircraft which were capable of dogfighting. Combat was more equal (than on the Russian front) even if the enemy were superior by five or six times more.

"The Flak which covered the invasion fleet was impressive. But it was nothing compared to that which protected Leningrad. The allies profited from the quantity of their materials; the Russians used what they had with remarkable precision" - Leutnant Günther Heckmann, 7th Staffel, Jagdgeschwader 51.

On 20th June, II. Gruppe and its supplementary Staffel, 7./JG 51, joined up with I. Gruppe. At 08:30 hours eight Fw 190 A-8s of 7./JG 51 and four of I. Gruppe took off for a free chase mission over the coast. A sharp combat with Lightnings soon ensued. Unteroffizier Walter Dobrath recorded his 4th and 5th victories, the latter coming as a result of colliding with a P-38. Three other Lightnings were claimed, Leutnant Siegfried Stoffel being among

Three views of the Bf 109 G-6/AS, "Black 14", of Unteroffizier Hugo Hausotter of 8th Staffel, seen at La Fère in July 1944. In this aircraft he shot down a Spitfire on 25th July, but had to bail out a few seconds later after being hit in turn.

An outstanding pilot of JG 1 was Hauptmann Alfred Grislawski, Staffelkapitän of 8th Staffel. He left the unit at the end of the Normany campaign to become Staffelkapitän of 11th Staffel, JG 53.

the claimants. However several German pilots were lost. Dobrath's fourth victory was probably the Lightning of 307th Fighter Group piloted by Lieutenant Robert Rice. This Lightning became separated during the engagement, and there was no American witness to what had happened. The aircraft crashed between Trun and Gacé, in the Argentan area. The fifth victory, which could only have been an accident, came shortly afterwards near Nonant-le-Pin. The victim, a Lightning of the same unit, was piloted by Lieutenant Roger. H. Wainwright. Lieutenant Lawrence Watson, who took part in the combat, remembered: "We were returning from an armed reconnaissance mission in the Le Mans region when our attention was drawn to enemy aircraft at seven o'clock. Coming out of the sun, they dived towards us. We took up defensive positions. Lieutenant Wainwright and myself turned towards the first Fw 190. I fired for ten seconds and then changed course. At that moment I saw a P-38 and a Fw 190 in flames diving towards the ground, the two left wings locked together. A parachute emerged, and I was convinced it was a German pilot. The two aircraft disappeared under the cloud base at 1,300 metres". Apart from the Fw190 attributed to Wainwright, Lawrence Watson, Lieutenant Horace Plummer and Captain James Gordy of 370th Group each claimed a Fw 190.

Five victories in Normandy were reached on 22nd June by Leutnant Siegfried Stoffel (a Thunderbolt), but he was killed in action the following day at around 22:00 hours near Alençon, during combat with 20 P-47s. In the afternoon of 23rd June, Oberfeldwebel Rudolf Hübl recorded his nineteenth and last victory with Jagdgeschwader 1. His formation of eight machines attacked two P-51s near Caen at 15:30 hours. One German and one American were shot down.

In I. Gruppe, Dobrath was wounded, Stoffel killed, Hübl was wounded by Flak on 27th June and Rathofer was killed three days later after taking his Normandy score to five. The losses were heavy; by the evening of 30th June, I. Gruppe could only count on four serviceable Fw 190s.

With II. Gruppe things were not much better. Shortly after arriving at Semallé they received a further attack. On 25th June, at about 13:00 hours, fifteen Mustangs (although other reports say Thunderbolts) machine-gunned the airfield and destroyed fifteen Fw 190s. These aircraft proved difficult to replace. On the same evening twenty pilots took off in a Ju 52 and He 111 for Köln-Ostheim to seek out new Fw 190s. II. Gruppe was therefore out of action until mid-July. During this period Oberleutnant Georg Eder, Staffelkapitän of 6th Staffel, was awarded a well-deserved Ritterkreuz. He had 49 victories to his credit, the last being over a P-47 on 21st June near Le Mans. On 1st July he was promoted to Hauptmann and transferred to Jagdgeschwader 26.

These promotions and decorations were a necessary psychological boost. June had been a catastrophe for the Luftwaffe. After three weeks of combat it was on its knees. The Allies claimed the destruction of over 1,000 German aircraft. In numerous units the few experienced pilots had gone.

On 4th July, eleven Fw 190 A-8s of I. Gruppe and 7./JG 51 took off shortly before 14:00 hours. They met the Americans of 404th Fighter Group in the Coutances region. Combat was joined and three German pilots were shot down. Two were from 7./JG 51, including the Staffelführer, the Austrian Leutnant Friedrich Krakowitzer, who had 20 victories in the east. The third pilot lost, Unteroffizier Karl Grube, was missing until 1990, when his body was found in the remains of his aircraft.

I. Gruppe were grateful for the acquisition of an additonal Staffel, 9th Staffel, Jagdgeschwader 77. Led by Oberleutnant Wolfgang Ernst, 9./JG 77 joined I. Gruppe at Lonrai. Training for conversion from the Bf 109 to the Fw 190 had been poor: on average six hours flying per pilot, part of which was taken up with flying with a 250 kilogram bomb.

On 6th July four pilots of 9./JG 77 carried out their first Normandy mission. In conjunction with seven other

Invasion front, summer 1944. Officers of III. Gruppe relax in the shade of trees. From left: Dr. Bernd Kettner (Gruppe doctor); Hauptmann Marschall (Adjutant) and Oberleutnant Erich Buchholz, an old pilot of 5th Staffel who would later become Gruppenadjutant of III. Gruppe, and Staffelkapitän of 8th Staffel.

Wunsdorf in early July 1944. Hauptmann Woitke presents his men to General Galland. In the forthcoming days of action on the invasion front, most of these men would be shot down.

pilots, they took off at 15:35 hours for a patrol in the Nogent-le-Rotrou/Mamers region. The 9./JG 77 Schwarm suddenly found itself in the presence of four P-38s of 428 Fighter Squadron, USAAF, who were providing top cover for the 429th, who were on a strafing mission. A short and violent combat then ensued. Quickly, Captain John Hewitt, leading the Americans, ordered his pilots to break off combat in view of the presence of the other Fw 190s. However two of his P-38s had already been shot down in flames, by Oberleutnant Ernst and Feldwebel Loch. Simultaneously, a Fw 190 was shot down, and shortly afterwards another. The two German victims were Unteroffizier Maximov and his Staffelkapitän, Oberleutnant Ernst, who described the end of the engagement thus: "I had just shot down a P-38 when I, in turn, was hit. I had to bail out but I waited until the last second before jumping: we all knew the Americans did not hesitate to machine-gun our pilots hanging on their parachutes. I got out of the cockpit, and the air current caught me and I hit the rudder. My right arm was broken with the impact. Shortly afterwards the parachute canopy opened and I finally landed. My misgivings had not disappeared, as a group of civilians were heading towards the wood where I landed. Maquis? If they were, they were coming to finish me off. By chance, German Field Police arrived and the local populace disappeared". Oberleutnant Wolfgang Ernst underwent long months of

recovery, then moved to Jagdgeschwader 53. In the meantime almost all of his men of 9./JG 77 had been posted missing.
On the following day, 7th July, 9./JG 77 were re-named 4./JG 1. On this day, Leutnant Gerhard Hanf, who took over from Oberleutnant Ernst, shot down his first Thunderbolt of the campaign (he was to claim another on 30th July).
On 5th July, at 13:10 hours, III. Gruppe left Wunsdorf and returned to the front via Wiesbaden and Metz. The strength was again up to 50 pilots, but they were of doubtful quality due to inexperience. The officer-strength of the unit was weakened by the illness of the Staffelkapitän of 7th Staffel, Oberleutnant Lutz-Wilhelm Burckhardt, with malaria. A month later the Gruppe would lose Hauptmann Alfred Grislawski, moving from 8th Staffel to 11th Staffel, Jagdgeschwader 53."Recovered from the wound I received at the end of January 1944 when I was with I. Gruppe, I was appointed Staffelkapitän of 8th Staffel. Continuallly under surveillance, the situation in Normandy was unbearable. After landing we hurried to eat our rations. Half an hour later we were once again in the air defending our skin. I recall we all had stomach trouble.
"The "Amis" (the slang term given by German pilots to their American counterparts) circled above our airfields waiting for easy prey, which we were during take-offs and landings. One saw with helpless rage the enemy diving on our comrades and inflicting heavy losses. No-one was spared by the Americans, not even the pilot

Feldwebel Rudolf Rauhaus, after having flown with II. and III. Gruppe, and as wingman to Oesau, flew with the Stab, I. Gruppe during the Normany campaign. He was killed in action near Caen on 31/7/44.

Fw 190 A-8 of 5th Staffel in the summer of 1944 during the Normany campaign. Note the loose spiral on the spinner.

La Fère, July 1944. Leutnant Hans Düsterbeck, Nachrichtensoffizier of III. Gruppe, (right) chats with Feldwebel Herbert Kaiser, Ritterkreuzträger.

Posing on the steps of a château which served as their operations quarters are Leutnant Hubert Swoboda (left) of 5th Staffel and Leutnant Helmut Weissbrodt of 7./JG 51.

hanging on the end of his parachute. Soon we were sent back to Wunstorf, where the Gruppe was reorganised. Then we left for France again, being based to the south of Paris. There were hardly any officers. From day to day, young pilots became Leutnant, Staffelführer, and then eventually shot down. I had the feeling that I would follow my predecessors on the list of losses" - Hauptmann Alfred Grislawski, 8th Staffel.

Losses soon began to mount. On 12th July two pilots of the Gruppe were killed and Leutnant Kurt Ibing, formerly of II. Gruppe, was wounded. By contrast, Kommodore Ihlefield recorded a 'triplet', three Spitfires falling to his guns. Unteroffizier Moser (P-51) and Oberfeldwebel Kaiser (Spitfire) were also victorious.

On the 13th, towards 20:00 hours, a flight encountered a formation of Spitfires, Typhoons and Thunderbolts, and one pilot was killed. However two Typhoons were shot down by two of the most experienced pilots of the unit: Hauptmann Grislawski and Oberfeldwebel Kaiser.

On the 14th, Ihlefield claimed a P-51 and a Spitfire. Two other Spitfires, a P-47 (by Hauptmann Woitke) and a P-51 (by Hauptmann Grislawski) were also claimed by his men.

On the 18th, a further three pilots of III. Gruppe were killed in action, with Ihlefield and Woitke each claiming a P-38.

The 19th resulted in a major success for III. Gruppe. No less than seven Typhoons were shot down east of Caen at around 21:00 hours. Among the seven victorious pilots were Hauptmann Grislawski and Unteroffizier Hausotter, both of 8th Staffel.

On 20th July, 30 aircraft took off at 12:30 hours. Flying at 700 metres in the Brétigny region, the formation was taken by surprise by Spitfires and Thunderbolts. Seven pilots were lost (killed, missing or prisoners). In the evening a pilot of 7./JG 51, Gefreiter Johannes Kamutzki, was also lost during a transfer flight from Alençon to Le Mans.

On 23rd July in the early evening, 40 P-38s of the 370th Fighter Group were returning from a mission against the marshalling yards at Limours. They encountered ten Fw 190s of II. Gruppe. Fierce combat developed between Etampes and the south of Versailles. Four P-38s were shot down, their pilots killed. The Fw 190 A-7 of Unteroffizier Erich Rahner of 7./JG 51 was behind that of Oberfeldwebel Leo Schuhmacher. In his rear view mirror, Schuhmacher realised that something was wrong: the Fw 190 A-7 appeared out of control and the undercarriage was partly lowered. Schuhmacher shouted to the unfortunate pilot over the radio to make a wheels-up belly landing. The impact was to severe that Rahner was in a coma for three days. Schuhmacher belly-landed alongside his comrade. He enlisted the help of civilians and two soldiers to get the canopy off, save Rahner and take him to hospital in Chartres. It appeared that Rahner had lost consciousness due to fumes from the supplementary fuel tank seeping into the cockpit.

On 24th July, two pilots of 7th Staffel were killed in action against Spitfires near Caen, with Oberfeldwebel Kaniss of 8th Staffel recording two victories over P-38s.

On 25th July, the first patrol of III. Gruppe took off at 06:25 hours and attacked a formation of Spitfires over

Members of II. Gruppe in front of a Fw 190 A-8 in summer 1944.

Lisieux. Feldwebel Fritz Haspel of 8th Staffel was hit in the left arm by a burst. He managed to bail out but injured his legs on landing. Helped by a woman and child, he was handed over to German soldiers and taken to hospital. Kommodore Ihlefield was more fortunate on this day, recording victories over a Lancaster and a Spitfire. His last victory on the Invasion front would be a P-51 on 27th July. Other victors were Hauptmann Mätzke: Spitfire; Feldwebel Lau: P-51 and P-47 and Unteroffizier Esser: two P-47s.
The month of July had cost III. Gruppe fifteen pilots wounded or killed, mainly in the Caen area. On the other hand, the Gruppe had claimed a total of 30 victories.
I. Gruppe's situation was critical: on 25th July the Gruppe had no Fw 190s on charge. Thirty pilots were sent to Köln to take possession of new aircraft. Pilots and aircraft would return to France by the 29th.

Sorely tested during the Normandy campaign, II. Gruppe returned to Reinsehlen to 'rest and re-equip'. Commanding officers are seen in this view, from left to right: Oberleutnant Otto Bach (Staffelkapitän, 7th Staffel); Hauptmann Staiger (Gruppenkommandeur); Oberleutnant Wegner (Staffelführer, 6th Staffel); Hauptmann Ludewig (Staffelkapitän, 8th Staffel) and Leutnant Swoboda (Staffelführer, 5th Staffel).

Reinsehlen, late summer 1944. Pilots at the front of this group are, from right to left: Oberfeldwebel Hutter; unknown; Unteroffizier Weichard; unknown; Leutnant Swoboda; Oberfeldwebel Flecks; unknown; unknown and Leutnant Kremer.

AUGUST 1944 - RETREAT

Up to 1st August, the Germans had succeeded in containing the allied forces in the Cotentin peninsula. However the front broke and the allies broke through in the Avranches region. Heading northwards, they encircled important German forces in the Falaise pocket. The defence of France was crumbling; the route to the Seine and Paris was open. The French capital was liberated on 25th August.
For the German fighter units bled white, there was no possibility of remaining in France. On the ground, the allied troops quickly approached the airfields evacuated urgently. Fuel was not coming through. The same applied to replacement aircraft. The sky was black with aircraft carrying stars and cockades. German aircraft were run to ground everywhere.
At the beginning of August, at Lonrai, I. Gruppe could only call upon eleven serviceable Fw 190 A-8s. On 4th and 5th August, the Gruppe moved to Oysonville where they carried out two to three sorties a day. On 7th August at 14:10 hours, fifteen Fw 190 A-8s took off on a ground attack mission in the region of Courandes. The formation was intercepted by American fighters. Four German pilots were killed. Four hours later nine machines took off and gained revenge by shooting down three P-47s, one falling to the guns of Leutnant Emil Demuth, Staffelkapitän of 3rd Staffel. On 11th August I. Gruppe left Oysonville for Aulnay-aux-Planches, from where limited operations were conducted. On 22nd August they returned to Schleswig-Holstein in Germany for a period of rest.
It is difficult to arrive at an accurate balance sheet for I. Gruppe's action in Normandy. However, they lost around forty pilots (killed, wounded or prisoners) and claimed forty one victories.
During the Normany campaign, II. Gruppe lost fifteen pilots, most of these losses suffered in a terrible combat over St. Lô on 20th July. During August, missions became more rare as the Gruppe progressively retreated eastwards.
In contrast to II. Gruppe, III. Gruppe remained very active for the whole of August. It was placed under the control of Geschwaderstab, Jagdgeschwader 27 along with II./JG 6 and II./JG 11. Herbert Kaiser of 7th Staffel recalled: "We were regularly in action against the fighter-bombers attacking our ground troops. Take offs were carried out in small formations (two to four aircraft), since enemy fighters were always lying in wait above the clouds over our airfields. We only ever flew at a few metres above ground level, and more than one aircraft

struck small hills. We only gained height when preparing to attack. On one day, one of my three companions indicated a formation of Spitfires. At the point of taking up an attacking position, we were attacked by a second formation which shot down my companions in seconds. By chance, but also thanks to my experience, I escaped them".

On 30th July and 1st August, Oberfähnrich Heckmann of 9th Staffel distinguished himself by shooting down a Spitfire, then a P-51. During this latter combat his Staffel camarad, Unteroffizier Wolf also recorded a victory over a Mustang. Two days later, Wolf was victorious again, this time over a Spitfire.

On 5th August III. Gruppe moved to Brétigny airfield. The following day, twelve pilots took off at 11:45 hours to intercept about 100 Lancasters escorted by 150 fighters in the Paris area. Only four Germans returned. Fahnenjunker Oberfeldwebel Herbert Kaiser, a Ritterkreuzträger with 68 victories (of which six were gained with Jagdgeschwader 1), had to bail out. Colliding with the rudder, he was seriously wounded. Operations and convalescense kept him away from the front until February 1945. Two experienced pilots, Oberfeldwebel Zander of 8th Staffel and Oberleutnant Bilfinger of 7th Staffel were victorious: the former shot down a Lancaster; the latter a P-47.

On 7th August, two P-47s were claimed by two pilots of 7th Staffel, one being Oberleutnant Bilfinger. On the debit side, Oberfeldwebel Kaniss was wounded by a Thunderbolt after having probably shot down another.

On 10th August, towards 14:00 hours, two pilots of 8th Staffel claimed two victories over Typhoons shortly after taking off from Brétigny. Oberfeldwebel Friedrich Zander and Unteroffizier Hugo Hausotter were the successful pilots, the latter scoring his third and final victory. As with his second victory, Hausotter had to bail out several seconds after his victory.

On 12th August Hauptmann Grislawski recorded his last victory with Jagdgeschwader 1 - a Spitfire.

The wounded Hauptmann Erich Woitke was replaced by a pilot returning from convalescense, an old boy of the unit, Hauptmann Heinz Knoke. Knoke was surprised to hear that he would be succeeding his old boss from the days when they were in Jagdgeschwader 52 in 1941. The surprise was even greater when Knoke found out that Woitke had received no promotions since those days, this in spite of having numerous victories.

It was a long time since Hauptmann Knoke had slung bombs under his fighter and attacked B-17s in 1943! A Staffelkapitän in Jagdgeschwader 11, he had shown many of the required qualities since being given command, and to date he had nearly 30 victories, including 19 "Viermots". At the end of April 1944 he had been wounded in combat, and was not yet fully recovered. Nevertheless, it did not stop him recording a further seven victories and becoming one of the highest scorers of the French campaign.

"During the night of 13th and 14th August I reached the base of my new Gruppe by car. To my surprise I met up with my first commanding officer from the eastern campaign: Hauptmann Woitke. He received me warmly. The heavy strapping he had around his left shoulder and his body made him look like a medieval horseman.

"From the morning of the 14th I was in action with my new unit, and during a combat with six Thunderbolts near Rennes I managed to hit one, which then exploded in the air. On the way home, we attacked a column of enemy vehicles. I set one Jeep on fire.

"On the 15th, we carried out an escort to fighter-bombers and in the combat which ensued, I scored my 28th victory over a Thunderbolt. On the 16th, Spitfires attacked our base. I took off in pursuit and managed to shoot one down near Etampes".

On 17th August Knoke shot down a Lightning near the village of Auxonette, and later in the day a Marauder, with three others being claimed by his comrades. On the 18th two Mustangs were added to his score.

"On 27th August, in six unsuccessful attacks against heavily defended pontoon bridges over the Seine, we lost twelve aircraft, two of which were in a poor state. I flew one of them, my Adjutant, Obergefreiter Döring took the other. Unfortunately he crashed on take-off and was killed.

"Eventually we engaged about 60 Mustangs and Thunderbolts. My companions quickly disappeared and I found myself alone with my wingman, Unteroffizier Ickes, who stoically followed my desperate manoeuvres to shake off a pursuing Mustang. With a risky move, I was able to surprise him and turn the situation to my advantage. He went down in flames. Then came a terrible shaking! Debris from my victim hit my aircraft. I had no other option but to bail out. On the ground, I was able to pass myself off as an American to four Maquisards, and to eventually regain our lines. The allies had broken through near Soissons. That night we had to retreat towards Cerfontaine in Belgium. I found out, sadly, that Ickes also had to bail out but was machine gunned on his parachute and was found dead on the ground" - Heinz Knoke.

"On that day, Knoke, Ickes, Döring, Freydank and myself were in action. Döring placed himself in front of me for take-off, but I signalled to him that I would go before him. He only had a few more seconds to live: his left wing touched the ground, the aircraft turned over and exploded. When the groundcrew arrived, it was already too late. We circled over the airfield, but his aircraft was just a heap of burning metal. The remaining aircraft joined up; I flew close to Knoke. We headed for Compiègne. At a height of 3,500 metres we sighted eight Mustangs, who first of all thought we were friendly aircraft. We turned left, and the enemy also turned. At a distance of between 400 and 500 metres they hit us with their first burst. My aircraft was lightly hit. Knoke and the others continued to circle while I, with four "Amis" on my tail, did a climbing turn. Thanks to methanol injection for the engine, I gradually pulled away. Only the Mustang which had hit me did not give up the chase. However he was not able to bring his guns to bear. I slowly regained my calm, and saw that my comrades were in a situation from which it was difficult to escape. Americans were

In September 1944 I. Gruppe were based at Eggebek, near Husum. Many training flights were undertaken, one of which ended with the port undercarriage leg collapsing with Unteroffizier Hans Caris at the controls. The aircraft was Fw 190 A-8, "White 8" normally flown by Leutnant Hans Berger.

arriving from all directions, Lightnings, Thunderbolts... Suddenly, I dipped my aircraft, my "Yellow 4" and dived fast. I then found myself all alone - there were no enemy in the vicinity. A little farther away, the remains of two aircraft were burning on the ground. Heading for Reims, I descended to 1,000 metres and landed at base. None of my companions were able to do likewise. On the ground, I could check the damage: my adversary had hit me seven times, including single hits in the radiator and propellor. The following night Knoke returned to Vailly with his parachute under his arm" - Unteroffizier Ullrich Wagner, 11th Staffel.

Contrary to the recollections of these pilots, it was on 23rd August that Obergefreiter Döring was killed taking-off, and the 25th when the final "Normandy" combat for III. Gruppe took place in which Hauptmann Knoke bailed out and the unfortunate Unteroffizier Friedrich Ickes was shot while hanging defenceless on his parachute.

Hauptmann Knoke's victories were gained at a heavy cost: a conversation recorded between two prisoners of the unit captured in the latter part of August elicited the information that: "Our Gruppenkommandeur recently carried out three missions. He shot down two Spitfires and a P-51, but each time he lost his No.2, No.3 and No.4".

RETURN TO THE REICH - END OF AUGUST 1944

"We were ten days on the road, via Cologne and Hamburg, before reaching Husum. At this time we received young pilots to fill the gaps following the last campaign. Generally, they were little more than boys. Each day, our chief would take the Staffeln into the air in different formations: Rotte, Schwarm, Staffel and Gruppe. Everything had to be taught to these youngsters, who arrived with only a few hours flying time. Ehlers, our Gruppenkommandeur, was very diplomatic with the Mayor and population of Husum: they had to understand and accept the noise" - Hauptmann Ludwig Siegfried, Oberzahlmeister, I. Gruppe.

At the beginning of October I. Gruppe was commanded as follows:

Stab and I. Gruppe at Husum (Greifswald from 7th October) with Fw 190 A-8s.

Stab - Hauptmann Hans Ehlers;
1st Staffel - Leutnant Lüpke;
2nd Staffel - Oberlutnant Hans Vermaaten;
3rd Staffel - Oberleutnant Emil Demuth; and
4th Staffel - Leutnant Gerhard Hanf.

"Recovered from my wounds suffered on 22nd April

Gruppenkommandeur, I. Gruppe, Hauptmann Hans Ehlers and Kommodore Herbert Ihlefield (right), plot the course of the enemy incursion.

1944, I rejoined my 2nd Staffel on 1st September at Husum. Gottfried Just was the only former friend I found there. Like myself, he had been promoted to Leutnant during the summer. All the other pilots were inexperienced, even the Staffel leader, Oberleutnant Hans Vermaaten, who arrived from a Flak unit. All our time was dedicated to training. Eventually, we moved to a new base: Greifswald. During the transfer flight, Oberleutnant Vermaaten's wing touched the ground and the aircraft, carrying a supplementary fuel tank, exploded. Leutnant Just took over the Staffel. We transformed the field at Greifswald into an excellent airstrip, with camouflaged pens in the woods for our Fw 190s. We continued exercises there" - Leutnant Herbert Neuner, 2nd Staffel.

II. Gruppe was established at Reinsehlen, in the Lüneburg area. Once again they operated from a field converted into an airfield. Fresh young pilots arrived to bring the Gruppe up to strength. The new Gruppenkommandeur, Hauptmann Hermann Staiger, rejoined the Gruppe during the French campaign. At the beginning of October, II. Gruppe's command structure was as follows:

Stab and II. Gruppe based at Reinsehlen (later Tutow) with Fw 190 A-8s.

Stab	- Hauptmann Hermann Staiger;
5th Staffel	- Leutnant Hubert Swoboda;
6th Staffel	- Oberleutnant Fritz Wegner;
7th Staffel	- Leutnant Otto Bach; and
8th Staffel	- Leutnant Günther Heckmann.

Leutnant Karl-Heinz Sundermeier remembered the end of the French campaign for III. Gruppe: "On 23rd August, I arrived at Vailly. On the runway, a Bf 109 was burnt out - a pilot had crashed on taking off. Hauptmann Grislawski, Staffelkapitän of 8th Staffel, had just left the unit and I was the only officer in the Staffel. I was also the youngest pilot. Three days after I arrived, we heard that the Gruppe had been disbanded. Accompanied by several other surviving pilots, I travelled to Beaurieux, where we were incorporated into 5th Staffel, Jagdgeschwader 11. This unit soon left French soil. On 1st September, after a short stop-over in Cerfontaine, in Belgium, we landed at Wiesbaden. It was exactly five years since the war began, and we were evacuating France!

II. Gruppe, Jagdgeschwader 11, was based on the airfield at Gymnich. Our small group of pilots from II. Gruppe, Jagdgeschwader 11, was assigned to an officer who had recently finished convalescense: Oberleutnant Fritz Bilfinger. After two combat missions from Gymnich, we moved to Breitschneid/Burbach in Westerwald. Not far away was Knoke and other remnants of III. Gruppe, Jagdgeschwader 1. Soon, we were moved to Wesel to oppose allied troops parachuted into the Arnhem area. Finally, on 2nd October 1944, we received the order to return to III. Gruppe, Jagdgeschwader 1, who were at Fels-am-Wagram, where they were building up strength. We then moved on to Anklam to take up combat again in defence of the Reich".

After being based in France and Belgium, Hauptmann Heinz Knoke received a new transfer order: Vienna. The Gruppe left their remaining aircraft in the Reims area. Three days were spent in Austria, then a further move to Anklam ensued. The road convoy only had a day and a half to cover a good 1,000 kilometres over damaged roads and with the added problem of finding food supplies. On 9th October 1944 III. Gruppe once again lost its Gruppenkommandeur. On the journey Knoke, driving his car, suffered a bad accident. He managed to avoid having his leg amputated, but his career as a pilot was over. It had been an illustrious career, which included 44 victories in the west, and was rounded off with the award of the Ritterkreuz on 27th April 1945.

Recovered from his injuries, Hauptmann Woitke once again took his place at the head of his unit:

Stab and III. Gruppe based at Anklam with Bf 109 G-10s.

Stab	- Hauptmann Erich Woitke;
9th Staffel	- Oberleutnant Helmut Müller;
10th Staffel	- Oberleutnant Fritz Bilfinger;
11th Staffel	- Oberleutnant Jochen Janke; and
12th Staffel	- Hauptmann Harald Moldenhauer.

Although it had not achieved all its objectives, the allied landings in Normandy had been a success. From mid-November the allies reached the frontiers of the Reich at certain points along the front. In aerial matters, the end of the French campaign led to the re-commencement of the systematic bombing of Germany.

The Geschwader was brought up to strength again, with manpower never having been so high before. However there was a certain loss of quality. The enthusiasm of the very young pilots was real enough, perhaps more so than before, but it was not enough to fill the gaps with young pilots who had received accelerated training.

I. Gruppe had the difficult task of being the first to take up combat again. On 21st November, at 10:42 hours, in dreadful weather, Hauptmann Ehlers took off from Greifswald at the head of 56 Fw 190 A-8s. The USAAF

Anklam late autumn 1944. A Bf 109 G-6/AS shows clearly the Geschwader emblem on the engine cowling and the red band on the rear fuselage.

sent nearly 1,300 "Viermots"; 1st Bomb Division represented a quarter of his number and had as its objective the oil refineries at Merseburg, 350 kilometres to the south of Greifswald. They were escorted by 310 Mustangs out of a total of 954 allied fighters committed.
Leutnant Herbert Neuner of 2nd Staffel recalled: "On 21st November combats began again in dreadful weather: rain and fog. Our formation was directed due south towards a formation of "Viermots". Suddenly, voices crackled over the intercom: "Attention, Indianer behind us!". Our Gruppe was split up. I dived but was hit several times. Having noticed that I was not being followed, I gained altitude and saw a large circle of aircraft. In the circle, aircraft, one behind the other, were weaving. I picked up speed, got behind a P-47 and shot it down. I broke away immediately and set course for home. By chance, the direction was good and I landed at Greifswald. If my memory is correct, only two or three of my companions joined me. We waited for further news. It was very bad: the absentees were posted missing, and hour by hour their deaths were confirmed."
The losses were numerous. It only took the Americans a couple of minutes to shoot down eight of their adversaries. In the combats which followed, seven other Germans were killed and four wounded. More than 20 aircraft were lost, including eight over Erfurt. On the credit side, only two victories were recorded over B-17s, one each to Leutnant Demuth and Unteroffizier Enderle. As previously recounted, Leutnant Neuner claimed a P-47, and Feldwebel Oswald a "Herausschuss".
On 26th November American forces, having diverse targets in the Ruhr area, sent over 1,137 bombers escorted by nearly 700 fighters. I. Gruppe, who could only call upon 32 Fw 190s, took off at 11:20 hours led by Leutnant Gottfried Just, who temporarily replaced Ehlers. II. Gruppe was also in action. Heavy losses once again followed: eleven killed or missing, including the Staffelkapitän of 7th Staffel, Leutnant Otto Bach, who had been with the unit since the formation of IV. Gruppe. Three pilots were also wounded.
On 5th December matters reached a peak, or rather hit the depths. The complete Geschwader took off at about 10:30 hours. B-17s of the 1st and 3rd Bomb Divisions escorted by 700 Mustangs were paying a return visit to Berlin. I. Gruppe were able to put 42 Fw 190s in the air. By evening the losses read:
Geschwaderstab: 2 killed;
I. Gruppe : 6 killed and 10 wounded;
II. Gruppe : 13 killed and 2 wounded; and
III. Gruppe : 5 killed and 2 wounded.
Among those killed were the new Staffelkapitän of 7th Staffel, Oberleutnant Rudolf Diesem, and Oberleutnant Helmut Müller, Staffelkapitän of 9th Staffel.
I. Gruppe claimed nine Mustangs; Leutnants Neuner, Just and Lüpke were among the victors. In III. Gruppe, Hauptmann Moldenhauer recorded a victory over a P-51. After a week of relative calm, matters once again moved quickly. On 16th December the Germans launched their last offensive in the west. Under cover of poor weather, they hoped to break through in the Ardennes region, cross the Meuse and push on to Antwerp. The allied forces would be cut in two. A hoped-for-peace in the west might then ensue, alllowing the Germans freedom to continue the fight in the east.
To this end, on 17th December shortly before 10:00 hours, I. Gruppe left Greifswald, their Fw 190s flying at low level guided by a Ju 88, and landed at Twente. Only a small strip of the airfield was useable. II. Gruppe

Greifswald, early December 1944. Pilots of I. Gruppe around Leutnants Demuth and Just on the motorcycles. From left to right: Stenschke; Birnbaum; Millers; Eck; Voss; Lüpke (open jacket); Schlarb; Kilian; Hofmann; Caris; Roschinski; Riemer; Hortemann and Stiemer.

On 24th December 1944 Hauptmann Erich Woitke was killed in action near Aachen. His place at the head of III. Gruppe was taken by Hauptmann Harald Moldenhauer. Moldenhauer (right) is seen talking to the Staffelkapitän of 11th Staffel, Oberleutnant Jochen Janke.

reached Drope, and III. Gruppe took off from Anklam at 09:47 hours and took up station at Rheine.
During the Ardennes offensive, the Geschwader's high rate of attrition continued. On 18th December towards 11:30 hours, 28 Fw 190 A-8s of I. Gruppe were in action in the Malmédy region. One pilot was reported missing. At the same time, III. Gruppe were confronting B-17s in the Cologne region. Several pilots were shot down and had to bail out, one of them seriously wounded.

On the 23rd losses continued with two pilots killed and two wounded from I. Gruppe (including Leutnant Neuner hit by his own Flak). The Gruppe recorded two victories over Thunderbolts through Hauptmann Ehlers and Leutnant Demuth. Towards mid-day Oberleutnant Jochen Janke of 11th Staffel shot down a B-17 and was then shot down himself, having to bail out.
On 24th December at 11:26 hours III. Gruppe took off and shortly afterwards suffered the loss of its Gruppenkommandeur, Hauptmann Erich Woitke, who was shot down by a Spitfire and remained in his Bf 109 G-14, "Grey 20" when it crashed near Aachen. He was 33 years old, and had registered 28 victories. He was succeeded by Hauptmann Harald Moldenhauer, the Staffelkapitän of 12th Staffel. The Gruppe at this point could only count on a dozen serviceable Bf 109 G-14s.
Leutnant Hans Halbey of Stab, III. Gruppe, recalled the action: "Shortly after take-off, Woitke called to us to release the supplementary fuel tanks as enemy aircraft were in the area and to be able to escape them we had to lighten our load. The action was not long in coming. Woitke's aircraft was hit by a full burst and was transformed into a ball of fire. Shortly after the explosion, I shot down a Spitfire in a circling combat; one of my comrades confirmed the victory over the radio. I was the only pilot of our formation to regain Rheine safe and sound. In accordance with instructions, I made out a combat report which was sent, as usual, to the Kommodore.

Feldwebel Hans-Georg Sperling of III. Gruppe, with Bf 109 Gs in the background, at Anklam in autumn 1944. To the right is a "G-10" with an extended tailwheel. On 25/12/44 he was wounded in combat against B-17s.

"In the evening, I was called to the telephone: "The Kommodore wants to speak to you!". I waited for his congratulations on my victory. This was not to be the case. On the contrary, I received a telling-off, which made me angry. In effect, I was the only pilot of the Gruppe to release the fuel tank just after take-off. Because of this, it being impossible to become involved in a long combat, I returned to base far earlier than my comrades. He announced his intention to place me before a court-martial for cowardice in the face of the enemy. I argued vehemently against these accusations, gave him a piece of my mind concerning my honour, and slammed the 'phone down. I was beside myself with anger. My fellow-officers intervened on my behalf, and later, the Kommodore appeared to have completely forgotten about our telephone conversation. On the following day, 25th December, the day was sunny, but cold. I was shot down (my fifth time) by a Spitfire and had to bail out".

There was no rest on Christmas day. Nearly 400 B-17s and B-24s carried out raids on communications centres in western Germany. All three Gruppen were in action, with I. Gruppe being particularly successful: seven Liberators shot down. However the price paid for these victories was high, with III. Gruppe suffering the heaviest losses with seven pilots killed or missing. Oberleutnant Fritz Bilfinger, Staffelkapitän of 10th Staffel was killed; a complete Schwarm from 10th Staffel led by Oberfeldwebel Friedrich Zander did not return, and Leutnant Rudolf Schnappauf, a very experienced pilot of I. Gruppe and former wingman of Oesau, was found in the wreckage of his Fw 190 A-8 a week later, on 1st January.

26th December showed no respite with eight pilots missing, including three of the more experienced pilots of II. Gruppe, Leutnant Horst Ertmann, Oberfeldwebel Georg Hutter and Oberfeldwebel Reinhard Flecks.

Worse was to come on the following day, and it was the turn of I. Gruppe to be heavily hit. At 10:15 hours

JG 1 lost many experienced pilots at the end of 1944, such as Leutnant Otto Bach, killed on 26/11/44 (right) and Oberfeldwebel Georg Hutter, killed on 26/12/44.

Hauptmann Hans Ehlers led off 18 Fw 190s on a mission to cover ground troops in the area of Dinant-Rochefort. They were challenged to the west of Mayen by a swarm of Mustangs of 364th Fighter Group and suffered the loss of six pilots killed. Among those killed were Leutnant Gottfried Just, Staffelkapitän of 2nd Staffel, and Gruppenkommandeur Hans Ehlers, shot down in his Fw 190 A-8, "White 20". At the time of his death, Ehlers had 55 victories, including 23 over 4-engined bombers. His final tally was probably higher, as details of his successes during the Normandy campaign were never brought to account. Ehlers was a respected figure among his men, and the Gruppe never quite got over his loss. Another Staffelkapitän, Leutnant Richard Förster of 4th Staffel, was also killed. Set against these losses were claims for six P-51s by I. Gruppe, including one by Leutnant Demuth and two by Leutnant Lüpke.

The year ended on a low note with 6th Staffel suffering three pilots killed on 31st December. The Ardennes action had hit the Geschwader very hard - 51 pilots killed, missing or wounded. The war situation did not offer the hope of any easement in the new year.

Hauptmann Hans Ehlers successor was Hauptmann Hans Georg Hachbarth, who had joined the unit on 1st November 1944. Formerly with II. Gruppe Jagdgeschwader 51, he had thirteen victories to his credit. Shortly after his appointment, Hachbarth learned of the major Luftwaffe fighter effort slated for New Year's day, under the code name "Operation Bodenplatte".

These views, and on the following pages, show action at Greifswald in December 1944 as aircraft of I. Gruppe (Stab, 1st, 2nd, 3rd and 4th Staffeln) prepare for take off.

LOSS TABLES - 1944

Date	Name of Crew and Rank	Staffel	Fate	Aircraft, W.Nr & Code	Damage /Loss	Reason for Casualty	Place
04.01.44	Uffz. Dietrich Hempler	3	Killed	Fw 190 A-5 Yellow 1 (1325)	100%	Shot down on combat mission.	Münster
04.01.44	Uffz. Robert Hain	3	Killed	Fw 190 A-7 Yellow 4 (430184)	100%	Shot down on combat mission.	Münster
04.01.44	Uffz. Karl-Heinz Hauptmann	5		Fw 190 A ( )	100%	Shot down in combat	
04.01.44		II. Gruppe		Fw 190 A ( )	8%	Belly landing following combat.	
04.01.44	FjF. Albert Lindenschmidt	9	Killed	Bf 109 G-4 Yellow 8 (19432)	100%	Aircraft crashed due to pilot's air sickness.	Hilnarennbeek
05.01.44	Fw. Alfred Müller	1	Killed	Fw 190 A-7y White 10 (430183)	100%	Shot down in combat with USAAF bombers.	
05.01.44	Ofhr. Heinz Rutzhofer	2	Killed	Fw 190 A-6 Black 4 (550788)	100%	Shot down in combat with USAAF bombers.	Prüm
05.01.44	Fw. Bernhard Kunze	2	Killed	Fw 190 A-6 Black 1 (550884)	100%	Shot down on combat mission.	Bergisch-Gladbach
11.01.44	Fw. Günther Kirchner	5	Wounded	Fw 190 A-7 Black 10 (430168)		Emergency landing following combat.	Nordhausen
11.01.44	Uffz. Erwin Mietho	6	Killed	Fw 190 A-6 Yellow 13 (550466)	100%	Shot down in combat with USAAF bombers.	Ohrbeck
11.01.44	Ofhr. Dagobert Schattner	8	Killed	Bf 109 G-6 Black 13 (410517)	100%	Shot down in combat with USAAF P-47s.	Osnabrück
24.01.44	Hptm. Alfred Grislawski	1	Wounded	Fw 190 A-7y White 1 (430167)	100%	Shot down in combat with USAAF bombers.	Baske
24.01.44	Fw. Martin Saller	3	Killed	Fw 190 A-5 Yellow 3 (410194)	100%	Shot down in combat with USAAF bombers.	Erlenbach
24.01.44	Ofw. Benno Liper	4	Killed	Fw 190 A-4 White 3 (2334)		Overturned on landing.	Venlo
24.01.44	Lt. Harald Schilling	5	Killed	Fw 190 A-6 Black 3 (550887)	100%	Shot down in combat with USAAF P-47s.	Near Tournai
24.01.44	Stf. Rudolf Mertens	5	Killed	Fw 190 A-6 Black 9 (550755)	100%	Shot down in combat with USAAF P-47s.	Near Tournai
24.01.44	Ofhr. Karl Kremer	5	Wounded	Fw 190 A-6 Black 6 (550759)	100%	Shot down in combat with USAAF fighters.	Antwerp
24.01.44	Lt. Bernhard von Kortzfleisch	6	Wounded	Fw 190 A-6 Yellow 1 (550871)	100%	Shot down in combat with USAAF fighters.	Near Tournai
30.1.44	Uffz. Alex Krones	2	Killed	Fw 190 A-7 Black 4 (430684)	100%	Shot down in combat with USAAF bombers.	Schapen
30.01.44	Uffz. Erich Rütter	2	Killed	Fw 190 A-7 Black 7 (430177)	100%	Shot down in combat with USAAF bombers.	Hannover
30.01.44	Uffz. Heinz Groller	3	Killed	Fw 190 A-7/R-6 Yellow 10 (430485)	100%	Shot down in combat with USAAF bombers.	Blomberg
30.01.44	Hptm. Friedrich Eberle	III. Gruppe	Wounded	Bf 109 G-6 White 20 (160303)	100%	Shot down in combat with USAAF P-47s.	Apeldoorn
30.01.44	Hptm. Albert Kind	7	Killed	Bf 109 G-6 White 1 (410565)	100%	Shot down in combat with USAAF P-47s.	South of Zwolle

Date	Name of Crew and Rank	Staffel	Fate	Aircraft, W.Nr & Code	Damage /Loss	Reason for Casualty	Place
30.01.44	Fw. Max Finsterwald	7	Killed	Bf 109 G-6 White 15 (15946)	100%	Shot down in combat with USAAF P-47s.	South of Zwolle
30.01.44	Ogefr. Rudolf Theyssen	7	Wounded	Bf 109 G-6 White 5 (160670)		Emergency landing due to fuel shortage following combat.	Gronau
30.01.44	Fw. Georg Reinfelder	7	Killed	Bf 109 G-6 White 12 (15727)	100%	Shot down in combat.	Lutherberg
30.01.44	Uffz. Georg Graf zu Ortenburg	7	Killed	Bf 109 G-6 White 23 (410213)	100%	Shot down in combat.	Zwolle
30.01.44	Fw. Martin Fink	8	Wounded	Bf 109 G-6 Black 14 (410415)	100%	Shot down in combat with USAAF P-47s.	Enschede
30.01.44	Uffz. Otto Tillack	8	Killed	Bf 109 G-6 Black 10 (27023)	100%	Shot down in combat with USAAF P-47s.	Zwolle
30.01.44	Uffz. Otto Tillack	8	Killed	Bf 109 G-6 Black 10 (27023)	100%	Shot down in combat with USAAF P-47s.	Zwolle
30.01.44	Uffz. Theodor Hörwick	8	Killed	Bf 109 G-6 Black 7 (411134)	100%	Shot down in combat with fighters.	Schelde estuary
03.02.44	Gefr. Bernhard Boose	1	Killed	Fw 190 A-7 White 23 (430175)	100%	Crashed on non-combat flight.	Ostbüren
03.02.44	Ofw. Gerhard Flemming	9	Killed	Bf 109 G-6 Yellow 4 (410881)	100%	Shot down in combat.	Wachtum
08.02.44	Lt. Hans Berger	1		Fw 190 A White 8 ( )	100%	Shot down in combat with USAAF B-17s.	
08.02.44	Fw. Hermann Köhne	2	Killed	Fw 190 A-7 Black 7 (430686)	100%	Shot down in combat with USAAF bombers.	Charleville
08.02.44	Gefr. Siegfried Marek	2	Killed	Fw 190 A-7 Black 8 (430187)	100%	Shot down in combat with USAAF bombers.	Luxemburg
08.02,44	Fw. Gerhard Giese	3	Killed	Fw 190 A-7 Yellow 6 (340283)	100%	Shot down in combat with USAAF bombers.	Near Chimay
08.02.44	Ogefr. Kurt Kramss	4	Killed	Fw 190 A-6 White 11 (551145)	100%	Shot down in combat with USAAF fighters.	South-east of Brussels
08.02.44	Oblt. Eberhard Burath	II. Gruppe		Fw 190 A ( )		Belly landing due to fuel shortage.	South of Luttich
08.02.44	Oblt. Günther Witt	7	Wounded	Bf 109 G-6 White 2 (15406)	100%	Shot down in combat with USAAF P-47s.	Luxemburg
08.02.44	Uffz. Wilhelm Kräuter	7	Wounded	Bf 109 G-6 White 11 (410515)	100%	Shot down in combat with USAAF P-47s.	Dinant
08.02.44	Fw. Gustav Schulze	7	Killed	Bf 109 G-6 White 24 (411029)	100%	Shot down in combat with USAAF P-47s.	Arlon
08.02.44	Fw. Richard Guthmann	9	Killed	Bf 109 G-6 Yellow 15 (411081)	100%	Shot down in combat with USAAF P-47s.	Polleur
10.02.44	Lt. Rudolf Kasischke	4	Killed	Fw 190 A-7 White 2 (430673)	100%	Shot down in combat with USAAF fighters.	North-east of
10.02.44	Uffz. Helmut Stiegler	4		Fw 190 A		Belly landing following combat.	25 kilometres south of Diepholz
10.02.44	Uffz. Harald Feist	5		Fw 190 A		Belly landing following combat.	Watenstedt
10.02.44	Oblt. Eberhard Burath	II. Gruppe		Fw 190 A ( )	100%	Shot down in combat.	Watenstedt
10.02.44	Uffz. Hans Hitter	9	Killed	Bf 109 G-6 Yellow 12 (160719)	100%	Shot down in combat with USAAF fighters.	Ahaus

Date	Name of Crew and Rank	Staffel	Fate	Aircraft, W.Nr & Code	Damage /Loss	Reason for Casualty	Place
11.02.44	Uffz. Lothar Hänert	3	Killed	Fw 190 A-7 Yellow 10 (340277)	100%	Overturned on take off.	Rheine
11.02.44	Uffz. Erich Negraszus	5	Killed	Fw 190 A-7 Black 1 (430172)		Overturned on landing.	Karthause
11.02.44	Uffz. Werner Veid	III. Gruppe	Killed			Shot down in combat.	Brusthem
12.02.44	Fw Walter Scholz	1	Killed	Fw 190 A-7z White 11 (430670)		Overturned on take off.	Dortmund
14.02.44	Fw. Fritz Haspel	8		Bf 109 G		Machine caught fire after take off.	Volkel
20.02.44	Hptm. Harald Römer	2	Killed	Fw 190 A-7 Black 10 (430465)	100%	Shot down in combat.	Eschwege
20.02.44	Uffz. Heinrich Bartzen	2	Wounded	Fw 190 A-7 Black 8 (430359)	100%	Shot down in combat with USAAF bombers.	Altenwalde
20.02.44	Gefr. Alfons Martini	2	Killed	Fw 190 A-7 White 9 (430965)	100%	Shot down in combat with USAAF bombers.	Hamburg
20.02.44	Uffz. Karl-Heinz Hauptmann	5	Killed	Fw 190 A-6 Black 3 (470076)	100%	Shot down in combat.	Einbeck
20.02.44	Uffz. Heinrich Jacobsen	II. Gruppe	Killed	Fw 190 A-7 White 21 (430256)	100%	Shot down in combat with fighters.	Northeim
20.02.44		II. Gruppe		Fw 190 A	65%	Belly landing following combat.	Göttingen
20.02.44	Fw. Paul Pfingst	8	Wounded	Bf 109 G-6 Yellow 14 (111042)	100%	Shot down in combat.	Huy
21.02.44	Uffz. Fritz Rathofer	3	Wounded	Fw 190 A-7 White 7 (430354)	100%	Shot down in combat with USAAF bombers.	Steinheim
21.02.44	Uffz. Hans Rau	4	Killed	Fw 190 A-7 White 15 (340271)	100%	Shot down in combat.	Lüstringen
21.02.44	Lt. Helmut Proff	4	Wounded	Fw 190 A-7 White 15 (430468)	100%	Shot down in combat.	Osnabrück
21.02.44	Uffz. Helmut Stiegler	4	Wounded	Fw 190 A		Emergency landing following combat.	Rheine
21.02.44	Fw. Otto Schmid	5	Wounded	Fw 190 A-7 Black 10 (430644)		Emergency landing following combat.	Rheine
21.02.44	Uffz. Harald Feist	5	Killed	Fw 190 A-7 Black 13 (642987)	100%	Shot down in combat.	Schledehausen
21.02.44	Uffz. Fritz Feier	7	Wounded	Bf 109 G-5 White 11 (110074)	100%	Shot down in combat.	Zwolle
21.02.44	FjF. Erich Mattern	8	Killed	Bf 109 G-6 Black 6 (410874)	100%	Shot down in combat with USAAF P-47s.	Zuider Zee
21.02.44	Fw. Fritz Haspel	8		Bf 109 G Black 3 ( )	100%	Shot down in combat.	Zuider Zee
21.02.44	Uffz. Helmut Sainisch	9	Killed	Bf 109 G-6 Yellow 5 (410141)	100%	Shot down in combat.	Zuider Zee
21.02.44	Lt. Helmut Müller	III. Gruppe	Killed	Bf 109 G-6 White 22 (410569)	100%	Shot down in combat.	Apeldoorn
22.02.44	Uffz. Kurt Krüger	3	Killed	Fw 190 A-7 White 10 (642989)	100%	Shot down in combat with USAAF bombers.	Gelsenkirchen
22.02.44	Uffz. Herbert Dosch	5	Wounded	Fw 190 A-6 Black 12 (550874)	100%	Shot down in combat.	Wesel

Date	Name of Crew and Rank	Staffel	Fate	Aircraft, W.Nr & Code	Damage /Loss	Reason for Casualty	Place
22.02.44		II. Gruppe		Fw 190 A ( )	100%	Shot down in combat.	
22.02.44	Uffz. Friedrich Kratz	8	Killed	Bf 109 G-6 Black 1 (16353)	100%	Shot down in combat.	Tilburg
23.02.44	Lt. Hans Halbey	III. Gruppe		Bf 109 G-6 White 23 ( )		Belly landing on non-combat flight.	Volkel
24.02.44	Uffz. Walter Kunze	2	Killed	Fw 190 A-7 Black 9 (430356)	100%	Shot down in combat with USAAF bombers.	Memeringen
24.02.44	Uffz. Joachim Schmidt	2	Killed	Fw 190 A-7 White 20 (430668)	100%	Shot down in combat with USAAF bombers.	Nijmegen
24.02.44	Uffz. Stefan Lux	2	Wounded	Fw 190 A-7 Yellow 10 (340027)	100%	Shot down in combat with USAAF bombers.	Holzhausen
24.02.44	Ogefr. Horst Gabel	3	Wounded	Fw 190 A-4 White 6 (2336)	100%	Shot down in combat with USAAF bombers.	Minden
24.02.44	Uffz. Horst Samenfeld	3	Killed	Fw 190 A-7 Yellow 11 (642994)	100%	Shot down in combat with USAAF bombers.	Minden
24.02.44	Uffz. Robert Eberhardt	4	Killed	Fw 190 A-6 White 5 (146)	100%	Shot down in combat.	South of Minden
24.02.44	Fw. Heinz Fuchs	4	Killed	Fw 190 A-7 White 7 (340314)	100%	Shot down in combat with USAAF B-24s.	South of Minden
24.02.44	Ofw. Leo Schuhmacher	6		Fw 190 A ( )	100%	Shot down in combat with USAAF P-47s.	
25.02.44	Lt. Fritz Wegner	5		Fw 190 A ( )	100%	Shot down in combat with USAAF bombers.	
02.03.44	Ofhr. Hans Hilbers	7	Killed	Bf 109 G-5 White 10 (26083)	100%	Shot down in combat.	Romsee, near Liege
02.03.44	Gefr. Alfons Salhofer	7	Killed	Bf 109 G-5 White 11 (27088)	100%	Shot down in combat.	Aachen
03.03.44	Fw. Willi Schmidt	4	Killed	Fw 190 A-7 White 14 (430654)	100%	Shot down in combat with fighters.	Hannover
03.03.44	Uffz. Hans-Joachim Tüngler	5	Killed	Fw 190 A-7 Black 15 (430501)	100%	Shot down in combat with fighters.	Amelinghausen
06.03.44	Fw. Werner Dotzauer	1	Killed	Fw 190 A-7 White 11 (340003)	100%	Shot down in combat with USAAF bombers.	Dalen
06.03.44	Uffz. Alfred Haupt	2	Killed	Fw 190 A-7 Black 3 (340002)	100%	Shot down in combat with USAAF bombers.	Almelo
06.03.44	FjOf. Erich Demuth	2	Wounded	Fw 190 A-7 Black 11 (642558)	100%	Shot down in combat.	Minden
06.03.44	Oblt. Wolfgang Kretschmer	4	Wounded	Fw 190 A-7 White 3 (643000)	100%	Shot down in combat with fighters.	Quakenbrück
06.03.44	Ofw. Detlev Lüth	4	Killed	Fw 190 A-7 White 9 (430680)	100%	Shot down in combat with USAAF B-17s.	Barnstorf
06.03.44	Ofw. Rudolf Haninger	4		Fw 190 A ( )		Belly landing following combat.	
07.03.44	Uffz. Paul Stuckenbrodt	6	Killed	Fw 190 A-7 Yellow 3 (430179)	100%	Crashed on test flight.	Rheine
08.03.44	Fw. Rudolf Lehmann	4		Fw 190 A ( )		Belly landing following combat.	
08.03.44	Uffz. Hubert Swoboda	5		Fw 190 A ( )		Belly landing following combat.	
08.03.44	Ofw. Reinhold Flecks	6		Fw 190 A ( )	100%	Shot down in combat.	

Date	Name of Crew and Rank	Staffel	Fate	Aircraft, W.Nr & Code	Damage /Loss	Reason for Casualty	Place
08.03.44	Hptm. Hermann Segatz	II. Gruppe	Killed	Fw 190 A-7 White 23 (43315)	100%	Shot down in combat with fighters.	South of Luckau
08.03.44	Oblt. Edgar Witzmann	6	Killed	Fw 190 A-7 Green 8 (550146)	100%	Shot down in combat with USAAF P-47s.	Hesepe
08.03.44	Uffz. Anton Krampert	6	Killed	Fw 190 A-5 Yellow 9 (410274)	100%	Shot down in combat with fighters.	Brelingen
12.03.44	Oblt. Heinrich Overhagen	8	Killed	Bf 109 G-6 (760016)	100%	Crashed on test flight.	Fels Am Wagram
15.03.44	Uffz. Rudolf Martin	1	Wounded	Fw 190 A-7 White 14 (340043)		Pilot wounded in combat with fighters.	Rheine
15.03.44	Uffz. Hans Dorn	4	Killed	Fw 190 A-5 White 1 (550888)	100%	Shot down in combat with fighters.	Fürstenau
15.03.44	Lt. Günther Buchholz	6	Wounded	Fw 190 A ( )		Belly landing following combat.	
23.03.44	Uffz. Johann Rühl	3	Killled	Fw 190 A-7 Yellow 8 (642977)	100%	Shot down in combat with USAAF bombers.	Diepholz
23.03.44	Uffz. Helmut Stiegler	4		Fw 190 A ( )	10%	Belly landing following combat.	
23.03.44	Fw. Wolfgang Brunner	6		Fw 190 A ( )	30%	Belly landing following combat.	
23.03.44		II. Gruppe		Fw 190 A ( )		Belly landing following combat.	
23.03.44		II. Gruppe		Fw 190 A ( )	100%	Pilot bailed out following combat.	Near Wittingen
28.03.44	Uffz. Wilhelm Peine	2	Wounded	Fw 190 A-4 Black 14 (6236)	100%	Overturned on landing on non-combat flight.	Hopsten
29.03.44	Hptm. Günther Wrobel	Sonderstaffel	Killed	Fw 190 A-7/R-2 Yellow 5 (643910)	100%	Shot down in combat.	Schlahnstedt
29.03.44	Uffz. Harry Kubon	Sonderstaffel	Killed	Fw 190 A-7 White 10 (340342)	100%	Shot down in combat.	Wohlsdorf
29.03.44	Uffz. Rudolf Martin	1	Killed	Fw 190 A-7 White 2 (340332)	100%	Shot down in combat.	Dedeleben
29.03.44	Fw. Werner Wiegand	2	Killed	Fw 190 A-7 Black 11 (340033)	100%	Shot down in combat with fighters.	Helmstedt
29.03.44	Uffz. Hans Eisenberger	2	Killed	Fw 190 A-7 Black 17 (643726)	100%	Shot down in combat.	Hannover
29.03.44	Uffz. Alfred Hoyer	3	Killed	Fw 190 A-7 Yellow 11 (643940)	100%	Shot down in combat.	Schöppenstedt
29.03.44	Uffz. Hans Nieskens	4	Killed	Fw 190 A-7 White 9 (430358)	100%	Shot down in combat with fighters.	Badersleben
29.03.44	Oblt. Eberhard Burath	4		Fw 190 A Blue 1 ( )	100%	Shot down in combat.	
29.03.44	Flgr. Georg Blech	5		Fw 190 A ( )	100%	Shot down in combat.	Near Badersleben
29.03.44	FjF. Max Sauer	II. Gruppe	Killed	Fw 190 A-7 Red 21 (430704)	100%	Shot down in combat with fighters.	Badersleben
31.03.44	Uffz. Eberhard Clemen	Gesch. Stab	Wounded	Fw 190 A-7 Green 21 (642534)		Emergency landing on non-combat flight.	Neuenkirchen
01.04.44	Fw. Josef Kehrle	8	Wounded	Bf 109 G-6 Black 7 (110066)		Emergency landing following combat with USAAF P-47s.	Zwolle
04.04.44	Uffz. Friedrich Enderle	3	Wounded	Fw 190 A-7 Yellow 16 (430687)		Emergency landing on non-combat flight.	Hopsten

Date	Name of Crew and Rank	Staffel	Fate	Aircraft, W.Nr & Code	Damage /Loss	Reason for Casualty	Place
07.04.44	Ofhr. Erich Zulauf	8	Killed	Bf 109 G-5 Black 5 (27092)	100%	Shot down in combat.	Paderborn
08.04.44	Ofhr. Rudolf Piffer	2	Wounded	Fw 190 A-8 Black 3 (170044)	100%	Shot down in combat with USAAF bombers.	West of Salzwedel
08.04.44	Uffz. Helmut Riehl	2	Wounded	Fw 190 A-7 Black 19 (643942)	100%	Shot down in combat with USAAF bombers.	West of Salzwedel
08.04.44	Uffz. Johann Pomberger	3	Killed	Fw 190 A-5 Yellow 16 (410244)	100%	Shot down in combat.	Stendal
08.04.44	Ofw. Georg Hutter	4		Fw 190 A ( )	100%	Collided with aircraft of Uffz. Dippold.	West of Salzwedel
08.04.44	Uffz. Helmut Dippold	5		Fw 190 A ( )	100%	Collided with aircraft of Ofw. Hutter.	West of Salzwedel
08.04.44	Uffz. Heinz Ebert	4	Killed	Fw 190 A-7 White 18 (340268)	100%	Shot down in combat wth fighters.	Gardelegen
09.04.44	Lt. Heinz Günther Lück	1	Wounded	Fw 190 A-8 White 14 (170050)		Belly landing following combat.	Erö Island
09.04.44		1	Wounded	Fw 190 A-8 White 3 ( )		Belly landing following combat.	Erö Island
09.04.44	Ogefr. Martin Finger	3	Killed	Fw 190 A-7 Yellow 6 (643707)	100%	Shot down in combat with USAAF bombers.	Norby
09.04.44	Lt. Meinhard Quack	4	Killed	Fw 190 A-6 White 8 (470795)	100%	Shot down in combat with USAAF bombers.	North Sea
09.04.44	Flgr. Georg Blech	5		Fw 190 A ( )	100%	Belly landing following combat.	
09.04.44	Uffz. Zinkl	6		Fw 190 A ( )	100%	Shot down in combat.	
09.04.44	Uffz. Günther Koch	7	Killed	Bf 109 G-5 White 7 (110059)	100%	Shot down in combat with USAAF bombers.	Stade
11.04.44	Uffz. Helmut Manikowski	Sonderstaffel	Killed	Fw 190 A-7 White 16 (643941)	100%	Shot down in combat with USAAF bombers.	Brunswick
11.04.44	Ofw. Kurt Barein	4	Killed	Fw 190 A-6 White 15 (470609)	100%	Shot down in combat with USAAF P-51s.	Brunswick
11.04.44	Uffz. Werner Nobis	5	Killed	Fw 190 A-7 Black 13 (340304)	100%	Shot down in combat with fighters.	Celle
11.04.44	Gefr. Hans Flick	6	Killed	Fw 190 A-7 Yellow 14 (431137)	100%	Shot down in combat with fighters.	Bernburg
11.04.44	Fw. Martin Fink	8	Wounded	Bf 109 G-5 Black 9 (110238)	100%	Belly landing when attacked by fighters while landing.	Burg
11.04.44	Uffz. Siegfried Weberirsch	9	Killed	Bf 109 G-5 Yellow 5 (161306)	100%	Shot down in combat with USAAF P-51s.	Magdeburg
11.04.44	Oblt. Erwin Achtermann	9	Killed	Bf 109 G-6 Yellow 17 (410722)	100%	Shot down in combat with USAAF P-51s.	Magdeburg
12.04.44	Fw. Josef Löhr	7	Killed	Bf 109 G-6 Yellow 9 (160752)	100%	Shot down in combat with USAAF P-47s and P-51s.	Wetzlar
13.04.44	Fw. Alfred Umlauf	2	Killed	Fw 190 A-7 Black 15 (643919)	100%	Shot down in combat.	Viernheim
13.04.44	Lt. Ernst Terborg	3	Killed	Fw 190 A-8 Yellow 3 (170027)	100%	Shot down in combat.	Heppenheim
13.04.44	Oblt. Hans Ehlers	3	Wounded	Fw 190 A-8 Yellow 5 (170046)	100%	Belly landing following combat.	Gutersdorf

Date	Name of Crew and Rank	Staffel	Fate	Aircraft, W.Nr & Code	Damage /Loss	Reason for Casualty	Place
13.04.44	Uffz. Alfons Schulz	4	Wounded	Fw 190 A-7/R-2 White 10 (643933)	100%	Shot down in combat with USAAF P-51s.	Worms
13.04.44	Uffz. Hubert Swoboda	5	Wounded	Fw 190 A-7/R-2 Black 4 (643950)	100%	Shot down in combat.	Near Ittlingen
13.04.44	Uffz. Wilhelm Kräuter	7	Wounded	Bf 109 G-5 White 13 (110049)	100%	Shot down in combat with USAAF P-47s.	Burgen
13.04.44	Ofhr. Josef Krebsbach	9	Killed	Bf 109 G-6 Yellow 16 (20428)	100%	Shot down in combat.	Affolterbach
13.04.44	Fhr. Gerhard Kramer	9	Killed	Bf 109 G-6 Yellow 20 (161176)	100%	Shot down in combat.	Affolterbach
16.04.44	Hptm. Emil Schnoor	I. Gruppe	Wounded	Fw 190 A-7 White 20 (340035)		Emergency landing on non-combat flight.	Detmold
16.04.44	Uffz. Schumann	II. Gruppe		Fw 190 A-7 ( )	70%	Damaged on landing on non-combat flight.	Erbenheim
19.04.44	Fw. Wilhelm Knöller	1	Killed	Fw 190 A-8y White 11 (170392)	100%	Shot down in combat.	Waldkappel
19.04.44	Uffz. Xaver Gschwend	1	Killed	Fw 190 A-7 White 5 (642965)	100%	Shot down in combat.	Melsungen
19.04.44	Gefr. Johannes Zitzmann	1	Wounded	Fw 190 A-7/R-2y White 17 (643930)	100%	Shot down in combat.	Alsfeld
19.04.44	Uffz. Gerhard Lippmann	2	Killed	Fw 190 A-7 Black 17 (431144)	100%	Shot down in combat.	Blankenburg
19.04.44	Lt. Otwin Zieger	2	Wounded	Fw 190 A-8 Black 14 (170025)		Crashed on take off on non-combat flight.	Lippspringe
19.04.44	Uffz. Helmut Dippold	5	Killed	Fw 190 A-7 Black 11 (340311)		Emergency landing following combat.	Eisenach
19.04.44	Flgr. Georg Blech	5		Fw 190 A ( )	25%	Belly landing following combat.	
19.04.44		II. Gruppe		Fw 190 A ( )	25%	Belly landing following combat.	Near Thale
22.04.44	Uffz. Arnold Giers	1	Killed	Fw 190 A-8 White 3 (170101)	100%	Shot down in combat with USAAF fighters.	Burbach
22.04.44	Ofhr. Herbert Neuner	2	Wounded	Fw 190 A-7 Black 16 (550839)		Crashed on landing.	Dortmund
22.04.44	Lt. Herbert Eh	3	Wounded	Fw 190 A-8 Yellow 2 (170097)	100%	Shot down in combat with USAAF fighters.	Ostbevern
22.04.44	Gefr. Heinrich Born	4	Killed	Fw 190 A-8 White 8 (580142)	100%	Shot down in combat with USAAF fighters.	Rhynern
22.04.44	Uffz. Johann Froschhauer	4	Wounded	Fw 190 A-7 White 5 (430483)	100%	Shot down in combat with USAAF fighters.	Schwerte
22.04.44	Uffz. Heinz Weber	5		Fw 190 A-8 Black 8 (170106)	100%	Crashed after ramming USAAF B-17.	Near Hilbeck
22.04.44	Flgr. Georg Blech	5		Fw 190 A-8 Black 10 (170102)	100%	Shot down in combat.	Near Unna
22.04.44	Hptm. Hotari Schmude	7	Killed	Bf 109 G-5 White 1 (110051)	100%	Shot down in combat.	Korbach
22.04.44	Lt. Kurt Ibing	7	Wounded	Bf 109 G-6 White 6 (440306)	100%	Shot down in combat with USAAF P-51s.	Arolsen
22.04.44	FjF. Gerhard Reimitz	7	Wounded	Bf 109 G-5 White 9 (110071)	100%	Shot down in combat with USAAF P-51s.	Korbach

Date	Name of Crew and Rank	Staffel	Fate	Aircraft, W.Nr & Code	Damage /Loss	Reason for Casualty	Place
22.04.44	Ogefr. Johann Peischl	7	Killed	Bf 109 G-5 White 10 (110081)	100%	Shot down in combat with USAAF P-51s.	Gemünden
22.04.44	Lt. Joachim Göhre	8	Killed	Bf 109 G-6 Yellow 9 (441028)	100%	Shot down in combat with USAAF P-51s.	Korbach
22.04.44	Gefr. Willi Klückmann	8	Killed	Bf 109 G-6 Yellow 11 (163066)	100%	Shot down in combat with USAAF P-51s.	Korbach
22.04.44	Ofw. Franz Wilhelm Heck	9	Killed	Bf 109 G-6 Yellow 19 (163085)	100%	Shot down in combat with USAAF P-51s.	Korbach
22.04.44	Ufz. Kurt Ziegenfuss	9	Killed	Bf 109 G-6 Yellow 17 (441011)	100%	Shot down in combat with USAAF P-51s.	Korbach
22.04.44	Ogefr. Konrad Fricke	9	Killed	Bf 109 G-6 Yellow 22 (163071)	100%	Shot down in combat with USAAF P-51s.	Fritzlar
27.04.44	Uffz. Herbert Strassemeier	1	Killed	Fw 190 A-5/U-12 White 16 (160416)		Crashed on landing on non-combat flight.	Münster
28.04.44	Uffz. Werner Humer	9	Killed	Bf 109 G-6 RH+JQ (15775)		Crashed on non-combat flight.	Paderborn
28.04.44	Ofw. Roman Heimbach	9	Killed	Bf 109 G-6 Yellow 1 (441154)		Crashed on non-combat flight.	Paderborn
29.04.44	Uffz. Rolf Eilken	1	Wounded	Fw 190 A-7 White 1 (430364)		Belly landing following combat.	Brunswick
29.04.44	Ogefr. Werner Triebel	6	Killed	Fw 190 A-8 Yellow 9 (170391)	100%	Shot down in combat.	Brunswick
29.04.44	Uffz. Hans-Hasso Hanfeld	6	Killed	Fw 190 A-7 Yellow 8 (431004)	100%	Shot down in combat.	Brunswick
29.04.44		II. Gruppe		Fw 190 A ( )	15%	Belly landing following combat.	
01.05.44		II. Gruppe		Fw 190 A ( )	80%	Belly landing following combat.	
04.05.44	Uffz. Claus Büchner	5	Killed	Fw 190 A-7 Black 6 (340048)	100%	Crashed on non-combat flight.	Störmede
04.05.44	Uffz. Willy Siewers	6	Wounded	Fw 190 A-7 Yellow 13 (652551)		Belly landing following combat with 2 USAAF P-51s.	Göttingen
04.05.44	Gefr. Otto Wurst	7	Killed	Bf 109 G-6 White 4 (440750)	100%	Shot down in combat with USAAF P-47s.	Greven
07.05.44	Uffz. Werner Preuss	5	Killed	Fw 190 A-8 Black 7 (680148)	100%	Crashed on non-combat flight.	Halver
-8.05.44	Fw. Hans Jörg Karl	1	Killed	Fw 190 A-7 White 15 (643908)	100%	Shot down in combat.	Nordburg
08.05.44	Uffz. Kurt Geberth	1	Killed	Fw 190 A-8 White 17 (174004)	100%	Shot down in combat.	Altena
08.05.44	Ofw. Rudolf Hübl	2	Wounded	Fw 190 A-8 Black 3 (174005)	100%	Shot down in combat with USAAF bombers.	Cielde
08.05.44	Uffz. Ernst Kay	2	Killed	Fw 190 A-8 Black 5 (170109)	100%	Shot down in combat.	Celle
08.05.44	Uffz. Wilhelm Peine	2	Wounded	Fw 190 A-8 Black 14 (730315)	100%	Shot down in combat with USAAF bombers.	Celle
08.05.44	Uffz. Karl Dietrich Ewald	2	Killed	Fw 190 A-8 Black 17 (170432)	100%	Shot down in combat.	Celle

Date	Name of Crew and Rank	Staffel	Fate	Aircraft, W.Nr & Code	Damage /Loss	Reason for Casualty	Place
08.05.44	Fw. Arnold Jansen	5	Wounded	Fw 190 A-8 Black 11 (170338)	100%	Shot down in combat.	Bonnemühlen
08.05.44	Uffz. Erich Landgrebe	6	Wounded	Fw 190 A-7 White 3 (340049)		Belly landing following combat.	Nienburg
08.05.44	Uffz. Wilhelm Odenthal	7	Killed	Bf 109 G-6 White 31 (440678)	100%	Shot down in combat with USAAF P-47s.	Soltau
08.05.44	Fw. Benvenuto Gartmann	7	Wounded	Bf 109 G-6 White 2 (440558)	100%	Shot down in combat with USAAF bombers.	Hengelo
08.05.44	Fw. Felix Karenitz	8	Killed	Bf 109 G-6/AS Black 5 (20629)	100%	Shot down in combat with USAAF P-47s.	Dedelsdorf
08.05.44	Gefr. Alfred Kampf-Mücher	9	Killed	Bf 109 G-6 Yellow 18 (440621)	100%	Shot down in combat.	Hoyahagen
09.05.44	Lt. Werner Stockert	5	Killed	Fw 190 A-8 (730299)	100%	Crashed on non-combat flight.	Störmede
09.05.44	Uffz. Friedrich Remy	8	Wounded	Bf 109 G-6/AS Black 13 (15415)		Crashed on take off.	Paderborn
11.05.44	Oberst Walter Oesau	Gesch. stab	Killed	Bf 109 G-6/AS Green 13 (20601)	100%	Shot down in combat with five USAAF P-38s.	South-west of St.Vith
11.05.44	Ofhr. Adolf Stibane	7	Wounded	Bf 109 G-6 White 19 (708419)		Belly landing following combat with USAAF P-47s.	Lachen-Speyerdorf
11.05.44	Fw. Kurt Friedrichs	9	Killed	Bf 109 G-6 Yellow 14 (440650)	100%	Shot down in combat with USAAF P-47s and P-51s.	St. Wendel
12.05.44	Ofhr. Gottfried Just	2	Wounded	Fw 190 A-8 Black 9 (170082)		Crashed into another Fw 190 on landing following combat.	Limburg
12.05.44	Ofw. Günther Treptau	2	Wounded	Fw 190 A-8 Black 10 (170405)	100%	Shot down in combat with fighters.	Giessen
12.05.44	Uffz. Gerhard Neukotter	2	Killed	Fw 190 A-8 Black 13 (170375)	100%	Shot down in combat with fighters.	Wetzlar
12.05.44	Fw. Heinz Kahl	4	Killed	Fw 190 A-8 White 3 (730408)	100%	Shot down in combat.	Wendel
12.05.44	Uffz. Hermann Blanck	4	Killed	Fw 190 A-7 White 2 (431126)	100%	Shot down in combat.	Cochem
12.05.44	Uffz. Helmut Stiegler	4	Killed	Fw 190 A-5/U-12 White 6 (410247)	100%	Shot down in combat.	Zell/Mosel
12.05.44	Uffz. Gerold Braun	4	Killed	Fw 190 A-8 White 14 (174006)	100%	Shot down in combat with fighters.	Thalfang
12.05.44	Uffz. Richard Joscht	5	Killed	Fw 190 A-7 Black 5 (430481)	100%	Shot down in combat.	Weblen/Mosel
12.05.44	Uffz. Hubert Swoboda	5		Fw 190 A ( )	30%	Damaged in combat.	
12.05.44	Flgr. Georg Blech	5		Fw 190 A ( )	30%	Emergency landing following combat.	4 Kilometres south-west of Cochem
12.05.44	Fw. Hans Joachim Gebser	7	Killed	Bf 109 G-6 White 5 (440626)	100%	Shot down in combat with USAAF P-51s.	Schiffenberg
13.05.44	Uffz. Wolfgang Kappler	7	Killed	Fw 190 A-8 Yellow 11 (680149)	100%	Shot down in combat.	Stade
13.05.44	Uffz. Fritz Wurl	6		Fw 190 A ( )		Belly landing on non-combat flight.	
13.05.44	Gefr. Pankraz Spiegelsberger	8	Killed	Bf 109 G-6/AS Black 25 (440402)	100%	Shot down in combat with USAAF P-51s.	Stade

Date	Name of Crew and Rank	Staffel	Fate	Aircraft, W.Nr & Code	Damage /Loss	Reason for Casualty	Place
15.05.44	Uffz. Kurt Baten	9	Wounded	Bf 109 G-6 Yellow 16 (440642)		Crashed. Reason not known.	Paderborn
16.05.44	Uffz. Heinrich Weber	5	Killed	Fw 190 A-7 Black 15 (642542)	100%	Crashed on non-combat flight.	Neuhaus
16.05.44	Uffz. Fritz Schneider	6	Killed	Fw 190 A-8 Yellow 8 (170436)	100%	Crashed on non-combat flight.	Störmede
19.05.44	Gefr. Kurt Vocke	2	Killed	Fw 190 A-7 Black 4 (430347)	100%	Shot down in combat.	Hannover
19.05.44	Gefr. Wolfgang Hartung	3	Wounded	Fw 190 A-7 Yellow 16 (643727)		Emergency landing following combat.	Oldenburg
19.05.44	Uffz. Hans Sudikatis	4	Killed	Fw 190 A-7 White 5 (170332)	100%	Shot down in combat.	Flensburg
19.05.44	Fhr. Friedheim Petry	6	Killed	Fw 190 A-7 Yellow 6 (340280)	100%	Shot down in combat.	Rheine
19.05.44	Lt. Günther Munz	7	Killed	Bf 109 G-6 White 11 (110065)	100%	Shot down in combat with USAAF P-51s.	Lübeck
22.05.44		II. Gruppe		Fw 190 A ( )	35%	Belly landing following combat.	
22.05.44	Uffz. Josef Wohlrab	7	Killed	Bf 109 G-6 White 12 (170004)	100%	Shot down in combat.	Rendsburg
22.05.44	Ofhr. Klaus Holz	9	Wounded	Bf 109 G-6/AS Yellow 7 (440936)		Belly landing following combat with USAAF P-51s.	Bramstedt
25.05.44	Ofhr. Manfred Büttner	1	Wounded	Fw 190 A-8 White 14 (730330)	100%	Shot down in combat with USAAF fighters.	North-west of Stuttgart
25.05.44	Ogefr. Kurt Homola	9	Killed	Bf 109 G-6/AS Yellow 9 (440489)	100%	Shot down on landing by USAAF P-51s.	Besigheim
28.05.44	Oblt. Eugen Kotiza	3	Killed	Fw 190 A-8 Yellow 1 (730483)	100%	Shot down in combat.	Hannover
28.05.44	Gefr. Karl Heinz Schmidt	3	Killed	Fw 190 A-8 Yellow 3 (680153)	100%	Shot down in combat.	Helmstedt
28.05.44	Ofhr. Gustav Knoll	3	Wounded	Fw 190 A-7/R-6 Yellow 18 (430688)	100%	Shot down in combat.	Wolmirsleben
28.05.44	Uffz. Bernhard Gollinger	6	Wounded	Fw 190 A-8 Yellow 12 (730388)	100%	Shot down in combat with USAAF fighters.	Near Eilsleben
28.05.44	Ofw. Kurt Brodbeck	6		Fw 190 A ( )		Belly landing following combat.	Goslar
28.05.44		II. Gruppe		Fw 190 A ( )	100%	Shot down in combat.	Near Brustau
28.05.44	Gefr. Josef Körner	9	Wounded	Bf 109 G-6/AS White 4 (440939)	100%	Emergency landing with engine damage.	Sondershausen
28.05.44	Ofw. Fritz Timm	9	Killed	Bf 109 G-6 Yellow 3 (440700)	100%	Shot down in combat with USAAF P-51s.	Elsdorf/Köln
29.05.44	Uffz. Adolf Höffler	4	Killed	Fw 190 A-8 White 7 (680137)	100%	Overturned in bomb crater on landing following combat.	Cottbus
29.05.44	Lt. Otto Bach	4		Fw 190 A ( )		Overturned in bomb crater on landing following combat.	Cottbus
29.05.44	Fw. Adolf Schulz	4		Fw 190 A-8 White 8 (730331)		Belly landing following combat.	Züllsdorf
29.05.44	Fw. Rudolf Lehmann	4		Fw 190 A-8 White 13 (170416)		Belly landing following combat.	Züllsdorf

Date	*Name of Crew and Rank*	*Staffel*	*Fate*	*Aircraft, W.Nr & Code*	*Damage /Loss*	*Reason for Casualty*	*Place*
29.05.44	Uffz. Erwin Steeb	6	Wounded	Fw 190 A-8 Yellow 16 (340282)	100%	Shot down in combat.	Zwittau
29.05.44	Uffz. Wazulek	II. Gruppe	Wounded	Fw 190 A-8 ( )		Bellly landing following combat.	Brunswick
29.05.44	Fw. Walter Zimmer	7	Killed	Bf 109 G-6 White 13 (440953)	100%	Shot down in combat.	Burg
30.05.44	Gefr. Johannes Zitzmann	1	Killed	Fw 190 A-8 Yellow 7 (730410)	100%	Crashed on take off.	Dresden
30.05.44	Uffz. Adolf Zeller	1	Killed	Fw 190 A-8 Yellow 15 (170029)	100%	Shot down in combat.	Pretzier
30.05.44	Fhr. Karl Brucker	2	Wounded	Fw 190 A-8 Black 12 (170063)	100%	Shot down in combat.	Salzwedel
30.05.44	Uffz. Max Bierbaum	6	Killed	Fw 190 A-8 Yellow 8 (171011)	100%	Shot down in combat.	Magdeburg
30.05.44	Uffz Horst Steinburg	7	Wounded	Bf 109 G-6 White 15 (440932)	100%	Shot down in combat.	Fallersleben
30.05.44	Uffz. Ferdinand Spychinger	9	Killed	Bf 109 G-6 Yellow 17 (440644)	100%	Shot down in combat with fighters.	Salzwedel
31.05.44	Fw. Adolf Schulz	4	Killed	Fw 190 A-8 White 19 (550541)	100%	Shot down in combat with fighters.	Bornholte
31.05.44	Uffz. Anton Sinek	4	Killed	Fw 190 A-8 White 1 (643946)	100%	Shot down in combat with fighters.	Bornholte
31.05.44	Flgr. Georg Blech	5	Wounded	Fw 190 A-8 Black 11 (680521)	100%	Shot down in combat with fighters.	Bornholte
31.05.44	Lt. Günther Buchholz	6	Killed	Fw 190 A-8 Yellow 7 (680534)	100%	Shot down in combat with fighters.	Osterwiehe
31.05.44	Fw. Alfred Bindseil	6		Fw 190 A ( )		Belly landing following combat.	Störmede
01.06.44	Ofw. Kurt Brodbeck	6		Fw 190 A ( )		Belly landing on non-combat flight.	Störmede
01.06.44	Fw. Ernst Seefeldt	8	Wounded	Bf 109 G-6 Black 10 (410696)	100%	Crashed on take off.	Paderborn
03.06.44	Uffz. Franz Michel	1	Killed	Fw 190 A-6 White 12 (530122)	100%	Crashed on test flight.	Lippspringe
04.06.44	Lt. Wolfgang Kiefer	8	Killed	Bf 109 G-6 Black 4 (160740)	100%	Collided with aircraft of Lt. Gerhard Bosse.	Paderborn
04.06.44	Lt. Gerhard Bosse	8	Killed	Bf 109 G-6/AS Black 12 (163771)	100%	Collided with aircraft of Lt. Wolfgang Kiefer.	Paderborn
06.06.44	Uffz. Gerhard Bachmann	9	Killed	Bf 109 G-6 Yellow 15 (163796)	100%	Crashed on non-combat flight.	Hameln
07.06.44	Hptm. Karl-Heinz Weber	III. Gruppe	Killed	Bf 109 G-6 White 20 (410399)	100%	Shot down in combat with USAAF P-47s.	Caen
07.06.44	Uffz. Günther Koschinski	7	Wounded	Bf 109 G-6 White 9 (440649)	100%	Shot down in combat.	Caen
07.06.44	Gefr. Werner Penke	9	Killed	Bf 109 G-6 Yellow 13 (440926)	100%	Shot down on take off by USAAF P-47.	Beauvais
07.06.44	Lt. Johann Brünnler	7./JG 51	Killed	Fw 190 A-8 Black 18 (680552)	100%	Shot down in combat with six USAAF P-51s.	Chateaudun
09.06.44	Uffz. Helmut Riehl	2	Wounded	Fw 190 A-8 Black 16 (730513)		Damaged on landing.	Le Mans

Date	Name of Crew and Rank	Staffel	Fate	Aircraft, W.Nr & Code	Damage /Loss	Reason for Casualty	Place
13.06.44	Uffz. Friedrich Henke	1	Wounded	Fw 190 A-8 White 4 (730476)		Pilot wounded in combat.	St. Mère Eglise
13.06.44	Uffz. Franz Schnabel	1		Fw 190 A-8 White 4 (730476)		Belly landing following combat.	
13.06.44	Uffz. Friedrich Enderle	3	Wounded	Fw 190 A-8 Yellow 3 (680536)		Pilot wounded in combat.	Gorronne
14.06.44	Uffz. Ferdinand von Nickisch	8	Killed	Bf 109 G-6 White 13 (440553)	100%	Shot down in combat with USAAF B-26s.	Caen
14.06.44	Ofw. Gustav Dilling	9	Killed	Bf 109 G-6 Chevron 0 (411491)	100%	Shot down in combat with USAAF B0-26s.	Caen
15.06.44	Lt. Hans Gareis	1	Killed	Fw 190 A-8 White 13 (170737)	100%	Shot down in combat.	St. Pol
15.06.44	Uffz. Wilhelm Woite	2		Fw 190 A-8 ( )	100%	Shot down in combat.	
15.06.44	Uffz. Horst Gabel	3	Killed	Fw 190 A-8 Yellow 10 (170735)	100%	Shot down in combat.	Rabodanges
16.06.44	Fw. Alois Wenke	2	Killed	Fw 190 A-8 Black 2 (680564)	100%	Shot down in combat.	Caen
16.06.44	Uffz. Fritz Hofmann	3	Wounded	Fw 190 A-8 Yellow 6 (170062)	100%	Shot down in combat.	Calais
17.06.44	Lt. Rudolf Piffer	1	Killed	Fw 190 A-8 White 3 (172604)	100%	Shot down in combat.	Argentan
17.06.44	Ofhr. Friedrich Wilhelm Brandt	1	Killed	Fw 190 A-8 White 5 (730389)	100%	Shot down in combat.	Argentan
17.06.44	Gefr. Gustav Neissl	9	Wounded	Bf 109 G-6 Yellow 7 (440956)	100%	Crashed. Reason not known.	Amfreville
17.06.44	Fw. Helmuth Heidemann Uffz. Herbert Redlich	7./ JG 51	Killed	Fw 190 A-8 White 12	100%	Shot down in combat with 20 USAAF P-51s.	Alençon
17.06.44	Uffz. Günther Henschel	7./ JG 51	Missing	Fw 190 A-8 Blue 4 (730473)	100%	Shot down in combat with 20 USAAF P-51s.	Alençon
17.06.44	Uffz. Franz Zechner	7./	Missing	Fw 190 A-8 Blue 15 (171015)	100%	Shot down in combat.	Alençon
18.06.44	Uffz. Benno Oberhauser	2		Fw 190 A-8 ( )	100%	Shot down in combat.	Alençon
20.06.44	Uffz. Walter Dobrat	1	Wounded	Fw 190 A-8 White 11 (680568)	100%	Rammed USAAF fighter.	Alençon
20.06.44	Uffz. Hermann	I. Gruppe	Missing	Fw 190 A-8 ( )	100%	Shot down in combat.	
20.06.44	Uffz. Löwe	I. Gruppe		Fw 190 A-8 ( )	100%	Shot down in combat.	
20.06.44	Ofw. Kurt Brodbeck	6		Fw 190 A-8 Black 12 (170643)	100%	Shot down in combat.	Argentan
20.06.44	Uffz. Horst Jürklies	7	Killed	Bf 109 G-6 White 12 (440250)	100%	Shot down in combat.	Clastres
20.06.44	Uffz. Willi Herzberg	8	Killed	Bf 109 G-6 Black 9 (165183)	100%	Shot down in combat.	Noyon
20.06.44	Uffz. Jürgen Zarte	9	Killed	Bf 109 G-6 Yellow 12 (165196)	100%	Shot down in combat with USAAF P-47s.	Clastres
20.06.44	Fw. Richard Henner	7./ JG 51	POW	Fw 190 A-8 Blue 8 (730407)	100%	Shot down in combat	Caen

Date	Name of Crew and Rank	Staffel	Fate	Aircraft, W.Nr & Code	Damage /Loss	Reason for Casualty	Place
22.06.44	Uffz. Helmut Faltin	2	Killed	Fw 190 A-8 Black 9 (730984)	100%	Shot down in combat.	St. Lô
22.06.44	Uffz. Karl Grube	3	Wounded	Fw 190 A-8 Red 2 (172661)	100%	Shot down in combat.	Lonrai
22.06.44	Fw. Hans Knabben	6	POW	Fw 190 A-8 Black 13 (730940)	100%	Shot down in combat.	St. Lô
23.06.44	Lt. Siegfried Stoffel	1	Killed	Fw 190 A-8 White 7 (680539)	100%	Shot down in combat.	Alençon
23.06.44	Uffz. Franz Schnabel	1	Killed	Fw 190 A-8 White 15 (680555)	100%	Shot down in combat.	Alençon
23.06.44	Uffz. Wilhelm Woite	2	POW	Fw 190 A-8 Black 14 (170093)	100%	Shot down in combat.	Caen
27.06.44	Ofw. Rudolf Hübl	2	Wounded	Fw 190 A-8 Black 1 (730515)	100%	Emergency landing after being hit by Flak.	Lonrai
27.06.44	Uffz. Benno Oberhauser	2	Killed	Fw 190 A-8 Black 7 (730461)	100%	Shot down in combat.	Caen
28.06.44	Ofhr. Aloysius Kaatz	5	Killed	Fw 190 A-8 Black 7 (680523)	100%	Shot down in combat with Spitfires.	Flers
29.06.44	Uffz. Walter Ruffing	7./ JG 51	Killed	Fw 190 A-8 White 123 (172713)	100%	Shot down in combat.	Flers
30.06.44	Uffz. Fritz Rathofer	3	Killed	Fw 190 A-8 Yellow 10 (730500)	100%	Shot down in combat.	Caen
04.07.44	Uffz. Karl Grube	3	Killed	Fw 190 A-8 Yellow 8 (680546)	100%	Shot down in combat.	St. Lô
04.07.44	Gefr. Karl Friedrich Ernst	4	Killed	Fw 190 A-8 Red 23 (170430)	100%	Shot down in combat.	St. Lô
04.07.44	Ogefr. Friedel Pallas	5	Wounded	Fw 190 A-8 White 226 (731462)		Overturned on landing on non-combat flight.	Semallé
04.07.44	Lt. Weissbrodt	7./JG 51	Killed	Fw 190 A-8 Blue 2 (730923)	100%	Shot down in combat.	St. Lô
04.07.44	Lt. Friedrich Krakowitzer	7./JG 51	Killed	Fw 190 A-8 Blue 11 (170094)	100%	Shot down in combat.	St. Lô
06.07.44	Oblt. Wolfgang Ernst	9./JG 77	Wounded	Fw 190 A-8 White 231 (350151)	100%	Shot down in combat.	Argentan
06.07.44	Uffz. Hans Maximow	9./JG 77	Killed	Fw 190 A-8 White 232 (731094)	100%	Shot down in combat.	Argentan
07.07.44	Uffz. Hans Böhmer	2	Wounded	Fw 190 A-8 Black 3 (174005)		Emergency landing following combat.	Lonrai
07.07.44	Gefr. Günther Petri	2	Wounded	Fw 190 A-8 Black 17 (730512)		Emergency landing following combat.	Argentan
12.07.44	Hptm. Friedrich Kasuhn	7	Killed	Bf 109 G-6 White 13 (164908)		Shot down in combat with Spitfires.	Caen
12.07.44	Oblt. Heinz Lammich	7	Killed	Bf 109 G-6 White 15 (163990)	100%	Shot down in combat.	Caen
12.07.44	Lt. Kurt Ibing	III. Gruppe		Bf 109 G-6 White 5 (412011)		Shot down in combat with Spitfires and Typhoons.	Caen
13.07.44	Uffz. Kurt Senger	7	Killed	Bf 109 G-6 White 9 (163831)	100%	Shot down in combat with Spitfires.	Epaignes

Date	Name of Crew and Rank	Staffel	Fate	Aircraft, W.Nr & Code	Damage /Loss	Reason for Casualty	Place
14.07.44	Uffz. Ferdinand Strohmeyer	1	Killed	Fw 190 A-8 Blue 5 (680538)	100%	Shot down in combat with USAAF fighters.	Caen
14.07.44	Uffz. Rolf Stromer	7	Missing	Bf 109 G-6 White 12 (163969)	100%	Shot down in combat	Caen
14.07.44	Uffz. Kurt Mann	9./JG 77		Bf 109 G-6 ( )		Belly landing following combat.	
14.07.44	Uffz. Viktor Orend	9	POW	Bf 109 G-6 Yellow 16 (163968)	100%	Shot down in combat.	Caen
14.07.44	Uffz. Paul Taube	9./JG 77	Wounded	Fw 190 A-8 White 242 (170941)	100%	Emergency landing due to fuel shortage following combat.	Aube
17.07.44	Ogefr. Thomas Rauth	1	Killed	Fw 190 A-8 White 6 (171081)	100%	Shot down in combat with USAAF fighters.	Caen
16.07.44	Ofhr. Anton Iller	6	Killed	Fw 190 A-8 White 2 (680567)	100%	Crashed into trees on take off.	Alençon
17.07.44	Uffz. Rudolf Hoffmann	5	Missing	Fw 190 A-8 Black 7 (170973)	100%	Shot down in combat with fighters.	Flers
17.07.44	Uffz. Josef Gold	6	Wounded	Fw 190 A-8 Black 5 (731397)	100%	Shot down in combat with USAAF P-51s.	Flers
18.07.44	Uffz. Julius Mangerich	7	Killed	Bf 109 G-6 Black 15 (163811)	100%	Belly landing following combat with USAAF P-38s.	Rouen
18.07.44	Uffz. Gottfried Döhnert	9	Killed	Bf 109 G-6 Yellow 6 (163984)	100%	Belly landing following combat.	Bray
18.07.44	Fw. Karl Heinz Kutzera	9	Missing	Bf 109 G-6 Yellow 13 (163988)	100%	Shot down in combat.	Caen
20.07.44	Lt. Helmut Proff	4	Killed	Fw 190 A-8 White 3 (731398)	10%	Shot down in combat with Spitfires.	St. Lô
20.07.44	Uffz. Christian Knoblauch	4	Missing	Fw 190 A-8 White 1 (680554)	100%	Shot down in combat with Spitfires.	St. Lô
20.07.44	Gefr. Walter Gehr	4	Killed	Fw 190 A-8 White 4 (170972)	100%	Shot down in combat with Spitfires.	St. Lô
20.07.44	Lt. Christian Steven	6	Missing	Fw 190 A-8 Yellow 1 (731064)	100%	Shot down in combat with Spitfires.	St. Lô
20.07.44	Ofhr. Rudolf Kaltenhauser	6	Wounded/Died 24/7/44	Fw 190 A-8 Yellow 2 (730403)	100%	Belly landing following combat with Spitfires.	Alençon
20.07.44	Gefr. Johannes Kamutzki	7./JG 51	Missing	Fw 190 A-8 Blue 4 (731739)	100%	Shot down in combat with Spitfires.	St. Lô
22.07.44	Uffz. Jacob Vogel	8	POW	Bf 109 G-6 Black 7 (413601)	100%	Became ill during flight.	Caen
23.07.44	Uffz. Erich Rahner	7./JG 51	Wounded	Fw 190 A-7 Blue 13 (170975)		Overturned on landing following combat.	Chartres
23.07.44	Ofw. Leo Schuhmacher	6		Fw 190 A-8 ( )		Belly landed to help Uffz. Rahner.	Chartres
24.07.44	Fw. Hans Fordemann	7	Killed	Bf 109 G-6 White 10 (163973)	100%	Shot down in combat with Spitfires.	Caen
24.07.44	Uffz. Albert Düsterhöft	7	Killed	Bf 109 G-6 White 16 (412187)	100%	Shot down in combat with Spitfires.	Caen
25.07.44	Gefr. Helmut Walter	5	Killed	Fw 190 A-8 Black 1 (731410)	100%	Shot down in combat.	Laigle

Date	Name of Crew and Rank	Staffel	Fate	Aircraft, W.Nr & Code	Damage /Loss	Reason for Casualty	Place
25.07.44	Fw. Eugen Grünenwald	7	Killed	Bf 109 G-6 White 17 (413535)	100%	Shot down in combat.	Rouen
25.07.44	Uffz. Hermann Käser	8	Wounded	Bf 109 G-6 Black 7 (413604)	100%	Shot down in combat.	Caen
25.07.44	Uffz. Alfons Wolfgang Habig	8	Wounded	Bf 109 G-6 Black 8 (165871)	100%	Shot down in combat.	Caen
25.07.44	Uffz. Hugo Hausotter	8		Bf 109 G-6/AS Black 14 ( )	100%	Shot down in combat by Spitfire.	Near Rouen
25.07.44	Ofhr. Bebbo Krätzer	8	Killed	Bf 109 G-6 Black 16 (110386)	100%	Shot down in combat.	Caen
25.07.44	Uffz. Heinrich Esser	9	Wounded	Bf 109 G-6 Yellow 1 (411471)	100%	Shot down in combat.	Rouen
25.07.44	Oblt. Wolfgang Meyer	III. Gruppe	Killed	Bf 109 G-6 Blue 211 (165411)	100%	Shot down in combat.	Caen
27.07.44	Ofw. Gerhard Roschinsky	1	Wounded	Fw 190 A-8 Black 8 (172729)	100%	Shot down in combat	St. Lô
27.07.44	Lt. Ulrich Brenner	2	Wounded	Fw 190 A-8 Black 2 (172991)	100%	Shot down in combat with USAAF fighters.	St. Martin
27.07.44	Lt. Gottfried Krumme	3	Killed	Fw 190 A-8 Yellow 5 (171451)	100%	Shot down in combat with USAAF fighters.	St. Lô
27.07.44	Fw. Eugen Busch	3	Missing	Fw 190 A-8 Yellow 11 (173005)	100%	Shot down in combat with USAAF fighters.	St. Lô
27.07.44	Uffz. Fritz Milde	5	Killed	Fw 190 A-8 Black 21 (171062)	100%	Shot down in combat with USAAF fighters.	Alençon
27.07.44	Fw. Fritz Haspel	8	Wounded	Bf 109 G-6 Black 2 (15391)	100%	Shot down in combat with fighters.	Lisieux
27.07.44	Uffz. Werner Moser	8	Wounded	Bf 109 G-6 Black 14 (413619)	100%	Shot down in combat with fighters.	Rouen
28.07.44	Uffz. Franz Moser	2	Wounded	Fw 190 A-8 Black 18 (680551)	100%	Shot down in combat with USAAF fighters.	St. Lô
28.07.44	Ogefr. Max Ulrich Förster	2	Missing	Fw 190 A-8 Black 5 (171612)	100%	Shot down in combat with USAAF fighters.	St. Lô
28.07.44	FjFhr. Jürgen Post	9./JG 77	Killed	Fw 190 A-8 (173045)		Crashed on non-combat flight.	Alençon
29.07.44	Uffz. Heinz Franke	2	Killed	Fw 190 A-8 (170953)		Crashed on non-combat flight.	Le Mans
29.07.44	Ogefr. Herbert Wehlte	3	POW	Fw 190 A-8 Yellow 3 (170966)	100%	Shot down in combat with USAAF fighters.	St.Lô
30.07.44	Uffz. Erwin Minzenmay	2	Missing	Fw 190 A-8 Black 1 (171087)	100%	Shot down in combat with USAAF fighters.	St. Lô
30.07.44	Ofhr. Werner Hostermann	2	Wounded	Fw 190 A-8 Black 7 (173033)	100%	Shot down by own Flak.	St. De Fleur
30.07.44	Uffz. Fritz Arndt	3	Killed	Fw 190 A-8 Yellow 6 (171662)	100%	Shot down in combat with USAAF fighters.	St. Lô
30.07.44	Uffz. Hans Knüpfer	8	Wounded	Bf 109 G-6 Black 15 (165856)	100%	Shot down in combat with fighters.	West of Paris
30.07.44	Ofhr. Lothar Lutz	9	Wounded	Bf 109 G-6 Yellow 2 (413553)	100%	Shot down in combat with Spitfires.	Nogent le Rotrou

Date	Name of Crew and Rank	Staffel	Fate	Aircraft, W.Nr & Code	Damage /Loss	Reason for Casualty	Place
30.07.44	Lt. Hans Halbey	III. Gruppe		Bf 109 G Black 1 ( )	100%	Shot down in combat with Spitfires.	Nogent le Rotrou
30.07.44	Uffz. Wolfgang Boye	7./JG 51	Missing	Fw 190 A-8 White 5 (690133)	100%	Shot down in combat with USAAF P-47s.	Avranches
31.07.44	Lt. Heinz Kottucz	3	Killed	Fw 190 A-8 Yellow 8 (173024)	100%	Shot down in combat with USAAF fighters.	Caen
31.07.44	Uffz. Heinz Fleischhauer	3	Missing	Fw 190 A-8 Yellow 7 (171004)	100%	Shot down in combat with USAAF fighters.	Caen
31.07.44	Fw. Rudolf Rauhaus	I. Gruppe	Killed	Fw 190 A-8 White 20 (172606)	100%	Shot down in combat with USAAF fighters.	Caen
31.07.44	Uffz. Hans Freitag	7	Wounded Died on 12/9/44	Bf 109 G-6 White 10 (413581)		Crashed on take off.	Tergnier
01.08.44	Uffz. Fritz Wurl	6	Killed	Fw 190 A-7 Black 1 (340032)		Crashed on landing.	Normandy
02.08.44	Lt. Franz Koplik	9	Killed	Bf 109 G-6 Yellow 12 (413583)	100%	Shot down in combat	Compiègne
05.08.44	Fw. Max Lau	9	Killed	Bf 109 G-6 Yellow 6 (413583)	100%	Shot down in combat with USAAF P-38s.	Compiègne
05.08.44	Ofhr. Hubert Heckmann	9	Wounded	Bf 109 G-6 Yellow 13 (165873)	100%	Shot down in combat with USAAF P-38s.	Compiègne
05.08.44	Uffz. Kurt Engfer	9./JG 77		Fw 190 A-8 White 6 (731066)	100%	Shot down in combat with USAAF fighters.	Avranches
06.08.44	FjOfw. Herbert Kaiser	7	Wounded	Bf 109 G-6 White 12 (413577)	100%	Shot down in combat.	Near Paris
06.08.44	Ogefr. Robert Kocaurek	7	Wounded	Bf 109 G-6 Black 11 (412259)	100%	Emergency landing following combat.	Near Paris
07.08.44	Ofhr. Günther Bernsau	1	Killed	Fw 190 A-8 White 12 (732039)	100%	Shot down in combat with USAAF fighters.	Angerville
07.08.44	Uffz. Herbert Havemann	1	Killed	Fw 190 A-8 White 1 (680738)	100%	Shot down when landing by USAAF fighters.	Chartres
07.08.44	Uffz. Gerhard Veil	1	Killed	Fw 190 A-8 White 4 (172979)	100%	Shot down in combat with USAAF fighters.	Avranches
07.08.44	Uffz. Walter Hiernerwadel	3	Killed	Fw 190 A-8 Yellow 2 (731743)	100%	Overturned on landing following combat.	Chateaudun
07.08.44	Ofw. Hans Kaniss	8	Wounded	Bf 109 G-6 Black 13 (412192)	100%	Shot down in combat with USAAF P-47s.	Rennes
07.08.44	Uffz. Hans Hermann	7./JG 51	Missing	Fw 190 A-8 Blue 5 (172739)	100%	Shot down in combat with Spitfires.	Mortain
07.08.44	Uffz. Friedrich Mai	7./ JG 51	Missing	Fw 190 A-8 Black 21 (680838)	100%	Shot down in combat with Spitfires.	Mortain
08.08.44	Hptm. Eberhardt Mätzke	9	Killed	Bf 109 G-6 Yellow 20 (413613)	100%	Shot down in combat with USAAF P-38s.	Alençon
09.08.44	Lt. Paul Himmelmann	7	Killed	Bf 109 G-6 White 2 (164909)	100%	Shot down in combat with USAAF P-47s.	Alençon
09.08.44	Uffz. Hans Georg Meyer	9./ JG 77	Killed	Fw 190 A-8 (731737)	100%	Shot down in combat with USAAF fighters.	Oysonville
10.08.44	Uffz. Wilhelm Wölper	3	Wounded	Fw 190 A-8 Yellow 6 (680177)	100%	Crashed on landing with aircraft of Uffz. Mann.	Oysonville

Date	Name of Crew and Rank	Staffel	Fate	Aircraft, W.Nr & Code	Damage /Loss	Reason for Casualty	Place
10.08.44	Uffz. Wilhelm Wäschle	4	Killed	Fw 190 A-8 Black 25 (731785)	100%	Shot down in combat with fighters.	Montreau
10.08.44	Uffz. Hugo Hausotter	8		Bf 109 G-6 Blue 17 ( )	100%	Shot down by USAAF P-47s.	
10.08.44	Uffz. Wilhelm Müller	9	Killed	Bf 109 G-6 White 5 (165833)	100%		Le Plessis
10.08.44	Uffz. Kurt Mann	9./JG 77	Killed	Fw 190 A-8 Red 1 (731791)	100%	Crashed on landing with aircraft of Uffz. Wölper.	Oysonville
11.08.44	Lt. Ulrich Brenner	2	Killed	Fw 190 A-8 Black 2 (731439)	100%	Crashed on landing.	Oysonville
12.08.44	Uffz. Wolfram Brechthold	9		Bf 109 G-6 Yellow 16 (165870)	100%	Shot down in combat with USAAF fighters.	Amy
14.08.44	FjFw. Fritz Junge	1	Wounded	Fw 190 A-8 White 13 (171665)		Emergency landing following combat with fighters.	Fere Champenoise
15.08.44	Ofhr. Werner Forchert	10	Missing	Bf 109 G-6 White 3 (412342)	100%	Shot down in combat with USAAF P-51s.	Dreux
15.08.44	Uffz. Karl Dunkel	10	Missing	Bf 109 G-6 Black 7 (164912)	100%	Shot down in combat with USAAF P-51s.	Dreux
15.08.44	Uffz. Josef Seubert	10	POW	Bf 109 G-6 White 10 (163987)	100%	Forced down by 6 USAAF P-38s.	6 miles west of St. Léger-en-Yvelinies
18.08.44	Uffz. Egon Schultz	10	Wounded Died on 19/8/44	Bf 109 G-6 White 16 (165384)		Crashed on take off.	Vailly
21.08.44	Lt. Kurt Ibing	10	POW	Bf 109 G-6 White 3 (413582)	100%	Shot down by light Flak.	Between Vermon and Mantes
21.08.44	Uffz. Paul Ost	10	Killed	Bf 109 G-6 White 6 (412168)	100%	Exact cause of loss not known.	Evreux
21.08.44	Gefr. Franz Schlusche	10	Wounded	Bf 109 G-6 White 13 (165834)		Emergency landing after being shot down by Flak.	Evreux
22.08.44	Gefr. Hans Thein	10	POW	Bf 109 G-6 White 9 (658381)	100%	Shot down by Flak.	Near Rouilly sur Seine
23.08.44	Oblt. Elmar Resch	9	POW	Bf 109 G-6 Black 15 (163856)	100%	Shot down in combat with USAAF P-47s.	Near Thorigny
23.08.44	Ogefr. Horst Döring	11	Killed	Bf 109 G-6 Black 1 (165819)	100%	Crashed on take off.	Vailly
23.08.44	Ogefr. Otto Messmer	11	POW	Bf 109 G-6 Black 2 (412352)	100%	Crashed on landing following engine trouble.	25 miles south of Paris
25.08.44	Ogefr. Alfred Finking	11	Killed	Bf 109 G-6 Black 23 (165811)	100%	Shot down in combat with USAAF P-51s.	Soisson
25.08.44	Uffz. Friedrich Ickes	11	Killed	Bf 109 G-6 Black 6 (412171)	100%	Shot down in combat.	Soisson
25.08.44	Hptm. Heinz Knoke	III. Gruppe		Bf 109 G ( )	100%	Shot down in combat.	
28.08.44	Uffz. Ewald Roth	10	Killed	Bf 109 G-6 White 15 (413584)	100%	Crashed with another German fighter during combat.	Cerfontaine
12.09.44	Uffz. Karl Heinz Virnau	8	Killed	Fw 190 A-8 Black 14 (171644)	100%	Crashed on non-combat flight.	Reinsehlen
19.09.44	Fw. Heinrich Bartzen	3	Wounded	Fw 190 A-8 Yellow 7 (173858)		Overturned on landing on non-combat flight.	Husum

Date	Name of Crew and Rank	Staffel	Fate	Aircraft, W.Nr & Code	Damage /Loss	Reason for Casualty	Place
19.09.44	Uffz. Erich Lorenz	8	Wounded	Fw 190 A-8 Black 13 (175197)	100%	Crashed on non-combat flight.	Soltau
22.09.44	Gefr. Gerd Cress	4	Killed	Fw 190 A-8 Red 8 (173097)	100%	Crashed on non-combat flight.	Husum
22.09.44	Fhr. Walter Schneider	4	Killed	Fw 190 A-8 Red 10 (175008)	100%	Crashed on non-combat flight.	Husum
22.09.44	Fhr. Walter Eitemeier	7	Killed	Fw 190 A-8 Red 10 (173920)		Crashed on non-combat flight.	Soltau
27.09.44	Uffz. Albert Friedmann	4	Wounded	Fw 190 A-8 Red 11 (173937)		Overturned on landing on non-combat flight.	Husum
01.10.44	Fw. Karl Dähn	4	Wounded	Fw 190 A-8 Red 12 (173923)		Emergency landing on non-combat flight.	Husum
13.10.44	Lt. Hans Berger	1		Fw 190 A-8 White 7 ( )		Belly landing on non-combat flight.	Wismar
14.10.44	Oblt. Hans Vermaaten	2	Killed	Fw 190 A-8 Red 12 (173865)		Crashed on non-combat flight.	Husum
15.11.44	Fw. Wolfram Murach		Killed	Fw 190 A-8 Yellow 20 (380163)	100%	Crashed on non-combat flight.	Mark. Friedland
18.11.44	Uffz. Ernst Adolf Schaumberg	2	Wounded	Fw 190 A-8 Black 1 (175238)	100%	Emergency landing on non-combat flight.	Ferdinandshof
18.11.44	Uffz. Helmut Bregulla	5	Wounded	Fw 190 A-8 White 17 (350216)	100%	Crashed on non-combat flight.	Tutow
21.11.44	Lt. Gerhard Nobereit	1	Killed	Fw 190 A-8 White 13 (171658)	100%	Shot down in combat with USAAF fighters.	Berga
21.11.44	Fhr. Kurt Fiedler	1	Killed	Fw 190 A-8 White 4 (173854)	100%	Shot down in combat with USAAF fighters.	Riefstadt
21.11.44	Oblt. Wilhelm Bergmann	2	Missing	Fw 190 A-8 Black 2 (173949)	100%	Shot down in combat with USAAF fighters.	Weimar
21.11.44	Fhr. Walter Fiedler	2	Killed	Fw 190 A-8 Black 4 (173855)	100%	Shot down in combat with USAAF fighters.	Gardelegen
21.11.44	Uffz. Helmut Lang	2	Wounded	Fw 190 A-8 Black 7 (175015)	100%	Shot down in combat with USAAF fighters.	Weimar
21.11.44	Fhr. Heinz Sieberg	2	Killed	Fw 190 A-8 Black 8 (681029)	100%	Shot down in combat with USAAF fighters.	Weimar
21.11.44	Ofw. Georg Fröhlich	2	Killed	Fw 190 A-8 Black 10 (173928)	100%	Shot down in combat with USAAF fighters.	South of Jena
21.11.44	Uffz. Günther Quentin	2	Wounded	Fw 190 A-8 Black 16 (175010)	100%	Shot down in combat with USAAF fighters.	Erfurt
21.11.44	Ofhr. Reinhard Seume	3	Wounded	Fw 190 A-8 Yellow 3 (171154)	100%	Shot down in combat.	Alsdorf
21.11.44	Ofhr. Gustav Knoll	3	Killed	Fw 190 A-8 Yellow 4 (173860)	100%	Shot down in combat.	Eisleben
21.11.44	Fhr. Karl Brücker	3	Killed	Fw 190 A-8 Yellow 7 (173913)	100%	Shot down in combat.	Langensalza
21.11.44	Gefr. Reinhard Simmel	3	Killed	Fw 190 A-8 Yellow 14 (173942)	100%	Shot down in combat.	Sangershausen
21.11.44	Fhr. Helmut Schreck	3	Killed	Fw 190 A-8 Yellow 16 (173874)	100%	Shot down in combat.	Blankenheim

Date	Name of Crew and Rank	Staffel	Fate	Aircraft, W.Nr & Code	Damage /Loss	Reason for Casualty	Place
21.11.44	Uffz. Gerhard Fendler	4	Wounded	Fw 190 A-8 Red 4 (175025)	100%	Shot down in combat with USAAF fighters.	Erfurt
21.11.44	Ofw. Arno Potzel	4	Killed	Fw 190 A-8 Red 6 (175007)	100%	Shot down in combat with USAAF fighters.	Roda
21.11.44	Fhr. Georg Müthel	4	Missing	Fw 190 A-8 Red 7 (171477)	100%	Shot down in combat with USAAF fighters.	Erfurt
21.11.44	Fhr. Joachim Horlbeck	4	Missing	Fw 190 A-8 Red 9 (175229)	100%	Shot down in combat with USAAF fighters.	Erfurt
21.11.44	Uffz. Alfred Thienert	4	Wounded	Fw 190 A-8 Red 13 (171151)	100%	Shot down in combat with USAAF fighters.	Erfurt
21.11.44	Uffz. Heinz Hempel	4	Wounded	Fw 190 A-8 Red 14 (175017)	100%	Shot down in combat with USAAF fighters.	Erfurt
21.11.44	Ofhr. Bruno Lüst	4	Missing	Fw 190 A-8 Red 15 (173926)	100%	Shot down in combat with USAAF fighters.	Erfurt
21.11.44	Uffz. Heinz Gwojdzinski	7	Killed	Fw 190 A-8 Yellow 9 (175178)	100%	Landed in bomb crater on landing on non-combat flight.	Roggentien
25.11.44	Uffz. Adolf Weichert	Stab,III. Gruppe	Killed	Bf 109 G-14 Grey 23 (784969)		Crashed on non-combat flight.	Anklam
26.11.44	Gefr. Ernst Nikoleizak	Gesch. Stab	Killed	Fw 190 A-9 Green 7 (205028)	100%	Shot down in combat.	Lewfreda
26.11.44	Uffz. Wolfgang Albrecht	2	Killed	Fw 190 A-8 Black 14 (175011)	100%	Shot down in combat.	Perleberg
26.11.44	Uffz. Heinz Reichardt	5	Wounded	Fw 190 A-8 White 8 (175159)	100%	Shot down in combat with USAAF P-51s.	Salzwedel
26.11.44	Lt. Karl Kremer	5	Wounded	Fw 190 A-8 White 12 (175004)	100%	Shot down in combat with USAAF P-51s.	Helmstedt
26.11.44	Lt. Hubert Swoboda	5	Wounded	Fw 190 A-8 White 13 (175207)	100%	Shot down in combat.	Wolmirstedt
26.11.44	Uffz. Walter Köbler	5	Killed	Fw 190 A-8 White 16 (178214)	100%	Shot down in combat with USAAF P-51s.	Sachau
26.11.44	Fhr. Harald Hinrichs	5	Killed	Fw 190 A-8 White 7 (175146)	100%	Collided with Fw 190 of Fhr. Erich Peters.	Ülzen
26.11.44	Gefr. Georg Blech	5	Killed	Fw 190 A-8 White 4 (175150)	100%	Shot down in combat.	Ülzen
26.11.44	Uffz. Alfred Wirth	7	Killed	Fw 190 A-8 Yellow 2 (171609)	100%	Shot down in combat.	Salzwedel
26.11.44	Uffz. Herbert Achenbach	7	Killed	Fw 190 A-8 Yellow 4 (173889)	100%	Shot down in combat.	Ülzen
26.11.44	Lt. Otto Bach	7	Killed	Fw 190 A-9 Yellow 15 (205186)	100%	Shot down in combat with USAAF P-51s.	Stendal
26.11.44	Uffz. Willi Siewers	7	Killed	Fw 190 A-8 Yellow 16 (738191)	100%	Shot down in combat.	Ülzen
26.11.44	Fhr. Erich Peters	8	Killed	Fw 190 A-8 Blue 16 (350220)	100%	Collided with Fw 190 of Fhr. Harald Hinrichs.	Ülzen
26.11.44	Uffz. Willi Lind	8	Killed	Fw 190 A-8 Blue 14 (173931)	100%	Shot down in combat with USAAF P-51s.	Peine
05.12.44	Uffz. Ernst Rheinbay	Gesch. Stab	Killed	Fw 190 A-8 Black 22 (960656)	100%	Shot down in combat.	Waren

Date	Name of Crew and Rank	Staffel	Fate	Aircraft, W.Nr & Code	Damage /Loss	Reason for Casualty	Place
05.12.44	Ofhr. Alfred Rossmeissl	Gesch. Stab	Killed	Fw 190 A-8 Black 23 (175158)	100%	Shot down in combat.	Waren
05.12.44	Ofhr. August Bohm	1	Missing	Fw 190 A-8 White 1 (960262)	100%	Shot down in combat.	Neuruppin
05.12.44	Fw. Franz Richter	1	Wounded	Fw 190 A-8 White 3 (173861)	100%	Shot down in combat.	Neuruppin
05.12.44	Uffz. Walter Stasch	1	Killed	Fw 190 A-8 White 6 (175020)	100%	Shot down in combat.	Dannenwalde
05.12.44	FjOfw. Hans Engelhaupt	1	Wounded	Fw 190 A-8 White 9 (171153)	100%	Shot down in combat.	Fürstenberg
05.12.44	Gefr. Heinz Hoppe	1	Wounded	Fw 190 A-8 White 11 (350856)	100%	Shot down in combat.	Dannenwalde
05.12.44	Fw. Kurt Weible	1	Wounded	Fw 190 A-8 White 12 (171548)	100%	Shot down in combat.	Liebenwalde
05.12.44	Ofhr. Manfred Büttner	1	Wounded	Fw 190 A-8 White 14 (350857)	100%	Belly landing following combat.	Schönwalde
05.12.44	Ofw. Gerhard Roschinsky	1	Wounded	Fw 190 A-8 White 15 (738169)	100%	Shot down in combat.	Fürstenberg
05.12.44	Uffz. Ernst Adolf Schaumburg	2	Wounded	Fw 190 A-8 Black 1 (750105)	100%	Shot down in combat.	Schwansee
05.12.44	Frh. Horst Köhler	2	Killed	Fw 190 A-8 Black 6 (960556)	100%	Shot down in combat.	Rheinsberg
05.12.44	Uffz. Günther Quentin	2	Missing	Fw 190 A-8 Red 12 (350217)	100%	Shot down in combat.	Stendal
05.12.44	Lt. Janis Lecis	3	Wounded	Fw 190 A-8 Yellow 3 (738248)	100%	Shot down in combat.	Neuruppin
05.12.44	Fw. Friedrich Enderle	3	Wounded	Fw 190 A-8 Yellow 7 (739263)	100%	Shot down in combat.	Rechlin
05.12.44	Uffz. Helmut Werner	3	Wounded	Fw 190 A-8 Yellow 10 (171152)	100%	Shot down in combat.	Fürstenwalde
05.12.44	Uffz. Paul Taube	4	Missing	Fw 190 A-8 Red 4 (960521)	100%	Shot down in combat.	Stendal
05.12.44	Ofhr. Gerhard Essig	4	Killed	Fw 190 A-8 Red 8 (380368)	100%	Shot down in combat.	Rheinsberg
05.12.44	Uffz. Johannes Wätzlich	5	Killed	Fw 190 A-8 White 6 (171607)	100%	Shot down in combat.	Bornkrug
05.12.44	Uffz. Hans Weichardt	5	Killed	Fw 190 A-8 White 11 (173917)	100%	Shot down in combat.	Waren
05.12.44	Uffz. Karlheinz Hässler	5	Killed	Fw 190 A-8 White 15 (175217)	100%	Shot down in combat.	Loppin
05.12.44	Lt. Herbert Nock	6	Killed	Fw 190 A-8 Black 9 (175189)	100%	Shot down in combat.	Waren
05.12.44	Uffz. Ferdinand Nüsse	6	Killed	Fw 190 A-8 Black 12 (173924)	100%	Shot down in combat.	Waren
05.12.44	Uffz. Johannes Bröckelmann	6	Killed	Fw 190 A-8 Black 13 (738171)	100%	Shot down in combat.	Waren
05.12.44	Lt. Wilhelm Hasse	6	Killed	Fw 190 A-8 Black 14 (350296)	100%	Shot down in combat.	Waren

Date	Name of Crew and Rank	Staffel	Fate	Aircraft, W.Nr & Code	Damage /Loss	Reason for Casualty	Place
05.12.44	Oblt. Rudolf Diesem	7	Killed	Fw 190 A-8 Yellow 2 (960655)	100%	Shot down in combat.	Waren
05.12.44	FjFw. Karleheinz Teckel	7	Killed	Fw 190 A-8 Yellow 3 (175157)	100%	Shot down in combat.	Waren
05.12.44	Uffz. Wilhelm Wiedenbeck	7	Wounded	Fw 190 A-8 Yellow 8 (713901)	100%	Shot down in combat	Waren
05.12.44	Fw. Werner Hartlieb	7	Missing	Fw 190 A-8 Yellow 10 (175192)	100%	Shot down in combat.	Waren
05.12.44	Uffz. Walter Schwan	7	Killed	Fw 190 A-8 Yellow 11 (173911)	100%	Shot down in combat.	Waren
05.12.44	Uffz. Ferdinand Moser	8	Killed	Fw 190 A-8 Blue 1 (170981)	100%	Shot down in combat.	Waren
05.12.44	Lt. Helmut Weissbrodt	8		Fw 190 A-8 Blue 2 (173875)	100%	Shot down in combat.	Waren
05.12.44	Ogefr. Wolfgang Boy	8	Killed	Fw 190 A-8 Blue 9 (175193)	100%	Shot down in combat.	Waren
05.12.44	Uffz. Alfred Fischer	8	Missing	Fw 190 A-8 Blue 15 (175203)	100%	Shot down in combat.	Waren
05.12.44	Oblt. Helmut Müller	9	Killed	Bf 109 G-6 White 1 (734154)	100%	Shot down in combat with USAAF P-51s.	Buberow
05.12.44	Uffz. Rudolf Prokay	9	Missing	Bf 109 G-14 White 11 (784102)	100%	Shot down in combat.	Neustrelitz
05.12.44	Uffz. Karl Dammeyer	11	Killed	Bf 109 G-14 Yellow 6 (785107)	100%	Shot down in combat.	Neustrelitz
05.12.44	Fw. Hugo Hausotter	11		Bf 109 G Yellow 16 ( )	100%	Shot down in combat with USAAF Mustangs.	Neustrelitz
05.12.44	Lt. Heinz Schöne	11		Bf 109 G ( )	100%	Shot down in combat with USAAF Mustangs.	
05.12.44	Ofhr. Hans-Werner Kroll	12	Killed	Bf 109 G-10 Blue 3 (490625)	100%	Shot down in combat with USAAF P-51s.	Zehdenick
05.12.44	Ofw. Heinz Mittrach	12	Wounded	Bf 109 G	100%	Shot down in combat.	Neustrelitz
05.12.44	Uffz. Hermann Käser	14	Wounded	Bf 109 G-14 Yellow 3 (784134)	100%	Shot down in combat.	Neustrelitz
11.12.44	Ofhr. Friedrich Wilhelm Voss	1	Killed	Fw 190 A-8 White 5 (793341)		Overturned on landing on non-combat flight.	Boltenhagen
11.12.44	Uffz. Hermann Büchert	8	Killed	Fw 190 A-8 Blue 3 (170982)	100%	Crashed after ramming enemy aircraft.	Loitz
11.12.44	Uffz. Ernst Brennecke	8	Killed	Fw 190 A-8 Blue 10 (173915)	100%	Crashed after ramming enemy aircraft.	Tutow
17.12.44	Uffz. Alfred Podszuweit	Gesch. Stab	Wounded	Fw 190 A-9 Green 14 (205032)		Hit bomb crater on landing.	Twente
18.12.44	Uffz. Lothar Mietling	4	Missing	Fw 190 A-8 Red 14 (960521)	100%	Shot down in combat.	Malmedy
18.12.44	Lt. Klaus Holz	9	Wounded	Bf 109 G-14 White 5 (784116)	100%	Shot down in combat with USAAF bombers.	Bonn
18.12.44	Lt. Ottokar Henning	12	Wounded	Bf 109 G-10 Blue 4 (490740)	100%	Crashed on take off.	Anklam
23.12.44	Uffz. Karl Fürstenau	1	Missing	Fw 190 A-8 White 9 (739371)	100%	Shot down in combat.	Wesel

Date	Name of Crew and Rank	Staffel	Fate	Aircraft, W.Nr & Code	Damage /Loss	Reason for Casualty	Place
23.12.44	Lt. Herbert Neuner	2	Wounded	Fw 190 A-8 Black 15 (171155)	100%	Shot down in combat.	Bocholt
23.12.44	Uffz. Alfred Thienert	4	Killed	Fw 190 A-8 Red 8 (171192)	100%	Shot down in combat.	South of Dortmund
23.12.44	Uffz. urt Malkwitz	9	Wounded	Bf 109 G-14 White 17 (784112)	100%	Shot down in combat with USAAF bombers.	Frankfurt/Main
24.12.44	Fhr. Wilhelm Grundmeier	1	Killed	Fw 190 A-8 White 4 (733986)	100%	Shot down in combat.	St. Vith
24.12.44	Uffz. Helmut Rechenbach	4	Wounded	Fw 190 A-8 Red 4 (490026)	100%	Emergency landing following combat with RAF fighters.	Enschede
24.12.44	Uffz. Paul Kolbe	8	Killed	Fw 190 A-8 Brown 9 (960683)	100%	Crashed on landing following combat.	Fürstenau
24.12.44	Lt. Heinz Schöne	11	Killed	Bf 109 G-14 Yellow 11 (780374)	100%	Shot down in combat with USAAF bombers.	Mönchen-Gladbach
24.12.44	Hptm. Erich Woitke	III. Gruppe	Killed	Bf 109 G-14 Grey 20 (490723)	100%	Shot down in combat with Spitfires.	Aachen
25.12.44	Lt. Rudolf Schnappauf	Gesch. Stab	Killed	Fw 190 A-8 Green 21 (960668)	100%	Shot down in combat.	Bastogne
25.12.44	Fw. Günther Gensch	II. Gruppe	Wounded	Fw 190 A-8 Black 22 (739407)		Pilot wounded in combat.	Münster
25.12.44	Fw. Rudolf Lehmann	7	Killed	Fw 190 A-8 Yellow 5 (960506)	100%	Shot down in combat.	Münster
25.12.44	Oblt. Fritz Bilfinger	10	Killed	Bf 109 G-14 Black 17 (780760)	100%	Shot down in combat.	Meckenheim
25.12.44	Uffz. Harri Kühn	10	Missing	Bf 109 G-14 Black 9 (784146)	100%	Shot down in combat.	Marche
25.12.44	Ofw. Friedrich Zander	10	Killed	Bf 109 G-14 Black 11 (784141)	100%	Shot down in combat.	Bastogne
25.12.44	Uffz. Heinz Zinnen	11	Missing	Bf 109 G-14 Yellow 6 (784111)	100%	Shot down in combat with USAAF bombers.	Venn
25.12.44	Fw. Hans Joachim Sperling	11		Bf 109 G-14 Yellow 8 (784158)	100%	Shot down in combat with USAAF bombers.	Venn
25.12.44	Oblt. Jakob Schneider	12	Wounded Died on 26/12/44	Bf 109 G-10 Blue 6 (490665)	100%	Shot down in combat with USAAF bombers.	Lüttich
25.12.44	Lt. Hans Adolf Halbey	12	Wounded	Bf 109 G-10 Blue 5 (490663)	100%	Shot down in combat.	Nettersheim
25.12.44	Ofw. Otto Soetbeer	12	Wounded	Bf 109 G-10 Blue 2 (490653)	100%	Shot down in combat with USAAF bombers.	Lüttich
26.12.44	Ofw. Georg Hutter	5	Missing	Fw 190 A-8 White 11 (171163)	100%	Shot down in combat.	Bastogne
26.12.44	Lt. Horst Ertmann	6	Missing	Fw 190 A-8 Black 2 (173890)	100%	Shot down in combat.	Bastogne
26.12.44	Ofw. Reinhard Flecks	6	Missing	Fw 190 A-8 Black 10 (960678)	100%	Shot down in combat.	Bastogne
26.12.44	Uffz. Ferdinand Nüsse	6	Killed	Fw 190 A-8 Black 5 (739252)	100%	Shot down in combat.	Bastogne
26.12.44	Fw. Johann Ruberg	7	Missing	Fw 190 A-8 Yellow 1 (173887)	100%	Shot down in combat.	Bastogne

Date	Name of Crew and Rank	Staffel	Fate	Aircraft, W.Nr & Code	Damage /Loss	Reason for Casualty	Place
26.12.44	Lt. Heinz Fresia	8	Killed	Fw 190 A-8 Black 13 (175005)	100%	Shot down in combat.	Bastogne
26.12.44	Ofhr. Paul Brühl	8	Killed	Fw 190 A-8 Black 8 (171639)	100%	Shot down in combat.	Bastogne
26.12.44	Ofhr. Helmut Bullenkamp	8	Killed	Fw 190 A-8 Black 12 (175003)	100%	Shot down in combat.	Bastogne
27.12.44	Hptm. Hans Ehlers	I. Gruppe	Killed	Fw 190 A-8 White 20 (739363)	100%	Shot down in combat.	Dinant
27.12.44	Oblt. Eduard Millers	1		Fw 190 A-8 White 22 (739385)	100%	Shot down in combat.	Dinant
27.12.44	Lt. Johannes Birnbaum	1	Missing	Fw 190 A-8 White 14 (960864)	100%	Shot down in combat.	Dinant
27.12.44	Uffz. Adolf Schiller	1	Killed	Fw 190 A-8 White 8 (350854)	100%	Shot down in combat.	Acht
27.12.44	Lt. Gottfried Just	2	Killed	Fw 190 A-8 Black 9 (960553)	100%	Shot down in combat.	Dinant
27.12.44	Uffz. Ernst Adolf Schaumberg	2	Wounded	Fw 190 A-8 Black 1 (960559)	100%	Belly landing following combat.	Behndorf
27.12.44	Uffz. Helmut Riehl	2	Wounded	Fw 190 A-8 Black 4 (960293)	100%	Belly landing following combat.	Bocholt
27.12.44	Ofhr. Gerhard Stiemer	3	Wounded	Fw 190 A-8 Yellow 3 (739274)	100%	Shot down in combat.	Euskirchen
27.12.44	Fw. Wolf Oswald	3	Missing	Fw 190 A-8 Yellow 6 (639163)	100%	Shot down in combat.	Dinant

Anklam, late 1944. Bf 109 G-10/R-3 of 11th Staffel.

Date	Name of Crew and Rank	Staffel	Fate	Aircraft, W.Nr & Code	Damage /Loss	Reason for Casualty	Place
27.12.44	Oblt. Walter Pörsch	3	Killed	Fw 190 A-8 Red 10 (175176)	100%	Shot down in combat.	Dinant
27.12.44	Lt. Richard Förster	3	Missing	Fw 190 A-8 Red 16 (350219)	100%	Shot down in combat.	Dinant
27.12.44	Fw. Herbert Mehl	I. Gruppe	Killed	Fw 190 A-9 White 21 (750102)	100%	Shot down in combat.	Dinant
27.12.44	Fw. Albrecht Kirschner	6	Wounded	Fw 190 A-8 White 3 (175145)	100%	Shot down in combat.	Plantlünne
27.12.44	Ogefr. Erich Franze	8	Killed	Fw 190 A-8 White 7 (739417)	100%	Shot down in combat.	Plantlünne
27.12.44	Lt. Wolfgang Schönfelder	10	Killed	Bf 109 G-14 Black 11 ((784139)	100%	Shot down in combat with USAAF bombers.	Münstereifel
31.12.44	Fhr. Horst Heimlich	6	Killed	Fw 190 A-8 Black 1 (960685)	100%	Shot down in combat.	Emsdetten
31.12.44	Uffz. Gerhard Hartig	6	Killed	Fw 190 A-8 Black 12 (733995)	100%	Shot down in combat.	Mesum
31.12.44	Uffz. Rudolf Wezulek	6	Killed	Fw 190 A-8 Black 14 (739286)	100%	Shot down in combat.	Mesum
31.12.44	Ofw. Werner Essinger	8	Wounded	Fw 190 A-8 Blue 6 (177003)	100%	Shot down in combat.	Burgsteinfurt

Pilots of the unit in front of a Fw 190 A at Greifswald in December 1944.

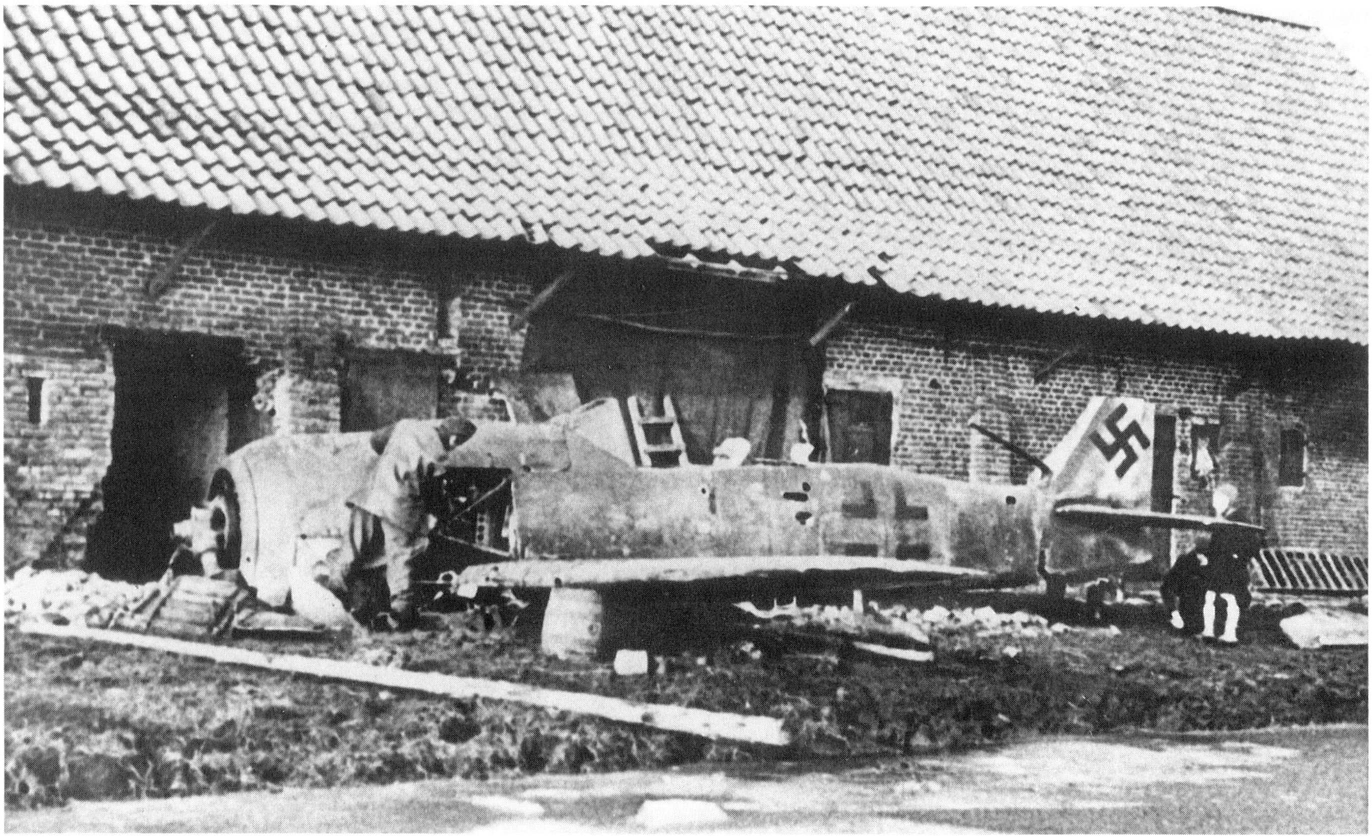

JG 1 suffered many losses on 1/1/45. This wreckage of a Fw 190 at St. Denis-Westrem is almost certainly a machine of the unit.

Viennese Major and Ritterkreuzträger Bernd Gallowitsch (centre), previously of JG 51, who became Staffelkapitän of 7th Staffel on 1/2/45. At the war's end he was Staffelkapitän of 4th Staffel.

Unteroffizier Gerhard Behrens of 8th Staffel, killed in action on 1/1/45.

CHAPTER 7 - 1945

BODENPLATTE - 1st JANUARY 1945

The High Command of the Luftwaffe were aware of the inability of the fighter force to carry out its allotted task. It was more depleted than ever. It was apparent that the few experienced pilots could not shoulder all the burden of combat. The Ardennes offensive appeared lost. With the improved weather conditions the intervention of the allied air forces meant that their ground troops received the necessary support, and the Luftwaffe was incapable of preventing this support. The plan, in preparation since mid-December, envisaged a mass attack on allied airfields in the Low Countries, Belgium and France. The thinking behind it was that if the Luftwaffe was not able to wrest control of the skies from the allies from the air, perhaps they could destroy them on the ground.
General Major Dietrich Pelz, the originator of the idea, waited only for favourable weather conditions before committing the expected thousand German fighters. The meteorological forecast pointed to 1st January being the best day for the attack. The Commanding Officers of the fighter units were called together, with senior officers communicating to them the details of the plan. On returning to airfields, Commanding Officers informed the pilots. New Year's Eve celebrations were out.
"On 31st December, just before nightfall, our chief came into our quarters, situated six or seven kilometres from the airfield, and told us to set to work. All the aircraft had to be in flying state by 05:00 hours in the morning. The Fw 190 which I was working on had serious damage in the oil sump. We worked without a break in the freezing cold. Towards midnight, the Flak fired, and brought down an aircraft. At 03:00 hours the aircraft were finally ready" - Unteroffizier August Michalski, groundcrew, 1st Staffel.
Oberleutnant Fritz Wegner of 5th Staffel recalled: "To understand what happened to our II. Gruppe during the operation, it is necessary to look back one week. On Christmas day my Gruppe had been involved in an important combat with Mustangs and Thunderbolts. Like a lot of our pilots, I was shot down and had to bail out. I reached my base again at nine o' clock on the morning of 26th December. The Gruppe had already received the order to mount an attack on the Bastogne area. Hauptmann Staiger and other pilots were already in their machines, and they took off without me. Arriving at the

objective, a murderous combat ensued, in which nearly all of our pilots were shot down. One of the few to escape was the Gruppenkommandeur Staiger. Badly shocked, he had to land near Frankfurt, some distance from our airfield. He was therefore not present for the "Operation Bodenplatte" attack. The strength of the Gruppe was further diluted by this bloodletting. I had to fill the gaps by retaining with II. Gruppe the fifteen ferry pilots who had brought fresh Fw 190s to us. Among these men were experienced pilots, retired from active service following injuries, never having flown these type of missions before. I kept them, however. On the morning of 31st December I was called to Fürstenau by the High Command, where I was appraised of the plan of attack for the following day. In the evening, having returned to our base at Drope, I called the pilots together and, swearing them to secrecy, outlined the plan of the operation".
1st January. At Twente, Drope and Rheine, the respective airfields of the three Gruppen of the unit, the pilots were roused from a nervous sleep shortly before 06:00 hours. Their leaders went over for the last time the plans for the mission: I. and III. Gruppen would attack the Belgian airfields of Maldegem, 15 kilometres to the east of Bruges, and Ursel, mid-way between Gent and Maldegem; II. Gruppe would pay a visit to the airfield of St. Denis-Westrem.
At 08:10 hours at Twente, two Ju 88 G night-fighters took off. They were to be the pathfinders for the single-engined fighters. Direction - due west. The twenty Fw 190 A-8s flew only 50 metres above the ground. Behind them, 30 small black dots showed up in the sombre sky. These were the Bf 109 G-14s of III. Gruppe, who had taken off from Rheine at 08:15 hours. The two formations joined up. Everything seemed to be going perfectly. The pilots were approaching Den Haag when all hell broke loose. The Flak batteries had not been advised of the flight of these important units. They opened fire with murderous precision. Several aircraft were hit, including the aircraft of Kommodore Herbert Ihlefield who had to make a forced landing.
Passing this obstacle, I. and III. Gruppen flew over the grey waters of the North Sea. They followed the Belgian coast and then set course south, for a point between Knokke and Blankenberge. They were only several minutes away from their objective.
At Drope, around 08:15 hours, a green flare cleared the 30 Fw 190 A-8s of II. Gruppe for take off. Their course was similar to that of their comrades of the other Gruppen. They also flew over the German flak batteries, which opened fire. Over the sea, the Gruppe changed course towards Gent. The pilots could now see the aircraft of I. and III. Gruppen.
Arriving over Bruges, Oberleutnant Hans Gottfried Meinhoff (a former reconnaissance pilot recently appointed Staffelführer of 4th Staffel) and four of his pilots split away from the rest of the formation as pre-arranged and headed for the allied airfield at Ursel. They made several passes and set alight a B-17 undergoing repair, a Mosquito and two Lancasters. The damage to aircraft would have been greater had not the majority of Spitfires based there returned to England the previous day.
I. and III. Gruppen, overtaken by II. Gruppe, split up: certain pilots, including Gruppenkommandeur Hackbarth, launched an attack on St. Denis-Westrem, while others attacked Maldegem, where the confusion was total. The airfield lacked anti-aircraft defences, which had been withdrawn a few days earlier. Coming in at tree-top height, the German aircraft had trouble finding their targets: the Spitfires had been dispersed well, and the dense smoke from a burning tank partly obscured the aerodrome from the attackers. Towards 09:30 hours the German fighters left, leaving twelve smoking carcasses of Spitfires behind, as well as a further two damaged. 485 Squadron, composed of New Zealand pilots, lost three-quarters of their aircraft.
II. Gruppe, together with some aircraft of I. Gruppe who had joined up with them, emerged over the airfield of St. Denis-Westrem, the base of 131 Polish Wing. The Spitfires of the three squadrons (302, 308 and 317) had taken off at about the same time as the German pilots to carry out attacks in the Woensdrecht area. As the Focke-Wulfs arrived, so also did 302 Squadron, who had returned from their mission and were in the course of landing. Flying Officer Chojnacki of 308 Squadron, who was flying with 302, closed quickly on the German aircraft and engaged them. He shot down a Fw 190 which crashed into a building on the airfield and finished up on a Fying Fortress. Seconds later, chased by three German aircraft, Chojnacki was shot down and killed. The German pilots were machine-gunning the airfield when Flight Sergeant Josef Stanowski of 308 Squadron appeared. Short of fuel, he preceded the other aircraft of his squadron. He saw the Fw 190s, and shot two down, one to the south of Gent, the other in the centre of town. The Polish pilot then made a belly landing. 308 Squadron, having successfully tussled with other Fw 190s a few minutes earlier near Lokeren, headed for St. Denis Westrem. The Polish pilots caught the Germans unawares, and claimed five shot down (with one German bailing out). One Spitfire, having been hit, made a belly landing.
The circling combats continued above, and in the general vicinity of, the airfield. 317 Squadron, called back to help, attacked in their turn. These latter arrivals claimed six Fw 190s shot down for the loss of two Spitfires, one making an emergency landing and the other crashing, killing the pilot.
After a quarter of an hour of this tough action, the signal to retire was given, and the Fw 190s headed east. They left behind nearly 25 wrecks of Spitfires, the greater part of which had been destroyed on the ground, as well as a Flying Fortress and a Stirling.
The return flight was also troublesome. Oberleutnant Meinhoff, Staffelführer of 4th Staffel, was hit by anti-aircraft fire and crashed to his death near Breda. Upon return, at about 10:40 hours, the news was bad: 17 pilots killed (including Hauptmann Hackbarth and the Latvian pilot, Feldwebel Harry Klints) and six prisoners of war. The Staffel hardest hit was 5th, with five pilots missing. A Pyrrhic victory! Leutnant Hans Berger claimed one Spitfire.

Two views of a Fw 190 A-8 of II. Gruppe at Garz/Usedom in February 1945.

AN EVENTFUL NEW YEAR

After the losses of the previous two months, the German fighter arm played a minor rôle in the future strategy of the war. Of the mass of young pilots in action at the end of the year, the only survivors were the lucky ones. Even in those surviving units, depth of experience was rare.
The shortage of responsible officers in I. Gruppe was evident. Hauptmann Hackbarth had only led the Gruppe for five days when he fell in combat on 1st January. Officially, the responsibility for leading the Gruppe in the air fell once again to Leutnant Emil Demuth. Nevertheless on 3rd January Major G. Capito, a former bomber pilot, nominated to take over I. Gruppe, arrived at Twente.
"During the night of 3rd-4th January, after a bad train journey, I presented myself before Oberstleutnant Ihlefield. He conferred to me the leadership of I. Gruppe, but immediately stated one condition: in the air, the chief of 3rd Staffel, Leutnant Demuth, was to lead the Gruppe. This restriction of my duties was made with the best of intentions: I lacked experience of leading a Gruppe, as well as being a fighter pilot.
"During the early days, fresh young pilots from training schools arrived, together with new machines. Around 11th January we were back up to strength again, although experience was cruelly lacking. We carried out our first formation flight under the direction of Demuth. I flew the number "6".
"On the 12th, following the Russian offensive and the establishment of the bridgehead at Baranow, we had to leave for the east. The Kommodore left the same evening to discuss matters with his superiors. On the morning of the 14th we were due to leave but an intense fog enveloped the region that a take off, on top of taking "green" pilots, was too perilous. A message arrived: an important formation of "Indians" was reported over the North Sea. Towards 09:00 hours the mist lifted slightly and I gave the order to take off. Following the Stabsschwarm, I saw one Staffel take off while the three others were lining up to take off. We flew for less than a quarter of an hour at 50 metres altitude when we hit a blanket of fog. Over the radio I heard Demuth's voice: "Airfield beneath us, everybody land". Not seeing him, I ordered the pilots to carry on. I had great experience of blind flying and could evaluate the danger precisely. "Rabe 6 (Raven 6) here, don't land, gain height and reassemble around the machine waggling its wings". I repeated this order several times. Five machines joined me and we landed at Fassberg without problem. The others were lost from sight. Arriving at Werneuchen in the afternoon, I finally received information about my men: the Stabschwarm and two Staffeln had, in effect, taken off with us. Now the pilots were completely scattered over the whole of northern Germany, from Hamburg to Brandenburg-Briest. It was on this airfield that Demuth and two other pilots had landed. I was also advised of the loss of two or three aircraft.
More serious, 1st and 2nd Staffeln were not able to leave at the same time as us, as the fog came down suddenly and prevented them from joining us. After fifteen minutes the two Staffeln were finally able to take off. The "Indians" arrived at that precise moment..." - Major G. Capito, I. Gruppe Gruppenkommandeur.
Twente, 09:15 hours. The delayed Focke-Wulfs started their take off routine. At this moment Spitfires of 2nd Tactical Air Force dropped out of the sky. The German pilots were completely taken by surprise. Eleven smoking craters littered the airfield. Lack of height meant that the German pilots were unable to bail out. Two Spitfires were shot down. Among the German losses were Unteroffizier Günter Sill of Stab, I. Gruppe, killed flying a Fw 190 D-9, one of the few aircraft of this type delivered to the Geschwaderstab and Gruppenstab, I. Gruppe of the unit shortly beforehand.
"... Ihlefield threatened me with arrest and court-martial. I avoided having to present myself before him on the airfield at Königsberg due to a transfer which had been arranged for me three days before. The threats to me were dropped and I learned later that the pilots of I. Gruppe were able to reassemble on 15th January at Werneuchen, from where they reached their destination" - Major G. Capito.

Pilots of II. Gruppe at Garz/Usedom in late February/ early March 1945. Extreme left is Feldwebel Erwin Steeb.

Pilots of the unit at Garz, late February/early March 1945. Unteroffizier Herbert Dosch is in the centre.

Unteroffizier Alvo von Alvensleben of 1st Staffel, recently arrived at the unit, completes the story: "On 14th January I was delayed by my Fw 190 being a victim of mechanical trouble. At 08:00 hours I reported to my Staffelkapitän and rejoined my friend, Unteroffizier Heidrich, to help him finish his preparations. The Schwärme, four aircraft wingtip to wingtip, from all Staffeln began to move on the airfield. The first aircraft took off and disappeared beyond the horizon. During this succession of take-offs, just as the Schwarm of my friend Heidrich reached take-off speed and left the ground about ten Spitfires emerged from the clouds and placed themselves behind the surprised German aircraft. The Spitfires cannon opened up, followed by German MGs replying. While I was taking shelter, I saw several Fw 190s crash and explode. My friend was among them. There was nothing more to say about the engagement. Remaining alone at Twente, I was not able to take off and rejoin my unit at Heiligenbeil until 1st February, in view of the intense enemy aerial activity".

JAGDGESCHWADER 1 IN THE EAST

On 16th January two trains left Holland and headed east. They carried the ground personnel of I. Gruppe, as well as all the necessary equipment required at their new base on the eastern front. The military situation was developing into a catastrophe. The Soviets could count on 6 million combatants, the Reich half that number. In material terms, the German strength was about one fifth of that of the Soviets. On the northern front the German forces had been isolated in Kurland since mid-October 1944. Kurland would be the theatre of operations of Jagdgeschwader 1. After a journey of four days the first train arrived at Jürgenfelde, near Insterburg. Immediately coming under Russian fire, it had to retreat. The second train was diverted to Heiligenbeil, where the pilots who had evacuated Jürgenfelde were awaited. Heiligenbeil was reached on 22nd January at 16:00 hours. A new transfer order arrived because the Russians continued to break through. The retreat was due west. At Heiligenbeil there was a large number of refugees, having been caused by the Russian army rolling everything before them. The four field kitchens of I. Gruppe arrived in the nick of time.

On 24th January the move by rail to Königsberg was possible, but two days later the train had to be abandoned, and personnel reached an aerodrome near Neukuhren. At -22 degrees the weather was inclement. On 30th January fresh information arrived to the effect that the Russians were barely 20 kilometres away. After further moves, at 22:30 hours on 4th February, the column, numbering 65 wagons, finally arrived at Rahmel airfield, near Danzig, where it was once again at the disposal of the Gruppenkommandeur and the flying personnel. The men were not to know that a further transfer order awaited them the following day. This account is only one example. Nearly every unit moving from west to east encountered similar difficulties.

The worries of the pilots moving east were of a completely different order. They were up against not only Russian tanks, but anti-aircraft batteries as renowned as their own. Their duties were to escort maritime convoys in the Baltic Sea, the only hope for troops and civilians encircled in the Kurland pocket.

After the catastrophic departure of 14th January, I. Gruppe could only muster ten pilots. The first five arrived at Jürgenfelde four days later under Oberleutnant Demüth; the rest, led by Leutnant Lüpke, arrived the following day. On 20th January, combat began for these ten pilots. Two of them were counted missing following an engagement with Russian Laggs, with Fähnrich Richde claiming one of the enemy. They soon had to evacuate Jürgenfelde in the face of the advancing Soviets, moving to Gutenfelde (23rd January), Neukuhren (26th January); Heiligenbeil (28th January) and Danzig (2nd February) in turn. These continuing changes of base left little time for missions: ground attacks and escort to transport aircraft. On 30th January Oberleutnant Emil Demuth recorded his seventeenth and last victory: a Yak-9.

On 7th February, while Demuth and his men were at Garz (on Usedom Island), a new order reached them: they were to pass their Fw 190 A-8s and A-9s to II. Gruppe and head for the Heinkel works at Parchim, 70

kilometres south of Rostock.
For their part, II. Gruppe left for the Eastern front under the control of Oberleutnant Fritz Wegner, Staffelführer of 6th Staffel. Major Hermann Staiger had been given command of one of the Gruppen of Jagdgeschwader 7 equipped with jet fighters. Arriving at Insterburg airfield on 18th January, II. Gruppe immediately went into action. Pilots encountered for the first time the Yak-3 and Yak-9 Russian fighters. Two were killed during this first engagement. Returning to Insterburg, the airfield had been bombed to the point where it was impossible to land. They were therefore diverted to Jürgenfelde. On the two following days several more missions were flown in the Insterburg region, resulting in further losses of pilots, among them Hauptmann Friedrich Strich, leading 7th Staffel. Bad weather and fog were ever present. Russian tanks continued their advance, and the retreating pilots took their first mechanic in the rear of their aircraft. Not being able to evacuate all the aircraft, II. Gruppe destroyed ten Fw 190 A-8s and A-9s between 21st and 23rd January.
In the air, the escaping aircraft lost their way somewhat during the transfer flight, but the majority arrived at Gerdauen, near Königsberg. The retreat continued through Heiligenbeil, Kolberg, Samland and finally Garz/ Usedom. On 4th February the unit was reformed there in order to take up combat once again against the allied four-engined bombers. These now had one objective: Berlin. The defence of the test bases of secret weapons of the Luftwaffe at Peenemünde and Swinemünde was also delegated to Jagdgeschwader 1. Installations at Garz were small, resulting in there being no blast pens for aircraft. They had to park along the side of the airstrip. After a week's work, the shelters were built and the aerodrome became operational.
"On 2nd January I was posted as an instructor to Jagdgeschwader 106 at Garz. The Russians had reached the Oder, and I carried out fighter-bomber missions against the pontoons with a 250 kilogram bomb. The Russians held the important crossroads in the town of Naugart, where five routes crossed, and we attacked there also. Shortly after my arrival at Garz, II. Gruppe, Jagdgeschwader 1 took up quarters there. I was surprised to find among the pilots Hauptmann Wolfgang Ludewig, who had been my Staffelkapitän when we were both with Jagdgeschwader 102 at Zerbst. It was he who, to my great disappointment, arranged my posting as an instructor rather than send me to the front. He advised me that the training units would soon be dissolved, and many of their personnel would be deployed as infantry. As Staffelkapitän of 8th Staffel, he suggested I became a Schwarmführer in his Staffel, which led to certain pilots being jealous. In February, we regularly escorted the maritime convoys evacuating those trapped in the enormous Kurland pocket.
"On 25th March, towards 16:00 hours, we were on alert. On the previous mission, a pilot had been shot down by our own Flak (this pilot, Gefreiter Amandus Strickrock of 6th Staffel was killed). We were waiting in the cockpits of the aircraft. The order for take-off was given, but as we moved off, it was cancelled. Four or five minutes later came a further instruction. Take off in four minutes to escort vessels in map-square "PM" (in the Bornholm area). Shortly afterwards, "Take off, course 60 degrees, height 4,000 metres". This course would take us right into the middle of a forbidden zone: the base at Swinemünde covered by an artificial fog. Not being able to see the smallest ship, we descended, and drew intense fire from the defences. I fired a signal flare and accelerated. I just had time to put another flare in position before I was far from this furnace. A glance to my left, my two comrades were there, to the right - my wingman had disappeared! I looked down, and saw a Fw 190 sinking in the sea. Right over it, I saw a white parachute. I immediately gave the position of Obergefreiter Neumann to the head of the unit. We had to carry on with the mission. Far from the coast, hunched up in our lifejackets, the sensation was very disagreeable. Finally, we found four long white trails of foam, our ships were there. We moved close. They were sailing in a north-easterly direction, while those we were due to escort should have been descending on Kurland. It was incomprehensible! A little further on, more trails. A dozen merchant ships of all sizes. In this uncertainty, we flew figures of eight while circling around the two convoys. As we lost altitude, a ship opened fire. We gained height again and continued escort at a safe distance. After an hour it was time to return. We set course 120 degrees and when we saw the chalk cliffs of the nearby Rügen island we were too far to the west, and we therefore headed eastwards. Over Peenemünde, we drew the fire of the anti-aircraft defences once again. Finally we reached Garz! Shortly after getting out of my Fw 190, a Kübelwagen sought me out to take me to HQ, where I made a report of the flight to Kommodore Ihlefield. On the following day a court-martial was arranged in my honour. A map was spread out on the table, and these gentlemen asked me to show our course. I did not do it, and Hauptmann Ludewig supported me: it was for them to prove that I had flown over the ships which we were to escort, and had got too close to them. I learned later that the ships carried nitroglycerine, which no doubt explained the nervousness of their gunners. It was a one-off situation" - Unteroffizier Konrad Augner, 8th Staffel.
At the end of February II. Gruppe received Major Staiger's successor: Hauptmann Paul-Heinrich Dähne. He was a young pilot, aged 23½, from Frankfurt-on-Oder. He had a hundred victories, gained with Jagdgeschwadern 52 and 11. His arrival coincided with the departure for a "Gruppenkommandeur" school of the Staffelkapitän of 6th Staffel, Oberleutnant Fritz Wegner. Wegner spent a month and a half at the Verbandsführerschule at Bad Wörishofen. He was then posted to II. Jagdgeschwader 300 at Holzkirchen, and on 24th April he was shot down by Flak and wounded. Post-war, he entered the new Luftwaffe, and retired in 1981 with the rank of Lieutenant-General. Combat missions undertaken by II. Gruppe out of Garz resulted in several losses, among them, on 11th

March, Leutnant Hubert Swoboda, Staffelkapitän of 5th Staffel. Feldwebel Erwin Steeb, a pilot of II. Gruppe for nearly a year, led 5th Staffel during the final combats. Leutnant Alfred Dürr, who had arrived at the unit at the end of January, became the official Staffelkapitän.
Like the other Gruppen, III. Gruppe were also sent east. The aircraft left Rheine airfield on 13th January at 14:05 hours. After a stop-over of three days at Straussberg, the pilots reached Schröttersburg, where two "free chase" missions were undertaken. A move to Thorn resulted in two further missions on the 20th. Thorn was then evacuated on 21st and 22nd January, and after that the Gruppe was rapidly plunged into the headlong German retreat. Pilots and essential ground personnel reached Marienburg and from there, on 23rd January, Berent, south-west of Danzig.
III. Gruppe were split up for a short time; pilots were sent to Jesau, Neukuhren and Pillau, where the aircraft were passed on to Jagdgeschwader 54. On 31st January, they regrouped at Stolp and received new machines. From this airfield they escorted Fw 190s of ground-attack units in the tank-busting rôle. They also flew escort to Oberst Hans-Ulrich Rudel's Schlachtgeschwader 2 "Immelman". During these missions, III. Gruppe recorded a dozen victories despite having major refuelling problems. It was believed by some that the lack of fuel was due to deliberate acts of sabotage.
At the beginning of February, a dozen technicians of III. Gruppe were trapped when Thorn was encircled. In effect, each time a unit took possession of a base, or when they left, a small detachment arrived in advance, or remained behind after all had left. It was usually composed of the best mechanics, to either receive the first machines, or get the remaining aircraft up to flying state. At Thorn, the rearguard reported to the commander of Thorn, who told them Thorn would be defended to the last man. The Technical Officer responsible for the technicians maintained radio contact with the unit's headquarters, and they received a promise that a Ju 52 would take off to collect them. To the east of the airfield, as the noise of battle grew louder, the tracks of the Russian tanks could be heard. At midnight, when all hope had nearly disappeared, a Ju 52 set down at Thorn and collected the remaining men of the unit.
On 3rd and 4th March, III. Gruppe left Stolp for Anklam airfield for "rest and refreshment". They were required to protect the test centres of Swinemünde and Peenemünde, and cover the Baltic, from where there was a flood of refugees.

THE PEOPLE'S FIGHTER - FEBRUARY TO APRIL 1945

Destroyed by constant bombing, the Third Reich no longer had enough quality materials, fuel, or experienced pilots. Hitler's Germany had little time left. The research bureaux worked tirelessly on new projects which might perhaps change the course of the war. Strong forces therefore protected the test centres such as Peenemünde. On 8th September 1944 the German Air Ministry issued an order to the German aircraft companies: construct a jet fighter able to reach 750 kilometres per hour whose construction was so simple that it could be mass-produced. The aircraft had to be ready before 1st January 1945. The design bureaux of the different companies put forward their designs: Heinkel, who had designed the first jet fighter in 1939, secured the contract. On 30th October the plans were ready and thousands of workers were mobilised. There was talk of forming and training the "Hitler Youth Airforce" on these small aircraft whose handling characteristics were such that it was considered that adolescents could fly it in combat!
The first prototype of the He 162 "Volksjäger" flew on 6th December 1944 from the aerodrome of Vienna-Schwechat, not far from the assembly line. The speed of completion was no doubt a unique feat in the field of aviation. Four days later, before a gathering of senior officials, the same aircraft, the He 162 V-1, crashed, taking its test pilot to his death. Heinkel, conscious of the aircraft's fragility, and certain defects, was opposed to this flight, but had to see this catastrophic demonstration through. The dream was over, reality returned. To construct such an aircraft took time.
Despite immense technical problems and wide scale dispersion of production lines to minimise the effect of bombing, the aircraft was put into series production and deliveries to the Luftwaffe began towards the end of January 1945. Military tests were conducted on the aircraft, and attempts were made to improve the aircraft through Erprobungs Kommando 162 under the command of Oberstleutnant Heinz Bär, who once again features in the history of Jagdgeschwader 1. His unit was initially based at Rechlin, then at Lechfeld and finally at München-Riem.
In the early part of February 1945 Vienna saw a gathering of those responsible for the He 162 project and the General of Fighters, Oberst Gordon Gollob, accompanied by Oberstleutnant Walter Dahl. The project finally reached fruition with the creation at Goslar of a new unit, Jagdgeschwader 80, to exclusively fly the He 162. It was decided to convert Jagdgeschwader 1 to this new aircraft. To this end, on 8th February, I. Gruppe handed over their 23 Focke-Wulf 190s to II. Gruppe and, led by Oberleutnant Emil Demuth, headed for Parchim. In a convoy of 65 wagons, they reached their destination at 02:00 hours on the 9th. The pilots received their theoretical training from the technicians and test pilots from the Heinkel-Nord works. 4th Staffel was disbanded and its pilots were distributed among the other three Staffeln of the Gruppe. Eventually rejoined by the Geschwader-

Two views of a line-up of aircraft of I. Gruppe at Leck in May 1945. In the foreground is He 162, "White 4", W.Nr. 120067 of 1st Staffel.

February 1945. One of the first and very rare He 162 A-1 "Spatz" of I. Gruppe. This aircraft was fitted with two 30 mm. MK 108 Kanone - the standard armament on the 'A-2' version was the 20 mm. Kanone.

stab, I. Gruppe spent nearly two months at Parchim. On 27th February ten pilots of 2nd Staffel under Leutnant Hachtel were sent to Vienna to collect the He 162s coming from the factory. The technicians noted: "These men were incredibly impatient to take on the He 162s which had been cleared by our technicians. As soon as they were ready, the pilots took over the aircraft".
Training began prudently. Nevertheless, on 14th March, Unteroffizier Tautz was killed on his first flight due to pilot error. Hachtel's men returned without aircraft - no combat-ready aircraft were yet available from the factory.
During the second half of March, ten pilots of I. Gruppe were sent briefly to Marienehe near Rostock, another source of He 162s. In fact, the principal production works of Heinkel was there. Lodging in a luxurious hotel at Warnemünde, they took charge of a formation of aircraft thoroughly tested by mechanics and test pilots of the company. At the beginning of April this detachment returned to Parchim where the pilots rejoined the rest of the Gruppe, who had made their first flights at the end of March. The flights, however, were of between 10 and 20 minutes only.
"When the engine was started up, an unusual, strident noise came from the turbine. The aircraft, small and light, with a huge engine on its back, made such a din rolling on the runway that one was relieved when the aircraft lifted off. The wheels left the ground when a speed of 220 kilometres per hour was attained. Acceleration was good and a normal runway sufficed. In flight, the aircraft was stable, and quiet. It responded easily to the controls. In general, training speeds were between 500 and 700 kilometres per hour. In the dive, according to factory information, we could reach the speed of sound. As for myself, I was able to reach 1,000 kilometres per hour once. We did not have the opportunity to try aerobatics with it. Lacking experience on the type, and having doubts as to the solidity of the undercarriage, I always touched down as gently as possible. After a very short flight, it would land, and once again the noise became appalling. I flew the aircraft on ten occasions" - Unteroffizier Alvo von Alvensleben, 1st Staffel.
On 8th April, Parchim was bombed by the British. Pilots and He 162s transferred to Ludwiglust, 17 kilometres south-west of Parchim. From there, several test flights were made. On 15th and 16th April, I. Gruppe had to quit its new base - the front line had nearly reached it. The Gruppe reached the airfield of Leck, in Schleswig-Holstein, some arriving via Husum.
Brand new He 162s continued to arrive at the unit: several pilots ferried aircraft from Marienehe to Leck while others of the unit provided air cover in the region.
On 19th April, Feldwebel Günther Kirchner, a veteran of II. Gruppe who had been posted to I. Gruppe following a recent break, shot down a British aircraft. This was admitted by the British pilot when he was captured. A Flak unit was, however, attributed with the victory. On the flight back to base, the He 162 crashed, killing the pilot. On 25th April at about 13:30 hours, Leutnant Hans Berger came across a group of Thunderbolts, but no combat occurred.
On 8th April, II. Gruppe left their Fw 190s at Garz and reached Rostock/Marienehe en route also to receive

Line-up of He 162 A-2s of 1st Staffel shortly before the end of the war.

Following the bombing of the base at Parchim, I. Gruppe could be found at Ludwiglust in mid-April 1945. Heinkel 162 A-2, "White 21" has an upper surface camouflage pattern which stops level with the cockpit.

training on the He 162.

"The officers were lodged in a hotel at Warnemünde, and the other pilots on the aerodrome. Each morning, as workers headed for work, a bus or wagon collected us and took us to the aerodrome of Marienehe. The place was unusual: three runways set out in a triangle in the middle of marsh land. First of all we received theoretical training on the aircraft we would be flying. Then we learned to start the engine, increase the throttle progressively, and move on the runway. We sat in this aircraft like in a glider. Starting the engine was a completely different procedure to that of the Bf 109. The revs had to be increased slowly, while holding the aircraft still with the help of the brakes, up to the moment when one decided that there was sufficient power for take off. Releasing the brakes, take off was achieved at around 180 kilometres per hour. After retracting the undercarriage, we also retracted the flaps. At around 450-500 kilometres we gained altitude. This aircraft had a mortal fault: at less than 300 kilometres per hour you had to be on your guard against tight turns. In this case, the aileron constrained the circulation of air around the turbine, the He 162 skidded and fell like a leaf without any possibility of correcting it. Generally we only flew for about 35 minutes at fairly low level. However we also made several flights at 8,000 metres. We would then be in the air for over an hour. The manoeuvrability of the aircraft was good. For landing, we approached the runway at about 250-260 kilometres per hour, and touch down at 200. It was a totally new flying sensation.

"On 24th April I was on the airfield looking skywards when a catastrophe occurred. Our Gruppenkommandeur, Hauptmann Dähne, did not seem to have confidence in this machine, and I think he retarded his training. On this day, towards 16:00 hours, he took off. We followed his manoeuvres - he was not flying higher than 500 metres. He started to turn, and the aircraft began to skid. I then saw the aircraft somersault. Small pieces of glass shone in the sun, and a trail of white smoke came from the turbine. The He 162 began to lose height. It fell like a dead leaf and crashed in the marsh at the mouth of the Warne. Our Gruppenkommandeur had probably tried to bail out without first having jettisoned the canopy, and had smashed his skull. That would explain the splinters of glass. We immediately jumped into boats to come to his aid. We searched in vain..." - Unteroffizier Konrad Augner, 8th Staffel.

Major Werner Zober, a veteran of the Spanish Civil War and decorated with the Spanish Cross with Diamonds, was appointed successor of Hauptmann Dähne. Dähne and Tautz were not the only losses of the unit with the He 162. Another ten pilots were killed. Numerous accidents accounted for others being wounded, particularly on 2nd May during a transfer flight from Rostock to Leck where II. Gruppe rejoined I. Gruppe.

Leck, May 1945. Hauptmann Heinz Künneke, Staffelkapitän of 1st Staffel, poses in front of a He 162 A-1, "White 5", which has covers over the cockpit and engine. Note the larger aperture on the "A-1" for the 30 mm. Kanone.

This He 162 A-2, "Yellow 3" at Leck carries an emblem of a Lion rampant holding a yellow 3. This emblem seems to have first appeared on JG 1 aircraft in the closing weeks of the war, and would appear to be the emblem of 3rd Staffel.

Well-known but nevertheless excellent view of officers of the unit. From left to right: Major Zober; Oberst Ihlefield; Hauptmann Künneke; Oberleutnant Demuth; Major Gallowitsch; Hauptmann Strasen and Hauptmann Reinbrecht. The last two named did not belong to JG 1.

THE END (APRIL - MAY 1945)

"Since January 1945, the war could be summed up for us as a succession of journeys by road and by rail. At the beginning of April we were at Ludwiglust. We then received the order to move to Husum. Having waited for nightfall, we set off. We were four officers in one car: Oberleutnant Wilhelm Krebs (Technical Officer of I. Gruppe); Major Bernd Gallowitsch (an Austrian "Ritterkreuzträger", 64 victories with Jagdgeschwader 51, recently posted to the unit by the head of Fighters, Oberst Gollob); Hauptmann Hans Blesser (HQ Company Chief) and myself Hauptmann Ludwig Siegfried, supply officer of I. Gruppe. We travelled for an hour before we were hit head-on by another car. This happened frequently due to the poor headlights in the darkness. Krebs and Gallowitsch were lightly injured and, more through good luck than judgement, we made it to Husum. It was crowded with retreating troops in northern Germany. We could only spend the rest of the night there. The following day, at mid-day, we finally reached Leck, where the remainder of the Gruppe were established.

On 2nd May, Stab and II. Gruppe left Marienehe urgently: the Russians had begun to take over the Heinkel installations. II. Gruppe joined I. Gruppe at Leck after a stop-over at Kaltenkirchen.

On the following day, the last re-organisation of Jagdgeschwader 1 took place. I. and II. Gruppen were redesignated I. (Einsatz)/JG 1 and II. (Sammel)/JG 1, Einsatz being combat, and Sammel replenishment. Commanding officers were as follows:

Geschwaderstab: Oberst Herbert Ihlefield;

Stab, I. Gruppe: Major Werner Zober;

1st Staffel	: Hauptmann Heinz Künneke;
2nd Staffel	: Hauptmann Wolfgang Ludewig;
3rd Staffel	: Oberleutnant Karl-Heinz Demuth.

Stab, II. Gruppe: Hauptmann Rahe;

4th Staffel	: Major Bernd Gallowitsch;
5th Staffel	: Hauptmann Bergholz;
6th Staffel	: Oberleutnant Zipprecht.

These two Gruppen had 50 pilots and an equivalent number of aircraft on charge. On Leck aerodrome, the

pilots carried out their last flights.
On 4th May, towards 11:45 hours, Leutnant Rudolf Schmitt of 1st Staffel, piloting He 162 "White 1", returned a victory over a Typhoon. This was never confirmed. For nearly two months, in effect, German fighters did not register claims officially. Furthermore, no Typhoon was lost on this day in the region. The victory tally of the unit closed on this controversial point.
"Our Commanding Officer, Ihlefield advised us of the death of Hitler, and told us to stay together until the allies captured our airfield. By so doing, no harm could come to us. He also told us that he no longer had the right to retain us. Everyone was free to go. I don't believe a single person left" - Unteroffizier Konrad Augner, 2nd Staffel.
"On 5th May around 08:00 hours we received the order from Headquarters: "Luftwaffe Mitte"", to cease action. We each placed one or two kilos of explosives in our aircraft. In the evening we received a new order: we were to leave our aircraft intact and to deliver them to the enemy. During the night we removed the explosives. On 6th May the British reached the aerodrome, which we had by then evacuated. We were on the way to Flensburg, to a camp at Schmörholm. Arms were collected and only the officers retained their pistols.
"On 8th May the allies took over the airfield, the British and Americans shared out our He 162s. They also took the technical personnel, who were required to keep the aircraft in flying condition. On 25th May our 25 female auxiliaries were released. Myself, I was set free on 13th July. Five days later, at 22:00 hours, I reached my family home at Wesermünde" - Hauptmann Ludwig Siegfried, Stab, I. Gruppe.
For III. Gruppe, the end of the war was more eventful. In mid-April, when it was envisaged that the pilots of III. Gruppe would start their conversion training on the He 162, they relinquished their aircraft and took up residence at Markgrafenheide/Warnemünde, near Rostock. Ground personnel took on charge several He 162s there, but they did not have time to prepare them for the training of their pilots: from 24th April III. Gruppe was officially disbanded. The most experienced pilots were transferred to other units, for example Oberfeldwebel Fritz Haspel and Unteroffizier Hugo Hausotter were posted to 5th Staffel, Jagdgeschwader 27, whom they joined in the Flensburg area.
A party of ground personnel was sent to Neustrelitz where they had to change their uniforms of the Luftwaffe for that of the infantry. They received arms and were told to make their way to Berlin to take part in its defence. A counter-order arrived rapidly: Berlin was encircled so they had to defend Neustrelitz.
"We were posted to the west of the city where white smoke was rising: artillery and russian armour were firing. The retreat westwards was made possible by the intervention of tanks and members of the "Hitler Youth" armed with Panzerfausts. The order to retreat was not waited for.
"In the night of 7th-8th May, our battalion, named "Eisen"

With He 162s lined up behind them are, from left to right: Major Zober; Hauptmann Ludewig; Hauptmann Künneke and Oberleutnant Demuth.

Following the dissolution of III. Gruppe at the end of April 1945, several experienced pilots of the Gruppe were posted to other units. Feldwebel Hausotter and Oberfeldwebel Haspel were transferred to 5th Staffel, JG 27.

was dissolved. We were given our papers and were told that the Russians were 100 metres to the east, with the Americans a similar distance to the west. Naturally we turned west and were very quickly captured, in the region of Neistadt-Kleve" - Feldwebel Ernst Webel, technician of III. Gruppe.

"On the last day of April 1945, the Commander of the airfield at Markgrafenheide told us that we would be engaged in the defence of the airfield. On the morning of 1st May our III. Gruppe was alone: the units which should have been alongside us had left during the night for Denmark. We were without arms or munitions, apart from several revolvers. Our Commander, Hauptmann Moldenhauer, took the decision to evacuate his men westwards. After a good breakfast, we shouldered our packs and started the march. Our objective was Leck. The first resting place was going to be Doberan. Our column was rapidly mixed in with a large mass of refugees. We reached Warnow-Fähre and headed towards Warnemünde. The group began to split up. I was walking in the front. The Commander told me and a comrade to try to regroup the men. The first to arrive dropped their baggage at the foot of a concrete wall two metres high and headed for a naval refreshment centre for their evening rations. My friend and I had hardly put down our packs when, suddenly, the war caught up with us. Sounds of battle came from the west. That was the way we were heading! All around us, people were running. My friend and I calmly remained seated whilst enemy fighters carried out strafing. We searched the horizon - the sky remained empty. New bursts were heard. Jumping up, we climbed onto the wall behind which were the tracks of Warnemünde station. Behind it, Russian tanks were firing without respite. We dropped down and, without having recovered from our surprise, saw our Commander with a half-dozen men. They were looking for their packs. "What are you doing here?" asked Moldenhauer, "come with us quickly". We picked up our packs and rejoined the small group. We headed quickly for the landing stage and the jetty. From there five naval boats were leaving, full of refugees and soldiers. The first four were heading out of the port, the fifth had just cut loose from the quay. The skipper saw us and told us to jump. One metres fifty from the quay there were wooden moorings. It was a metre higher than the quay, and it was not a simple matter to reach the boat. The boat continued to head away. We had to jump from mooring to mooring to reach it. Four strong hands lifted us on board. Hardly had the last one got on board

Two views of a He 162 A-2, "White 3" of 1st Staffel receiving attention from mechanics. Note the 20mm. cannon, the red tip at the front of the engine housing, and the absence of of the red arrow on the nose of the aircraft.

Following the end of hostilities these four officers await their final release by the allies. From left to right: Leutnant Hans Berger; Oberleutnant Emil Demuth; Leutnant Gerhard Hanf and Oberleutnant Wilhelm Krebs.

Oberleutnant Emil Demuth, Staffelkapitän of 3rd Staffel, poses in front of the fin and rudder of his He 162 A-2, W.Nr. 120074, which carries 16 kill markings gained on Fw 190s.

Five pilots of 3rd Staffel in March 1945. From left to right: Brune; Ackermann; Klein; Kirchner and Köhne. The two most experienced pilots, Ackermann and Kirchner, were killed on 23rd and 19th April 1945 respectively at the controls of He 162s.

than a violent shaking surprised us. The boat put on full steam to escape the port. Our ability to reach the boat was not due to any athletic prowess on our part, but to the real fear within us which gave us wings.
"On the beach, at the foot of the Warnemünde lighthouse, the first Russian tanks rolled. They had seen us. The marines took up their action stations and replied. We "passengers" took cover. To the right, and from behind, two aircraft appeared at great speed. The gunners quickly opened fire on them. We quickly recognised them as Arado 234s and shouted: "They are ours!". The fire stopped immediately. The four other boats did likewise. In between times, we had succeeded in getting out of the range of the Russians. They fired a last salvo, which posed us no danger. One craft which had been hit in the stern was towed by one of our other friends. Out at sea, soldiers and refugees transferred onto a Danish cargo vessel. Anything that was not necessary was abandoned. I only possessed what I was carrying. The ships separated. Ours followed the coastline west at a safe distance from the shore. In the early evening, anxiety returned: we were passing through a minefield and saw the anti-submarine nets in the port of Wismar. The mines were pushed away behind us by using poles. Strange sights for a flyer!
"We docked at Wismar, 50 kilometres west of Rostock, without knowing how much further the Russians had advanced. The enemy was no longer with us. The captain was able to bring his family on board. We sailed again and began our games with the mines once more.
"On the morning of 2nd May we followed the coast and entered the port of Orth, where the ship was camouflaged with fishing nets. The flotilla was replenished with fuel and food. We spent two quiet days on the Baltic, only broken by enemy fighter-bombers heading for inland targets. Several times we thought we had been spotted. However thanks to the ice-cool nerves of our captain, we remained safe from our attack. In the evening we entertained our saviour.
"Twenty four hours later, our captain announced that he would land us at Kappeln. Under the cover of darkness, the camouflage nets were removed and we put out to sea. During the night the flotilla cruised at slow speed in the Kiel straits. In the distance we saw flashes. The poor city was undergoing further bombardment.
At dawn on 4th May the other ships had disappeared. Our vessel penetrated the mouth of the Schlei and zigzagged to avoid the mines and anti-submarine nets. We landed at Kappeln and left the marines. The sun was shining, and we saluted the vessel, which was moving off. In front of a hangar, there was a long queue. As it seemed to be involved in distribution, we approached with interest. It was a naval depot whose contents were being distributed to the population. While our Commander spoke to the Quarter-master, we spoke to some young girls. I learned that my father, Major Hillmer, had his quarters nearby. I caught him by surprise while he was shaving. The re-union was very moving: he finally had one of his three sons returned to him. I introduced him to my friends. He put a vehicle at our dispersal. Our small group then split up. I remained with my friend, the others, including Moldenhauer, set off in the direction of Leck to rejoin the two other Gruppen of the unit.
My career as a flyer finished in that manner. Somewhat abruptly, but with a certain amount of luck. Interned, I was released by the British at Hamburg, at the end of August 1945" - Unteroffizier Dietmar Hillmer, 11th Staffel.
Thus the story of Jagdgeschwader 1 ended: in the final months with conversion to a revolutionary fighter and involvement in the general pell-mell of retreat which was symptomatic of the disintegration of the Luftwaffe. Jagdgeschwader 1 could truly be termed the premier fighter unit involved in defending the Reich.

LOSS TABLES - 1945

Date	Name of Crew and Rank	Staffel	Fate	Aircraft, W.Nr & Code	Damage /Loss	Reason for Casualty	Place
01.01.45	Hptm. Georg Hackbarth	I. Gruppe	Killed	Fw 190 A-8 ( )	100%	Shot down during Operation Bodenplatte.	Gent railway station
01.01.45	Uffz. Egon Comtesse	1	Wounded	Fw 190 A-8 White 3 (960729)	100%	Shot down during Operation Bodenplatte.	Gent
01.01.45	Uffz.. Paul Wunderlich	2	POW	Fw 190 A-8 Black 6 (739228)	100%	Shot down during Operation Bodenplatte.	Near Scheldt estuary
01.01.45	Gefr. Karl Heinz Bauch	2	Killed	Fw 190 A-8 Black 9 (960709)	100%	Shot down during Operation Bodenplatte.	Gent
01.01.45	Fw. Heinz Jürgan Killian	3	Killed	Fw 190 A-8 Yellow 6 (738159)	100%	Shot down during Operation Bodenplatte.	Gent
01.01.45	Fw. Fritz Hofmann	3	POW	Fw 190 A-8 Chevron 1 (175044)	100%	Shot down during Operation Bodenplatte.	Gent
01.01.45	Lt. Ernst von Johannides	5	Killed	Fw 190 A-8 White 1 (739429)	100%	Shot down during Operation Bodenplatte.	Gent
01.01.45	Lt. Walter Holick	5	Killed	Fw 190 A-8 White 6 (739230)	100%	Shot down during Operation Bodenplatte	Gent
01.01.45	Uffz. Otto Kuntzsch	5	Killed	Fw 190 A-8 White 4 (960679)	100%	Shot down during Operation Bodenplatte.	Gent
01.01.45	Uffz.Erich Wenniges	5	Killed	Fw 190 A-8 White 15 (960473)	100%	Shot down during Operation Bodenplatte.	Gent
01.01.45	Uffz. Edgar Ardner	5	POW	Fw 190 A-8 Black 4 (171513)	100%	Shot down during Operation Bodenplatte.	Ederkamp, 3 km. north-west of St. Denijs airfield
01.01.45	Fw. Karl Hahn	II. Gruppe	Killed	Fw 190 A-8 White 8 (352518)	100%	Shot down during Operation Bodenplatte.	Gent
01.01.45	Fw. Harry Klints	II. Gruppe	Killed	Fw 190 A-8 Black 5 (739235)	100%	Shot down during Operation Bodenplatte.	Gent, St. Denijs airfield
01.01.45	Ofhr. Hilmar Kreb	II. Gruppe	Killed	Fw 190 A-8 Yellow 4 (960659)	100%	Shot down during Operation Bodenplatte.	Gent
01.01.45	Ofw. Kurt Niedereicholz	7	Killed	Fw 190 A-8 Yellow 14 (173932)	100%	Shot down during Operation Bodenplatte.	Gent
01.01.45	Uffz. Oskar Vetter	7	Killed	Fw 190 A-8 Yellow 16 (173813)	100%	Shot down during Operation Bodenplatte.	Gent
01.01.45	Fw. Paul Mayr	8	Killed	Fw 190 A-8 Blue 10 (960547)	100%	Shot down during Operation Bodenplatte.	Gent
01.01.45	Uffz. Gerhard Behrens	8	Killed	Fw 190 A-8 Blue 14 (960677)	100%	Shot down during Operation Bodenplatte.	Gent
01.01.45	Uffz. Reinhold Schober	8	Killed	Fw 190 A-8 Blue 15 (733978)	100%	Shot down during Operation Bodenplatte.	Gent
01.01.45	FjFw. Willi Wichardt	9	POW	Bf 109 G-14 White 19 (782402)	100%	Shot down during Operation Bodenplatte.	Scheldt estuary
01.01.45	Lt. Anton Guha	10	POW	Bf 109 G-14 Grey 22 (780375)	100%	Shot down during Operation Bodenplatte.	Near Biervliet
01.01.45	Fw. Wilhelm Kräuter	10	Missing	Bf 109 G-14 Grey 23 (784090)	100%	Shot down during Operation Bodenplatte.	South Holland
02.01.45	Fw. Friedrich Steinborn	10	Killed	Bf 109 G-14 (785080)	100%	Crashed on non-combat flight.	Plantlünne

Date	*Name of Crew and Rank*	*Staffel*	*Fate*	*Aircraft, W.Nr & Code*	*Damage /Loss*	*Reason for Casualty*	*Place*
02.01.45	Ofw. Günther Treptau	2	Killed	Fw 190 A-8 Black 7 (739267)	100%	Shot down in combat with British fighters.	Oldenzaal
02.01.45	Ofhr. Dieter Stucken	2	Killed	Fw 190 A-8 Black 10 (173936)	100%	Shot down in combat with British fighters.	Oldenzaal
02.01.45	Uffz. Karl Greuel	2	Killed	Fw 190 A-8 Black 12 (177001)	100%		Oldenzaal
14.01.45	Lt. Bruno Honsek	1	Killed	Fw 190 A-9 White 6 (980207)	100%	Shot down in combat with British fighters.	Bentheim
14.01.45	Fw. Günther Rosemund	1	Killed	Fw 190 A-8 White 4 (960727)	100%	Shot down in combat with British fighters.	Bentheim
14.01.45	Uffz. Hans Heidrich	1	Killed	Fw 190 A-8 White 5 (739325)	100%	Shot down in combat with British fighters.	Twente
14.01.45	Ogefr. Walter Mämpel	1	Killed	Fw 190 A-8 White 5 ( )	100%	Crashed following combat.	Twente
14.01.45	Uffz. Heinz Franke	2	Killed	Fw 190 D-9 Black 7 (210111)	100%	Shot down in combat with British fighters.	Venlo
14.01.45	Ofhr. Helmut Schwager	2	Killed	Fw 190 A-8 ( )	100%	Crashed following combat.	Twente
14.01.45	Fw. Otto Schulz	2	Missing	Fw 190 A-9 Black 2 (980217)	100%	Shot down in combat with British fighters.	Twente
14.01.45	Ofhr. Wilhelm Ade	2	Wounded	Fw 190 A-9 Black 3 (980219)	100%	Shot down in combat with British fighters.	Lünten
14.01.45	Ofw. Gerhard Kühl	3	Missing	Fw 190 A-9 Green 21 ( )	100%	Shot down in combat with British fighters.	Twente
14.01.45	Uffz. Günther Sill	I. Gruppe	Killed	Fw 190 D-9 Green 8 (210224)	100%	Shot down in combat with British fighters.	Enschede
14.01.45	Oblt. Heinrich Greuner	4	Wounded	Fw 190 A-9 Red 1 (980216)		Emergency landing on non-combat flight.	Stolzenau
14.01.45	Uffz. Wolfgang Kindhaüser	4	Wounded	Fw 190 A-8 Red 4 (205226)		Shot down in combat with RAF fighters.	Twente
16.01.45		II. Gruppe		Fw 190 A-8 (380345)	15%	Damaged due to engine problem.	
17.01.45	Ofhr. Rudolf Müller	9	Killed	Bf 109 G-14 White 11 (782335)	100%	Collided on take off.	Schröttersburg
18.01.45	Uffz. Erwin Kurz	5	Killed	Fw 190 A-8 White 2 (173048)	100%	Shot down in combat with Yak-9s.	Insterburg
18.01.45	Fw. Günther Kuhlen	5	Killed	Fw 190 A-8 White 12 (734010)	100%		Insterburg
18.01.45		II. Gruppe		Fw 190 A-8 (739241)	100%	Shot down in combat.	
18.01.45		II. Gruppe		Fw 190 A-8 (737367)	25%	Engine problem.	
19.01.45		II. Gruppe		Fw 190 A-8 (739258)	30%	Damaged on combat mission.	
19.01.45	Uffz. Heinrich Kopton	7	Killed	Fw 190 A-8 Yellow 13 (173921)	100%	Shot down in combat with Yak-3s.	Schlossburg
19.01.45	Lt. Erwin Bender	8	Wounded	Fw 190 A-8 Brown 11 (490032)	100%	Shot down in combat.	Insterburg
20.01.45	Ofhr. Herbert Huss	1	Killed	Fw 190 A-9 White 3 (980203)	100%		Insterberg

Date	*Name of Crew and Rank*	*Staffel*	*Fate*	*Aircraft, W.Nr & Code*	*Damage /Loss*	*Reason for Casualty*	*Place*
20.01.45	Fhr. Horst Hergesell	3	Missing	Fw 190 A-9 Yellow 6 (960723)	100%		Insterburg
20.01.45		II. Gruppe		Fw 190 A-8 (750134)	15%	Damaged on combat mission.	
20.01.45	Hptm. Friedrich Strich	7	Killed	Fw 190 A-9 Yellow 4 (960033)	100%		Insterburg
22.01.45		II. Gruppe		Fw 190 A-9 (490030)	100%	Engine problem on combat mission.	
23.01.45	Ofhr. Werner Hostermann	3	Killed	Fw 190 A-9 Yellow 3 (980218)	100%	Crashed.	Danzig
23.01.45	Uffz. Werner Bornholdt	11	Killed	Bf 109 G-14 (785924)	100%	Crashed on take-off.	Riesa
24.01.45		II. Gruppe		Fw 190 A-8 (739381)	10%	Engine damage on non-combat mission.	
24.01.45		II. Gruppe		Fw 190 A-8 (173903)	15%	Damaged while taxiing.	
28.01.45	Fhr. Emil Jäger	8	Missing	Fw 190 A-8 Blue 4 (739240)	100%	Shot down in combat.	Königsberg
01.02.45		II. Gruppe	Wounded	Fw 190 A-8 ( )	80%	Belly landing.	
02.02.45	Uffz. Alvo von Alvensleben	1	Wounded	Fw 190 A-8 White 11 (960267)		Emergency landing.	Danzig
03.02.45	Ogefr. Max Schiochol	5	Killed	Fw 190 A-9 White 1 (980212)	100%	Shot down in combat.	Werneuchen
03.02.45	FjU. Karl Elbertzhagen	7	Killed	Fw 190 A-8 Yellow 5 (734033)	100%	Shot down in combat.	Werneuchen
03.02.45	Uffz. Heinz Henn	8	Killed	Fw 190 A-9 Black 11 (980548)	100%	Shot down in combat.	Werneuchen
03.02.45		II. Gruppe		Fw 190 A-8 (738168)	20%	Emergency landing due to pilot getting lost.	
05.02.45	Oblt. Willi Krüger	3	Missing	Fw 190 A (980563)	100%		
05.02.45	Uffz. Bodo Henn	II. Gruppe		Fw 190 A Black 11 (180548)	100%		
05.02.45		II. Gruppe		Fw 190 A-9 (205205)	100%	Shot down in combat.	Near Wiezen
07.02.45		II. Gruppe		Fw 190 A-8 (931017)	60%	Damage due to servicing fault.	
09.02.45	Fhr. Herbert Dönch	9	Killed	Bf 109 G-14 White 9 (785109)	60%	Emergency landing.	Stolp-Reitz
10.02.45		II. Gruppe		Fw 190 A-8 (584338)	30%	Damage due to servicing fault.	
11.02.45	Uffz. Hans Gummel	I. Gruppe	Wounded	Bf 109 G-6 (41066)	100%	Belly landing due to engine fire.	
14.02.45		II. Gruppe		Fw 190 A-8 (738227)	60%	Damage due to engine problem.	
14.02.45		II. Gruppe		Fw 190 A-8 (739540)	15%	Damaged while taxiing.	
14.02.45		II. Gruppe		Fw 190 A-8 (732293)	15%	Belly landing.	
16.02.45	Oblt. Georg von Friesen	1	Killed	Fw 190 A-8 (739570)		Crashed on take off.	
20.02.45				Bf 109 G-6 (170006)	10%	Damage due to servicing fault.	Erding airfield
21.02.45		I. Gruppe		Fw 190 A-9 (980550)	10%	Belly landing due to technical problems.	Prossnitz
27.02.45		III. Gruppe		Bf 109 K-4 (332760)	50%	Damaged on landing.	Vietzker-Strand airfield
28.02.45		III. Gruppe		Bf 109 G-14 (785843)	30%	Tipped over onto nose on landing.	Vietzker-Strand airfield

Date	Name of Crew and Rank	Staffel	Fate	Aircraft, W.Nr & Code	Damage /Loss	Reason for Casualty	Place
01.03.45	Uffz. Hermann Volz	11	Killed	Bf 109 G-14 (452742)		Crashed.	Stolp-Reitz
02.03.45		II. Gruppe		Bf 109 G-14 (464131)	30%	Belly landing due to pilot getting lost.	North-east of Wertheim
04.03.45		III. Gruppe		Bf 109 K-4 (332784)	40%	Crashed on landing.	
05.03.45	Lt. Gottfried Grasl	9	Missing	Bf 109 G-14 White 13 (781115)		Emergency landing in enemy territory.	Konitz
05.03.45	Uffz. Max Heller	10	Killed	Bf 109 G-14 Black 8 (785997)	100%	Shot down in combat with fighters.	Rummelsburg
05.03.45		III. Gruppe		Bf 109 G-14 (785828)	10%	Emergency landing due to fuel shortage.	
06.03.45		III. Gruppe		Bf 109 G-14 (785992)	20%	Damaged while taxiing.	Stolp-Reitz airfield
14.03.45	Uffz. Tautz	2		He 162 ( )			Vienna
17.03.45	Lt. Hubert Swoboda	5	Wounded	Fw 190 A-9 White 13 (980369)	100%	Shot down in combat with Russian fighters.	Brüssow
20.03.45		II. Gruppe		Fw 190 A-8 (739522)	30%	Damage due to servicing fault.	Garz airfield
25.03.45	Gefr. Amandus Strickrock	6	Killed	Fw 190 A-8 Yellow 8 (750085)	100%	Shot down by own Flak.	Usedom
25.03.45	Uffz. Herbert Neumann	8	Wounded	Fw 190 A-8 Brown 17 (426198)	100%	Shot down by own Flak.	Swinemünde

At the end of March/early April 1945 the following were killed in action; the date and place is unknown:

	Lt. Hubert Swoboda	5
	Lt. Erwin Bender	8

Date	Name of Crew and Rank	Staffel	Fate	Aircraft, W.Nr & Code	Damage /Loss	Reason for Casualty	Place
13.04.45	Uffz. Friedrich Enderle	I. Gruppe	Killed	He 162 ( )	100%		
19.04.45	Fw. Günther Kirchner	3	Killed	He 162 ( )	100%		Klintum
24.04.45	Hptm. Paul Dähne	II. Gruppe	Killed	He 162 ( )	100%		Warnemünde
30.04.45	Lt. Alfred Dürr	6	Killed	He 162 (120086)		Emergency landing due to fuel shortage.	Autobahn north of Danischburg, near Lübeck

The following further losses are known for the He 162 but are far from complete:

Date	Name of Crew and Rank	Staffel	Fate	Aircraft, W.Nr & Code	Damage /Loss	Reason for Casualty	Place
11.04.45	Mann	I. Gruppe	Missing	He 162 ( )			
18.04.45	Hartung	I. Gruppe	Killed	He 162 ( )			
23.04.45	Ackermann	I. Gruppe	Killed	He 162 ( )			
25.04.45	Uffz. Gerhard Steiner	I. Gruppe	Wounded	He 162 ( )			
Unknown	Ofw. Karl Beck	II. Gruppe	Killed	He 162 ( )		Emergency landing due to fuel shortage.	Klintum, near Leck
Unknown	Fw. Jupp Gold	II. Gruppe	Killed	He 162 ( )			
Unknown	Uffz. Stelter	II. Gruppe	Killed	He 162 ( )		Flying error caused crash.	Marienehe

APPENDIX 1

JAGDGESCHWADER 1 BASES

Jagdgeschwader 1 was generally split up, each Gruppe occupying different airfields. It happened that Staffeln of the same Gruppe, or even different Schwärme of the same Staffel, could be apart. They were often based on adjoining airfields. The following list shows the period of occupation of a base by a complete Gruppe, or its component parts.

JAGDGESCHWADER 1 IN HOLLAND AND THE RUHR

(1)	Bergen aan Zee:	I. Gruppe:	05/41	12/41
		II. Gruppe:	05/42	
		III. Gruppe:	01/42	
(2)	Bergen op Zoom:	IV. Gruppe:	05/42	07/42
(3)	Deelen/Arnhem:	I. Gruppe:	04/43	12/43
		II. Gruppe:	07/42	
		IV. Gruppe:	06/42	04/43
(4)	De Kooi:	I. Gruppe:	12/40	06/41
(5)	Dortmund:	I. Gruppe:	12/43	02/44
(6)	Düsseldorf:	II. Gruppe:	05/42	
		IV. Gruppe:	04/42	
(7)	Haamstede:	II. Gruppe:	02/42	07/42
(8)	Hopsten/Rheine:	I. Gruppe:	02/44	
		II. Gruppe:	07/43	04/44
(9)	Katwijk:	Geschwaderstab:	12/41	02/42
		I. Gruppe:	06/41	09/41
		II. Gruppe:	01/42	07/43
(10)	Leeuwarden:	II. Gruppe:	02/42	04/43
		III. Gruppe:	05/43	12/43
		IV. Gruppe:	05/42	
(11)	Mönchen-Gladbach:	IV. Gruppe:	06/42	02/43
(12)	Schipol/Amsterdam:	I. Gruppe:	06/43	07/43
		II. Gruppe:	03/42	05/43
(13)	Twente:	I. Gruppe:	02/44	04/44
			12/44	01/45
(14)	Venlo:	II. Gruppe:	07/42	09/42
(15)	Vlissingen:	II. Gruppe:	03/42	06/42
(16)	Volkel:	III. Gruppe:	12/43	02/44
(17)	Woensdrecht:	II. Gruppe:	02/42	07/43

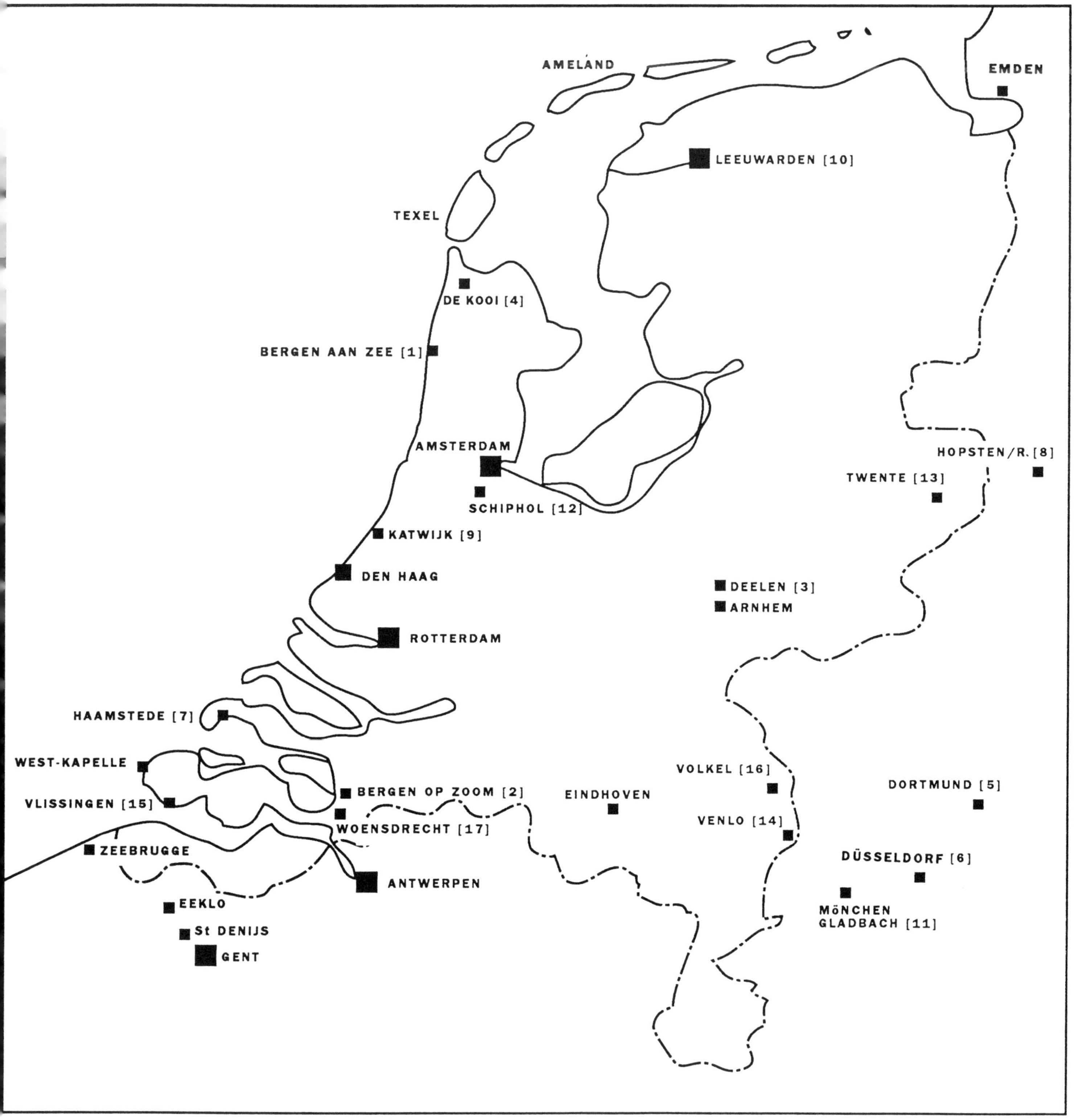
AMELAND
EMDEN
LEEUWARDEN [10]
TEXEL
DE KOOI [4]
BERGEN AAN ZEE [1]
AMSTERDAM
HOPSTEN/R. [8]
TWENTE [13]
SCHIPHOL [12]
KATWIJK [9]
DEN HAAG
DEELEN [3]
ARNHEM
ROTTERDAM
HAAMSTEDE [7]
WEST-KAPELLE
VOLKEL [16]
DORTMUND [5]
BERGEN OP ZOOM [2]
EINDHOVEN
VLISSINGEN [15]
VENLO [14]
WOENSDRECHT [17]
ZEEBRUGGE
DÜSSELDORF [6]
ANTWERPEN
EEKLO
MöNCHEN
GLADBACH [11]
St DENIJS
GENT

JAGDGESCHWADER 1 IN NORMANDY

(1)	Aulney:	I. Gruppe:	11/08/44	....	22/08/44
(2)	Bearieux:	III. Gruppe:	26/08/44		
(3)	Beauvais:	III. Gruppe:	06/06/44	....	30/06/44
(4)	Brétigny:	III. Gruppe:	06/08/44	....	15/08/44
(5)	Cuissai-Lonrai:	I. Gruppe:	12/06/44	....	05/08/44
		II. Gruppe:	17/07/44	....	/08/44
(6)	Essay:	II. Gruppe:	12/06/44	....	17/06/44
(7)	La Fére:	III. Gruppe:	11/07/44	....	05/08/44
(8)	Le Mans:	I. Gruppe:	07/06/44	....	12/06/44
		II. Gruppe:	07/06/44	....	12/06/44
(9)	Marolles:	III. Gruppe:	18/08/44	....	19/08/44
(10)	Montdidier:	I. Gruppe:	06/06/44		
		II. Gruppe:	06/06/44		
(11)	Oysonville:	I. Gruppe:	04/08/44	....	11/08/44
(12)	Semallé:	II. Gruppe:	18/06/44	....	/08/44
(13)	St. Quentin/Clastres	Stab:	15/06/44	....	?
(14)	Vailly:	III. Gruppe:	18/08/44	....	29/08/44

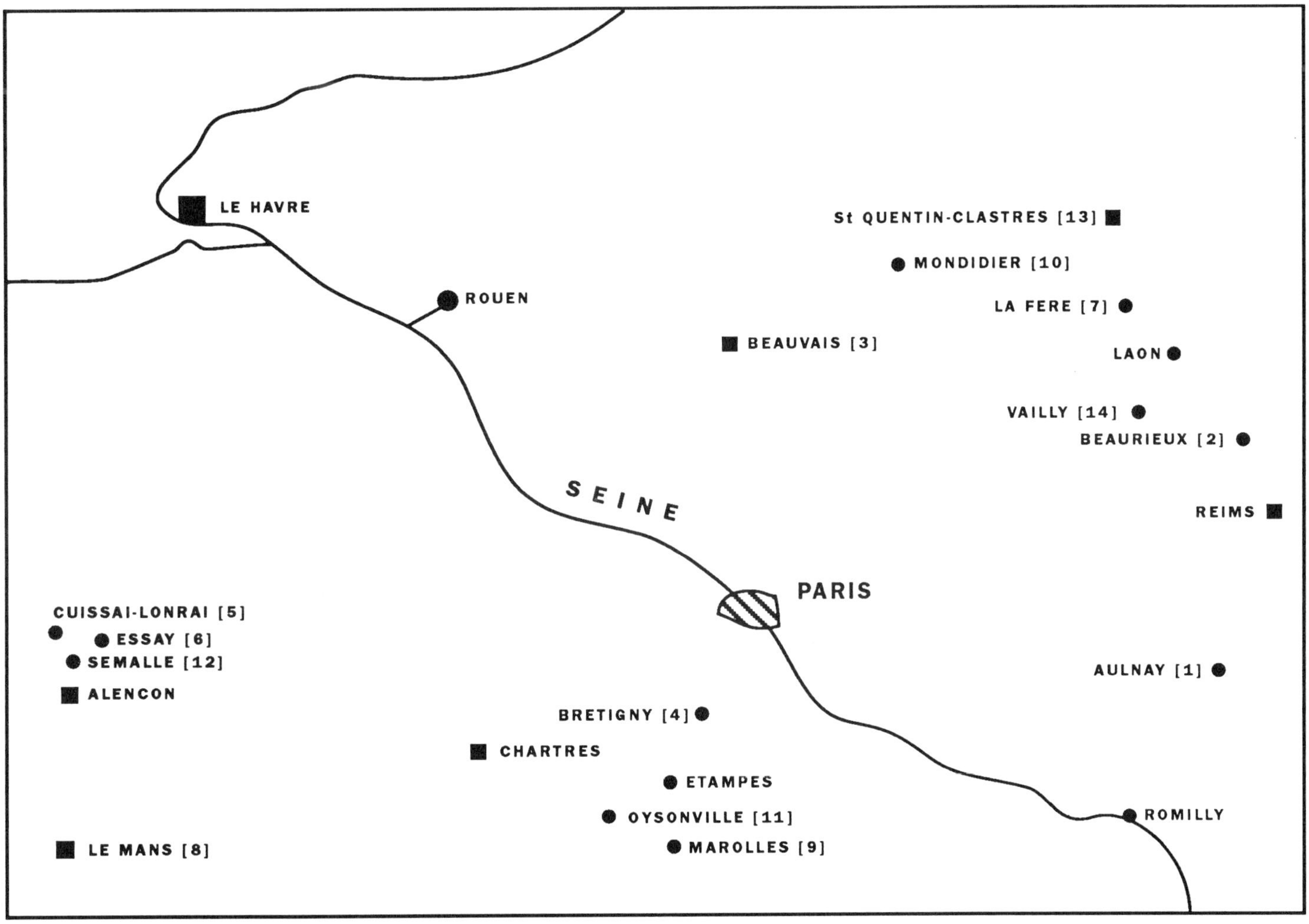

LE HAVRE
ROUEN
St QUENTIN-CLASTRES [13]
MONDIDIER [10]
LA FERE [7]
BEAUVAIS [3]
LAON
VAILLY [14]
BEAURIEUX [2]
SEINE
REIMS
PARIS
CUISSAI-LONRAI [5]
ESSAY [6]
SEMALLE [12]
ALENCON
AULNAY [1]
BRETIGNY [4]
CHARTRES
ETAMPES
OYSONVILLE [11]
ROMILLY
MAROLLES [9]
LE MANS [8]

JAGDGESCHWADER 1 IN THE EAST

(1)	Allenstein:	I. Gruppe:	09/39	
(2)	Anklam	III. Gruppe:	09/10/44	.... 17/12/44
			03/03/45	.... ?
(3)	Berent:	III. Gruppe:	23/01/45	.... ?
(4)	Brüsterort:	I. Gruppe:	30/01/45	
(5)	Danzig/Rahmel:	I. Gruppe:	04/02/45	
(6)	Garz:	I. Gruppe:	07/02/45	.... 09/02/45
		II. Gruppe:	early 02/45	.... 08/04/45
(7)	Gerdauen:	II. Gruppe:	21/01/45	
(8)	Greifswald:	I. Gruppe:	07/10/44	.... 17/12/44
(9)	Heiligenbeil:	I. Gruppe:	21/01/45	.... 01/02/45
		II. Gruppe:	22/01/45	
(10)	Insterburg:	II. Gruppe:	18/01/45	
	In./Jürgenfelde:	I. Gruppe:	14/01/45	
		II. Gruppe:	18/01/45	
(11)	Kolberg:	I. Gruppe:	07/02/45	
		II. Gruppe:	early 02/45	
(12)	Marienburg:	III. Gruppe:	21/01/45	.... 23/01/45
(13)	Markgrafenheide:	III. Gruppe:	mid 04/45	.... 01/05/45
(14)	Neu Kuhren:	I. Gruppe:	24/01/45	
		III. Gruppe:	end 01/45	
(15)	Parchim:	I. Gruppe:	09/02/45	.... 09/04/45
(16)	Pillau:	III. Gruppe:	end 01/45	
(17)	Rostock/Marienehe:	I.Gruppe:	mid 03/45	.... early 04/45
		II. Gruppe:	08/04/45	.... 02/05/45
(18)	Schröttersburg:	III. Gruppe:	15/01/45	.... 19/01/45
(19)	Stolp:	III. Gruppe:	31/01/45	.... 04/03/45
(20)	Thorn:	III. Gruppe:	19/01/45	.... 02/02/45

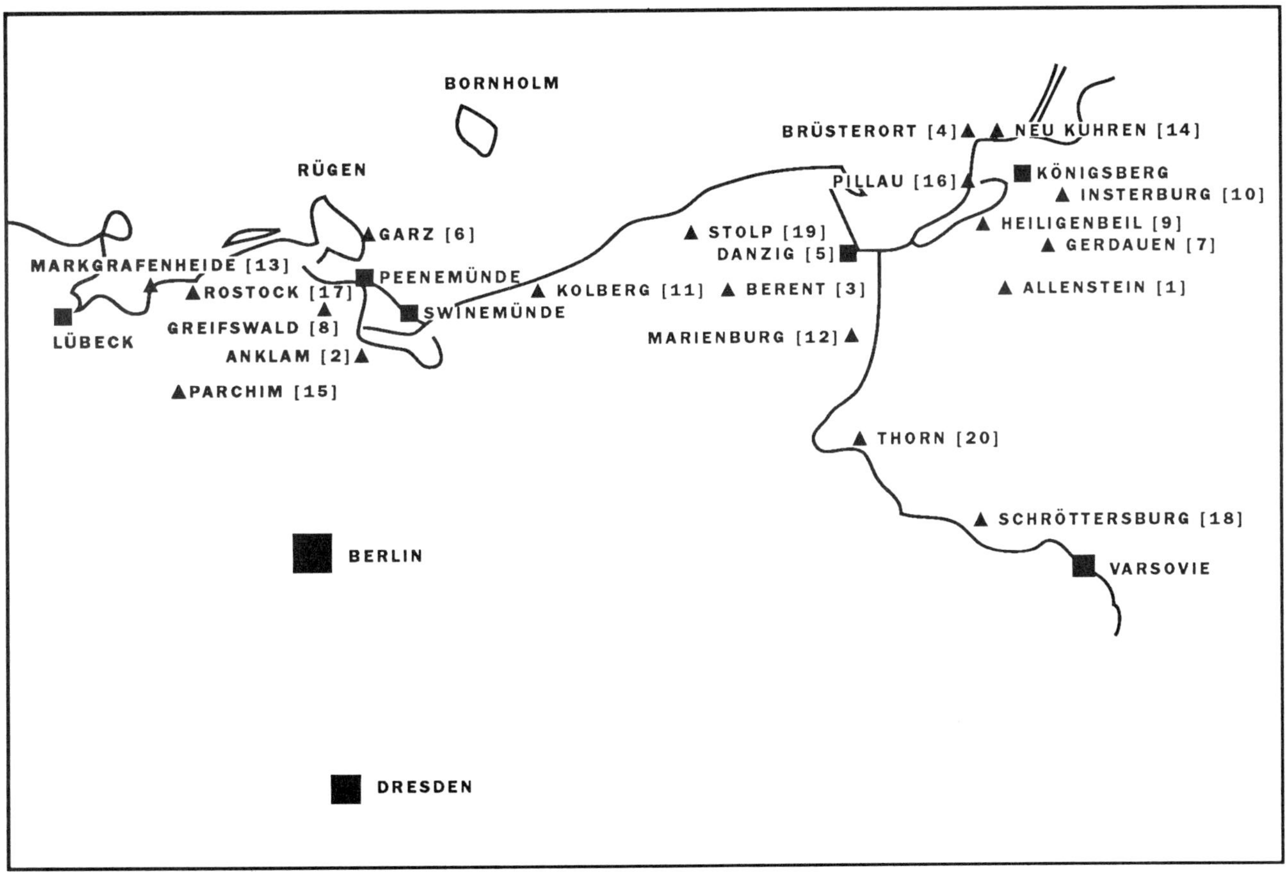
BORNHOLM
RÜGEN
BRÜSTERORT [4]
NEU KUHREN [14]
PILLAU [16]
KÖNIGSBERG
INSTERBURG [10]
HEILIGENBEIL [9]
GERDAUEN [7]
ALLENSTEIN [1]
GARZ [6]
STOLP [19]
DANZIG [5]
MARKGRAFENHEIDE [13]
ROSTOCK [17]
PEENEMÜNDE
KOLBERG [11]
BERENT [3]
SWINEMÜNDE
LÜBECK
GREIFSWALD [8]
ANKLAM [2]
MARIENBURG [12]
PARCHIM [15]
THORN [20]
SCHRÖTTERSBURG [18]
BERLIN
VARSOVIE
DRESDEN

Major Erich Mix in his Bf 109 F at Husum, August 1941. Note part of the Gruppenkommandeur's chevron just visible on the fuselage. The armoured windscreen is also evident in this view.

On 6th January 1942 Major Erich von Selle left I. Gruppe Jagdgeschwader 54 to take up post as Kommodore of Jagdgeschwader 1, which he would occupy for seven months.

A change occurred at the head of the unit when Major Hans Philipp left JG 54 to become Kommodore of JG 1 from 1/4/43. He is seen here still wearing a coat of Russian front origin.

APPENDIX 2

PRINCIPAL OFFICERS OF JAGDGESCHWADER 1

The head of a Geschwader was the Kommodore. Theoretically, he led the unit in action, accompanied by his Stabsschwarm, usually the Adjutant, Technical Officer and another experienced pilot. The Kommodore led three, sometimes four, Gruppen.

Each of these Gruppen had at their head an experienced officer, occupying the official post of Gruppenkommandeur. Following the loss of one of them, a Gruppenführer (Gruppe leader) would be appointed, usually the most experienced Staffelkapitän. He would then lead the Gruppe until a new Gruppenkommandeur was appointed. The non-combat administrative tasks were often delegated to the Gruppenadjutant, who was not always a pilot.

Each Gruppe was composed of three, sometimes four, Staffeln, of which the Kapitän was an officer, usually a Hauptmann or Oberleutnant. When the loss of a Staffelkapitän occurred, a Staffelführer was appointed from within the ranks of officers of the Staffel, this being usually a Leutnant. If the necessary leadership qualities were shown, he would probably be given the appointment of Staffelkapitän some time later. As was often the case, however, the Staffelführer was often less experienced than one or more NCO pilots (usually Oberfeldwebel or Feldwebel) of the Staffel. Then it often happened that the more experienced junior rank led the Staffel in combat.

To tackle the massed Allied formations, Geschwadern were often grouped together, for example Jagdgeschwader 1 and Jagdgeschwader 11.Then the complete formation was led by a Verbandsführer, who would not necessarily be the most senior officer, nor the one holding the higher post. It could be a Staffelkapitän whose tactical qualities were recognised as being first-class.

KOMMODOREN OF JAGDGESCHWADER 1

Oberst Carl Schuhmacher	12/11/39	-	05/01/42
Major Erich von Selle	06/01/42	-	27/08/42
Oberstleutnant Dr. Erich Mix	28/08/42	-	31/03/43
Oberstleutnant Hans Philipp	01/04/43	-	08/10/43
Oberst Walter Oesau	10/10/43	-	11/05/44
Major Heinz Bär	12/05/44	-	19/05/44
Oberst Herbert Ihlefield	20/05/44	-	end

GRUPPENKOMMANDEURE (FÜHRERN) OF JAGDGESCHWADER 1

I. Gruppe (1st Formation):

Hauptmann Bernhard Woldenga:	01/04/37	-	31/01/40
Hauptmann Joachim Schlicting	01/02/40	-	05/07/40

(On 05/07/40 I. Gruppe became III. Gruppe, Jagdgeschwader 27).

I. Gruppe (2nd Formation):

Major Dr. Erich Mix	26/09/41	-	27/08/42
Hauptmann Günter Beise	19/09/42	-	01/04/43

(On 01/04/43 I. Gruppe became III. Gruppe, Jagdgeschwader 11).

I. Gruppe (3rd Formation):

Major Fritz Losigkeit	01/04/43	-	20/05/43
Hauptmann Emil Rudolf Schnoor	21/05/43	-	16/04/44
Oberleutnant Hans Ehlers	17/04/44	-	27/12/44
Hauptmann Georg Hackbarth	28/12/44	-	01/01/45
Major Günter Capito	03/01/45	-	14/01/45
Oberleutnant Emil Demuth	15/01/45	-	02/05/45

Oberstleutnant Walter Oesau, see here when a Hauptmann succeeded Hans Philipp as Kommodore of the unit.

One famous fighter pilot replaced another. Oesau's replacement was Oberstleutnant Herbert Ihlefield, who was only the ninth pilot of the German forces to receive the Swords to his Knights Cross with Oakleaves. Ihlefield led the unit until the war's end.

Hauptmann Hans von Hahn, Gruppenkommandeur, I./JG 3, later II./JG 1. His victory tally stood at 34 when he arrived in Holland from the eastern front.

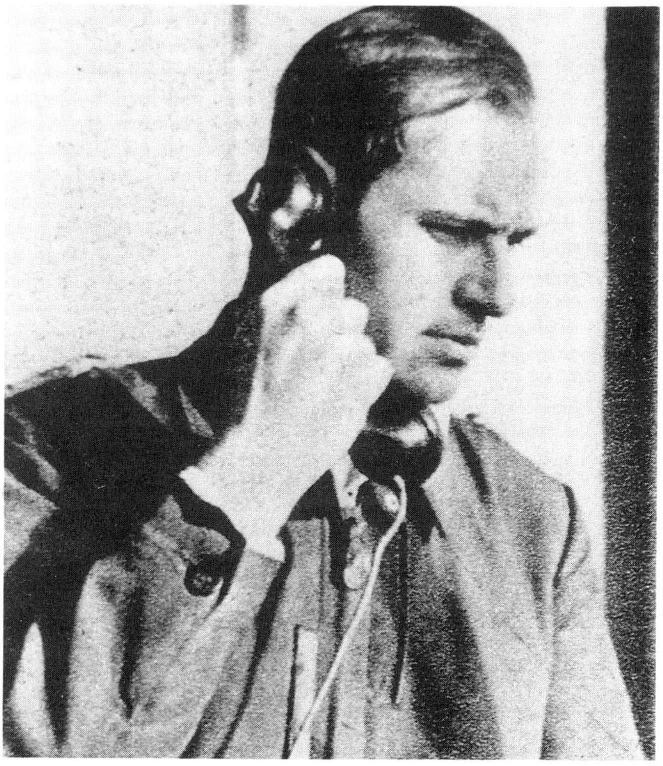

Hauptmann Schnoor, who left 8th Staffel to take command of I. Gruppe upon Hauptmann Losigkeit's transfer.

I. Gruppe (4th Formation):
Major Werner Zober 03/05/45 - end

II. Gruppe (1st Formation):
Hauptmann Hans von Hahn 15/01/42 - /03/42
Oberleutnant Robert Olejnik /03/42 - 19/06/42
Oberleutnant Detlev Rohwer 20/06/42 - 14/10/42
Hauptmann Robert Kijewski 15/10/42 - 16/04/43
Hauptmann Dietrich Wickop 16/04/43 - 16/05/43
Hauptmann Robert Olejnik 17/05/43 - 27/06/43
Hauptmann Walter Hoeckner 28/06/43 - 04/02/44
Hauptmann Hermann Segatz 05/02/44 - 08/03/44
Major Heinz Bär 09/03/44 - 12/05/44
Hauptmann Karl-Heinz Weber 28/05/44 - 07/06/44
Oberleutnant Georg Eder 08/06/44 - 31/07/44
Major Hermann Staiger 01/08/44 - /02/45
Hauptmann Paul-Heinrich Dähne /02/45 - 24/04/45

II. Gruppe (2nd Formation):
Hauptmann Rahe 03/05/45 - end

III. Gruppe (1st Formation):
Hauptmann Herbert Kijewski 06/01/42 - 15/10/42
Hauptmann Emil Rudolf Schnoor 16/10/42 - 31/03/43
(On 01/04/43 III. Gruppe became I. Gruppe, Jagdgeschwader 11).

III. Gruppe (2nd Formation):
Major Karl-Heinz Leesmann 01/04/43 - 25/07/43
Hauptmann Robert Olejnik 26/07/43 - 08/10/43
Hauptmann Friedrich Eberle 09/10/43 - 27/04/44
Hauptmann Hartmann Grasser 28/04/44 - /05/44
Hauptmann Erich Woitke /05/44 - 12/08/44
Hauptmann Heinz Knoke 13/08/44 - 09/10/44
Hauptmann Erich Woitke 10/10/44 - 24/12/44
Hauptmann Harald Moldenhauer 25/12/44 - end

IV. Gruppe:
Hauptmann Fritz Losigkeit 04/04/42 - 31/03/43
(On 01/04/43 IV Gruppe became I. Gruppe, Jagdgeschwader 1).

STAFFELKAPITANE OF JAGDGESCHWADER 1

1st Staffel (1st Formation):
Oberleutnant Wilhelm Balthasar / /39 - 05/07/40
(On 05/07/40 1st Staffel became 7th Staffel, Jagdgeschwader 27).

1st Staffel (2nd Formation):
Oberleutnant Müller
(On 01/04/43 1st Staffel became 4th Staffel, Jagdgeschwader 11).

1st Staffel (3rd Formation) (ex-10./JG 1):
Oberleutnant Alfons Raich 01/04/43 - 12/05/43
Oberleutnant Hans Munz 13/05/43 - 21/05/43
Oberleutnant Georg Schott 01/06/43 - 27/09/43
Oberleutnant Rudolf Engleder 01/10/43 - 06/11/43
Oberleutnant Alfred Grislawski 06/11/43 - 24/01/44
Leutnant Heinz-Günther Lück 24/01/44 - 09/04/44
Leutnant Anton-Rudolf Piffer 01/05/44 - 17/06/44

Hauptmann Olejnik (seen here at readiness) took over command of III. Gruppe when Gruppenkommandeur Karl-Heinz Leesmann was lost in action on 25/7/43.

Major Heinz Bär arrived at Rheine in early January 1944. He is seen here wearing the Knights Cross with Oakleaves and Swords.

On 15/10/43 Hauptmann Herbert Kijewski became Gruppenkommandeur of II. Gruppe.

Hauptmann Georg Peter Eder, who led II. Gruppe during the Normandy campaign. He recorded his 50th victory on 21 June, and was awarded the Ritterkreuz three days later.

Oberleutnant Siegfried Stoffel	17/06/44	-	23/06/44
Leutnant Lüpke	24/07/44	-	15/02/45
Hauptmann Heinz Künneke	16/02/45	-	end

2nd Staffel (1st Formation):

Oberleutnant Walter Adolph	/ /39	-	05/07/40

(On 05/07/40 2nd Staffel became 8th Staffel, Jagdgeschwader 27).

2nd Staffel (2nd Formation):

Oberleutnant Wolfgang Wedding	/07/41	-	30/09/41
Oberleutnant Werner Dolenga	01/10/41	-	24/10/42
Oberleutnant Heinz Knoke	25/10/42	-	01/04/43

(On 01/04/43 2nd Staffel became 5th Staffel, Jagdgeschwader 11).

2nd Staffel (3rd Formation) (ex-11./JG 1):

Oberleutnant Rainer Framm	01/04/43	-	10/06/43
Leutnant Peter Marxen	11/06/43	-	30/07/43
Leutnant Hans Feustel	31/07/43	-	17/08/43
Leutnant Wolfgang Steffen	18/08/43	-	30/08/43
Leutnant Hans Ehlers	31/08/43	-	31/10/43
Oberleutnant Rudolf Engleder	07/11/43	-	16/12/43
Leutnant Hans Windblicher	17/12/43	-	31/01/44
Hauptmann Harald Römer	01/02/44	-	20/02/44
Oberleutnant Helmut Biederbick	27/02/44	-	10/03/44
Oberleutnant Rudolf Engleder	10/03/44	-	01/05/44
Oberleutnant Helmut Biederbick	02/05/44	-	05/06/44
Leutnant Hans Windblicher	16/07/44	-	20/08/44
Oberleutnant Hans Vermaaten	21/08/44	-	14/10/44
Oberleutnant Wilhelm Bergmann	15/10/44	-	21/11/44
Leutnant Gottfried Just	22/11/44	-	27/12/44
Leutnant Hans Berger	01/01/45	-	04/01/45
Leutnant Gerhard Hanf	14/02/45	-	03/05/45
Hauptmann Wolfgang Ludewig	04/05/45	to end	

3rd Staffel (1st Formation):

Oberleutnant Max Dobislav	01/01/38	-	05/07/40

(On 05/07/40 3rd Staffel became 9th Staffel, Jagdgeschwader 27).

3rd Staffel (2nd Formation):

Oberleutnant Paul Stolte			
Oberleutnant Werner Heidrich	/ /	-	12/01/43
Hauptmann Egon Falkensammer	01/01/43	-	01/04/43

(On 01/04/43 3rd Staffel became 6th Staffel, Jagdgeschwader 11).

3rd Staffel (3rd Formation): (ex.-12./JG 1)

Oberleutnant Karl Becker	01/04/43	-	30/07/43
Oberleutnant S'trohal	30/07/43	-	30/09/43
Oberleutnant Hans Ehlers	01/11/43	-	16/04/44
Oberleutnant Eugen Kotiza	01/05/44	-	28/05/44
Hauptmann Maier	01/07/44	-	20/07/44
Leutnant Emil Demuth	01/08/44	-	15/01/45
Hauptmann Heinz Künneke	16/01/45	-	12/02/45
Leutnant Hans Berger	13/02/45	-	03/05/45
Leutnant Emil Demuth	04/05/45	to end	

4th Staffel (1st Formation):

Oberleutnant Robert Olejnik	06/01/42	-	15/05/43
Leutnannt Heinz Tröger	16/05/43	-	17/06/43
Leutnant Richard Haug	17/06/43	-	24/06/43

Hauptmann Robert Olejnik	28/06/43	-	26/07/43
Oberleutnant Eugen Kotiza	27/07/43	-	end of 43
Oberleutnant Wolfgang Kretschmer	/01/44	-	06/03/44
Oberleutnant Eberhard Burath	07/03/44	-	01/06/44

4th Staffel (2nd Formation) (ex-9./JG 77):

Oberleutnant Wolfgang Ernst	01/07/44	-	10/07/44
Leutnant Gerhard Hanf	11/07/44	-	16/12/44
Leutnant Richard Förster	17/12/44	-	27/12/44
Oberleutnant Hans Gottfried Meinhof	28/12/44	-	01/01/45
Oberleutnant Heinrich Greuner	02/01/45	-	14/01/45
Leutnant Gerhard Hanf	15/01/45	-	14/02/45

4th Staffel (3rd Formation):

Hauptmann Bernd Gallowitsch	03/05/45	-	end

5th Staffel (1st Formation):

Oberleutnant Max Buchholz	06/01/42	-	end of 42
Hauptmann Dietrich Wickop	/01/43	-	16/04/43
Leutnant Wilhelm Tschira	16/04/43	-	21/06/43
Leutnant Rüdiger von Kirchmayr	22/06/43	-	31/05/44
Leutnant Fritz Wegner	01/06/44	-	14/07/44

5th Staffel (2nd Formation) (ex.6./JG 1)

Leutnant Hubert Swoboda	15/07/44	-	11/03/45

5th Staffel (3rd Formation):

Hauptmann Bergholz	03/05/45	-	end

6th Staffel (1st Formation):

Oberleutnant Eberhard Bock	06/01/42	-	19/03/42
Oberleutnant Detlev Rohwer	20/03/42	-	03/10/42
Leutnant Walter Leonhardt	04/10/42	-	04/02/43
Hauptmann Harry Koch	/02/43	-	22/12/43
Feldwebel Leo Schuhmacher	23/12/43	-	20/01/44
Major Heinz Bär	21/01/44	-	14/03/44
Hauptmann Georg-Peter Eder	15/03/44	-	07/06/44
Feldwebel Reinhard Flecks	08/06/44	-	14/07/44

6th Staffel (2nd Formation) (ex. 5./JG 1):

Leutnant Fritz Wegner	15/07/44	-	01/03/45

6th Staffel (3rd Formation):

Oberleutnant Zipprecht	03/05/45	-	end

7th Staffel (1st Formation):

Hauptmann Harry Koch	06/01/42	-	/02/43

7th Staffel (2nd Formation):

Oberleutnant Heinrich Klöpper	01/04/43	-	29/11/43
Hauptmann Albert Wind		-	30/01/44
Oberleutnant Günther Witt		-	08/02/44
Hauptmann Lutz-Wilhelm Burckhardt	09/02/44	-	/05/44

7th Staffel (3rd Formation) (ex-4./JG 1)

Leutnant Otto Bach	15/07/44	-	26/11/44
Oberleutnant Rudolf Diesem	27/11/44	-	05/12/44
Hauptmann Friedrich Strich		-	20/01/45
Major Bernd Gallowitsch	01/02/45	-	02/05/45

8th Staffel (1st Formation):

Hauptmann Julius Henschel	06/01/42	-	07/11/42
Hauptmann Emil Rudolf Schnoor	08/12/42	-	01/04/43

(On 01/04/43 8th Staffel became 2nd Staffel, Jagdgeschwader 11).

8th Staffel (2nd Formation):

Oberleutnant Herwig Zuzic	01/04/43	-	19/08/43
Hauptmann Friedrich Eberle	11/09/43	-	08/10/43
Hauptmann Alfred Faber	09/10/43	-	03/11/43
Oberleutnant Heinrich Overhagen	04/11/43	-	12/03/44
Hauptmann Alfred Grislawski	13/03/44	-	23/08/44

8th Staffel (3rd Formation) (ex-7./JG 51):

Leutnant Günther Heckmann	15/07/44	-	23/03/45

9th Staffel (1st Formation):

Oberleutnant Werner Gutowski	06/01/42	-	31/03/43

(On 01/04/43 9th Staffel became 3rd Staffel, Jagdgeschwader 11).

9th Staffel (2nd Formation):

Leutnant Eugen Wintergerst	01/04/43	-	04/09/43
Oberleutnant Rainer Framm	05/09/43	-	03/11/43
Oberleutnant Erich Buchholz			
Oberleutnant Helmut Müller	01/10/44	-	05/12/44
Oberleutnant Jentsch	06/12/44	-	25/12/44

10th Staffel (1st Formation):

Oberleutnant Friedrich Eberle	03/04/42	-	11/03/43
Oberleutnant Herwig Zuzic	12/03/43	-	18/03/43
Oberleutnant Alfons Raich	19/03/43	-	01/04/43

(On 01/04/43 10th Staffel became 1st Staffel Jagdgeschwader 1).

Hauptmann and Ritterkreuzträger, Hauptmann Hans Ehlers was killed in action on 27/12/44. Kommandeur of I. Gruppe, Ehlers had recorded 60 victories, including 23 four-engined bombers.

10th Staffel (2nd Formation) (ex-7./JG 1):			
Oberleutnant Elmer Resch	15/07/44	-	23/08/44
Oberleutnant Fritz Bilfinger	01/10/44	-	25/12/44
Feldwebel Koschinski	26/12/44	-	

11th Staffel (1st Formation):			
Hauptmann Wilhelm Moritz	01/04/42	-	10/09/42
Oberleutnant Rainer Framm	10/09/42	-	01/04/43

(On 01/04/43 11th Staffel became 2nd Staffel, Jagdgeschwader 1).

11th Staffel (2nd Formation) (ex-8./JG 1):			
Oberleutnant Joachim Janke	01/10/44	-	20/04/45
Oberleutnant Rudolf	21/04/45	-	end

12th Staffel (1st Formation):			
Oberleutnant Franz Eisenach	03/04/42	-	24/04/42
Oberleutnat Stöcker	24/04/42	-	04/05/42
Hauptmann Bier	04/05/42	-	30/06/42
Hauptmann Karl-Heinz Schulz	01/07/42	-	30/03/42

(On 01/04/43 12th Staffel became 3rd Staffel, Jagdgeschwader 1).

12th Staffel (2nd Formation) (ex-KG 2):			
Hauptmann Harald Moldenhauer	01/10/44	-	25/12/44
Oberleutnant Jentsch	25/12/44	-	

At the end of the war the allies showed a great interest in the German jet fighters, and the He 162 aircraft were taken by the Americans, British and French for evaluation. This He 162 was taken on charge by the French.

APPENDIX 3

KOMPANIE OESAU

Although this work deals with Jagdgeschwader 1, reference needs also to be made to the existence of "Kompanie Oesau". It illustrates the desperate measures which Germany was prepared to take towards the end of the war. Kompanie Oesau had no direct link with Jagdgeschwader 1 but such a link had been envisaged by the High Command. During the overall re-equipment with the He-162, the unit would have been reinforced with adolescents who, despite their lack of experience, would have been pitched into combat in the hope of their gaining victories.

On 20th October 1944 the name "Kompanie Oesau" appeared for the first time when an order was issued to the 1. Flieger Schule Göppingen which advised that a company of pilot school FFS A should be re-named "Kompanie Oesau". This unit, situated at Danzig-Langfuhr, was commanded by a former pilot of JG 1 and 27, Major Max Dobislav.

The Air Ministry launched an appeal for the formation of a special volunteer unit. Officer-cadets (1927 class) and other ranks (1928 class) came, in the main, from the "Flieger Hitler Jugend" (Hitler Youth Flyers). The adolescents joined with a written promise to take part in combat as pilots. To be accepted into the unit, and to be involved in action as quickly as possible, they had to forfeit officer candidature. Their advancement was dependent on their courage. These pilot-candidates would make their first solo flights after only seven glider flights in the two-seater "Kranich". That done, training would be accelerated to enable them to fly the He 162, or other jet aircraft. It was impressed upon them that the important aspects were being able to take off and to guide the aircraft; landing again was not the most important thing!

Many volunteers reported for duty. To infuse them with the necessary morale, they passed through Berlin, and there met several pilots, including Oberst Herbert Ihlefield.

The ranks of the unit swelled quickly, and in January 1945 it left Danzig-Langfuhur for Goslar. The young pilots waited in vain for the famous fighter aircraft.

On 1st April 1945, Kompanie Oesau, with 1500 men on charge, was re-named "Parachute Battalion Oesau". Five days later, the three companies of 500 combatants headed for the nearby front and went into action against American tanks arriving in their sector. The action was tough: by 21st April, for example, only 65 soldiers were fit for action with the 3rd Company.

It seems that He 162s were delivered to Goslar shortly after as confirmed by Oberst Adolf Dickfield, formerly of JG 2 and 11. As Inspector of the Flieger Hitler Jugend he recalled discussions with those responsible for German military aircraft on the subject of utilising new types of aircraft by adolescents. The creation of a new unit from the Hitler Youth was given to him.

"At the beginning of March 1945, I went to Goslar to bring into being a unit, as yet un-named, under the overall responsibility of the General of Fighters, Oberst Gollob. The ground personnel came from various units which had been disbanded. In mid-April we received a dozen He 162s and the recently-arrived pilots from various training schools began their training. This in itself proved difficult, due to lack of fuel. After an initial combat flight without enemy contact, I shot down a P-47 on 21st April 1945. The following day a similar victory was recorded by Leutnant Bartz. These two were the only victories of this un-named unit, destined to be called "Jagdgeschwader Hitler Jugend". Soon, the Americans approached Goslar, and we evacuated our He 162s towards Travemünde while the rest of the unit were engaged in ground fighting ...". - Oberst Adolf Dickfield.

ACKNOWLEDGEMENTS

This work, in preparation for six years, would not have been possible without the help of a considerable number of people who showed great patience during my requests for assistance, or during long correspondence. Many researchers did not hesitate to open up their files and took an active interest in the work. I would like to make particular mention of ongoing assistance from Jean-Louis Roba, and the important rôle played by Regis Decobecq, Jean-Yves Lorant and Jean-Pierre Van Mol. To all these people I offer my grateful thanks.

Former members of Jagdgeschwader 1 and families (F) of pilots:

A. von Alvesleben; K. Augner; H. Berger; K. Bekker; H. Biederbick; L. Blumel (F); E. Burath; W. Dietrich; A. Dürr; F. Eberle (F); G. Eder (F); H. Eh; K. Ell; R. Engleder; W. Ernst; G. Framm (F); A. Freudendorfer; E. Friedrich; G. von Friesen (F); L. Gerold; A. Grislawski; W. Gutowski; H. Halbey; W. Harder; F. Haspel; H. Hausotter; G. Heckmann; G. Hildenbrand; D. Hillmer; W. Hoeckner (F); W. Hoepfner; F. Hofmann; Hollmann; R. Hübl; K. Ibing; H. Ihlefield; A. Job; H. Kaiser; J. Kehrle; F. Kinsky (F); R. von Kirchmayr; W. Koeditz; G. Krell; K. Kremer; W. Kretschmer; H. Künneke; H-G. Lehmann; A. Lindeschmidt (F); F. Losigkeit; H. Meissner; A. Michalski; A. Miksch (F); E. Mix (F); H. Moldenhauer; W. Moritz; H. Neuner; F. Pirkenseer; H. Pretsch von Lerchenhorst; E. Rahner; R. Rauhaus (F); T. Rauth (F); H. Rettich; H-G. Reinhardt; H. Riediger; S. Rudschinat; O. Schiele; O. Schmid; R. Schnappauf (F); L. Schreiner; L. Schuhmacher; E. von Selle (F); L. Siegfried; H-J. Sperrling; F. Snaidero; Staerk (F); E. Steeb; F. Steiner; K-H. Sundermaier;F. Timpe; W. Wedding; E. Wedel; F. Wegner; H-G. Wennekers; D. Wickop (F); W. Widnmann; L. Wingenfeld; E. Wintergerst (F); W. Wollenweber.

Oesaukorps: G. Magenau; H. Riediger; A. Dickfield.

Helpers and friends:

Belgium: D. Campion; R. Decobecq; J-L. Roba; C. Vanhee; J-P. Van Mol.
Germany: B. Barbas; G. Leonhardt; M. Meyer; P. Petrick; H. Ring; F. Zimmermann.
Austria: A. Hiller.
England: A. Stewart; J. Vasco.
United States: J. Crow; J. Kitchens; D. Caldwell.
France: R. Chuinard; J-Y. Lorant.
Norway: K. Maesel.
Low Countries: R. W. de Visser; A. Neeven.

Photographs came from the collections of the following:

Augner; Barbas; Berger; Biederbick; v. Bülow (F); Burath; Crow; Decobecq; de Visser; Dürr; Ell; Engleder; Framm (F); Frappé; Friedrich; Halbey; Haspel; Hausotter; Heckmann; Hillmer; Holmann; Ibing; Grislawski; Job; Junker; v. Kageneck (F); Kehrle; v. Kirchmayr; Köhne; Krell; Lächler; Lehmann; Lorant; Losigkeit; Meissner; Meyer; Michalski; Miksch (F); Mix (F); Moritz; Petrick; Pretsch v. Lerchenhorst; Peinemann (F); Rauhaus (F); Rettich; Riebl; Roba; Rodeike; Rudschinat; Schmid; Schnappauf (F); Schreiner; Schuhmacher; v. Selle (F); Siegfried; Snaidero; Stärk (F); Steeb; Timpe; Van Mol; Wedel; Wegner; Wennekers; Wingenfeld; Wintergerst (F); Wollenweber.

Bundesarchiv Koblenz; ECPA and SHAA.

SOURCES

A work such as this has its base in documents of the era, but the majority of documents of the Third Reich have been destroyed. While the War Diary of II. Gruppe, Jagdgeschwader 1 survives for the period 1942 to 6th June 1944, the existence of other documents relating to Jagdgeschwader 1 is not known. What are left are the recollections of action and the personal documents of former members of the unit. The Loss Lists are relatively complete in official German archives, and they represent indispensible material. Aside from drawing information from the survivors, or families of those lost in action, the following works were of assistance:

Aders G. and Held W. - Jagdgeschwader 51 "Mölders". Stuttgart, Motorbuch Verlag. 1985.
Balke U. - Die Operativen Einsätze des KG 2 im zweiten Weltkrieg. Koblenz, Bernard and Graefe Verlag. 1990.
Freeman R. - The Mighty Eighth War Diary. London, Janes. 1981.
Galland A. - The First and the Last. London, Methuen. 1955.
Girbig W. - Six Months to Oblivion. London, Ian Allan. 1975.
Girbig W. - Jagdgeschwader 5 "Eismeerjäger". Stuttgart, Motorbuch Verlag. 1975.
Held W., Trautloft H., and Bob E. - Die Grünherzjäger. Friedberg, Podzun-Pallas Verlag. 1985.
Knoke H. - I flew for the Führer. London, Evans Brothers. 1953.
Lorant J-Y. and Frappé J-B. - The Focke-Wulf 190. Paris, Docavia.1981.
Obermaier E. - Die Ritterkreuzträger der Luftwaffe 1939-1945 (Band 1 Jagdflieger). Mainz, Dieter Hoffmann. 1989.
Olynyk F. - USAAF (European Theatre) Credits for the Destruction of Enemy Aircraft in Air-to-Air Combat in World War II. Aurora. OH. 1987.
Priller J. - JG 26. Heidelburg, Kurt Vowinkel Verlag. 1956.
Rinng H. and Girbig W. - Jagdgeschwader 27. Stuttgart, Motorbuch Verlag. 1971.
Skawran P. - Ikaros. Steinebach. Luftfahrt-Verlag W. Zuerl. 1969.
Wood D. and Gunston B. - Hitler's Luftwaffe. London, Salamander Books. 1977.

INDEX

This index does not include entries in the Loss Tables and Appendices.

FORTHCOMING PUBLICATIONS

THE HISTORY OF THE MESSERSCHMITT 110 AND ITS UNITS IN 1940